Gender, Heteroglossia and Power

Language, Power and Social Process　4

Editors

Monica Heller
Richard J. Watts

Mouton de Gruyter
Berlin · New York

Gender, Heteroglossia and Power
A Sociolinguistic Study of Youth Culture

by

Joan Pujolar

Mouton de Gruyter
Berlin · New York 2001

Mouton de Gruyter (formerly Mouton, The Hague)
is a Division of Walter de Gruyter GmbH & Co. KG, Berlin.

♾ Printed on acid-free paper which falls within the guidelines
of the ANSI to ensure permanence and durability.

Library of Congress Cataloging-in-Publication Data

Pujolar, Joan, 1964.
    Gender, heteroglossia and power : a sociolinguistic study of youth
culture / by Joan Pujolar.
       p.   cm. − (Language, power, and social process)
Includes bibliographical references and index.
    ISBN 3-11-016797-2 (cloth : alk. paper) − ISBN 3-11-016796-4
(pbk. : alk. paper)
    1. Youth−Spain−Barcelona−Language.   2. Sociolinguistics−
Spain−Barcelona. 3. Language and languages−Sex differences.
4. Bilingualism−Spain−Barcelona. 5. Discourse analysis. I. Title.
II. Series.
PI20. Y68 P85 2000
306.44'0946'72−dc21
                                        00-052092

Die Deutsche Bibliothek − Cataloging-in-Publication Data

Pujolar, Joan:
Gender, heteroglossia and power : a sociolinguistic study of youth
culture / by Joan Pojular. − Berlin ; New York : Mouton de Gruyter, 2001
    (Language, power and social process ; 4)
    ISBN 3-11-016796-4 brosch.
    ISBN 3-11-016797-2 Gb.

Printing: Druckerei Gerike, Berlin.
Binding: Lüderitz & Bauer GmbH, Berlin.
Cover design: Christopher Schneider, Berlin.
Printed in Germany.

"...how life, from being made up of little separate incidents which one lived one by one, became curled and whole like a wave which bore one up with it and threw one down with it, there, with a dash on the beach."

Virginia Woolf, *To the Lighthouse* (1927: 76)

Acknowledgements

This book would not have been possible if I had not received substantial support from a good number of people who have helped me in many different ways, often without really being aware of how important their assistance was. First of all, I am greatly indebted to Marilyn Martin-Jones, who helped me to open many theoretical and methodological doors and also gave me the opportunity to participate in the Bilingualism Research Group at Lancaster University. I also have a deep debt of gratitude towards Joan Albert Argenter from the Universitat Autònoma de Barcelona, who has given me encouragement and support for many years. My study is based on fieldwork carried out amongst two groups of young working-class people from Barcelona. I did not know these people beforehand. They agreed to integrate me in their groups and their lives, to help me with my research, and they only expected my friendship in return. I am not sure that they understood the importance of what they did for me and how grateful I feel. I would also like to extend my gratitude to all those who helped me in my fieldwork and whose names I do not mention in order to ensure the confidentiality of the participants in my study. These were youth workers at various civic centers and *casals*, as well as the staff of the training school where the members of one of the groups were working. I would also like to thank Péter Bodor, Emili Boix, Raimon Bonal, Roger Hewitt, Sally Johnson, Alfons López, Luci Nussbaum, Simon Pardoe, Ben Rampton, Amparo Tusón and Ruth Wodak for their very useful suggestions at different stages of my analysis. Dankmute Pohl and Lilie Chouliaraki have read the drafts of this book and have given me helpful and often challenging ideas. My friends Joan Bassets and Judith Bosch allowed me to stay in their flat in Barcelona during my fieldwork. Without their generosity, my life would have been much more complicated. I am grateful to Jordi Portabella, Natàlia Ramon and Xeixi Planagumà for their hospitality. The assistance of Tena Busquets at the early stages of fieldwork was essential.

I also want to thank the *Institut de Sociolingüística Catalana* for their financial assistance and encouragement in a previous research project that served as a pilot study for the present one. My research would not have been possible without the financial assistance of the *Comissió Interdepartamental de Recerca i Innovació Tecnològica* (CIRIT) and of the Institut viii *Acknowledgements*

d'Estudis Catalans. I am also thankful for the support received from the *Fundació Jaume Bofill*.

Contents

Notes to the reader

The analysis presented in this book is based on an ethnographic study of two groups of young people, the "Rambleros" and the "Trepas", and contains a large number of transcripts from conversations and interviews. In order to ensure the confidentiality of the research participants, I decided to change their names while preserving some characteristics of their original names, such as their gender and their linguistic ascription (i.e. whether their names took Catalan or Spanish forms). I have also changed occasional details about their lives for the same purpose. The names of the groups are invented. The name "Rambleros" comes from "Rambla", a typically Catalan pedestrian promenade that can be found in many neighborhoods of Barcelona. The Rambleros used to meet on one of them. The word "trepa" is an old fashioned epithet which, according to some Trepas, was used by parents when their children were being naughty. I felt it was an appropriate name for a group which was very much oriented towards transgressive practices. The design of figure 1 below is meant to give the reader a sense of the characteristics of the two groups at a glance.

Transcription conventions

For the numerous extracts from natural conversations, interviews, group discussions and fieldnotes, I have adopted a very simplified version of the usual transcription conventions in order to make reading as fast and comfortable as possible. Because many episodes contain people speaking in either Catalan or Spanish, these languages are represented consistently throughout the book.

> Stretches in Catalan are always represented in normal characters
> The English translation of a Catalan utterance is also in normal type.
>
> *Stretches in Spanish are always represented in italics*
> *Their English translation is always in italics as well.*

Rambleros   Trepas

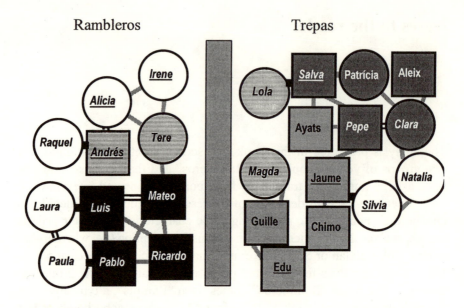

Key

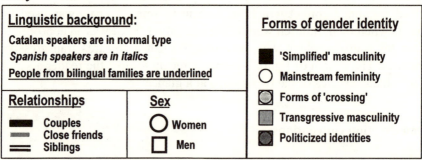

Figure 1

Note: Here "bilingual family" refers to those who had one Catalan-speaking and one Spanish-speaking parent. Jaume was, however, a special case, as he had a Portuguese-speaking mother and a Catalan-speaking father, who had become accustomed to speaking Spanish at home. The father had reportedly begun to speak Catalan to his children after a few years when he realized that linguistic winds were changing. The different typographical representations of these "bilinguals" (some in normal type and some in italics) reflect the fact that their linguistic practices were, in some cases, generally equivalent to those of other Catalan speakers and, in other cases, similar to those of other Spanish speakers.

In the transcripts, speakers' names are written in normal characters or in italics according to whether they were speakers of one language or the other (according to the classification displayed in figure 1). I never use capital letters or punctuation for the text in the original language. Because translation usually forces us to make more detailed interpretive choices than the transcriptions, I do include punctuation in the English version to make reading easier. In many cases, I considered that the original version of an extract was not strictly necessary and I provided the English translation only. In these cases, the original versions of the extracts are provided in the appendix.

In addition to these conventions, I use the following signs in the transcriptions:

··· Dots indicate pauses

·   One dot indicates any short pause that is of significance for the understanding of a particular utterance.

··   The second dot onwards indicates the approximate duration of a pause in seconds.

(xxx) Brackets indicate stretches that are either inaudible or difficult to interpret.

[xxx] I use Square brackets to give contextual information, including interrogative intonation in question tags, such as "no[?]". In the English translation, I also include in square brackets fragments of text that do not appear in the original but which may help to understand what is being said or meant.

> This sign indicates the beginning of an overlap between the current speaker's turn and the turn of another speaker (which is transcribed immediately below).

< This sign marks the beginning of the utterance that overlaps with the previous one.

= This sign at the end of an utterance indicates that the next speaker has begun speaking immediately after the previous one and without allowing any perceptible pause between turns. It is used to indicate that an interruption may have occurred. The utterance of the next speaker begins with a "=" as well.

"xxx xxxx" In the English translation, I have used quotation marks to indicate changes of voice or character dramatizations in people's speech.

Underlined text indicates the particular elements of an extract that are relevant to the discussion. They can be examples of argot, code-switching, opinions, etc. When these indications appear, both the original version and the English translation are underlined.

In many of the episodes I transcribed, speakers use dirty language and unconventional expressions that have no clear equivalent in either Standard English or unconventional English. I have sought to translate these stretches by drawing upon the most common forms of English slang. When this has not been possible, I have provided the equivalents in Standard English only and I have indicated which expressions were unconventional in the original version when this was of importance to the discussion. Finally, it is important to bear in mind that the Catalan and Spanish equivalents of the slang words *guy*, *bloke* or *man* have masculine and feminine forms (tiu, tia, *tío*, *tía*). This is why I have often preferred to translate them as "boy" or "girl", that is, to preserve the gender distinction in the translation.

Introduction

This book is a sociolinguistic study of youth culture. It is concerned with the way young people speak and how they construct their identities when they get together beyond the controlling grasp of parents, teachers, police officers, priests, law-abiding neighbors and any other full members of the adult world. In the peer-group context, young people engage in characteristic forms of leisure activities, interact in particular ways amongst themselves and speak in the well-known forms of slang. There have been many studies about young people under the academic label of *popular culture*, but very few detailed studies that focus on language and the way in which language contributes to shaping the world of youth cliques. In this study, I intend to show that discourse analysis, in the form of a close analysis of patterns of social and linguistic interaction, can make a significant contribution to our knowledge of the social world. More specifically, I will argue that the development of particular speech styles in the contexts of young people's leisure activities is intimately connected with struggles over gender, ethnicity and class relations.

Gender is, as I will show, the most important aspect of social identity in the peer-group context, as it constitutes the key forms of participation and self-presentation in this domain. Ethnicity and class are also important if we wish to understand many aspects of young people's cultural practices, especially the way they use language, that is, the way they manage heteroglossia, which is the socially stratified diversity of speech forms. By incorporating the ways of speaking of various social groups in different ways, young people construct and express in a symbolic way their position vis-à-vis the relations of power that exist between these groups.

The study is based on data I collected amongst two cliques of young working class people in Barcelona by means of ethnographic participation, observation, tape-recording of conversations and in-depth interviewing. Barcelona, the capital of Catalonia, is a bilingual city, which means that young people there combine the use of youth slang and dialects with switching between the Catalan and Spanish languages. In this context, an analysis of everyday conversations can provide a source of very rich and complex sociolinguistic data. I have tried to explain and lay out very clearly the procedures of data analysis so that this book can be useful not only for specialists in the fields mentioned, but also for students who wish to bring some form of discourse analysis, and particularly an analysis of face-to-face interaction, into their own research.

The book is not meant to be a mere description put together for academic audiences only. There is a political agenda behind it; not one of indoctrination, of course, but one of exploration of issues and ideas that may eventually be useful to address particular social problems. This is partly due to the motivations that led me to study language use amongst young people, namely my interest in assessing the results of the linguistic policies aimed at promoting the use of the Catalan language. Thus, I was not only interested in describing *how* young people speak, but also in finding out *why* they happen to speak or decide to speak the way they do. This is why I became interested in Critical Discourse Analysis (Fairclough 1989, 1992a) and Bourdieu's theories of practice and of social reproduction (1972, 1990, 1991a), as these models have been devised with a political agenda in mind, that is, in order to produce a politically relevant understanding of how society works and how it can be changed in positive directions. Therefore, what I try to do here is to develop an explanatory framework that can be useful to address the concerns of various social actors outside the academic field; in this case, language planners, social workers, cultural activists and the like. This does not mean that I will engage in any detailed discussion about particular policy initiatives that might be relevant to these interest groups. Rather, what I do is interrogate the data in ways that I believe are relevant to them. This interrogation involves three main questions:

1. Why do so many young people in Barcelona refuse to use Catalan or, in some cases, even develop anti-Catalan feelings? This question connects with more general issues, such as racism and ethnolinguistic relations in Western societies.
2. Why do many youth cliques engage in risky and antisocial practices (heavy drugs, dangerous driving, aggression and the like)?
3. In what ways do gender relations and identities within youth cliques contribute toward reproducing the social inequalities between the sexes?

Issue 1 was what prompted me to do this study, as a Catalan linguist concerned with the ways in which the Catalan language was appropriated by the new generations. I came to develop an interest in 2 and 3 because they touch on aspects that seem to be common to all youth cliques and essential to understanding what youth culture is about. The problematic practices of 2 are the most extreme expression of social processes that seem to be present in virtually all youth cliques. There is always some risk being taken and some form of misbehavior or misdemeanor taking place. With regard to 3, I realized very early on that gender divisions were a key feature of peer-group relations.

Therefore, this study constitutes an exploration of the world of youth culture carried out with the tools of discourse analysis and based on ethnographic and conversational data, the data analysis being done under the guiding principle that it should connect with the interests of people concerned with the social problems described. Let us look into all these aspects in more detail.

Let us begin with the most common perceptions of what youth culture is about. It would be quite easy for any researcher to fall into the trap of treating the world of young people as inherently problematic and somewhat mystifying, as is often done in many public arenas and within the family. Researchers are almost by definition adults (at least by the time we manage to get our work published), and this adult gaze can quite easily lead to downplaying the inner coherence and cogency that youth culture provides for its participants. In any case, the goal of this study is not to judge whether the practices of young people or the discourses *about* young people are right or wrong, strange or natural. The goal is to try to understand how and why these practices become meaningful for young people so that we can begin to address what we perceive as problematic in them.

In any case, when it comes to discussing the young, we cannot claim that there is a lack of knowledge and understanding due to restricted contact, as happens with some segregated minority groups. However, despite the fact that we have all been young, we seem to be unable to address some of the problems associated with young people. Thus Paul Willis (1977) finds that many working-class males develop a counter-school culture that leads them to value violent and disruptive behavior, as well as sexist and anti-intellectual attitudes, so that they actively produce their destiny as an unqualified and uneducated workforce in the job market. Hewitt (1986) and Rampton (1995) also show that racist attitudes appear in many youth cliques even when schools try to discourage them. The studies by Maltz and Borker (1982), Goodwin (1990), Thorne (1993) and many others demonstrate that children and adolescents reproduce gender divisions in informal contexts, even when they have attended progressive schools which actively encourage equal treatment of both sexes. In the particular context of

Barcelona, many young people are associated with yet another problematic issue: apparently, they have not been sensitive to the policies of linguistic promotion deployed by the Catalan government. In the early 1990s, the Catalan autonomous government invested a great deal of effort and public money to ensure that all young people would learn both the Catalan and Spanish languages at school. This policy was set up in order to promote the use of the local language, Catalan, which had suffered heavy political persecution during the dictatorship of General Francisco Franco in Spain (1939-1975). However, research carried out by sociolinguists showed that young people used less Catalan than was initially expected.[1] And not only this: many teachers and observers also were under the impression that some of them actually made a point of not using it.

Now it is common to look outside the world of youth culture proper for causes and explanations for all these problems: social deprivation, the media, bad education, bad role models and so on. With regard to the use of the Catalan language, a similar exercise could be done by recalling that the patterns of language use amongst young people are not substantially different from those of the Catalan population as a whole (see subsection 1.1. for details). Such general statements may be true, in a manner of speaking; but they do not really help to understand how and why particular forms of practice come to *make sense* in the particular social contexts in which young people organize their leisure activities. This is what I will try to do in this study: to explore how it makes sense for some young people to talk and behave in particular ways, that is, to try to narrow the gulf of mystery and mystification that sometimes seems to surround the world of the young.

Social anthropology has traditionally considered that any instance of social practice can only be understood on the basis of the values, worldviews and relations that constitute the community under study. No action can thus have meaning on its own; just like words, which, if they did not have a place in the linguistic repertoire of a speech community, would be simply noise. This means that to understand a particular feature of the behavior of a given social group (say language choice, risky driving, sexism), one needs to take a comprehensive, i.e. holistic, approach that illuminates this feature from the perspective of the whole set of cultural practices where it is inserted (in this case, youth culture). From this viewpoint, I took it that "youth culture" refers to the whole set of social practices young people organize as they gather together in their leisure time: typical games, conversations and fun-making activities. Thus, I had to consider as relevant everything young people did in the peer-group context, and particularly all those elements commonly associated with youth culture: musical tastes, drug-consumption habits, unconventional speech, particular conversational styles, typical games and activities. I had to look into the interrelations between all these elements on the basis of a detailed analysis of the social practices found in real-life contexts, and I also needed to gather extensive knowledge about each particular context and the participants involved.

This is why I decided to focus on the study of two particular cliques. I also considered that the method of participant observation was best suited for the particular purposes I had in mind. Therefore, this book is not a general description and classification of forms of youth culture and patterns of speech, as this would have forced me to adopt a much more superficial, and probably quantitative, approach. My fieldwork consisted of joining two groups of young people from working-class neighborhoods in Barcelona. During a period of approximately five months, I participated in the leisure activities of these people as a member of their own clique. The data were collected via fieldnotes and recordings of conversations, interviews and group discussions. The analysis presented here is based on transcriptions from these data sources.

To summarize, this study is articulated around three basic questions, which correspond to the three parts of the book:

Part 1: What was youth culture about in these particular contexts? In this part, I analyze the conversations and activities of the two groups. I try to uncover the values, meanings and views about the world that underlay their typical games, tastes and forms of relation. Gender identity emerges here as the leading thread in understanding the most important features of social organization of the two cliques. As I was analyzing my data, I gradually realized that gender was the central issue around which many other issues revolved: differences in tastes, preferences, forms of participation and even language attitudes clearly followed gender divisions. This is why this part is devoted to describing how the activities of the groups served to create and maintain various forms of masculinity and femininity.

Part 2: What role did language play in these processes? This part deals with the sociolinguistic aspects, not only how the two groups used Catalan and Spanish, but also how they used the whole set of linguistic resources available to young people in Barcelona. These are the following: a) a characteristic Spanish-based speech style that integrated elements from the

Andalusian dialect of Southern Spain, b) the common slang of young people, which contained some elements of inner-city argot and which could be used when speaking both languages, and c) other forms of Spanish and Catalan associated with social groups or activities that the Rambleros and the Trepas evoked or mimicked in their speech. In this part, I try to show that these speech forms were intimately connected with the practices, identities, values and worldviews described in part 1. In particular, I will describe the interesting connections that existed between forms of gender identity and patterns of language use. In this sense, the study of a bilingual community is especially interesting because bilingual discourse makes visible subtle phenomena that are normally harder to perceive in other monolingual contexts.

Part 3: What are the connections between these local practices and social processes of a wider scale? Here I basically explore both the causes and the sociopolitical implications of the practices described. These are, of course, complex matters that affect questions that are central to sociology, such as the relationship between structure and action, the extent to which individual action can be seen as predetermined or as the product of free choice, the processes that contribute to the reproduction or transformation of social relations and so on. I will ponder in what ways we can see some aspects of the cultural forms analyzed as determined by the actors' position in the social structure and in what ways we can see them as the product of free decisions and creativity. All these questions are obviously very relevant to political activists and policy makers who seek to bring about social changes at various levels (e.g. gender equality, ethnic and classrelations, promotion of minority languages). In a way, I seek to extrapolate the findings in two main directions: a) a political one, by pondering what sort of policy approach could help to tackle some of the social problems discussed throughout the book (e.g. young people's risky practices, unequal relations between the sexes or between linguistic communities); b) a theoretical one, by explicitly reflecting on the conceptual framework that might justify such an extrapolation. These two aspects, the political and the theoretical, are closely connected in the sense that any form of political action is based onim plicit or explicit conceptions about how the social world works. My overall objective is thus to develop a framework that can be used, tested and refined in the social arena as a basis for political consciousness, organization and action.

The main argument of this book is that the use of particular speech varieties in the context of youth culture is an important part of the processes whereby young people construct their views about the world and their relationships amongst themselves and with other social groups. These processes occur in social interaction as individuals seek to project particular images of themselves as men and women and as members of particular communities by adopting particular forms of self-presentation and by incorporating particular discourses and speech styles. Finally, these processes are in part a product of people's position in the social structure and they may either contribute toward reproducing or changing existing patterns of social relations. Thus, in the particular context of Barcelona, young people may incorporate different speech styles as they construct alternative and often conflicting forms of gender relations and as they act out their understanding of what it means to speak Catalan and Spanish, an understanding which is largely mediated by the social position of the Catalan and Spanish-speaking communities in that context.

To conceptualize and explore these processes, I have had to draw upon ideas, theories and methods from various disciplines: basically linguistic anthropology, interactional sociolinguistics, critical discourse analysis and the works of singular authors such as Erving Goffman, Mikhail Bakhtin or Pierre Bourdieu. As these approaches and authors belong to rather different research traditions, they address different issues and they provide very different concepts and terminology. Therefore, I have felt the need to produce some explanations and clarifications as to the ideas and concepts I have incorporated from these various sources. What remains of this introductory chapter will be devoted to describing how this research has been done. In the first section, I will give a brief background information about the Catalan language and the particular sociolinguistic situation of Barcelona. This information is useful to understand aspects of the data analysis, as well as the reasons that led me to do this research and to choose the particular groups I studied. In the second section, I describe how I did the fieldwork and how I recorded and analyzed the data. In the third and last section, I present my theoretical and methodological position in more detail.

The main body of the book is divided into three parts. I have sought to write parts 1 and 2 in a way that is accessible to a variety of audiences, as I believe that the content of this book can be relevant not only to sociolinguists or discourse analysts, but also to researchers who are working in other fields, such as gender studies, cultural studies and ethnic relations, as

well as other people outside the academic world: feminist or language activists, language planners, teachers, social workers and even parents interested in understanding the workings of youth culture and its conflictual relation with the school and family contexts. Part 1 contains chapters 1, 2 and
3. These are devoted to the analysis of the social practices of the young
people studied, and particularly to the different forms of gender identity
that they constructed through these practices. Here I will show how the
processes of construction of gender identities are essential to understand
young people's different forms of involvement and investment in the features generally associated with youth culture: music tastes, drug-
consumption habits, the values of transgressive and risky activities and so
on. Part 2 contains chapters 4, 5 and 6. The first deals with the use various
forms of youth slang. I try to show how people interpreted the meanings of
various speech styles as linked to particular social groups, mainly marginal-
ized groups, and how they incorporated these forms of speech as a way of
incorporating or appropriating the world views and social relations associated with these groups. Chapters 5 and 6 deal with the social meanings and
conventions associated with the use of Catalan and Spanish, which, as I
will show, also depended on the types of social groups and life experiences
that my research participants associated with these languages. In part 3
there is a single chapter that contains reflections about the extent to which
the practices analyzed can be seen as the product of the low socioeconomic
position of the groups and the extent to which they can be seen as creative
responses and as means of symbolic resistance. The book concludes with a
discussion about the implications of these findings for sociolinguistic theory and for political initiatives.

1. Historical and social background of this research

As I have already indicated, my own entrance door into sociolinguistics
was the study of the social and political aspects of bilingualism, and particularly, of the processes of maintenance and shift of minority languages.
One of the objectives of this research was to explore how young people
used the Spanish and Catalan languages in their informal conversations and
to assess the implications of my findings for local language policies. Therefore, it will be useful to explain some basic facts about the history and the
present sociolinguistic situation of Catalonia. This will help to understand
some parts of the analysis, especially the issues discussed in chapters 5 and

6, as well as the reasons that led me to choose the particular groups of young people I studied.

1.1. The politics of language in Catalonia

The Catalan language is spoken in the Mediterranean coast of the Iberian Peninsula, basically in the regions of Catalonia, Valencia and the Balearic Islands, as well as in Andorra, the French Eastern Pyrenees Department, the Aragonese "strip" (*La Franja*) and the enclave of L'Alguer (Italian: *Alghero*) in Sardinia. The total population of these territories is about 10 million, of which about 7 million are reckoned to be native speakers of Catalan (Mollà and Palanca 1987).

These regions were part of a loose confederation of states, the *Corona d'Aragó* 'Aragonese Crown', which lost their sovereignty in 1714, following the Spanish war of succession, when a joint French-Spanish army occupied them and abolished their parliaments and governments. From then on, the Spanish Crown set out an agenda of turning Spain into a politically and culturally unified country. The historian and politician Francesc Ferrer (1985) describes with interesting detail how the crown started a policy of appointing Castilians for all public offices at the same time that legislation was gradually passed banishing the use of the Catalan language in the administration, the school, the church and the public sphere as a whole.

During the Second Spanish Republic (1931–1939), an autonomous Catalan government was re-established and the language recovered its official status for a short while. However, the military rebellion led by general Francisco Franco, inspired and supported by fascist groups, put an end to democracy and unleashed the darkest anti-Catalan feelings of many Spanish nationalists. During the period between 1939 and 1975, any manifestation of "Catalan culture", including the use of the language, was generally treated as seditious. As reported by Josep Benet (1995), all public uses of Catalan were prohibited: press, broadcasting, theater, governmental departments, schools, posters, street signs, shop signs, advertising, private correspondence, telephone calls, names of ships. Even the first names of people in the registry had to be hispanicized. A large number of publishing companies, newspapers, schools and even Barcelona Autonomous University were closed down, while official propaganda treated Catalan as a "dialect".

Figure 2: Map of the Catalan-speaking territories and of the regions where Catalan enjoys official status.

After democracy was restored in Spain, the autonomous Catalan government and parliament were re-established (1980). In 1983, the parliament passed a new language law, called *Llei de Normalització Lingüística*, which set out the basic principles of a policy which was to bring Catalan back to public life as the "normal" language of use in all social arenas. The term *Normalització* had originated in the works of Aracil (1965) and it designated a process whereby a particular language became fully operational and effectively used for all the communicative functions of a modern society. However, in the early eighties, the population of Catalonia was much more diverse than it had been in the pre-war period. Despite the secular persecution of the language, Catalans had never ceased to use it for everyday informal communication, although the majority of adults could not write it properly. But now, Spanish was the first language of many workers who had moved to Catalonia in search of work. Having been Spain's leading industrial region, Catalonia had always attracted population from Spain's rural and economically depressed areas, but never in the numbers seen in those years. Between 1950 and 1975, an estimated 1.4 million people settled in the outskirts of the main industrial towns, first in improvised shantytowns and later moving to hastily developed new neighborhoods, with poor services and communications (Recolons et al. 1979; and Miró et al. 1974: 101–104). On the basis of census data from 1975, Strubell calculated that the proportion of immigrants ranged from 34.1 % to 78.7 % in towns of over 50,000 inhabitants (1981: 75). The highest proportions of immigrants were to be found in the Barcelona Metropolitan Area, an area that nowadays contains half of Catalonia's total population of 6 million. In addition to this, the first immigrants had higher fertility rates than the locals, which means that the proportion of Spanish speakers has increased steadily ever since.[2] Through Figure 3, we can get a rough idea of this process. Although the data come from different sources and are not, strictly speaking, comparable, the overall trend can be seen very clearly: Spanish-speakers have come to predominate amongst the younger generations (compare the four first columns with the last one).

These migration movements, coupled with the process of economic expansion, created a very particular social arrangement. The immigrants occupied the unskilled levels of the job market, while the autochthonous working-class was gradually pushed up to skilled and managerial posts in industries and services. So despite the fact that Catalans are a cultural minority, they control key sectors of the economy in Spain's most industrialized region. The position of Spanish speakers is, in this sense, comparable to that of immigrant minorities in many industrialized countries. However, these "immigrants" belong to the cultural majority that controls the state apparatus.[3]

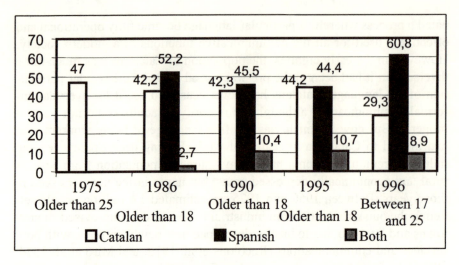

Figure 3: Evolution of linguistic groups in Barcelona in percentages of speakers. Sources: Strubell (1981: 132); Institut d'Estudis Metropolitans de Barcelona (1991: 9; 1997a: 61) and Argenter et al. (1999).[4]

As a consequence, the social values and prestige attached to the two languages can be particularly varied and complex. Spanish is seen as a language of wider communication and it is the only official language of the state. On the other hand, for many Catalans, it is still seen as a language imposed "from above" through military and political means. Moreover, the use of Spanish is associated locally with people belonging to the lower ranks of the social ladder, although economic differences between natives and immigrants appear to be gradually decreasing. Conversely, the Catalan language is associated with the middle classes, a better standard of living and with Catalan national allegiances.

Hence the new language policies were established in a context of resentment on the part of native Catalans for the brutality with which they were treated during the dictatorship. But, on the other hand, some Spanish-speaking people had misgivings about the prospect of a Catalan administration that would give more power to the already economically powerful (see Woolard 1989). Therefore, language policy became a politically sensitive issue *within* Catalonia, in addition to a source of conflict with Spain's government. During the 1980s and 1990s, knowledge of the Catalan language has become an implicit or explicit requirement for access to most jobs except some manual ones. It has gradually become the main language of education at all levels, and an extensive immersion program has been organized for all Spanish-speaking children in the public school system (see Vila 1993: 17, 24). It is also predominant in the administration, although some services run by the central state (such as mail, railways, police) and the recently privatized telephone company still use mainly Spanish. There are two television channels, several newspapers, magazines and radio stations in Catalan which get a good share of the audience, although Spanish still predominates in the media. Spanish is also the language most widely used in business, despite Catalan social predominance in this sector (see Carulla 1990; Departament de Cultura 1991 and Pujolar 1991a).

During this process of linguistic "normalization", most Catalans expected that the children of immigrants would integrate or assimilate into Catalan society by means of adopting the language (see Pujolar 1995b). However, at the beginning of the 1990s, it became clear that this was not really happening. Even in schools where Catalan was the medium of instruction, children would use mainly Spanish in the playground and in their peer-group activities (Vila 1996). Moreover, informal exchanges between speakers of both languages were commonly carried out in Spanish, as Catalan speakers were generally more proficient in Spanish than the converse. This meant that, in some contexts, Spanish would become the more widely used language even when Catalan speakers were more numerous.

This state of affairs caused alarm amongst language planners, sociolinguists and linguistic activists. They feared that the Catalan language was losing its last stronghold of resistance, i.e. the more informal contexts, and that it might be in the early stages of a process of extinction. In the opinion of some commentators, Catalan was in danger of becoming an "academic" language which, as happened with Latin, would only be learned at school and used just for some formal official functions.

1.2. My research agenda

When I began to do research on language and identity, I had this debate in mind. My idea was that future trends of language use would depend very much on the linguistic conventions that the young generations would adopt as a response to the new language policies. In an earlier study, I had observed and interviewed a group of students to find out what language they spoke to whom and why (Pujolar 1991b, 1993). My results had not led to any definite conclusion in terms of what fate awaited the language, as I found that the linguistic behavior of people was much more diverse and complex than I had expected. However, this apparent failure did not really deter me from exploring the issue further. The experience of interviewing and listening to people had radically changed my idea of how sociolinguistic processes worked. It was obvious to me that the very general descriptions of social norms and general trends found in many studies were but a poor reflection of what was actually going on in Catalan society. In a general sense, my findings confirmed the ideas that Kathryn Woolard had put forward in her study on language and ethnicity in Catalonia (1989). Drawing from Barth's ideas about ethnicity (1969), Woolard argued that the use of Catalan and Spanish in Barcelona served to create and maintain an ethnolinguistic boundary between the locals and the immigrants. This boundary separated the predominantly middle class "Catalans" from the mainly working-class Spanish-speaking population, who were generally called "Castilians" (*castellans*). As a result, the use of the two languages was effectively fraught with a multiplicity of social significations. Language loyalties, feelings of nationhood, political ideologies and social prejudices had made of language choice a very sensitive and complex issue.

So I thought it would be interesting to explore how young working-class people experienced and reconstructed this class/ethnic divide that Woolard had described. Besides, the social segment I chose had a special significance for Catalan language policies. Most of the members of the groups I studied were the children of immigrant workers, i.e. "second-generation immigrants", as they are often called. The majority of them spoke Spanish at home and belonged to the first generation of children who had experienced the reintroduction of the Catalan language at school. Therefore, I decided to study how these policies had affected the linguistic practices of these people: how they used their linguistic repertoire in their everyday lives, how they negotiated their language choices, to what extent people had opportunities to use Catalan, to what extent they wished to do it, what it meant for them to use one language or the other, why they used much less Catalan than had been expected or desired and what social factors appeared to have an important bearing on these issues.

To do so, I felt I had to get as close as possible to the ordinary lives and everyday social conditions of working-class youths. This is why I chose participant observation as a research method. I also decided to focus mainly on the leisure activities that young people organized with their groups of friends. This was because I considered that peer-groups are a social space that is central to the identities of the young. The peer-group is where children, adolescents and young people can organize activities and adopt their preferred forms of behavior without direct control from adults. Although most youth cliques are formed at school or in other educational contexts, they are "natural" groups in the sense that they are based on personal affinities and operate outside the constraints of any formal institution. People are probably more committed or emotionally attached (at least for some years) to the views and values developed in these contexts. Additionally, the peer-group is one of the social spaces where people develop the forms of interaction typical of informal contexts, precisely where the Catalan language appeared to be receding. Finally, although there were many studies of language use amongst adolescents and young people, these were usually done by researchers approaching them through educational or social welfare institutions, the data being usually gathered in playgrounds and premises of schools, youth clubs and so on. Now, in Catalonia, these institutions usually encourage the use of Catalan and I wanted to study precisely the linguistic practices of young people when they were away from institutional pressures. Finally, I thought it would also be interesting to go a bit further than previous studies and seek a fuller integration and a closer relationship with the people researched, as this might facilitate access to richer and more varied data.

I chose to do research on people who were beyond early adolescence (18 to 23 year-olds) because, at this age, expectations about work, economic independence and stability of couples start gaining significance. As Figure 4 shows, this age range covers the transition from school to work:

I took it that, in such a transitional period, people would be most likely to feel conflicting pressures on their identities. Conflicts could arise, I speculated, between the types of practices and values promoted by the peer-group and those expected within the job-market. I hoped to gain interesting insights into how these pressures were felt by young people of this age. In choosing the two groups, I took special care to ensure that they differed in many ways, while still falling within the particular type of population that my study was targeting. I did so because differences would allow me a) to make conceptual comparisons and b) to try to establish relationships between concepts or categories.

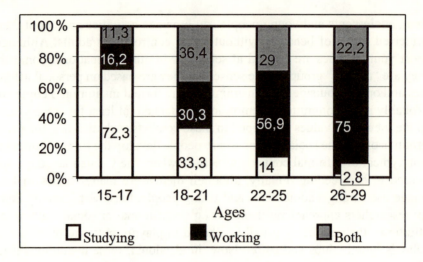

Figure 4: Are you studying or working. Source: Gabinet d'Estudis Socials 1991: 34.[5]

I use the word "group" in a loose sense here, meaning the social space of leisure created by people who meet with some regularity, people who would call each other "friends". I was not interested in particularly rough gangs who were involved in petty criminal activities, as I wanted to focus on people who felt somehow integrated into society. I therefore decided to study one Spanish-speaking group and a linguistically "mixed" one. I also chose gender-mixed groups in order to be able to explore gender relations.

The sociolinguistic situation of Barcelona has both similarities and differences with the typical pattern of social and linguistic stratification found in most cities of the industrialized world. Linguistic and ethnic diversity is a common feature of modern cities. Young people in Barcelona possess a repertoire of unconventional linguistic expressions similar to the varieties found elsewhere. However, the scenario arising from Catalan-Spanish bilingualism is relatively unique. First, it is not common that the local population gets so clearly outnumbered by the newcomers. Secondly, the population of native origin does not normally learn the language(s) of the immigrants. In Barcelona, Catalan-speakers are generally fluent bilinguals, whereas linguistic skills amongst Spanish speakers can vary quite significantly. Finally, as they are closely related languages, both Catalan and Spanish are universally understood and often used together in many conversations where members of both linguistic groups participate. This means

that an additional ingredient is added to the pattern of linguistic stratification found in monolingual urban contexts. Thus, the use of the various
forms of slang and the two languages creates a complex crisscrossing of
symbolic meanings. Old and new patterns of language choice and codeswitching are being created and recreated as young people seek to construct
their positions, both at the (micro) interactional level and at the (macro)
level of ethnolinguistic and class relations. In this context, the analysis of
conversational practices becomes in some ways more complex and challenging, but also more revealing and suggestive.

2. How I did the fieldwork

This study is based on data collected through ethnographic methods: basically participant observation and tape recordings of spontaneous conversations, group discussions and interviews. To get these data, I sought to integrate myself as much as possible within the groups I wished to study. This
meant joining them in their get-togethers and trying to participate in the
games and conversations they organized. At the time, I was 28, which
means that I still looked young enough not to appear the odd one out in the
cliques. I could speak the two languages and I could also use the typical
slang of young people, although I learned some new expressions that were
not around at the time I was studying in Barcelona (up to 1988).

As I did not know the people I researched beforehand, the contacts were
made via youth clubs and social services situated in working-class
neighborhoods of Barcelona. This was in June 1992. I met the people working in these services, explained to them the aims of my research and asked
for help to get in contact with groups of young people. I also worked for a
while for a voluntary association that organized cultural activities in one of
the target neighborhoods. Eventually, I was introduced to two youth workers who in turn introduced me to two members of (what I later named as)
the *Rambleros* group. Almost at the same time, one director of a special
training school for young unemployed people introduced me to one member of the other group, which I called the *Trepas*. After the first meeting
with both groups, I stopped seeing my contacts in the youth club and the
training school. Initially, I talked with one or two members of each group
and explained to them that I wished to do a study about young people, their
customs and ways of speaking. After this, they introduced me to their
friends and I asked them whether it would be possible to hang around with

the whole group for a while. Some found it interesting and some found it curious, but everybody reacted to my proposal in a positive way. I will now proceed to give a brief description of the characteristics of each group.

2.1. The Rambleros and the Trepas

The Rambleros were a group of 11 people (6 women and 5 men) who lived very close to each other. The group had many characteristics of a close-knit network (Milroy 1980) in that it was held together by strong ties of kinship, friendship and couple relationships. Some had been friends since the early school years. Some had even worked for the same employers for some periods of time. The Rambleros lived in a peripheral, working-class neighborhood, away from the city center, with restricted public transport and disastrous city planning. There the streets are unbelievably narrow and crowded and they can hardly cope with Barcelona's deficit of parking space. Although other people now and then joined the group, it had a demarcated membership and a clear entity: members would often refer to it as *el grupo*. In the summer of 1992, almost everybody was either employed or (in the case of some women) studying. Nevertheless, after the employment peak caused by the Barcelona Olympic Games, many lost their jobs and remained unemployed or doing occasional black market jobs for many months. They all spoke Spanish amongst themselves, although some members were known to be using Catalan at work or had one Catalan-speaking parent. Economically, they appeared to be reasonably well off, dressed in neat clothes and some even drove cars that they had bought out of their earnings.

A short character cast of the group can begin with Mateo and Luis, who were half brothers (the former's mother had died many years ago) and whose father worked for an electricity company. Mateo had a steady job in a car factory and Luis worked for a while in a supermarket until his contract expired. A younger brother, Javi, often joined us when we met in the neighborhood. Laura and Paula were sisters and their parents owned a small café just outside the neighborhood, where Laura worked while she was looking for other jobs. Paula worked as administrative assistant for a car selling business. She was clearly one of the group's leaders, together with Luis, although they were rather different in character. By "leader" I mean, in this case, the ones who often assumed coordination, consultation and decision tasks where some group management work had to be done.

Paula was by far the most outspoken of all the women and probably the only one who showed an interest in talking about politics or other social issues. She was the one who decided that I was to be allowed into the group. Luis, on the contrary, sought to produce an impression of unsophisticatedness, boldness and, sometimes, aggressiveness, which, colored by his strong Andalusian accent, made him the very model of masculinity that the group's men seemed to be after. The same could be said of Pablo, Paula's boyfriend, who never drank alcohol due to a liver condition, but often wore a T-shirt displaying the trademark of a well-known whisky. He spent a long while living on unemployment benefit until he got a job as a bus driver, which had been his father's job. Paula's sister Laura was also Luis' girlfriend. As these two couples were (and have remained) stable, they constituted the core of the group. Ricardo, the son of a lorry driver, worked as a waiter in a small café and was a first cousin of Paula and Laura's. His sisters, Marina and Marta, also often joined us to chat with them. They belonged to a section of the group that had split a few months before after having some sort of conflict, I gathered, with the men. Marina's boyfriend, Ángel, had also left the group but remained a good friend of the men. Andrés, although being an old friend of all the above-mentioned, did not share many of the preferences and tastes of his male friends. He spent most of the time with his girlfriend Raquel or chatting with some of the women. Raquel, who worked as an assistant hairdresser, was the only relatively new acquaintance for everybody, as she had joined the group because of her relationship with Andrés. Andrés worked as a waiter in his father's business, a well known fashion café. Alicia was his sister, who had Irene as her best friend. Alicia and Irene were trying very hard to finish their vocational training and were seriously considering rejoining the university track, which they finally did not (despite the fact that Irene left her administrative job to concentrate on her studies). They were the closest friends of Tere, who was going through a tough period, as she received intensive teasing from many group members due to her slightly rough or "unfeminine" manners and tastes and also due to an ambivalent friendship with Mateo, which the others sought to portray as a romance. Except for Laura and Paula's mother, who worked at the family café, all the mothers of the Rambleros worked as housewives and exceptionally as cleaning ladies.

Almost all the Trepas worked and studied in a training school for unemployed people that was located in a working-class neighborhood. Some group members (Pepe, Guille, Patrícia and Aleix) actually lived just outside of this neighborhood but very close to the school, at the rims of slightly better-off areas that could probably be labeled as lower middle-class. But most group members lived in that same neighborhood, which is also in one of Barcelona's peripheral districts. It is a bit more spacious than the Rambleros' area. It consists of many clusters of huge apartment blocks built in the high-tide of the migration movements. It had few services but was slightly better connected transport-wise. The school was part of a government scheme where trainees attended courses and worked as apprentices in various professions. The group had therefore been brought together by the common experience of educational failure (all, except Chimo, had given up studying while they were at the secondary school level) and unemployment.

Probably because it had been formed in this fashion at the training school, the Trepas group was much looser in its organisation than the Rambleros, as most members had other close relationships. When I met them, they had just started to go out together with some regularity, but not everybody turned up all the time. It was made up of roughly 14 people (6 women and 8 men). The group contained some visible subgroups of older friendships. I had a closer relationship with the core-group than with the more 'peripheral' members. This core group was formed by 5 people who were very politicized. My first contact was with Clara, who was an active member of a feminist group and was still entertaining hopes to study "cultural anthropology" at the university, which she never did. Her situation was delicate, as she and Pepe, her brother, had left their home due to a conflict with their father, who worked as head of the supplies division of an important health organization. Pepe (who was living with an older sister and her partner) and Clara (who had rented a very run down flat with two friends) were living off their meager earnings and some handouts from their mother. This situation was probably behind the low spirits they often showed and their high absenteeism in the training school; but it did not prevent them from feeling very involved with my project, such that they took it as a personal duty to ensure my integration into the group. Although Clara and Pepe had Spanish as their family language, as their parents were of immigrant origin, they were the ones who made the most significant efforts to promote the use of Catalan within the group. Clara's closest friends were two Catalan speakers: Patricia, who participated in the same feminist group, and Aleix, who was also involved in antimilitary groups and was always much closer to the women than the men of the clique. Salva, Pepe's closest friend and the group's most charismatic member (maybe because he was tall, strong, blond and very affectionate), was also involved in antimilitary groups and made some unsuccessful attempts to establish Catalan as

was tall, strong, blond and very affectionate), was also involved in antimilitary groups and made some unsuccessful attempts to establish Catalan as
the language of communication with Ayats, who was a Catalan speaker
who did not share the others' interest in politics. Salva, Pepe and Ayats
shared an interest in hard-core music and eventually formed a band themselves, which rehearsed a lot but performed in public very little. The core
group of politicized members had another interesting common feature: except for Salva, they all had a complicated family situation. Clara, Pepe and
Aleix all had large families with six siblings. Aleix had also left his parents' home because he did not feel comfortable there. Salva had four siblings, but it appears that he did not experience special family tensions.
Patrícia lived with her parents, although her father was a salesman who was
more often than not away on his travels. She and her mother very often had
to take care of her sister's three children, who had no partner, was working
and often did not assume all her parental responsibilities. Patrícia tried
many times, unsuccessfully, to get her secondary school studies back on
track or to enter an arts school.

Out of these core members, who often met and discussed deep political
issues over considerable amounts of beer and joints, there were two couples
of more uncomplicated, merriment-seeking, Catalan-speaking male friends:
Jaume and Chimo, the permanent suppliers of cannabis derivatives, and
Edu and Guille, who turned up less often than the others. These generally
shared the musical tastes of the other men. Jaume, the son of a plant manager who had just been made redundant, had brought his new girlfriend
Silvia into the group, a very attractive woman who stood out in the group
because she presented a much more middle-class style of dress and demeanor. Chimo, the son of a taxi driver, was the only one who made it to
the university. Lola did not turn up so often either, although she was
Salva's partner (in a relatively loose way) until Salva and Clara got involved. Natalia was another training-school recruit who became gradually
very close to, and also very dependent on, Clara, who had "seen more of
the world". She was going to evening classes, as she was trying (unsuccessfully) to get a secondary school certificate. Magda used to turn up with a
guitar at some training-school events and sang with a beautiful voice. However, at normal weekends her position in the group became more peripheral, probably because her Andalusian style (one of the indicators of her
rough-masculine style and tastes), her more conservative apolitical attitudes
(amongst them, the principle of never speaking in Catalan) and her musical
tastes set her apart, in one way or another, from the various sectors of the

to take care of her four children on the basis of state benefits and house cleaning services.

It is interesting to note that all the Rambleros presented smaller-sized families that appeared to be generally more stable and integrated than those of the Trepas. However, the professional profiles of the Trepas' fathers (the mothers rarely worked outside their homes) were generally more middle-class. Salva and Ayats' fathers worked as clerks in banks; Lola's father was a medium-level manager and Aleix's father had worked as a sales manager, though he was unemployed at the time. It was also common for many of the Trepas to have brothers and sisters with university degrees and with good and stable jobs.

The neighborhoods where the Rambleros and the Trepas were based have a particularly bad reputation in Barcelona because they are associated with marginal criminal gangs who engage in drug dealing, heavy drug consumption, car theft, house breaking and so on. Indeed, I had witnessed this kind of atmosphere myself in the Rambleros' neighborhood a few years before, while I was studying at the university in the mid eighties. But by the time I started my fieldwork, the neighborhood had improved quite remarkably for a number of reasons. New public services, better lighting and other urban facilities had been installed or built in these areas. Community initiatives against drug dealing had also been relatively effective. One youth worker told me that all heroin takers were "either dead or in prison". I rarely had a sense of danger while I was doing my fieldwork, except perhaps in the late hours in the Trepas neighborhood. There, some of the women had also reported cases of serious sexual assaults.

2.2. Fieldwork relations and data collection

My general attitude during the fieldwork was to seek as much involvement as possible with the groups studied. In these matters, my approach owes a lot to the methodological and epistemological discussion contained in Cameron et al. (1992). The basic idea is that one should not try to create distance to ensure objectivity and to avoid biases, but to promote as much proximity and interaction as possible with the research participants, and even to encourage them to participate in the analysis or reflection on their own practices. I put these principles in practice as faithfully as I could, which means, in general terms, that I participated in the groups' activities pretty much as one of them, although I avoided doing and saying things that participants would have found incongruent or out of character. I also avoided issuing direct judgements and opinions about people's practices, especially on occasions when I was called upon as a sort of authority figure. All these matters forced me to keep difficult balances and ambivalences, but the result was satisfactory in the sense that most people felt that they could safely share their views with me and that they would be respected.

In any case, the process was not simple. I started going out with the two groups in the first week of July 1992. Typically, they went to pubs, bars, concerts or discos. They chatted, drank, smoked, took cannabis derivatives, teased each other, played table-football or video games and laughed a lot. Of course, at first, the whole situation was a bit awkward and embarrassing for me, as I did not know what was best to do or say and many of them did not know how to treat me either. Fortunately, various members of both groups made efforts to bail me out of the situation by showing interest in what I was doing or finding something to chat about. With the Rambleros, there was at first the problem that I did not have access to them during the week, and I had to find ways of getting invited without feeling that I was imposing too much on them. I eventually started joining them in a café where they met every afternoon. As the relationship developed, they started to count on me for trips, football matches and holidays. With the Trepas, my access to the group's activities was much easier because they met daily in a café outside the training school. However, it was a bit more difficult to make myself a space within this group: the Rambleros tended to organize activities which involved the whole group, whereas the Trepas usually divided themselves into smaller groups based on personal affinities.

In the first three months of the fieldwork, until September 1992, I kept a written record of everything that was going on. I did not write notes while I was with the participants because I did not want them to be constantly aware of being observed and I wanted to get involved in their activities myself. I made extensive notes, writing everything I could remember, when I was back home, often very late at night. In September, I also started to record samples of spontaneous speech until I had gathered some 25 hours of talk. I did this with an inconspicuous walkman recorder and a microphone, which I was carrying inside a small handbag. They knew I was doing it, although they were not aware of it all the time. Sometimes I had to stop recording because some people felt uncomfortable about it. At Christmas that year, I gave them a first draft of my analysis. It was a single-spaced ten-page account, with a Catalan and a Spanish version, where I described my general impression about the groups in relatively positive terms and accessible language. It was read and apparently enjoyed by most of the people in the groups. They seemed quite thrilled about the whole thing and began to understand better what I was doing. I then organized a group discussion for each group. The discussions went on for about 4 hours and touched on all sorts of issues related to family, work, gender, friendships and political consciousness. After these group discussions, I arranged a set of interviews with 20 group members. Five people declared that they preferred not to do them, four of them because they were allegedly "too busy" and one of them because she feared some kind of exposure (it was the Ramblero woman who was being so intensively teased by the whole group). In the interviews, which lasted an average of 45 minutes, I inquired in great detail about all sorts of issues related to their everyday lives in order to get enough biographical information (family situation, employment, qualifications, projects, economic situation, daily routines, tastes, hobbies) and I also explored with them some issues regarding the use of linguistic varieties and styles (swearing, slang, dialects, use of Catalan, Spanish and English). After this, I continued my observations in a more unsystematic manner. In Easter 1993, I went on a holiday trip with the Rambleros and there I stopped taking fieldnotes altogether. During the following three years, I paid some additional short visits two or three times a year. I have used as data some of the episodes I could recall or information from this later period, particularly in relation to their personal trajectories in employment. Nevertheless, my analysis is substantially based on data collected from July 1992 to January 1993.

2.3. How the data were organized and analyzed

I transcribed the fieldnotes, the interviews and the group discussions in entirety. I also scanned all the natural conversations by jotting down a quick summary of what was going on and keeping track of the position of every event in the tapes so that I could go back to it if I needed to transcribe it. It is quite an extensive body of data. The numbered texts occupy 2 Mb of hard disk memory for 76 text-only files. I used the application Ethnograph 3.0 to handle it by introducing thematic codes on stretches of text that can later be recovered in a reasonably convenient way.

In my analysis I have used all these types of data in different ways. To analyze face-to-face encounters, for instance, I used fieldnotes, my own memories, recordings and participants' reports if they appeared to be reasonably reliable in the context. I have used interviews and group discussions in various ways: a) to gather extensive biographical information about the participants which was not possible to get through simple participant observation, b) to get the participants' help in interpreting practices and situations whose origin and meaning were not clear to me as a newcomer, c) to get, as Potter and Wetherell put it, the fullest possible "range of accounting resources people use when constructing the social world" (1987: 164), d) to engage in explicit reflection on aspects of the research and the analysis (since research is, to a great extent, a process of making things explicit, it seemed appropriate to give the researched the opportunity of helping me out in my interpretative endeavors), and e) to locate mismatches between reported behavior and actual behavior, as these mismatches often point towards interesting conflicts and contradictions.

3. Conceptual framework

As I explained above, the particular characteristics of this study forced me to construct a theoretical and methodological approach that integrated ideas from a variety of sources. I have made an effort to do this in a coherent way. My starting point was the model developed by Norman Fairclough (1989, 1992a) for a critical discourse analysis, which he later called *Text Orientated Discourse Analysis* (henceforth TODA). TODA is an attempt to develop linguistic tools for sociological analysis. It places a heavy emphasis on identifying power relations on the basis of texts and, particularly, on pinpointing the processes that produce and reproduce social disadvantages or eventually lead to significant social changes. This is why this model is seen as a form of *critical* Discourse Analysis, as opposed to other forms of Discourse Analysis which study more aseptic aspects of texts and communicative processes. TODA also gives precedence to the empirical analysis of communicative processes, and therefore, to the study of concrete, *situated* social events. The assumption is that the experience of individuals as social subjects and their ideas about the world stem from their participation in social interaction. From this viewpoint, discourse is seen as *constitutive* of social reality in a general sense. Social identities are constituted in discourse through the roles or positions adopted by individuals in particular social events. Knowledge about the social world, or *ideologies*, are developed by social subjects not only out of what is said in these events, but also out of what remains as implicit knowledge necessary to act as legitimate participants. In this sense, social practices are seen as *ideologically invested* (Fairclough 1992a: 67).

However, although discourse analysts have theorized a lot about the importance of language or discourse in general, they have not had much to say about the importance of particular *languages* or language varieties. This question appears to have been traditionally left to sociolinguists, particularly anthropological linguists, interactional sociolinguists or ethnographers of communication. The perspective developed here is an attempt to bring together these two perspectives: the critical-discourse-analytical and the sociolinguistic. On the one hand, I seek to show the importance of *what you speak* (i.e. what dialect, what register, what language) in the processes of constitution of the social world. Thus I argue that linguistic variation should be of central concern to discourse analysts. On the other hand, I also try to show how this discourse-analytical perspective can be useful to address some key issues of linguistic anthropology, particularly the interrelations among language, thought, identity and culture.

It was precisely through TODA that I became aware of the significance of intertextuality and interdiscursive processes in the constitution of social identities and ideologies; and this led me in turn to explore Bakhtin's dialogical conception of language in detail. A dialogical understanding of language is one that, as Bakhtin (1981, 1986) proposed, sees each utterance as inherently responsive (it responds to and incorporates previous utterances, thus becoming multivoiced) and also as formally and semantically anchored to the particular social context where it is produced, such that particular language styles constitute linguistic-ideological phenomena that encode the social relations and identities of particular social groups and activities.

Bakhtin's ideas have also helped me to avoid what I see as the most common "structuralist traps" of much sociolinguistic work, namely the assumption that linguistic and social phenomena can be treated separately and put in relation afterwards. In any case, it is from this perspective that I believe we can "rethink", as Gumperz and Levinson (1996) put it, linguistic relativity, that is, the notion that language determines the way we perceive and understand reality. According to Gumperz and Levinson, this rethinking consists of assuming the implications of the idea that meaning does not come entirely from the linguistic system, but also from the social context of communication where language is used. I believe that this book can make a contribution to this discussion via a dialogical understanding of the linguis-

tic-ideological processes associated with heteroglossia, i.e. the social stratification of language.

My study follows the main principles of TODA, though the method and
analytical procedures are somewhat different from those proposed by Fairclough, which often poses a heavy emphasis on text analysis rather than on
interactional analysis. My analysis of talk in interaction has relied heavily
on the works of Erving Goffman (1959, 1967, 1974, 1981) and Mikhail
Bakhtin (1981, 1986). For the analysis of face-to-face interaction, I have
drawn a lot upon Erving Goffman's dramaturgical view of social encounters together with a large number of concepts and ideas from his books
(1959, 1967, 1974). And to explore the connections between interactional
processes and the use of speech styles, register and languages, I adopted
Mikhail Bakhtin's dialogical view of language. This means that I seek to
identify the voices and genres of spoken conversation in order to explore
the ideological aspects of heteroglossia (1981, 1986). Finally, for the purposes of exploring the political and theoretical significance of the practices
analyzed, I have taken the work of Pierre Bourdieu as a reference point
(1972, 1991a). Here, rather than simply adopting and applying some of his
concepts and ideas in the analysis, I have brought together analysis and
conceptual discussion in order to explore what Bourdieu's model can and
cannot say about the significance of the practices studied. This additional
level of analysis implies an attempt to explore how the particular interactional practices observed can be seen as reproducing or transforming general patterns of relations between social groups defined in terms of ethnicity, gender and class (see also Pujolar 1995a).

In the following subsections, I give a brief outline of some concepts that
are used in this book and that will be useful to understand some parts of the
data analysis and discussion.

3.1. Towards a post-structuralist methodology

What Fairclough seeks to do is to develop an explicit and accessible methodology to investigate how power operates in modern society, a methodology that is very much centered on the analysis of texts. His departure point
is fundamentally Foucault and some of his critics (Foucault 1972, 1979;
Dreyfus and Rabinow 1982; Rabinow 1984). The basic principle is that our
frameworks for understanding the world and the social identities of individual actors are produced through discourse. Discourse is central to the

processes that produce the social relations and forms of organization associated with the exercise of power. One problem is, however, that Foucault
produces an inadequate conceptualization of resistance, contestation or
struggle: "the dominant impression is one of people being helplessly subjected to immovable systems of power" (Fairclough 1992a: 57). Foucault's
analyses and discussions are based, as he argues, on the assumption "that
one can extrapolate from structure to practice, that one can arrive at conclusions about practice without directly analyzing real instances of it, including texts" (ibid.: 57). From this perspective, Fairclough's proposal can be
summarized in two points: a) we need to study concrete, situated social
events or instances of practice; b) we need to assume more fully the implications of the *tactical polyvalence of discourses* (ibid.: 59), an idea hinted
at by Foucault himself and arguably by Bourdieu and many others, but
which has not been given enough weight so far. This *tactical polyvalence*
refers to the fact that "elements of an order of discourse do not have ideological values or modes of ideological investment *of a fixed sort*" (Fairclough 1992a: 98, my emphasis). This means that instances of practice cannot be seen as having fixed, predetermined values or meanings. These are
open to struggle.

This has important and wide-ranging implications for all levels of social
research, including the traditional discussions about its status as scientific
knowledge and about the types of statements it can or should provide. The
researcher's gaze is reconstituted as it stops scanning for closed rules and
structures and enters into more ambivalent and ambiguous spaces of struggle over values or meanings. In a way, it situates indeterminacy at the center of analysis, i.e. as the very object to focus on.

Fairclough argues that the values or meanings of the elements analyzed
(genres, discourse types, subject positions, conventions) depend on how
they are articulated within a given *order of discourse*. An order of discourse
consists of a given state of relations between a set of interrelated discourse
practices. He makes a distinction between *local* orders of discourse (the
"political state of affairs", so to speak, within a given network of relations
inside an institution or amongst a group of people) and the *societal* orders
of discourse, which consist of the complex sets of relations amongst society's groups and institutions. The values and meanings of particular practices are thus dependent on the processes that establish and maintain particular orders of discourse. For example, the significance of a particular
exchange (instance of practice) between one teacher and one pupil in terms
of their personal and professional relationships is very much dependent on

how affairs are run in that particular school (the local order of discourse) and within the educational system as a whole, including the interrelations between the educational system and other fields, such as the job market and the government (the societal order of discourse). Thus, equivalent exchanges can have different readings and implications if located within different orders of discourse, which means that a degree of local indeterminacy is always to be found and hence that there is no universal significance that can be accorded to a given practice. I will call this phenomenon *polyvalence*, i.e. the fact that utterances or practices can have different meaning potentials or values.

Any instance of practice can potentially be read off as reproducing the existing "status quo" or as opening up the possibility of some form of transformation (or both). The polyvalent character of the elements of an order of discourse implies that constant maintenance work is needed to preserve a given state of relations. Firstly, because more or less significant contradictions, dilemmas and problems are bound to arise: e.g. do I treat a colleague as just a fellow worker, a friend or a woman in a situation which stands at the boundary of all these orders? Secondly, contestation is always a possibility as well. If social actors can try to resolve dilemmas and contradictions by adapting and combining existing conventions in creative ways, they can also use their inventiveness to organize transgression and put the existing order under threat (ibid.: 96).

3.2. The voices and words of Bakhtin

I have developed some analytical procedures by adapting ideas from Mikhail Bakhtin (1981, 1984a, 1986) for the study of bilingual discourse and the speech genres of everyday life. I have found his concepts very useful to explore the ideological investment of linguistic varieties. Bakhtin's work rotates around the notion of *dialogism*, a concept that expresses his particular perspective on language, human consciousness, social interaction and culture. A dialogical vision is one that accepts the possibility of language only in as much as it enters a dialogue:

> any utterance, in addition to its own theme, always responds ... in one form or another to others' utterances that precede it... [T]he utterance is related not only to preceding, but also to subsequent links in the chain of speech communion... [T]he utterance is constructed

> by taking into account possible responsive reactions, for whose sake,
> in essence, it is actually created. (Bakhtin 1986: 94)

This principle implies that language is inherently contextual. Any utterance must, by definition, emerge from a given social situation: it can only be understood on the basis of its dialogical context, that is, as a response to previous utterances which, at the same time, anticipate posterior responses. This is also an inherently historical conception of communication. The utterance does not only involve a coder and a decoder, but also a particular (socially constructed) location, a place and a time.[6] It is because of this dialogism that any utterance can be seen as *polyphonic*, i.e. as containing multiple voices:

> Each utterance is filled with echoes and reverberations of other utterances to which it is related by the communality of the sphere of speech communication... Each utterance refutes, affirms, supplements, and relies on the others, presupposes them to be known...
> (Bakhtin 1986: 91)

According to Bakhtin, we incorporate other voices and discourses in different ways. Utterances are filled with "'others' words, varying degrees of other-ness and varying degrees of 'our-own-ness'" (ibid.: 89). The process whereby previous utterances are integrated into the new utterance is the cornerstone of this model. To understand how new meanings are created, we need to consider two basic aspects of the dialogical process:

1. The process of incorporation of voices from other utterances transforms the semantic qualities of these voices according to the situated expressive intention of the speaker: they get *reaccentuated* (Bakhtin 1986: 89). *Double-voicing* is one of the most common forms of re-accentuation: it refers to the author's "use of someone else's discourse for his[7] own purposes by inserting a new semantic intention into a discourse which already has, and which retains, an intention of its own" (1984b: 186–189). Ironical statements and quotations are typical examples of double-voicing. This idea reminds us, for instance, that quotations are not actually reproductions, but *representations*, of what was reportedly said. Double-voiced discourses are opposed to monologized discourses, which are intended to be seen as di-

rect, unmediated or exclusive, i.e. a discourse that "recognizes only itself and its object" (ibid.).

2. Linguistic forms become bound up with the meanings expressed in the contexts where they are used. Bakhtin claims that "form and content in discourse are one, once we understand that verbal discourse is a social phenomenon" (1981: 259). Words bring with them the contexts where they have lived (ibid.: 293), thus producing a synthesis of form, meaning and context which leads to the formation of *speech genres*. Genres are "relatively stable types" of utterance that can be described in terms of both content (a set of topics, a particular ideological perspective) and form (length, intonation, compositional structure, phonological and morphological features, etc.) (Bakhtin 1986: 60). According to Bakhtin, we master a very large array of speech genres such as greetings, farewells, congratulations, informative genres and so on. Genres are commonly defined in terms of the social situations where they appear or that they contribute toward creating.

It is therefore through the notion of genre that we can explore how language is embedded in the interactional processes where social reality is created. It is also important to point out that Bakhtin sees genre as a *constitutive dimension* of language, not as a property of a few conventionalized special texts. This means that any utterance can be seen as actualizing or recasting and, potentially, as reaccentuating and hence transforming a particular generic configuration (see ibid.: 78).

The notion of genre is particularly relevant for the purposes of my study because of its connection with *heteroglossia*, i.e. the social stratification of language. For Bakhtin, what we usually call "a language" is basically a particular code that has been sanctioned and unified by social institutions. This "unified language" is the result of a particular historical development, i.e. the political and cultural constitution of the nation state. It is an abstract image that we have created and which obscures many features of the social workings of language. Society, in fact, is always linguistically diverse, stratified or *heteroglossic*. The social stratification of language is parallel to the diversity of social groups (classes, generations, professions, groups of friends, etc.). As each social group is associated with particular activities, social relations and ideologies, each develops its own speech genres which, at the same time, gradually fashion differentiated accents, styles, dialects and languages. It is in this sense that these languages have both a formal side (phonological, morphological, lexical, syntactic, intonational) and a semantic one (sets of values and ideologies):

> What constitutes these different languages is something that is itself extralinguistic: a specific way of conceptualizing, understanding, and evaluating the world. A complex of experiences, shared (more or less) evaluations, ideas, and attitudes 'knit together' to produce a way of speaking. (Morson and Emerson 1990: 141)

The languages, dialects, styles and accents are thus a product of the dialogical processes outlined above. The idea is very suggestive, as it implies that there *must* be a functional asymmetry between different language varieties. This may help us to understand why particular linguistic forms become associated with particular contexts, meanings and social groups, thus giving rise to stereotypes (although values and meanings are themselves open to constant dialogical transformation as they are also adopted as voices subject to on-going re-accentuation). In this way, Bakhtin gives us a clear indication of how we may be able to connect particular speech forms with particular cultural forms. This connection is not between particular social features and linguistic variables, but it is an indirect relation via the insertion of linguistic structures in particular social practices.

Bakhtin's model contains interesting ideas as to how to explore these phenomena. By portraying meaning as unfinalized, open to re-accentuation and bound with linguistic forms in a way which is historically and situationally located, I believe it contains the core ideas for a social theory of meaning. In this sense, I concur with Gardiner's (1992) view that the writings of the Bakhtin circle point towards a view of language as constitutive of ideology and subjectivity in social practice, very much in tune with present-day post-structuralist views on these issues.

3.3. The organization of face-to-face encounters

I have extensively borrowed from Goffman for the analysis of casual talk and issues of self-presentation in face-to-face interaction. His ritual/theatrical conception of social interaction has proved very useful to identify what the stakes are in particular social encounters and to appreciate how a local order of discourse is subtly established and maintained. Goffman's work, or at least parts of it, is widely known amongst sociolinguists and researchers working in a variety of fields who have often been inspired by his phenomenological insights into the *interaction order*. His focus was always on the *processes* whereby social actors seek to arrive at shared understandings of what is going on in face-to-face encounters, at what he calls a "working consensus" (Goffman 1959: 21). It has often been said that Goffman's writings lay too much emphasis on the achievement of this interactional consensus, so that social struggles, disagreements and conflicts of interests appear to be ignored. However, my own reading is that he does see differences of interest and perspective as constitutive of social encounters. The idea of *working consensus* is not used as a theoretical presupposition to characterize all interactions. It is an *end* that participants, in principle, seek to achieve, but may also fail to achieve: Goffman's books contain abundant examples of breakdowns or failures to achieve this consensus, which can cause hostility or feelings of being "ill at ease, nonplussed, out of countenance, embarrassed..." (ibid.: 24). One of his most popular books, *The Presentation of Self in Everyday Life* (1959), is actually a study of how individuals or teams organize and endeavor to sustain particular *fronts*. Fronts comprise "that part of the individual's performance which regularly functions in a general and fixed fashion to define the situation for those who observe the performance" (ibid.: 32). I believe that it is precisely these processes of definition of situations, with their potential for both consensus and conflict, with their vulnerabilities, that should be central to a study of how people struggle to define and redefine their positions, roles or identities.

Another important feature of Goffman's work is his descriptive style or phraseology, which is based on the view that the behavior of individuals or teams can be described as *theatrical performances* (ibid.: 9). His use of the theatrical metaphor transmits a sense of a world where actors are presented as actively producing the features of their conduct, however unthinkingly or unwillingly (see Lyman 1973: 361, quoted in Williams 1988: 65). I have sought to adopt some of the features of this dramaturgical discourse. Because of this, it is possible that my analysis gives a distorted perspective of people's actions, as if they were always the products of careful and conscious reflection. To what extent individuals are *aware* of their practices and intentions is a complex question, which I have not tried to explore here. What was relevant for my study was to see all practices as somehow significant in that they were the product of complex processes of socialization and could, in some circumstances, be brought to consciousness and manipulated.

The performances of social actors involve the projection of a particular state of affairs, which involves in turn the creation of a character. Social actors seek to organize particular presentations of *self*, or *faces*. According to Goffman, in any encounter, the person tends to take a *line*, "a pattern of verbal and non-verbal acts by which he expresses his view of the situation" and his evaluation of the participants, including himself (1967: 5). The person is thus currently aware that the other participants are also evaluating him and that the current performance normally has a bearing on their expectations for future encounters. Therefore a person's performance amounts to a *display* of attributes and character which implies a claim to legitimate membership of and participation in that particular social milieu. In a word, the individual seeks to preserve *face*, which is defined as "the positive social value a person effectively claims for himself by the line others assume he has taken during a particular contact" (ibid.: 5). The possibility that the line one takes or the face one puts on might be discredited raises the issue of *face-work*, i.e. the complex array of resources, supportive actions and avoidance strategies that people adopt in interaction to protect their own and others' self-presentations.

Another of Goffman's notions, *frame*, is very productive analytically. It refers to the "basic frameworks of understanding available in our society for making sense out of events", particularly with regard to the processes whereby individuals regard something as "real" or as "a joke, or a dream, or an accident, or a mistake, or a misunderstanding, or a deception, or a theatrical performance, and so forth" (Goffman 1974: 10). Goffman proposes to distinguish, firstly, between two classes of *primary frames*: natural and social frames. The first correspond to "occurrences seen as undirected, unoriented, unanimated, unguided, 'purely physical'", whereas the second involve "will, aim, and controlling effort of an intelligence, a live agency, the chief one being the human being" (ibid.: 22). Primary frames provide the basis for *transformations*. The most relevant form of transformation here is *keying*, which consists of a systematic reconstitution of a primary frame on the basis of which an activity or situation can be understood (ibid.: 45). The most typical example of a keyed activity is play, where a primary activity is somehow reproduced but only playfully, as a joke and so on. The *theatrical frame*, in so far as it involves the organization of a fictional scene, can also be considered to be a type of keying (ibid.: 138). The concept of *out-of-frame activity* is relevant here as well. It refers to lines of activity or courses of action that are somehow simultaneous and segregated from what can be seen as the main "official" line (ibid.: 201). These can be, for instance, potentially distracting and threatening elements of the context, which may be treated by participants through a form of *active disattention* so that the main line of activity can continue. Out-of-frame activity also includes signals and undertakings (such as asides) which serve to regulate or co-ordinate the activity that enjoys "official" status.

Goffman develops the notion of frame to theorize about some important properties of talk. The basic idea is that talk can contain various types of frames, such as the ones described above. To illustrate how this works, Goffman proposes to see talk as a dramatic narrative, where the speaker effectively *replays* a given scene through constant realignments, switchings of roles, voices and alternating impersonations (Goffman 1974: 502). The idea of seeing linguistic performances as animations of scenes ties in with the works of Bakhtin (1981, 1986), and also of Voloshinov (1971), a member of the Bakhtin Circle, whom Goffman actually quotes. They all see speech as intrinsically multivoiced and *populated* with the words of many characters.

In my analysis, I have integrated Goffman's view of social interaction as involving particular presentations of self and dynamic shifts between interpretive frames. I have taken the position that an individual's front, self-presentation or face has to do with the positions that she or he is expected to take in the social activities where he or she participates. It would be, at an interactional level, what Foucault and Fairclough call *subject positions*, which I will analyze in terms of displays of socially relevant attributes and adoption of modes of participation or involvement (roles, types of alignment between actors and audiences). From this perspective, I will seek to study the processes whereby identities are produced, sustained or discredited in the organization of social activities.

I will also analyze the dynamic shifts between interpretive frames, particularly between primary and keyed frames, that occur in face-to-face encounters, and especially in talk. I will show how keying is fundamental for the construction of particular presentations of self which could not be sustained if the activities in question were carried out seriously (e.g. aggressive behavior). The analysis of talk as framed behavior or as *dramatization* can also help to make interesting connections between Goffman's ideas and Bakhtin's dialogical model. Firstly, the voices of others are commonly appropriated in a manifest way through the dramatization of more or less clearly delimited characters, i.e. through keyings. Secondly, the re-

accentuation of voices is often done by manipulating these voices in characteristic ways (for example, through exaggerated mimics and ironic intonation). I will thus use frame analysis to locate particular voices as evidence of particular processes in the construction of identities and ideologies. Of particular interest is here the analysis of how bilinguals switch
from one linguistic code to another as a procedure for *framing* and, thereby,
for *appropriating* the voices of other social groups in various ways. The
assumption is that the appropriation of particular speech styles and their
corresponding speech genres involve implicit statements as to the social
identities and ideologies associated with these genres and styles. Further
methodological details on this type of analysis are given in chapter 5.

3.4. Situated practices and social change

So far, I have laid a heavy emphasis on situated practice and interaction
processes as the starting point for the study of the processes of constitution
of the social world. From a TODA perspective, this corresponds to the description of local orders of discourse, which is done in parts 1 and 2 of this
book. However, we need to move beyond this level of analysis to get a
fuller picture of the significance of these practices. Otherwise, we would
get the distorted impression that the people studied acted in a completely
free and creative way, with their meanings and values being created almost
"on the spot". Clearly, some social determinants must be at work when ideologies, identities, speech styles and languages are appropriated by entire
social groups. Fairclough observes that discursive practice "inevitably takes
place within a constituted, material reality, with preconstituted 'objects'
and preconstituted social 'subjects'" (1992a: 60). We should therefore for-
mulate three basic questions:

1. To what extent the meanings, ideologies and identities described were
   the outcome of the actors' creativity or, on the contrary, contained elements that were predetermined or preconstituted by the social conditions in which actors lived?
2. In what ways did the practices analyzed contribute to reproducing or
   changing social structures?
3. What political initiatives could be put in place to tackle problematic aspects of the practices analyzed?

We need a discourse or a model that helps us situate the practices we analyze in terms of socially relevant processes that transcend the uniqueness of individuals and contexts. This is crucial to evaluate the political significance of the practices analyzed. For instance, if we wish to find out whether particular practices contribute to the reproduction of a sexist or racist society, we need to assess to what extent these practices effectively produce gender or ethnic discrimination and to what extent the social actors involved can introduce changes in their practices that make a significant contribution to improving social relations at the macro social level.To answer these questions, I have incorporated Bourdieu's ideas. Basically, I have explored the relations between orders of discourse at various levels, especially how the local orders produced by the youth cliques are articulated with the field of socioeconomic relations. To do so, I have drawn from his ideas on the workings of *social fields*. Social fields are abstract social spaces that constitute and, at the same time, are constituted by activities and relations that have a degree of internal coherence and also of autonomy with respect to those of other fields (e.g. education, the media, private enterprising). I decided to consider that Bourdieu's fields expressed some aspects of how orders of discourse operate (see also Chouliaraki and Fairclough in press). The notion of field allows us to hypothesize the existence of relatively integrated social spaces that contain a variety of positions and relations for social actors. Therefore, what I will do is seek to situate the practices of the Rambleros and the Trepas in relation to various social fields. This does not mean that I am going to try to simply fit my data into Bourdieu's scheme. In actual fact, his model contains some inadequacies and gaps that have been pointed out by a variety of authors, and which often refer to an inadequate conceptualization of resistance coupled with an overstressed emphasis on reproductive processes (see Calhoun et al. 1993; Williams 1973; Woolard 1985a). Rather, what I will do is discuss to what extent Bourdieu's model can cater for the analytical needs of studies based on situated data and in what way it can contribute to a *context sensitive* and politically committed sociology. To do so, I will bring together the theoretical discussion with the process of analysis, so that I will be exploring how his model can help us to link the practices of the Rambleros and the Trepas with issues of wider significance such as the risky games of the young or the production of inequalities between the sexes or between ethnolinguistic groups. I will deal with all these issues in part 3.

Concluding remarks

Thus, in the following chapters, I will try to show that the peer-group practices of the Rambleros and the Trepas can help us to learn a lot about the way in which language use shapes people's identities, relationships, values and views of the world. Through the forms of self-presentation adopted in their interactions, we will see how they construct subtle forms of gender identity. Through a detailed analysis of their speech forms, we will see how these are used to evoke particular characters and construct particular definitions of the situation that are consistent with people's aims to adopt those identities. We will also see that the use of Catalan and Spanish, and the frequent switching from one language to the other, is part and parcel of these processes. And finally, we will see how these patterns of identity and language use have a lot to do with the position of the Rambleros and the Trepas within the field of youth culture and within the fields of education and socioeconomic relations.

Part 1

Masculinities and femininities in youth culture

My first fieldwork observations were directed at detecting whether there were any significant relations between linguistic behavior and any type of social categorization, particularly ethnicity and gender, as class and age could be assumed to be the same for all the people I was researching. Ethnicity was clearly a relevant category, as demonstrated by Calsamiglia and Tusón (1980, 1984), Tusón (1985a), Woolard (1989) and particularly Boix (1993). I discuss relationships between language and ethnicity in chapter 6. Gender issues, on the contrary, had remained virtually unexplored in research on bilingualism.[8] Conversely, the burgeoning research fields of gender studies and language and gender had also had very little to say about bilingualism (see Coates and Cameron 1988; Johnson and Meinhoff 1997). In any case, already in the early stages of my fieldwork, I realized that there were some interesting relations between language attitudes and gender identities, particularly in the Rambleros group. Generally speaking, the Rambleros women tended to speak about the Catalan language in a more favorable light and were also more ready to use it in some situations. Additionally, the Rambleros men tended to speak with a particular *accent* associated with Spanish-speaking working-class contexts and which appeared only exceptionally amongst women (see also Pujolar 1997b).

In a way, these findings could be connected with those of many variationist researchers who had found that women tended to make greater use of "high status" linguistic varieties such as standard languages as opposed to vernaculars or dialects (Trudgill 1974; Cheshire 1982). If one accepted, as Woolard argued, that Catalan could be seen as a high status language because of its association with the local middle classes, then one could interpret that a similar trend was at work in Barcelona (maybe superposed to or overlapped with another standard/vernacular opposition between standard Spanish and the Rambleros' characteristic accent). However, there was much more in my data and in the Catalan situation as a whole than could be satisfactorily dealt with from this perspective. First of all, it was obviously difficult to see Spanish as taking the role of a dialect or of a vernacular within the boundaries of the Spanish state and in a context where it is clearly predominant in the mass media and the publishing industries.

Secondly, the linguistic practices of the second group, the Trepas, were quite different. Their attitudes towards bilingualism and their use of youth slang did not seem to follow the men/women divide found amongst the Rambleros. However, it was not a solution either to just discard gender as a relevant category. I realized very quickly that gender must have something to do with what was going on in those groups. Most of the activities they organized produced visible separations between men and women. Even though my fieldwork focused on informal, spontaneous, peer-group activities such as hanging around, drinking, smoking, dancing and chatting, gender identities seemed to have a huge bearing on people's preferences and ways of participating in the groups' events. Gender identities seemed to be essential to understanding both the workings of youth culture and the role of language in the processes whereby people constructed their identities and ideologies. The key to the problem was, of course, to conceptualize gender identity in a more adequate way, beyond the simple male/female division that is often implicit (and even explicit) in many studies. This analysis involved seeing gender as something people constructed, created and shaped in the social interactions in which they participated. Identities could thus be described in terms of the roles and relationships people developed on these occasions, the social attributes (skills, character) that they implicitly or explicitly claimed to have by acting, not acting or arranging their appearances in particular ways. As these processes were always located in particular social encounters, identities had to be *organized* through the complicity, mutual involvement and coordination of other people (in this case, their clique of friends).

Part one of this book, which includes chapters 1, 2 and 3, will be devoted to exploring this interactional production of gender amongst the Rambleros and the Trepas. I will build upon previous research on gender based on ethnographic methods, that is, on studies that assume that gender is about how people participate in particular social events. Studies of child peer-groups have found that boys tend to engage in activities that "provide objective criteria for making evaluations among group members" for "comparing their skill in a range of competitive endeavors" (Goodwin 1990: 135—136) and that "girls organize their actions in ways that display equality rather than differentiation, and emphasize cooperation" (ibid.: 64). Oppositions such as hierarchical-egalitarian (as masculine) and competition-cooperation (as feminine) are common themes in the literature. Transgression and opposition to authority are features commonly associated with working class young males as well (Willis 1977: 11—12). Willis described in interesting detail how his *lads* organized their opposition to the usual values held up by authority (diligence, deference, respect). They sought to display aggressiveness towards each other and especially towards the school conformist; they emphasized the use of dialect, swearing and argot; they engaged in drug taking and systematically sought to challenge school regulations. These types of behavior are found in many studies of working class young males (see also Labov 1972; Hewitt 1986; Tertilt 1996) The emphasized use of youth slang and swearing has also been identified as typically masculine because of the fact that it involves a certain transgression of social norms (see de Klerk 1997). Another common feature of many all-male conversations is the treatment of homosexuality and femininity as stigmas, not so much in relation to actual homosexual people or women, but in relation to other heterosexual men who may not measure up to the subtle standards of masculinity, i.e. who do not behave as "real men" (see Cameron 1997; Tertilt 1996).

On the other hand, women generally organize activities aimed at displaying equality and cooperation rather than hierarchy and competition. In school playgrounds, for instance, girls organize themselves predominantly in small groups from an early age (Maltz and Borker 1982). Their social organization is typically centered on dyads where they develop their friendship relationships, which consist of sharing secrets and weaknesses, monitoring emotions and states of mind and supporting each other's appearance (see Thorne 1993: 94; Goodwin 1990: 46—48).

However, this rather general level of description has its dangers, especially that of stereotyping and of fostering the impression that given patterns of behavior are "natural" to a given sex. This is why researchers on children's play, like Goodwin (1990), Thorne (1993) and Hughes (1988) have sought and found elements of competition, hierarchy and aggressiveness in girls' games and elements of care and collaborativeness in boys' games. The results of these studies essentially prove that social practices are much more ambiguous (or polyvalent) than is often assumed (see also Cameron 1997). In any case, the problem seems to lie, as Connell (1987) argues, in the tendency to take masculinity and femininity as discrete and uniform entities, which forces many researchers to construct excessively broad generalizations, to stress the differences between the sexes rather than the common features and even to distort the findings by ignoring exceptions and variability (see also Brittan 1987; Thorne 1993; Overing 1986 and Goodwin 1990). This epistemological attitude can even help to justify the doubtful psychological literature that treats non-canonical forms of gender as "deviant" or "queer" and produces such labels as "tomboyism" or "sissy boy syndrome" (see Thorne 1993: 117). What is relevant is to study the different patterns of gender found between individuals, classes and peoples, and to explore the relationships and struggles between different conceptions of masculinity and femininity (Connell 1987). Generalizations can only contribute to fostering and disseminating traditional gender stereotypes, while obscuring the ways in which society effectively creates and maintains gender divisions and inequalities.

Following this need to relativize gender, Goodwin (1990) and Thorne (1993: 44-47) have also sought to show that there are many activities where boys and girls play together, although some of them, such as girls-chase-the-boys or vice versa, dramatize gender boundaries and maintain "a sense of separation between the girls and the boys as distinctive groups" (ibid.: 46). Thorne has also investigated a relatively unexplored issue: *gender crossing*. It refers to the common phenomenon of people engaging in activities and developing identities usually ascribed to the other sex. It seems that the most conspicuous forms of crossing are generally stigmatized in our society, as illustrated by the derogatory terms "sissy" and "tomboy" (which also have equivalents in Catalan (*marieta, marimatxo*) and Spanish (*marica, marimacho*)). Thorne has shown how complex this phenomenon can be, with different individuals *crossing* the gender divide to different degrees and in different ways. In her examples, it is quite clear that children develop strategies for crossing while trying to avoid stigmatization. She gives the illuminating example of a boys' leader who engaged in girls' and little kids' games very often because he could afford it, as he was "tall, blonde, athletically and verbally skilled, widely respected, leader of the largest clique in the classroom" and the other boys could not cast doubts on his masculinity (ibid.: 122-123). She portrays the strategies of crossing as forming a *continuum* of different practices rather than an identity switch or a form of deviance.

Connell (1987) argues that we should start from the assumption that there exist a variety of forms of masculinity and femininity. Consequently, researchers should concentrate not so much on general descriptions of gender patterns, but on the processes whereby particular forms of masculinity become hegemonic. This is to an extent what Thorne (1993) does in the study quoted above: to analyze in interesting detail how children negotiate gender boundaries and how these boundaries are reproduced through the marginalization and stigmatization of those who do not conform to the dominant gender order at school, i.e. the gender crossers.

In this book, I will try to deal with these complex issues by analyzing in detail the talk and games of the Rambleros and Trepas. In this part 1, however, I will not yet explore how relations of domination are formed and reproduced. Later on, in chapters 4 and 7, I will suggest some interesting ways in which these questions can be framed. What I will seek to do first is to explore how individuals sought to produce and maintain particular images of themselves by negotiating their participation in particular social events. On the basis of the varied positions that Rambleros and Trepas created in their everyday doings, I will propose a working classification of various types of masculinity and femininity. In chapter 1, I will deal with the Rambleros group and I will argue that its members presented the more traditional patterns of gender construction. In this group, men organized agonistic and sometimes aggressive games to present themselves as tough, witty and as prepared to break rules (including linguistic ones) and experience risks, while they posed an implicit claim that they were simple people who followed their "natural" impulses. Women, on the contrary. sought to produce the impression of being orderly persons in whom one could trust, persons devoted to showing care and to maintaining a tidy self-presentation through dress and language style. Chapter 2 will deal with the forms of gender found amongst the Trepas, which were much more diverse. The group's leaders in particular presented relatively "aware" or "politicized" forms of gender identity which were, to an extent, a critical response to the ones found amongst the Rambleros. Thus chapters 1 and 2 will basically constitute a description of the peer-group practices of the Rambleros and the Trepas respectively, although at some points I will combine information and examples from both groups if this contributes to illustrate an argument more clearly. Chapter 3 will be devoted to some methodological qualifications, as the analysis performed in chapters 1and 2 might give the inadequate impression that the men and women I observed lead utterly separated and independent lives as they sought to produce their differing forms of gender identity. To dispel this implication, I will try to show that the categories and the genres I have proposed, rather than existing in a pure form, exist in their constant transformations and re-accentuation exerted within the complex flow of activities and conversations. One same social situation or speech event may provide space to construct differing, even conflicting forms of identity. Thus, chapter 3 will be devoted to showing a) how the analysis of gender identities can help to understand people's differing agendas in interaction, b) how gender influences the way people's contributions to conversation are understood, and c) how gender separation works even when people are "together".

Chapter 1

The Rambleros

In this chapter, I will seek to describe the patterns of social organization of the Rambleros group by focusing on the gendered aspects of their activities. I will begin by describing speech events and ways of talking associated with the Rambleros men, which led to the construction of what I call *simplified masculinity*. This term refers to the pattern of masculinity that is closer to our social stereotypes and which is based on displays of transgression, aggressiveness, naturalness and unsophistication. The term "simplified" evokes what I see as a very important ideological feature of this form of gender, namely that its "proponents" claim to have simple, unsophisticated personalities who merely follow natural, spontaneous drives and whims. Of course, this is one of the ways in which this form of masculinity claims legitimacy, that is, by claiming that things are simpler than they actually are and thus avoiding the need to justify or even stand by one's deeds. After this, I will also describe the predominant form of femininity, *mainstream femininity*, found in the group. The label "mainstream" is meant to suggest the fact that this constitutes the most predominant and widely legitimated model of female comportment, the one that most Rambleros women strove to live up to. A discussion on *crossing* will follow. Here I will focus on the people who sought to participate in practices associated with the other sex, thus creating situations that potentially contradicted the available models of gender. Particularly in this last section on crossing, but also in the previous ones, I will make occasional references to the Trepas group because the forms of gender found in each group cannot be neatly separated. Additional information on gender conflicts and struggles amongst the Rambleros can be found in section 1 of chapter 4.

1. Simplified masculinity

I will begin by analyzing one of the Rambleros men's favorite genres: verbal aggression, which is illustrated in the following encounter:

Extract 1 [Rambleros]

Transcription conventions can be found in page xi. This conversation took place on a Saturday night, around 2 o'clock; we had just parked our cars and were walking towards a kind of disco-pub along a silent street.

Andrés: [cridant] *eh vamos al bocatta aquel [?]*
    [Loud] *Hey, let's go to that sandwich place [?]*

Luis: mira ·· si quiereh comer · te puedes amorrar entre mis patas sabes [?]
    Look ··· if you wanna eat · you stick your snout between my legs, you know[?]

Ricardo: o entre lah mías
    Or between mine.

Joan: [riure]
    [Laughter]

Pablo: >(xx lah mías) · · · <tienes pa elegir
    (xx mine) · · · you've got quite a choice

Andrés: <la verdá eh que tengo mucha hambre>
    The truth is I'm very hungry.

Ricardo: (pues) amórrate >entre lah tres
    Then go for the three of them.

Andrés: pues chico <con esto no me llega pa nada
    Well kid, with this I would not have enough really.

Joan: *pues tienes muchas opciones*
    You've got many options anyway.

Pablo: (gili) pollas
    Cock (sucker).

Luis: calla · que si te la pongo en la boca parece el anuncio de (el tiempo) tiene razón (xxx)
    You shut up. If I stick it into your mouth, it'll be like this advert about "(Time) is right (xxx)."

Andrés: pero eso no me llena · la verdá · · · necesito por lo meno un beicon
    But this won't fill me up, honest. I need at least some bacon.

Unknown: (eh[?])

Luis: (xx) aquí
    (xx) here.

Ricardo: mira · te pongo yo la polla en la boca es que no te cabe colega
    Look. I stick my cock into your mouth, and there won't be room enough for it, mate.

A whole constellation of beliefs, ideas, past experiences and personal interests was needed so that the participants were able to conduct this type of exchange successfully. In a way, we could see this particular extract as a kind of microcosm where many elements of social relations, ideologies and identities are represented and form an intricate network of relations. Andrés started by letting people know that he wished to go to a particular place where they usually ate. To this, Luis reacted by suggesting that he could eat his genitalia instead. His reaction had two basic implications: first, that he did not want to go there; and second that Andrés might be willing to engage in a humiliating sexual practice. The humiliating character of the fellatio is, as I understand it, based on the assumption that sexual pleasure is centered on the penis. Any sexual activity is thus seen as a triumph, an achievement or a "service" from the perspective of the male penis. On the contrary, it can be seen as humiliating or downgrading for those who "render" the service. This is probably why the expression "*cómeme la polla*" (literally, 'eat my cock') was so popular among young people at the time, including the Rambleros men, who also used it as a provocation with their women friends. In this sense, Luis was hinting at the possibility of Andrés being a homosexual, a stigmatized identity, thus casting doubts on his masculinity (and, therefore, on the features of character which are the very condition for participation in this kind of talk).

Later on, Andrés responded to both potential meanings of Luis' utterance. After the other members of the group had insisted by offering their corresponding genitalia to placate Andrés' hunger, he affirmed that these were inadequate. In doing so, he firstly defended his proposal to go to eat, which was left open again, and, additionally, he indirectly cast doubts on the masculinity of his friends in return by suggesting that their genitalia were of inadequate size. The size of the genitalia was assumed to be a value associated with masculinity as well. In this sense Ricardo's final intervention implied a counterclaim to Andrés' suggestion.

To understand other aspects of Ricardo's contribution, I must also raise attention to some relevant prosodic features of his utterance, which are lost in the transcription: first the rising articulatory tension up to *boca* 'mouth', conveying a sense of threat; then the release of this tension suggesting that the concluding remark was so obvious that it was beyond discussion; and finally the term *colega* 'mate' conveyed a sense of forgiving friendliness. Although the threatening tone was diminished by his nearly bursting into laughter, Ricardo was playing the character of the street fighter defending his face while offering a way out of the conflict. He was calling upon an image similar to the deeply rooted Spanish *chulo* (literally: 'a pimp'), who treats the streets as if they were a bull-fighting ring.

Finally, Ricardo's half-repressed laughter points towards another very important feature of this conversation: the fact that it constitutes a *playful* confrontation. In Goffman's (1974) terms, the whole exchange was *keyed*: speakers were, so to speak, acting characters, not to be taken as really or seriously insulting or threatening each other. However, it is also important to see that this type of play allowed the Rambleros men to project their verbal dueling ability and to claim particular attributes of masculinity in an ambivalent way (see also Talbot 1998 for additional insights on this same extract).

Thus by uncovering the different layers of meaning in this interaction, it is possible to explore how particular cultural references were effectively present as the leading thread to understand and participate in everyday talk. There were particular themes (sizes of genitalia, homosexuality, conceptions about sex), genres (verbal dueling, face negotiations in fights) and voices (from pimps, imaginary or real). We could see these elements as constitutive of a particular discourse of masculinity, which is made available in particular social contexts, and from which the Rambleros were drawing to produce the meanings of this particular interaction. This discourse contained a set of appropriate subject positions, a set of roles and components of identity that individuals must adopt and which were implicit in its themes, genres and voices: a particular conception (or conceptions) about what it took to be a man.

Consequently, the meanings constructed in this encounter came in part from the relationship that the participants established with this previously existing discourse: an interdiscursive relationship. Would this mean that the Rambleros were not really producing meanings of their own? Were they simply repeating old clichés to signal their membership in the group, as many sociolinguistic studies claim? I believe that this is not the case. Bakhtin's ideas can help us to appreciate the extent to which these themes or cultural references were used to construct a space of creativity within this particular group. According to Bakhtin (1986), each new utterance constitutes, at one and the same time, a link in an ongoing dialogue and a unique contribution to it. If we take these cultural traditions metaphorically as an ongoing, latent dialogue, we can see extract 1 as a new creation which contributed toward maintaining a tradition by transforming it: by adapting it to a particular context. The themes of sex and threat were thus embedded in an organizational discussion about where to go and what to do at that particular moment. Across different occasions, the same themes were adopted and always adapted to produce new effects. After the discovery or invention of a new word or a new phrase, people would start experimenting, looking for occasions and events where it could be used and purposes it could serve to produce new verbal aggressions or hilarious effects. This explains, incidentally, why some expressions could become old or worn out. This particular discourse of masculinity could thus be seen not so much as a set of rules imposed on behavior, but as a set of resources available to produce and create particular games, situations and presentations of self.

1.1. Creative swearing

The taboo terms, expressions and images used in these contexts contained, basically, sexual, scatological (farting, burping) and religious themes. It was this commitment to the creative development of taboo resources which set apart the ways of speaking of most men and women of the Rambleros, rather than simple quantitative differences on who swore more or less. The use of swearing amongst men was one of the possible elements that could be used to produce what I saw as *ritual displays of transgression*. The transgressive character of these displays derived from the fact that these themes were known to be inappropriate for mention in "proper" social intercourse. As de Klerk points out, taboo expressions have a "covert attraction" because of the connotations of strength, masculinity and confidence that result from "defying linguistic or social convention" (1997: 147). The common formats of insults or face threatening moves analyzed above have an ingredient of this flouting of social standards of demeanor. They had a ritual character because these events were jointly organized to produce transgressive displays to which participants showed mutual appreciation and recognition. Appreciation was commonly expressed through laughter, where it was implicitly acknowledged that a breakdown of social propriety had occurred. This is best illustrated in the following example from the group discussions:

Extract 2 [Rambleros]
Joan: *And the other [topic]: speech*
Pablo: What speech!?
Woman1: What speech? [various voices are heard]
Woman2: (the way) of speaking
Pablo: [loud] *What speech!?*
Andrés: "(drop dead) you dirty swine, bitch", and things like that [laughters and voices] .

Ricardo: he he he he he!
Mateo: "Eat my cock", ha ha ha >ha ha!.
Ricardo: ho ho ho ho [very loud laughters from others as well].

The group discussion constituted for the Rambleros a situation of a special kind. They were keenly aware that they were producing a display of the group within a vaguely defined public sphere embodied by the tape recorder and by my identity as a researcher. And it was precisely the formality of the public sphere, with its symbolic relation to authority, which created particular opportunities for transgression. In this situation, just the words by themselves triggered the laughter as if they carried a special kind of magic with them; but the magic was given by a) the features of the situation, and b) its transgressive character in terms of common standards of proper speaking.

Other examples can be given to illustrate how the Rambleros men exploited swearing and tabooed themes creatively as a form of transgression. Sometimes, they would simply stand at the sidelines of other conversations and find ways of recasting what was being said into some scatological or pornographic scene, as Ricardo and Pablo did in the following episode.

Extract 3 [Rambleros]
Here the Rambleros were standing in a street of their neighborhood and waiting for all the members to turn up and get organized for a night out. In the meantime, people were doing some small talk. Raquel, a Ramblero woman was telling me the argument of a film, Alien 3.

Raquel: la nave · se estrella en unn · en una prisión no[?]> · en un planeta de una prisión
  The spaceship · crashes into a · into a prison, right?> in the planet of a prison

Joan: *<sí · · · sí*
  Yeah...Yeah.

Raquel: y entonces pues hay · violadores y >(xxx)
  And then, well, there are · rapists and >(xxx)

Ricardo: <(xxxx) la mimma cara de >(xxx) la película (xx) porque hay violadore
  <(xxxx) that same face of >(xxx) the film (xx) because there are rapists.

Joan: *<(xxx) · · · no veas qué >ambientorro de película no[?]*
  <(xxx) · · · gosh what an >atmosphere, this film, isn't it?

Raquel: <y entonces ella le decía a un- · de estos asesinos no[?] decía va venga
  <And then she was asking one- · of these murderers, right? she was asking "come on,

mátame mátame no[?] · pa' que · >(xx)
come on! Kill me! Kill me!" right? · so that >(xx)

Ricardo: <pa' que la violase
<so that he would rape her

Raquel: · · no hombre no
 · · No, not that!

Ricardo: he hehe
[laughter] He hehe!

Raquel: se enrolla con el médico de la prisión · · > (pero no se ve)
She gets involved with the prison doctor · · >(but it is now shown)

Pablo: <(otti)
<(gosh)

Raquel: y la rapan el >pelo así
And they shave her >hair, like that!

Pablo: <se vee[!?]
<not shown?

Raquel: se rapa el pelo porquee ee >y le dijo quee
She has her hair shaved because ee >and he tells her that

Ricardo: <y se va a la mili
<And she goes into the military service.

Raquel: le dijo el · que mandaba en la prisión que se tenía que rapar el pelo
porque=
She's told by the guy · in charge of the prison that she had to have her hair shaved
because=

Ricardo: =porque se iba a la mili
=because she was going into the military service.

Raquel: · hay · · no · había piojos
There's · · No. There were lice.

Joan: *hm*
Hm.

Raquel: y dice · · y dice · y dice cuandoo · te laves y tal dice · frota bien
And he says · · and he says · and he says "wheen · you wash yourself", he says "rub

tus · [curt titubeig de prevenció, baixada de veu] partes no[?]
your · [short hesitation of demureness, the voice is lowered] parts properly", right?

dice · porque puede haber ladillas no[?] · ha · · · [esclata a riure]
He says · "because there may be crab lice", right? · ha · · · [she bursts into laughter].

Ricardo: sí animaleh de >granja
Yes, >farm animals.

Pablo: <*animale de granja puede haber*
<farm animals, there might be

Raquel: [*rient*] *animale de granja* · · · · *por eso se rapa el (coño)* [*baixada*
[*laughing*] *farm animals* · · · · *that's way she shaves her (cunt)* [*Here the voice*

significativa de la veu]
has lowered a lot]

Joan: *Carai*
Gosh!

Pablo: yo tambieng me lo raparía si me dieran cuatrocientoh kiloh yo tambiéng
I would shave mine as well if they gave me four hundred millions, I would

me lo rapo vamos · · ·
shave mine as well, no doubt · · ·

Joan: [*mentre Raquel riu*] *ningún problema*
[*while Raquel laughs*] *no problem.*

Raquel: y encima dice · digo le digo yo al andrés le digo · mm esta chica · · tx ·
And, on top of that, he says · I say, I say to Andrés I say "Mm, this girl · · tsch ·

vale trabaja bien no[?] digo pero de guapa no tiene nada · · o sea · porque ·
OK she acts alright, right?" I say, "but, she's not pretty at all · · I mean, 'cause ·

parece muy basta no[?] · es muy bastorra · · y dice qué va · no · si está
she looks quite rough, right? · quite roughy" · · and he says "Not at all · No · She looks

muy bien · · y yo venga mirarla y digo · pero donde estará bien[?] · · digo
really good!" · · So I keep looking at her and I say · "Well, how come she looks so
good?" · · I say

[*comença a riure*] *porque* >*es que no · no la encuentro*=
[*she begins laughing*], *"because* > *the thing is I can't... I can't really see how come*=

Pablo: <*a mi me guhta tambieng*
<*I like her as well.*

Paula: =*quien[?]*
=*Who?*

Raquel: >*laa*
>*This...*

Pablo: <*laa · sigur · nina · huevoh* · ·
This ·"Sigurnina Balls" [Word play consisting of the hispanization of
Sigourney=Sigurnina and of Weaver=huevos, 'eggs', slang for 'balls'].

Raquel: la de alien
The one in "Alien".

Paula: no sé · es que no he visto alien
I don't know. I haven't seen "Alien".

Pablo: <(sigurni) uiber
  <*Sigourney Weaver [Pronunciation closer to the English one]*

Notice that Ricardo's attention was instantly caught by the reference to "rapists" and that he then sought to use the idea of "rape" to transform a dramatic situation in one in which the woman protagonist was simply seeking to have sex (where he says *"pa' que la violase"* 'so that he would rape her'; the joke has a sadomasochistic reading, but I believe that the special use of the idea of "rape" was rather provoked by Ricardo's wish to use it in some way or other). Raquel kept telling the story by carefully downplaying the elements that could be seen as dirty, by avoiding the use of bad language and by lowering her voice when tricky words such as *"partes"* 'parts' or *"coño"* 'cunt' had to be said. Ricardo and Pablo, on the contrary, focused their attention on these particular elements. Thus they joked about the reference to lice by portraying them as just any sort of farm animal. Finally, Pablo even engaged in a word-play by transforming the name of the actress into a very vulgar word for testicle.

Later on, I explained to Raquel the plot of the film *Gorillas in the Mist*, in which a woman biologist (played again by Sigourney Weaver) manages to keep illegal hunting at bay in an African nature reserve. Pablo then intervened to retell the plot of the film transformed into a pornographic movie where the protagonist had sexual liaisons with the Gorillas.

There was also a game consisting of smacking people's foreheads when someone produced a loud burp. The smack could only be avoided by placing one's thumb on one's forehead.

It is because displays of transgression were used to constitute masculine identities that these ways of talking or playing made sense and became constitutive of the group's culture. The speech genres of swearing and dirty language were constitutive of these particular social activities. It is in this sense that the use of such speech styles could be seen, not only as a "sign" of membership, but actually as a requirement for participation in these activities (and therefore for membership) in the male section of the group.

This transgressive principle is, I believe, useful to understand the meanings associated with many language varieties and styles. Their character does not come simply from their being ascribed to a particular social stratum, and their use does not necessarily seek to redefine social standards of language use and etiquette. In fact, their meanings and practices depend very much on the terms in which authority is defined at particular historical moments because, in a way, they are a negative reflection of it. This is probably why religious swearing is seemingly disappearing now that the church has acquired a much lower profile in public life.

However, the value of transgression is also open to contestation. I will deal with this issue in succeeding chapters. Now, in order to show the contrast between different ways of swearing, I will show how the Rambleros women used taboo expressions.

1.2. Women's appropriation of swearing

Common sense and much sociolinguistic research has traditionally associated women with more "correct" ways of speaking, the use of phonological forms closer to the standard and lesser use of vernacular styles such as slang and argot. Other researchers have challenged or qualified these findings (Cheshire 1982; de Klerk 1992). It is probably because most studies on these issues have relied basically on quantification that we possess little information on qualitative differences and similarities between the way women and men swear. Here I will try to explore this issue through a detailed analysis of conversational data. Let us look at the following example from the group discussion, in which Raquel was explaining why she did not want to wear high heels:

Extract 4 [Rambleros]
Raquel: ...If we have to stay all day standing, all night, for instance, if we go to
    dance or so · >with heels, short skirt ·
Luis: <You wanna wear a short skirt just to sit down?
Raquel: mmmm · Well, but, [Luis laughs] *>fuck!*
Paula: <No >(xx) now and then.
Raquel: <it's that · you haven't- you've never been >with- · with- with heels...

Here Raquel's second intervention was, in the original Spanish: "*Hombre, pero, joer!*". *Joer* comes from *joder*, a very worn out expression which means 'fuck', but with a much more diminished character than the English equivalent. Both *hombre* and *joer* were what Goffman (1981: 79) calls expressions, which is a type of self-remark or self-talk. Exclamations usually express a spontaneous reaction by the speaker towards a particular element of the situation. As such, they are not addressed to the audience, strictly speaking, although they may be used to convey to the audience a particular alignment of the speaker towards what is happening. The main characteristic of self-addressed remarks is that they are not meant to be responded to:

"*Hombre!*" (Spanish for 'man'), in this example, did not address any of the men in the room, and it could well have been uttered in a women-only conversation. Use of swearing in exclamations of this kind was very usual among the women in both groups. Because they were not addressed to the audience, they were not meant to involve them in a creative give-and-take of dirty expressions. Thus, this self-remark genre was not meant to be creative in the same way as men's swearing was. The Rambleros women were not involved in developing and renewing the usual themes of sex, religion and scatology. This is why they normally drew upon very worn out expressions, such as *hostia* (the communion wafer), *joder, mierda* 'shit' and often their euphemized forms: *hosti, jolín* or other expressions which would be considered as not really rough in these contexts.

Another form of swearing amongst the Rambleros women appeared inserted in narratives:

Extract 5 [Rambleros]
Paula: ...what- what I am not going to do, what I am not going to do, I am not the one who enters the group [woman laughs] · · *it- it's her, therefore · I'm not gonna go and* lick her ass *so that she stays*
Pablo: Uoow! how rough!

Here Paula was expressing her line of reasoning with respect to a particular situation. She did it by animating a dialogue through which the audience could appreciate why she had made a particular decision in the past. The underlined expression served to convey that, had she insisted on expressing interest in a woman's friendship, when this was not reciprocated, then she would have put herself in a demeaning situation. The expression referred was again a very common one, not an elaborated stylistic creation, although it had a lively effect on the audience in this situation because of the emphasis she put on it, and because the audience was paying attention very silently and was aware of being recorded. In this context, Pablo's reaction to Paula's rough language should not be taken at face value, but as ironical. He was a very insistent swearer. In my data, I have many instances of women chiding men for the use of bad language, for "mispronouncing" words, for not being dressed properly, for picking their noses, farting or burping. In this sense, the situations where men did so constituted a humorous recasting of the women's voices, which served both to expose them in an embarrassing position and to justify themselves by showing that women were not really an example of proper manners.

On some occasions, a woman would utter an exclamation about the dirty exclamation she had just uttered, and typically bring her hands to her mouth thus implying that the word had been uttered unintentionally. This occurred, of course, in situations where I was present, and where my presence was possibly one of the reasons for the embarrassment.

These examples suggest that the Rambleros women were especially sensitive as to the conditions in which they could safely swear without being seen in a negative light. They would tend to swear at particular junctures of a conversation or in situations where a sense of surprise or anger was conveyed. On such occasions, the subject had the potential claim of diminished responsibility, i.e. of having got carried away, of having said something unintentionally or exceptionally. Women thus swore in a kind of guarded way, as they tried to prevent loss of reputation. Very rarely did they engage in strong insults, except in some situations when they were angry for being teased or harassed by the men. Their swearing was like a voice they kept at a safe distance, not to be taken as a true aspect of themselves. Patricia, from the Trepas, illustrated this distinction when she described how she used to swear in the past, before she got accustomed to do so much more often as a result of her feminism:

Extract 6 [Trepas].
Patricia: I don't know. I- some things · · for me the so- when I used to say "son of a bitch" it was when I hit myself with a nai- when I was hitting a nail and I hit myself with the hammer. And I used to say "son of a bitch", or when something fell to the floor, like that, · but I didn't say "son of a bitch" like this [now], *come on*: "son of a bitch", or say "*it makes my [genitals] sweat*" I never used to say that either.

I do not mean by this that women were more sensitive than men to the way they displayed themselves to others, nor that men and women had different standards of hygiene and demeanor. It was rather that men and women manipulated the ideas of hygiene and demeanor in a different way according to the rituals they engaged in and the identities they sought to display. Masculine swearing had to go further if men were to produce interest and excitement in and around the particular games that they organized. Most women, as I will show in the next section, had different agendas.

1.3. The exploitation of risk: risk to face

The exploitation of risk, either symbolic or physical, was the feature that set the strongest contrast between the form of masculinity of the Rambleros and that of the Trepas people. Amongst the Rambleros, the organization of, and participation in, risky events of various kinds allowed for the display of wit, physical strength and aggressiveness usually associated with the imagery of masculinity. In this section, I will discuss symbolic risk, or risk to face, and I will deal with physical risk later. Although a risk to face can also be produced through the symbolic implications of physical acts, I will deal here only with threats to face produced through language. I call these *verbal aggressions*. Extract 1 above can be taken as a good example of this type. The game consisted of participants producing statements that discredited others and reacting in turn to others' discrediting statements. Threats to face commonly stood on the assumption that men should be heterosexual and should have remarkable physical strength and sexual prowess. Shorter genres such as insults, tellings-off, also usual amongst the Rambleros, can be included in this class as well.

However, although real dangers of momentary losses of face were often created for the participants, these events were always perceived as games, i.e. as keyed activities (Goffman 1974: 43). Luis said in his interview:

Extract 7 [Rambleros]
Luis: We are more · cut from another pattern, we are more brutish, right? More- ·
We like to hit and hassle each other, when we don't know what to talk about: to
insult each other to provoke and all that. · · Well, yes, we are more- [He laughs]
· Well you've already seen it that-. Hanging around, isn't it? You don't know
what to do: "'Ricky', you gonna eat my cock!", and the other one gets cross, (he
gives-), "I'm gonna hit you", "punch". · · Of course never- · but it is only, only
between us, I mean we never hassle [other] people or, · · to have a good time,
to- to- we always have something to laugh about right? Well, · when we don't
know what to laugh about, well, we insult each other [He laughs] · · without
doing it- I mean with no bad- intent, never, right? You've already seen it,
haven't you?

In the interviews, three out of the four Rambleros men dramatized verbal aggressions and said that they were not meant to cause *real* offense. The keyed character of verbal aggressions allowed people to insert them in almost any situation without endangering a particular course of action (which would happen if somebody's dignity was seriously put in doubt).

For example, when negotiating what movie to see in the cinema, strong insults and rejections could be distributed without endangering the line of discussion.

Although verbal aggression games such as those I have described did not have a name, as in Labov's (1972) study of inner city gangs, they were quite conventional. They consisted of presenting someone in a demeaning way (for instance, by producing a narrative where he or she was involved in a demeaning course of action). On the other hand, face-threatening actions, and the use of dirty language, offered opportunities for transgression from commonly accepted norms of respect to others and of linguistic propriety.

Nevertheless, some conditions had to be met so that this type of frame could be sustained. In a situation where one is very vociferously insulted, it is not that easy to ignore the potentially demeaning signification. Mateo, in his interview, mentioned that they could do this because they had known each other for a long time. The Rambleros men could accept verbal aggression because they knew in the context of their overall relationship that their reputation or their status was not really threatened. Such a state of affairs must have been made possible thanks to the group's history, where the members had shown that they counted upon and cared about each other. For instance, their strong rejection of Andrés' proposal that they should go and eat a sandwich was acceptable as long as there was the expectation that Andrés' needs would be somehow taken into consideration. In this sense, I felt that the people of this group, including the men, were quite considerate and responsible towards each other. This is evidence of how the meaning potential of utterances is dependent on the relationships that interlocutors have established in previous communicative encounters.

This frame started to crack, nonetheless, in situations where some member's interventions were repeatedly transformed into ridicule without consideration for the person's actual intentions. In both groups, there were some temporary lines of mocking insistently directed at particular persons, who could become for a while a kind of buffoon. In such cases, the person's possibilities for participation in discussions and games could become quite restricted because his or her interventions were never taken in their intended meaning. Sometimes these individuals ended up not getting any fun at all out of the game, and they could get really worked up or depressed.

Favored victims of verbal aggression were the women of the group. The "eat my cock" phrase, mentioned in relation to extract 1 was one of the games directed at them. I once saw Ricardo saying it to Irene, one of the women. She responded with a very strong disparagement of Ricardo's suitability as a sexual partner. This response, though, was not meant to be taken as an engagement in a verbal aggression game, but as a rejection of it. Precisely because Irene's intervention might have been taken as an excuse to keep "playing the game", she took care to go away immediately, thus implying that the interaction was over. Similar instances of women "telling off" men were common, not only as a reaction to verbal aggressions, but also to swearing or dirty narratives. Women found such games demeaning, sometimes even when they did not participate actively in them and were only expected to listen or show minimal appreciation. Men seemed to enjoy provoking these reactions as a game in itself.

Sometimes, women did participate as spectators of men's verbal aggressions and dirty jokes. It was perfectly possible for the women to laugh, show appreciation or even, exceptionally, contribute in particular situations. This was often done in a way that implied that this participation was involuntary: for instance, to laugh as if one could not avoid it, sometimes adding dismissive comments on the man who had produced the situation. The following anecdote illustrates this possibility:

Extract 8 [Rambleros]
We went on a holiday trip to a tourist resort in southern Spain. One day, as we were walking from the camping ground to the town, Pablo started a narrative describing, in a very scatological way, the supposed masturbative practices of one of the women present. At first he was told off by the other women but encouraged by the appreciation of the men. As he developed the narrative, he came up with such imaginative elements that the whole audience, men and women, broke into seemingly uncontrollable laughter. [My own recollection]

1.4. Diminished risk: teasing

Teasing is a genre common to any social group in society, although clearly not appropriate for any social occasion. It seems to have much in common with verbal aggression in that it consists of performing acts or producing utterances which in some way threaten the image of a person, but normally in an easily repairable way. The Rambleros women teased a lot, much of their teasing being directed at the men, one could say, as sweet revenge for being hassled verbally. In the following episode, Ricardo was teased because he had had his hair cut:

Extract 9 [Rambleros]

Noia 1: vaya pelada eh[?]
Woman 1: What a 'shearing', yeah?

Noia 2: es verdá
Woman 2: That's right!

Noia 3: eh verdá riquini te hah pelao
Woman 3: That's right! Riquini, you've been sheared!

Paula: (eh que) quiere ligar eh[?]
   (It's because) he wants to pick up [girls], yeah?

Pablo: [cridant] *riquini*
   [shouting] *Riquini!*

In this situation, the women's ironic intention came across basically through their tone, which was probably accompanied by caresses on Ricardo's (nicknamed "Riquini") hair. Paula's suggestion that the haircut had been done to "pick up girls" referred to a typical masculine theme, and it contained an insinuation that Ricardo was not completely successful in these matters. On another occasion, as the men were playing five-a-side football, Paula (who was watching the match together with the rest of the women) kept shouting deriding comments at Mateo for allegedly wearing sportswear that looked like a pyjamas or a skirt.

Cross-gender teasing is considered by Thorne (1993: 78–79) as *border-work*: a way of playfully acting out gender conflict in the form of fighting, teasing, bothering and hassling. The distinction I make between teasing and verbal aggression is to highlight the fact that, in teasing, one need not manipulate taboo elements. Here we are talking about themes such as minor accidents with no serious consequences, temporary losses of self control due to alcohol or distraction, failures to appreciate the nature of a state of affairs and producing wrong reactions, inadequate features of one's body such as posture, quality of dress, hair-style, sizes of bodily organs and so on. These elements were perfectly legitimate in women's talk as long as the teasing was conducted with appropriate tact. Paula also reported highly organized teasing on a night the women went out on their own:

Extract 10 [Rambleros]

Paula: ...look, we [women] went out · by ourselves, and we got into mimicking each other · on the way we dance. · Aand we picked · we picked on each other's defects...

Thus the moderate transgression of face-saving expectations is meant to be understood in the context of a long sustained relationship where the participants are effectively giving each other a lot. Conversely, it can be used to signal willingness to treat or to be treated in friendly terms even when the background relationship is not there. An important difference between teasing and verbal aggression can be shown through the way I was treated. I could very easily be the object of teasing, but not so easily of verbal aggression. One day, as we played table-football in pairs (another male competitive game), team mates regularly took to insulting and criticizing each other when things went wrong. Nevertheless, my team-mate did not feel he could do this with me and all the time we kept blaming ourselves for failures and fiascoes.

Paula's report in extract 10 about women's teasing is, in the context of this group, very significant. She talked about highly organized teasing during a significantly long period of time on a special occasion, that is, one night the women chose to go out by themselves. The implication seems to be that such activities could not be organized when men were around. Indeed, in the group discussion, the women said that they often resented the teasing from men. One sensitive issue of cross-gender relations was dress, hair-style and physical appearance in general. In my fieldwork, I did not hear women talking about dressing and hair-style extensively as is sometimes stereotypically reported, though they usually made supportive comments to each other about looks. In the following extract, Irene explained why she wore skirts and shorts when she went on holiday but did not dare to do so within the group:

Extract 11 [Rambleros]
Irene: But here I don't come down, yeah? Because I know that if I come down: "Hey lass, and so on and so forth". If you [don't] mock me because of my ass, you will mock me because of my legs.
Luis: And you would take it badly. Why? [Irene: yeah!] Because you think that we would not like to see you with a skirt?
Joan: No maybe because you wanna dress as you like and you don't like people commenting on it, throwing it at you
Irene: Of course
Raquel: Because it is all afternoon mocking Irene because of her...
Laura: And at the end, you get worn out, and you don't put it on.

The men's teasing was therefore perceived as too strong or too insistent. So my impression is that teasing between women involved an implicit agreement not to carry the lines beyond the limits of their own game, and especially not to make the jokes available to the men, who could make less tactful uses of them. This does not mean that women were necessarily more sensitive to teasing than men. As Irene implied in the following extract, men must also have had their weak points:

Extract 12 [Rambleros]

Irene: if we mock you you take it · you take it really bad.· But then, to us- No, you mock us and we cannot take it bad because "come on!"

1.5. Physical risk and aggressiveness

If I compare the impressions I have so far from living in Catalonia and Britain, and also from reading literature on youth culture in Catalonia, Britain and the US, I perceive significant differences with regard to fighting culture. Generally speaking, I would say that, in Catalonia, bullying and fighting does not have such a constitutive role in men's relationships as seems to be implied by the English and North American literature. The works of Willis (1977), Hewitt, (1986), Jackson (1990: 188), Phillips (1993: 225) and Labov (1972) suggest that real fighting has a very central role amongst the gangs of young men in these contexts. It remains to be seen whether the impression fostered by these studies and by media coverage of youth violence in Britain and the US is a really balanced one.

In my childhood, there were fights and confrontations, but fighting ability did not seem to play a significant role in establishing group membership or popularity ranking. I do remember recurrent stories of big fights and long-lasting feuds amongst groups of older boys from different towns. But these seemingly disappeared in the early 70s, which may be a sign of some social change that may have gone unnoticed. In Barcelona, only a few skinhead groups, extreme right activists and inner city gangs are known to be violent. Football fans are generally seen as very peaceful. I am not aware that Catalonia has ever had the inner-city riots that occur now and then in Britain or the United States. Nevertheless, there is a kind of fighting culture in Spain, in a way embodied by the stereotypical *chulo*, as mentioned above. In my native town, it is common amongst Catalan speakers to dramatize voices from fighting rituals with a switch to Spanish, which may reflect the fact that many aggressive gangs in my childhood were usually of working-class Spanish-speaking origin. However, it is clear that native

Catalans can participate in violent deeds as well. I remember, during my fieldwork in Barcelona, a Catalan speaker narrating in great detail how he had smashed a car with a baseball bat. The narrative contained a great deal of code-switching, which suggests that the fighting ethos may be constructed as a Spanish thing. Vandalism is, in any case, just as common in Catalonia as it appears to be in England: litter bins and most pub toilets must be repaired regularly.

I never saw the Rambleros men getting involved in street fights. Nevertheless, Luis reported having done so in the military service. He was telling me here that he occasionally joined a gang of people he had met when he was a conscript:

Extract 13 [Rambleros]

Luis: It's that it's another kind of ball-game. They are more "tacataca", right? *more the "lolailo" type* [people associated with some forms of Spanish folk music, typically lower class, also Romanies], *smoking lots of joints and creating the- · trouble in the streets, pushing people around, well, · · Hanging around and singing in the streets, and if somebody jumps up, then you go for trouble, right? Aand · · create trouble, right? er- · "Eeeh! what's up", · Well the typical thing in the [military] service, right? that- · · We did it in Segovia and: "we are the fourth of 90!", "eeh!". And when somebody from another turn came, · we always went foor er trouble. · Or · "we are Parashooters", "Well, we are from the Armoured Brigade". And there was a history of- of- · of fights for many years, right?. · "Where are the Armoured Brigade guys?", "They've gone to such and such pub". So there we go. Ugh, and we had real brawls there.*

Clearly Luis was happy to display readiness to fight; but engaging in actual fighting depends very much on the possibility of associating with people who are willing to organize fights and to respond to provocation. In this sense, the military service seemed to provide a sort of backstage for behavior which did not need to be brought home. The military service has many such traditions. Bullying and insulting new recruits, or even Catalan conscripts, are traditions transmitted across generations of soldiers.

As Luis' quote in extract 7 implies, verbal aggression has a kind of continuity with fighting. The Rambleros men would organize keyed, playful fights amongst themselves. They reported that they had fought playfully on the beach, a situation which I also witnessed with some of the Trepas men. Playful pushes and casual blows were also very usual, and here it was also possible for women to participate. Women hit men much more often than other women, which shows that this was a form of cross-gender *border-*

work (Thorne 1993). In the group discussions, both Paula and Andrés complained that the blows (from men and women respectively) were sometimes too strong. The problem with games of threat is precisely that players cannot disclose how far they are prepared to go because this would discredit any sense of threat. An acceptable level of potential damage seems to be necessary for the game to make sense. But then, women are known not to be prepared to go really far. Thorne (ibid.) mentions that girls' unserious fighting and chasing never gets really rough, whereas that of the boys usually does. This may be because boys are oriented to showing superiority (even if playfully) whereas women are not. These niceties of frame negotiation had a significant bearing on the way in which men and women approached teasing and fighting. In the following extract, there is an interesting discussion in which Raquel and Paula were explaining why women got the worst of teasing and fighting:

Extract 14 [Rambleros]
Luis: Well then just show me what the difference is between you-
Raquel: It's cause you > (xx be right)
Luis: <You can take the piss out of me and if the moment comes I get worked up, I
   say "look, you shut up or I'm gonna break your head."
Raquel: <u>But I am not capable of saying such thing</u>
Paula: Why, why
Raquel: Because I am >of a different character
Paula: <Luis · >(xx) I'm telling you something else
Luis: <Okay · Fine! · I'm saying something else > · not the strength alright.
Paula: <I'm · I'm telling yo- · · >I'm telling yoou
Raquel: <(because if I) tell >you "I'm gonna break your head"
Paula: <that I'm gonna break your head >and you'll burst out laughing!
Luis: <Okay. Not strength, not strength. She takes the piss out of me and I tell her:
   > Okay, okay?
Raquel: <And on top of all he breaks mine, · you know? [she laughs]

Women could not go as far as men in games of threat. One of the reasons might be that they were sensitive to the implications of presenting themselves as too rough. Raquel's statement that she was not capable of "saying such thing" did not mean, of course, that she was not capable literally, but that she felt unprepared to take on the implications of doing such thing. As an illustration of this, I can mention the fact that one of the women was very seriously singled out for criticism by a man *and* a woman for hitting too strongly, whereas no man was singled out in this discussion (see also section 3 on crossing). Women's inroads into displays of aggressivity were, therefore, of a limited scope. It was, in a way, the men's symbolic territory.

It is important to see these games as a way to organize particular displays of character. Performances need an audience, or they will not be performances at all. In the following extract, Luis owns up to the fact that not only group members, but also bystanders, could be treated as a potential audience:

Extract 15 [Rambleros]

Luis: ... when we don't know what to laugh about, well, we insult each other [He laughs] · · *without doing it- I mean with no bad- intent, never, right? You've already seen it, haven't you? Even- · even people who are not with us and are (not) paying attention can have a good time, they can laugh. When we take the underground and we hassle each other, · and people are around, they listen and la- laugh and all that.*

The common stereotype that associates some Mediterranean cultures with loud and boisterous behavior in some contexts might be due to this tendency to treat strangers as an audience. This was very clear in some situations amongst the Trepas, where long conversations were held between individuals at great distance. The individuals would shout at one another engaging in some absurd, allegedly meaningless or ludicrous conversation. This was seen as fun precisely because it was supposed to be overheard by other pedestrians.

Within the groups, I also perceived that the point of fighting, verbal aggression or teasing was not what happened between speaker (or doer) and addressee, but what the wider audience (other members of the group) assessed as happening between them. The point was not in what was being said or done but in the scene created. Similar observations can be found in Labov (1972) and Rampton's (1995) study of "ritual insults" or "jocular abuse", that is, that a third person role is necessary for these events to make sense. A consequence of this should be that people do not do certain things in isolation. This point is difficult to validate in the sense that any observer (such as a fieldworker) can automatically be constituted as a relevant audience, and two isolated participants could always have a reason to treat each other as an audience in a reciprocal way. In any case, I do believe that these events were possible because the group usually organized itself in a collective format, i.e. as having a common line rather than multiple groups having multiple lines. In this context, the displays analyzed always received relevant reactions and appreciation from others.

The Rambleros men displayed their readiness to fight quite often in implicit or explicit ways. However, I never saw that they sought to get involved in real fights when we went out. Occasionally, a low key form of violence could appear when playing football. Nevertheless, they would present themselves as not starting it. One day when we played five-a-side football, the other team had an exceedingly tough defender (I can corroborate it, my leg felt it). He was reportedly "cooled down" after a couple of special interventions made by members of my team. These occurred nevertheless within the frame of the game, not as direct aggression (just a foot going further than it should, as is customary in football).

In some hard-rock music concerts there is a game of strong pushes combined with dancing where individuals can be propelled across long distances, sometimes landing on distracted bystanders. It is probably a derivation of the Punk Slam Dance as described by Roman (1988). Luis suggested that wrangling was one of the attractions of heavy metal concerts. Indeed, the literature corroborates the stereotypical aggressiveness of heavy metal music, which is shown not only in its sound, but also in the artists' stage performances and the iconography (Straw 1990; Breen 1991). The typical heavy metal songs are characterized by a strong beat and a very amplified instrumental sound, which usually forces singers to adopt a very loud and high-pitched, and thereby distorted, voice. The heyday of heavy metal is considered to be the beginning of the seventies, with groups like Led Zeppelin, Deep Purple and Black Sabbath. It is associated with very histrionic performances, like those of Jimi Hendrix, and also with satanic, apocalyptic or necrophilic imageries. After a certain crisis during the eighties, heavy metal came back to the stage with a strong support of international record companies. Luis himself pointed out that he was the first in liking heavy metal amongst his siblings by saying "*At the beginning, I was the [only] violent heavy metal [of the group]*". Except one, all the Rambleros men were confessed "heavies" and would get together to read specialized magazines, attend concerts and go to "heavy" pubs. They were highly knowledgeable on all the issues linked to heavy metal music and rock music in general: once I was asked to buy a particular CD which they knew had only been issued in Britain.

The taste for heavy metal can be an example of another way of constructing an aggressive ethos: participating in aggressive shows as a spectator. The Rambleros men also liked to get near to the scenes of street fights,

even if they did not get involved in them. Sometimes, they even participated in the typical face-saving negotiations, even though they were not
acquainted with any of the offended parties. Women would keep away at a
greater distance, and later they would fish for an account of the story from
the men, who would be able to build exciting narratives and give a certain
impression of superiority with regard to people who fight for petty reasons.

2. Feminine agendas

Up to now, I have focused on themes that were central to the construction
of masculine identities. The activities and displays described so far probably match our general ideas about what young people do in their leisure
activities: swearing, playful or serious fighting, drinking, drug taking, listening to music (some of these aspects are further explored in chapter 2).
This may well be because our ideas about what young people do may be
based on what young men do. Indeed, the activities of young men are usually (they certainly were in this case) the most visible and audible in these
contexts. Thorne (1993) points out, for example, that in a school playground, the boys tend to occupy most of the physical space available. In the
events described, women seemed to participate in a peripheral way; or alternatively, they engaged in similar activities but in diminished or euphemized forms. They seemed to struggle between two agendas: that of gaining status as full participants in the general merriment (in order to enjoy
themselves, to have friends, to learn things) and that of maintaining and
developing the qualities, relationships and identities desired by and expected of young women in their social context.

On the basis of these considerations, we might be led to conclude that
the Rambleros were essentially a male-dominated group. While in chapter 4
I will argue that this is generally the case, such a partial account would not
do justice to the Rambleros women. I have offered a very fragmented view
of their behavior, always considering their ways of participation in activities associated with the men. As a result, I have stressed the features of
femininity that appeared to limit their suitability as participants in these
events. The view I have been giving of women is probably congruent with
many male-centered discourses which present femininity in terms of
women's inadequacies. Coates (1988: 121) has pointed out that research on
women's language, in focusing on cross-gender interaction, has traditionally described it in a "negative tone" by seeing it as "weak and tentative".

Cameron (1994) has also denounced popular and academic discourses on gender that are based on the assumption that masculine ways are the norm and feminine features are deviant and problematic. In this section, therefore, I will reverse my focus and try to conceptualize what women were seeking and what they brought into the social spaces I investigated. The question is, therefore: what were the agendas of women? What qualities, relationships and identities were they trying to develop?

2.1. Displays of intimacy

In the introduction to part 1, I have mentioned that much research on gender, particularly amongst children, has established that girls are generally interested in developing friendships or relationships. It is therefore typical that they organize their interactions in dyads, i.e. groups of two persons devoted to talk and to developing their relationships. In these events, participants are expected, or are given opportunities, to display intimacy, i.e. to express or imply interest in each other's lives, emotions, experiences, secrets, fears and happinesses. I will call these types of events *intimations*, by which I seek to stress that they constitute *active processes* where intimacy is produced (even if this is not the common meaning of the word in English). My definition of intimation is similar to what Jones (1980: 197) calls "chatting" as a particular form of gossip characterized by intimacy and mutual self-disclosure. In my data, intimation did not necessarily consist of sharing very sensitive secrets. Most of the conversations I had access to involved no serious dangers of exposure. One of their most common features was to catch up on news, where the participants simply updated each other on any new development in their respective lives: most of the "news items" were quite harmless to anybody. The following extract illustrates this point. In their joint interview, Silvia and Jaume (from the Trepas) had been discussing an event which had taken place the day before. Jaume was complaining that he and Chimo had felt left out because Silvia and Natalia had withdrawn to talk on their own. Silvia then described her conversation with Natalia:

Extract 16 [Rambleros]
Silvia: No, for instance · last night Natalia was telling me that she felt very
depressed, right? because she could see that she did not have any qualifications
and that · well that she did not have any qualifications, that's what she thought,
right? And, I mean she felt very bad, when she found herself with no job, her

studies halfway through, that · she had to start working but she had not found a
job and that, she has not actually started looking for one, right? And all- it's a
bit of everything, we were talking like that, rather, because I saw she was a bit
depressed I asked what was wrong. And I asked her that what was wrong,
(yeah?) · And I asked her, well· · what what was wrong, no and · · · And that's
why, right?. Th- They [the men] were smoking a joint so "what are we gonna
do?" So we started talking right? Also, I had not seen her since before
Christmas and all that right? [I didn't know] whether she had had a good time
in the village and all that, I asked her right? If she had been to the village. And
she did, well, [she asked] me just the same.

Interestingly enough, Jaume said that he had also asked Natalia what
was wrong with her, but that she had avoided the question and only engaged in conversation about it later with Silvia. Natalia, undoubtedly, had
seen the issue as not appropriate to talk about with Jaume. Natalia's intimations with Silvia were embedded in a developing relationship where such
events were a constitutive routine feature, whereas this was not the case
with Jaume. Clara, another woman of the Trepas, said that all the women in
her groups organized these intimations, so that they paid continuous attention to what each other felt on a day to day, sometimes on an hour to hour,
basis.

Later on, Silvia also implied that it was necessary that these events include a reduced number of participants:

Extract 17 [Trepas]
Silvia: but it may well happen that we arrange, and Natalia and I have have
arranged to meet. "Ah!" then says Clara, "Then I will come as well", I don't
know, or Patricia, right?: "Ah! Then I am coming as well". Then if we meet
four or five then it's a big fuss. If we st- start to talk again about sorrows · with
lots of people around, then, · it- it is not possible either, right?. Therefore, well,
of course we just seized the opportunity at that moment right? and said: "Now
we are gonna talk, yeah?"

Silvia must have known, as I did, that Natalia and Clara were also quite
intimate. In this sense, Clara could have participated just as well. Silvia was
merely implying that two or three participants was all right, but that four or
five were already too many. This is probably because too many participants
would have made displays of interest and intimacy more difficult in practical terms. Interest is expressed through involvement, reciprocity and sympathy. If the number of participants grows, it is likely that the interaction
will not supply opportunities to develop as far as intended: topics may not

be explored fully enough and all the participants' interests must be accommodated.

I believe that the women's ability to organize displays of intimacy and personal interest had an important bearing upon my own experience of socialization into the groups. In both groups, my entry and integration was facilitated by women, and it was with them that I had to talk and sort out the issues arising from my "intrusion". It was with them that I first engaged in sessions of exchange of news, negotiations and organization. Almost as a natural result, this created a situation where catching up and later confiding became a normal state of affairs. I also made an effort to extend this practice to as many women as I could, because I was interested in getting to know everyone. This was also made possible because, from the start, most women showed interest as well. Most of the time, they did this by coming straight to me and encouraging conversation, something that men rarely did. The first day I went out with the Rambleros, each woman came to me one by one and asked me who I was, what I was doing, whether I was having a good time and whether I would come back. On subsequent occasions, I could take these approaches as a signal that they would welcome an approach on my part.

Nevertheless, as a man, I must say that I did not find participation in these events easy. In the first stages of the fieldwork, I usually felt awkward and I was not sure of the point of some conversations. My interpretation is that my masculine assumptions led me to look for meaning in the topic that was being discussed rather than in the display of interest itself. I also felt there was awkwardness on their part, as if they were also sensing this mismatch. Sometimes I felt at such a loss that, when I decided to telephone them, I would write down a list of conversation topics to allow myself to relax and keep the conversation going smoothly. On the other side, I also found positive sides to this experience: I felt I could actually talk about any topic, anything, whereas with the men I felt constrained to adapt to their usual lines such as stories of outrageous intoxications, of funny incidents, sexual themes, music and so on. With the men, I felt I had to restrict myself to making good jokes or to telling particularly interesting or extraordinary things. With the women, I felt that legitimate topics included those that affected somebody personally in whatever way; jokes were also acceptable and all issues could be explored in more depth. In my own experience, I have also felt that in comparable situations women generally retell events and experiences with much more detail (for instance, explaining to a friend the vicissitudes of a trip or a holiday). I think that this was important in making my integration into the groups possible. For instance, I have plenty of conversations recorded where I talk with the Rambleros women about all kinds of details related to my research, particularly about the practical problems of recording talk. I am also convinced that the women also helped their male friends to understand what my situation was and what I was doing, which probably made things easier.

I also felt that the women were generally much better informed about what was going on in both groups. This impression must have been fostered by the fact that exchanging information was a legitimate activity for them. With the men, it was more difficult to find the right moment to ask a question. For instance, at the beginning, I could not understand jokes and stories because of my lack of background knowledge about what and who they were talking about. In order to understand what was going on, I had to ask questions about the assumptions behind what was said. I increasingly felt that many men did not like this, because it somehow made them step out of the game and felt it a bit disruptive, whereas women did not seem bothered at all by these interruptions and seemed to understand better why I asked the questions.

2.2. Chatting

I use the common terms *chatting* or *chat* to refer to a particular type of conversational activity organized by women. The difference between chats and the one-to-one displays of intimacy mentioned above is not clear-cut. As Silvia suggested in extract 17, when too many participants were involved, some types of intimation were not possible. I will call *chats* those situations where the conversation ceased to have a private, intimate character. They were typically situations with more than two participants, but this criterion cannot be strictly applied. This category would include the conversations of all-women groups that Coates (1988) portrays as engaging in *gossip*. When writing about women's talk, researchers do not usually make this distinction: they usually refer to both, intimation or chatting, as *gossip* (Gluckman 1963; Jones 1980). The continuities between intimation and chatting can certainly be detected in the atmosphere usually created in these situations. Coates (ibid.) points out that they involve a common exploration of issues and a certain ethos of equality and consideration for each person's contributions. On the basis of a convincing conversational analysis, she provides evidence of how the women she studied constructed their conversational lines in a very collaborative way.

If we accept that building relationships and ties is at the top of women's agendas (Gilligan 1982; Goodwin 1990; Thorne 1993), it is congruent to expect that women will also seek opportunities to display personal interest, sympathy and care in these chatting events. Amongst the women I studied, attention to each other's faces seemed to be a priority. Teasing was certainly done with much more circumspection than amongst males or in cross-gender talk. Also, it was common for them to make supportive comments about their appearance, particularly when somebody turned up with a new dress or hairstyle. In section 2 of chapter 2, I also show an example of how a politicized Trepas woman went through a *dress-appreciation ritual* by displaying role-distance. These events must have surely made women feel that they had to be mindful of their appearance. Even those who tried to redefine their femininity by adopting a typical masculine *I-don't-care-what-I-wear* style would show some concern about their appearance.

Other manifestations of this *building relationships* agenda could be found in the topics chosen and in the way people chose to present themselves in narratives:

Extract 18 [Rambleros]

I once overheard a conversation between Silvia and Lola of the Trepas group. Silvia was talking about her relationship with Jaume, her boyfriend. I noticed how much she used the pronoun *we*, thus representing herself from the perspective of her membership of the couple. At one moment she made the following statement:

> *"Se   me ha comprado unos pantalones violetas"*
> [He] himself me has bought some trousers   violet

This reflexive construction, which does not exist in English, can convey through the dative form *me* a sense of possession such as in *se me rompió el vaso* 'I broke my glass' or 'my glass got broken'. Salva, a man who also overheard the conversation, teased Silvia for implying that her relationship with Jaume was too steady or too formal.

Here Silvia was portraying herself as a member of the Silvia-Jaume relationship. And even as she described Jaume's activities, she would linguistically represent herself in the text as a participant, thus implying that whatever Jaume did affected her as well. Salva's reaction is consistent with Gilligan's (1982) claim that men prefer to construct themselves as free and independent individuals.

As I mentioned before, women's chats allowed them to discuss a wider range of topics and in more depth than was the case in men's conversations. I have a recording of the Rambleros women talking about a tax-raise which affected the business of one of the women's parents. One day Lola (of the Trepas) recounted that she had nearly been hit by a young teenager wildly riding a motorbike. Some two yards away from her, the teenager, who was wearing no helmet, collided head-on with a traffic fence and probably died. Lola was saying that she could not feel sorry for him because he knew he was acting dangerously and he could have killed her as well. Clara disagreed with her on the basis that this was too insensitive a view of the matter. They went on trying to find some common ground. This conversation seemed to have a lot in common with those analyzed by Coates (1988). I also remember getting involved with three or four Trepas women in a discussion about the Goliards, a religious order stemming from the Cathar movement, which was crushed by a French-led invasion of Provence in the 13th century.

The common belief that some topics of conversations are associated with women and others with men was, to a certain extent, true. For instance, it was common for women to talk about boyfriends, relationships, appearances or other people's problems and anecdotes. The Rambleros men usually talked about football, music and the military service. However, what made the conversations of women and men really different was the fact that the women seemed more prepared to engage in a focused conversation where each participant's points would be taken up seriously. This is the reason why, at the early stages of fieldwork, I got the impression that many conversations were dominated by the women. In mixed-gender talk, women did not necessarily hand conversational control to men, but kept developing their topics. In these situations, it was common for men to participate from the sidelines, teasing and making jokes about what was being said. Extract 18 above is an example of this and also the occasion where I was talking with Raquel about a film while Pablo kept chipping in with dirty comments. Extract 19 is another example of this:

Extract 19 [Rambleros]
This is with the Rambleros group. At this point, they had asked me why I had not done military service. I had answered that it was because in my year there was a population surplus. Paula, interestingly enough, had asked me whether I would have gone for conscientious objection, a possibility that the men of the group had not apparently considered themselves. Ricardo had commented on how lucky I

was. Paula had then pointed out that the schools had had lower intakes of children that year.

Ricardo: oye pueh que · no me ehtraña cada ve hay meno niña · · [Pausa llarga]
  Listen, well... I am not surprised, if there are less and less girls... · · [Long pause]

Joan: *en en donde en donde once mil men- niños menos en*
  Wh- Where eleven thousand le- kids less? Where...

Ricardo: en la ehcuelah
  In the schools.

Paula: en las escuelas
  In the schools.

Joan: *de toda España?*
  In the whole of Spain?

Ricardo: sí bueno en lo lo- en loh primario · · *o sea en >(xxxx)*
  Yes. Well, in the- in the primary levels. · · That is >(xxxx)

Pablo: <>(xxxxx)

Joan: *<pues son pocos entonces*
  It's not a lot then.

Ricardo: no aquí en cataluña eh?
  No. Here in Catalonia, right?

Paula: en cataluña.
  In Catalonia.

Joan: *cataluña cataluña sí*
  Catalonia, Catalonia, yes.

(···)

Pablo: cada veh meno ··· pueh meno decrecido
  [If there are] fewer and fewer... Then [we get] less 'dwarves'.

Paula: [veu alta] *idiota que eres cuando tengas tú un niño a ver si lo llamas tú*
  [Loud voice] What an idiot you are. When you have a child, are you going to call it

  también decrecido idiota
  a dwarf as well? You idiot!

Pablo: no pero lo llamaré cabezón.
  No, but I will call it big head.

Ricardo: cabezón no pero pequeño saldrá.
  Not big head. But small it is bound to be.

Here Paula and I had been developing a topic of conversation to which Pablo and Ricardo had been adding things now and then, particularly because the military service was a topic that men liked. The underlined stretches signal departures from the topic. In the first, Ricardo's tone indicated that he was trying to make a joke, probably with a sexual innuendo, which was not very successful. In the end, Pablo's intervention was meant to provoke Paula and to discredit the seriousness of the topic by calling children "dwarfs". Ricardo's final intervention was a tease directed at Paula because of her short stature. The conversation went on to a verbal tit-for-tat.

It was probably because of this tendency of the men to turn any situation into a joke (most usually the Rambleros men) that the women often preferred to organize their own private chats. The group discussion with the Rambleros was particularly anarchic due to the men's tendency to joke about the situation rather than getting involved in it. In both groups, the women sometimes organized women-only nights out. The following extract illustrates many of the points that I have been trying to make on women's talk:

Extract 20 [Rambleros]
The Rambleros were sitting around a table at a café, and Paula decided to move to the next table, where some women acquaintances of hers were chatting.

Paula: ei estoy (al lado) hablando un momento [anant a la taula de les germanes de Ricardo]
Hey, I'll be (there) talking for a minute [moving to the table where her acquaintances were sitting].

Pablo: llegar yyy
You get there aaand...

Ricardo: qué raro paula · · · >es raro
How strange, Paula · · · >That's strange.

Laura: <es raro que tu hables paula
<It is strange for you to talk, Paula.

Marta: ya que no viene la laura
'cause Laura is not coming...

Laura: [cridant] *cachuperru ven tuu*
[shouting a playful insult, literally "piece of dog" with phonological markers of a Spanish dialect or a catalanized phonology featuring an ignorant person] *"Cachuperru!"*.
Why don't you come!

Marina: [cridant] *renegada*
[shouting] *Renegade!*

[Laura throws something at her]

Pablo: >hala
  Gee!

Laura: <[rialla]
  [laughter].

Irene?: nena
  Girl!

Pablo: qué guarra >la tía
  How nasty, >that woman.

Ricardo: >si le (ha dao) en la cabesa se ha roto hombre
  > She's really (hit her) on the head it's broken, man.

Laura: no le he dao verdá[?]
  I didn't really hit her, did I?

Paula announced that she was joining the other group and that this "disconnection" was going to be short (*un momento*). Nevertheless, because short withdrawals did not need to be normally justified, people understood that she was actually announcing a longer disconnection and that she had the intention of spending a long while chatting with her acquaintances. Hence the teasing from Ricardo: "how strange", and Laura: "...of you to talk". Ricardo and Laura pretended to be surprised. They used a serious tone in order to deceive Paula, so that she thought that they were saying something serious. Their remark was understood as ironical because Paula was already known publicly to be a big talker.

Here a situation was created that caused Marta to respond to various explicit and implicit meanings. She was one of the women who had arranged for Paula to chat with her own group. So she justified why Paula had been selected, that is, because Laura was not prepared to come. The implications were that a) she acknowledged responsibility for Paula's withdrawal, and b) her decision was justified because she could not get Laura to do it instead. The implication was that Laura *should* have come as well, and therefore, that she was being unfriendly. Marta's voice indicated that she was pretending. The audience also knew that such statements, when serious, were not normally aired publicly. Consequently, Laura reacted to this teasing by playfully insulting Marta (*cachuperru*), and Marta retorted with an insult that insisted on Laura's doubtful faithfulness ("renegade!"). To continue the tit-for-tat, Laura threw an object at Marta. After that, the keyed frame broke down because some members of the audience considered that things had gone too far.

Notice the type of insults, which, as I discussed above, did not contain any typical masculine taboo word. Additionally, if we uncover the presuppositions behind the second example of teasing, we find quite a different theme from that of masculine verbal aggressions. These presuppositions spoke about a world of reciprocal duties of displaying friendship through participation in talk. Incidentally, the first teasing rested on the assumption that Paula talked too much, which is indicative of the status of women's talk amongst the Rambleros. I discuss this last issue in more depth below.

2.3. Men's intimation: the backstage of backstages

The stereotypical theme that women were "too talkative" was voiced often, especially amongst the Rambleros men. Ricardo told me once, as I was chatting with Paula, that I would get a headache by talking too often with the women. And when talking about the interviews, both Ricardo and Laura pointed out that interviewing women would also give me a headache. Jaume, of the Trepas, said once that he found many women's conversations boring. He also complained bitterly about women who withdrew their attention from the group and engaged in private talk:

Extract 21 [Trepas]
Jaume: What happens is that the women, they do it · at moments where we may be all together · A- at least that's what happened yesterday right? We are all together and suddenly, well, you see them, and we [are left] there, right? Amazed, right? And I may be willing to talk with Chimo, I may be keeping it to myself for two days, not speaking because there are other people around. And I don't do it to have (xxx), I don't do it so as not to spoil the fun for other people right? Or else I say "Hey Chimo, wh- · · what are you doing in the morning?" · "So and so", "okay so come down 'cause I want to talk to you", right? And that's it, right? · it's not- · · it's not to hide it so to speak, right? · but it is not to spoil the fun of the people...

Jaume clearly found that women's intimations did not constitute a legitimate activity in group gatherings. For him, they were diversions, peripheral activity, not an essential part of what a person seeks in the peer-group, not part of the fun. They were, in Goffman's (1957) terms, an illegitimate "alienation from the interaction" which fails to honor the main line of activity, as seen by the men. The Rambleros men's view of women as exceedingly talkative, as giving headaches (which can also be a metaphor for boredom), was also based on the assumption that women's talk was not a fun-making activity. This evidence gives an indication of how the women's agendas were delegitimized in these groups. Assumptions about what was public (for the whole group) and what was private, about what was fun and what was boring, gave legitimacy to men's understanding of what constituted proper social participation, such that even their disruptive humorous departures from the topic, as shown in extract 19, were considered as correct.

In order to understand the position of women's talk in the groups better, it is also necessary to explore the situations in which men engaged in displays of intimacy. In extract 21, Jaume implied that men also talked in an intimate way about their problems and things, but that this was a private matter not appropriate when they were all hanging around together. Amongst the Rambleros, I got indirect evidence that men shared their worries. In the group discussions, Luis and Pablo indicated with a certain clarity how they did it:

Extract 22 [Rambleros]
Luis: he and I, for instance, and er- in order to- · When some t- · Well we have gone out together the two of us alone · with nobody else · · And it's been in order to talk about- · I mean · · say · to let off steam, to tell things · (x) to tell things maybe because I needed to tell them to someone...

In the group discussion, Pablo also listed a number of friends with whom he claimed to share intimacies. Ricardo also acknowledged that he had talked with his friends when he broke up with his girlfriend. It was also commented that men were generally prepared to talk about their problems with women, but not the other way round. This raises the question of whether men expected reciprocity in the same way as women. Two members of the group were also censored for allegedly being too reserved on these matters.

By way of a conclusion, the data suggest that men's displays of intimacy generally occurred behind the scenes of common and public masculine performances. Men's intimations were, somehow, *backstage* activities (Goffman 1959). They were also conducted as an extraordinary, exceptional, activity: the concept of *desahogarse* 'letting off steam' conveys an accumulation of tension which eventually must be liberated, i.e. feelings must be let out when they are perceived to be suffocating, but not on an everyday basis (see Bruner and Kelso 1980 for similar accounts about the function of men's graffiti). Thorne (1993: 94) claims that reciprocal self-disclosure is a constitutive feature of girls' friendships, whereas between boys self-disclosure is "far more likely to be exposed to others through joking and a kind of collective shaming". Jackson (1990), in his critical autobiography, also explains how he learnt how to hide his feelings from his mates in order not to make himself vulnerable. The fear of exposure can explain partly why some men chose to confess things with trusted friends and in isolation, in a bid to control the potential implications and uses of what is done and said. However, I feel that this explanation is not fully satisfactory, as it does not explain why men find it quite natural to organize things in this way. In the conclusion to part 1, I will come back to this issue by bringing together some common threads to all the forms of gender identity found amongst the Rambleros and the Trepas.

3. Gender crossing

It is to be expected that not all individuals will be happy with the possibilities open (and closed) to the members of their sex. Thorne (1993) speaks of gender crossing when individuals seek to participate in some of the events usually associated with the other sex. She argues that crossing practices constitute a *continuum* rather than a categorical gender switch, as people *cross* gender boundaries in different degrees and in different ways. The literature also suggests that gender crossing decreases as children grow older, especially in adolescence. Thorne (1993: 132—133) says that crossing becomes very difficult amongst teenagers, as sexuality increases its bearing on the practices of the young. Jackson (1990: 125) gives an account of how his inroads into activities associated with femininity were hampered both by his teachers and by the pressure of the male peer-group. He also describes how the practices and discourses of homophobia were used to enforce hegemonic views of masculinity. As my participants were in their late teens and early twenties, it is probably understandable that crossing was not very visible. I did not even perceive it as a relevant issue during my fieldwork. It was much later, when I approached the data with the background of the literature, that I began finding connections between events and phenomena that I had considered as anecdotal. In the groups, I never saw anybody being called a "sissy" or a "tomboy". There was one man in the Trepas group who was with the women all the time. This was, however, a special case that I will discuss in chapter 2 (section 2), in the part devoted to *gender switching*.

In my analysis, I have identified as *crossers* (i.e. people who engaged in gender crossing) those who presented a cluster of features (appearance, tastes, interactive style, participation preferences) which, according to what I have said so far, were typical of members of the other sex. I have also considered as crossers people whose gender choices had nothing to do with a commitment to feminist mobilization, although in actual social practice both types of trajectory had interesting connections: amongst the Trepas, the politicized environment made it possible for features of crossing to be displayed more freely (see chapter 2).

The features which can be taken as evidence of gender crossing varied from individual to individual. As this issue could be particularly sensitive for some of the people involved, I have adopted a mode of writing about it which tends to avoid reference to specific incidents and individuals. In the case of women, in my data, gender crossing seemed to be invariably associated with adopting features of masculine speech: unmitigated swearing was common; amongst the Trepas women, extensive use of the inner-city argot repertoire; amongst the Rambleros women, aspiration of implosive /s/ or its deletion, and other features which distinguished men's and women's speech as described in chapter 4 (section 1). In the interviews and group discussions, people made interesting comments about women who liked to participate in verbal aggression games or playful physical aggression beyond the level expected of other women, or about women who drank a lot, were fond of men's styles of music and dressing, liked the establishments (pubs, bars) preferred by men and so on. Sometimes these women were mentioned as just exceptions to the rule, but sometimes they were also referred to in a humorous or even censoring tone. Interestingly enough I also detected in all women crossers a particular attraction for sport. This was manifested in various ways: similar alignments to football teams as men, or even willingness to play soccer or other sports either in the present or in childhood. In relation to dressing, though, I did not see that women crossers went as far as men in trying to display careless appearances. There was always the necessary tidiness through make-up, properly arranged hair and attention to detail.

In the case of men, crossing could be associated with displaying special concern for dress and appearance; conversely, with showing disinterest in masculine styles of music, in verbal aggression and heavy drinking. Speech patterns could get closer to the standard. There could be more readiness to show involvement in dancing (whereas most men would move in a sort of restrained, absent-minded, inconspicuous way) or to participate in activities which the other men avoided, such as singing romantic songs in a karaoke with the women. There could also be a fondness for forms of teenage or children's culture, from which other men distanced themselves.

I have no evidence that gender crossing hampered the individuals' possibilities of participating in events and activities with members of their own sex. Actually, in the case of men, there was little joining women in their talk and more playing with the effect of challenging existing patterns of appearance (by turning up, for instance, with a very flashy piece of clothing): it was a very assertive type of identity construction. But it is also true that not sharing some of the other men's tastes created some isolation with respect to the group of men. For women crossers, participation in feminine events seemed to be less problematic. Amongst the Trepas, crossers were half camouflaged amongst the (male and female) feminists. But among the Rambleros, because teasing was particularly frequent and intense, gender crossers provided material for other members to work with, such that these identities became more problematic. One of the women in particular seemed to have lost the right to expect the other women to attend to her face needs (in the sense that women would normally avoid teasing each other and would defend each other against teasing from the men).

The problem seemed to be that, in both groups, many events were organized in order to display the types of character or personal characteristics "naturally" associated with a particular sex. As gender identities are very often defined in terms of oppositions (see Cameron 1992), in a context where teasing was a conventional activity, crossers would always provide material for others to pick on them. So a male crosser would earn the qualification of "special" or "queer" and the female crosser that of "rough", as clearly happened among the young people I studied. This stretch below from a group discussion among the Rambleros illustrates this phenomenon:

Extract 23 [Rambleros]
Paula: about his nose I have never teased him.
Irene: quite right.
Andrés: about my nose, about my way of dancing, · about my teeth, about my teeth, about my way of dancing about my way of dressing, about the way I am, well, anything!

And from an interview:

Extract 24 [Rambleros]

Luis: ...just like when Tere used to say "el curro", right? "me voy al curro" [slang: I'm going to work] *"eeeh, what a laugh!", "el curro" damn, as if she waas · a kind of a miner right?* [He laughs].

Rampton (1991, 1995) also uses the term *crossing*, in this case to refer to the adoption of voices from other ethnic groups' language varieties in the activities of working-class adolescents. He points out that, given the multiple meaning potentials of these practices, crossing does not necessarily involve the emergence of new paradigms of ethnic relations. My data on gender crossing seem to point to a similar conclusion. Gender crossing does not involve the creation of new forms of gender display, but a kind of combination between available options which is bound to be problematic if it is not accompanied by skilful tact. Crossers did not constitute, strictly speaking, a class of their own with reasonably predictable patterns of participation and display. They all presented different ways of handling a delicate balance between the requirements and implications of participation in markedly gendered events of both sides. It was this necessary ambiguity which made crossing practices sometimes overlap with feminist forms of gender, which I analyze in the next chapter.

Concluding remarks

To conclude, the Rambleros was a group where the more traditional patterns of gender identity predominated: ritual insults, fights and transgression for men; displays of care and intimacy for women. This created a separation which also showed in musical tastes and drug-consumption habits, although it was generally not experienced as "a problem" by group members. They saw it as a natural part of life. In this context, things were not so easy for those who were not satisfied with the forms of social participation that were expected of them by reason of their sex. As these adopted what the others saw as deviant patterns of behavior, they became easily exposed to the customary insults and teasings, of which they became preferred targets. I think that we can easily begin to see how important gender identity can be in the peer-group context and also how subtly a particular gender "order" can be created and sustained.

Chapter 2

The Trepas

In this chapter, I will describe the gender identities constructed by the members of the Trepas group. I will pay special attention to what I have called "politicized identities", that is, the forms of gender found amongst the core group members, which were a direct result of their conscious political reflection. As I explained in the introduction, 5 members of the Trepas were or had been actively involved in leftist revolutionary parties, feminist groups or anti-military organizations that promoted conscientious objection. Apart from the work involved in such organizations, these people had also sought to transform their practices within the peer-group to make them consistent with their political ideas of equality and social justice. As a result, the politicized Trepas constructed forms of gender identity which were, to an extent, a creative and oppositional response to the more conventional gender identities such as the ones described in the previous chapter.

However, I will begin the chapter by describing the less unconventional type of gender identity of some *non-politicized* male members of the group. I have named this type of masculinity "transgressive masculinity" because it was significantly different from simplified masculinity. Basically, it did not involve displays of aggressivity. This will help to contextualize politicized identities because most politicized men presented features of this type of transgressive masculinity. Thus, I will later concentrate on what were the most characteristic features of politicized gender identities. Amongst the Trepas, there were also two women who presented a form of femininity similar to that of the Rambleros women, and another two could also be identified as women crossers. However, as I have dealt with these types of gender earlier, I will not study them here in detail.

1. Transgression and insubmission

I once saw some members of the Trepas men engaged in a playful fight on the beach together with other students of their training-school. This was, however, the only occasion in which I witnessed members of this group engaged in an activity that consisted of exploiting risk and displaying some aggressivity, which were the typical features of the Rambleros men's games. Otherwise, this type of practice was untypical in this group. Verbal aggression and emphasized use of dirty language was totally non-existent, and their swearing was not as creative as that of the Rambleros. The most significant references to aggression I have in my data are Pepe's portraying of himself as a victim of it. He once told me that he had decided not to attend a concert he wished to go to for fear of violence. And once he was beaten up by a group of American soldiers because he defiantly sang the international communist anthem as a provocation. Pepe and Salva usually presented themselves as victims of institutional violence, especially from the police (see extract 30, a song from their own music band, for an example of this). Pepe also told me that his brother was arrested when the police clamped down on illegal vendors and beggars in the period prior to the Olympics.

It is true that some of the Trepas' practices could be seen as containing elements of aggression. We could interpret their commitment to politics as a way of developing a confrontational ethos. Their preferred music style, hard-core, in addition to its politically oppositional attitude, was imbued with a patently aggressive vocal performance. And it may well be that, in a particular situation, a Trepas man might want to display aggressiveness in some way. However, this was certainly not what was looked for and was expected of their everyday interactions within the group.

What I argue in this section is that the Trepas men (and some women crossers) preferred to exploit the effects of *transgression* of dominant standards of demeanor and appearance to construct their particular form of masculinity. I have already mentioned the issue of transgression with regard to the Rambleros. Many of the points I will make here apply to them as well, particularly with regard to drug taking. The association of transgression with masculinity is often mentioned in the literature. Nevertheless, in the case of the Trepas, transgression was invested with their political outlook. Transgressive practices acquired an ambivalent value in the sense that they could also be seen as political *subversion*. This ambivalence allowed them to claim political correctness and, at the same time, to honour the forms of masculinity based on showing that one is good enough, or clever enough, to be able to break the rules and be one's own master. This also means that they experienced their transgressions as a much more serious issue than the playful Rambleros men.

Their appearance certainly manifested an insubmissive air. They wore much rougher clothing than the reasonably tidy Rambleros. In their way of dressing, body positions and gestures, the Trepas presented themselves as very laid back, as if they were always tired, as if they had put on the first T-shirt they had found, with or without holes or torn parts. This did not seem to be inconsistent, though, with wearing a nice, clean Rastafari hairstyle or a black leather jacket with carefully placed anarchist motifs. At weekends, men would not change their dressing patterns significantly and women would come with clothes that were just a bit tidier but also very austere. One woman, who used to dress quite smartly, explained to me that she had played down her appearance when she had joined the group.

1.1. Drug-taking

Consumption of legal (alcohol, tobacco) and illegal (cannabis derivatives, cocaine, stimulating pills) drugs is quite widespread amongst young Barcelonese. As for its potential transgressive value, it is worth bearing in mind that official discourses frame drug-taking in terms of its hazards to health and public safety. The law establishes some practices related to drugs as criminal and drugs are totally prohibited at school (although restricted consumption of alcohol and tobacco is sometimes permitted). In this context, drug consumption seemed to be almost obligatory amongst men. For instance, to drink a lot was valued and recognized as something worth commenting on and laughing about. Therefore, many men seemed to push themselves to drink more and more:

Extract 25 [Rambleros]
[Source: fieldnotes]
Yesterday [Mateo] did not go out because he did not have any money and he did not let his brother lend him any because he already owed too much money to too many people. He swallows the *Cuba libres* like water. Like Luis, who says that once he drank 27 *Cuba libres* as counted by his brother. And he says that they do not make him drunk.

A *Cuba libre* is generally a combination between a soft drink and a strong liquor such as gin, rum, vodka or whisky. The dose of liquor is of 8 to 10 cl.. Although nights-out in Barcelona can easily last up to 7 hours, I myself cannot drink more than four without losing, as Goffman puts it, "guiding control" of myself.

Apart from this kind of drinking competition, points were scored by a) going to bed as late as possible, b) ingesting a variety of other drugs in significant doses, c) ending up absolutely "pissed" and d) having extraordinary or funny things to tell as a consequence of this, such as uncommon sensorial effects (for instance, cocaine eliminates the feeling of tiredness and sometimes of drunkenness) or some misfortune or accident that can be transformed in a funny narrative. All this would provide material for things to tell later and would contribute to an assertion of the value of these activities within the group:

Extract 26 [Trepas]
Here I was sitting with some Trepas men at a café terrace in the afternoon.

Salva: el costa que se ha quedao too tonto tío
  You know Costa, he's gone quite nuts, man.

Pepe: sí[?]
  Has he?

Salva: porque el costa se ha pasao el verano de ajo · y se le va la olla ahora
  Because Costa has spent the summer tripping [taking LSD] · . And now his head drifts

  que te pasas
  away quite bad.

Pepe: todo el verano · comiendo ajos y ahora[?]
  All summer tripping, and now...?

Salva: se han pasado el Juli y el Quim todo el verano de ajos · y se ve que ahora
  Juli and Quim have spent all summer tripping. And it seems that now you

  pues que igual · te lo encuentras · normal no[?] pero al cabo de dos horas de
  may well meet him: [everything] normal, right? But after a couple of hours you've

  estar hablando con él · el pavo empieza a decir · bue bub bue bub yueb [riure]
  been talking to him, the guy starts saying "bue bub bue bub yueb" [laughter]

  como sí s- se le acabaran lah pilah no[?] [rialla].
  as if h- his batteries were running out, right? [laughter].

Joan: [rialla]
  [Laughter]

Salva: y el pavo no sabe lo que dice
  And the guy doesn't know what he's saying.

  Pepe: hub bub bub

In his interview, Salva said once "*yesterday...I was with* Juli, *smoking and drinking a bit...*". Men almost identified getting together with drug-taking, particularly amongst the Trepas. When they played truant from the training school, they went to "*drink a few beers*" and "*smoke a few joints*". One of the Rambleros men could not drink because of a permanent medical condition. This did not diminish his status in the group. Nevertheless, I found it interesting that he often wore a T-shirt featuring the logo of a popular whisky brand. The centrality of drug-taking for the construction of masculinity amongst the men of both groups can hardly be overstressed. Drinking took special precedence over other things such as buying records, clothing, food or transport (some of them regularly did fare dodging). This was particularly so amongst some Trepas men who were unemployed or very low paid. If one of them was short of money, he would be invited by his companions and helped to stay in the fun. Therefore unemployment helped to increase the daily intake dramatically. Once an experienced youth worker told me that he had totally forbidden people to take *litrones* into his youth club. *Litrones* are cheap one-liter beer bottles that many young people buy, typically to accompany their gatherings in the streets (together with their ghetto-blasters). Nevertheless, the same youth worker also said that he turned a blind eye on smaller bottles. He clearly perceived the importance of alcohol amongst young people and was seeking to find the right balance. In an inspiring study of youth criminality and drug abuse in a neighboring town, Funes (1982) recalls the time when young people abandoned the traditional wine-drinking and card or domino playing in bars and started gathering to take drugs in the streets. It was at the beginning of the sixties, when the hippy and other counter-cultural movements idealized narcotic experience and turned drug-taking into the central activity of many groups of young people. He points out that drug taking became so important that people started experimenting with all types of substances. Sometimes they would even take pills stolen from pharmacies that had no sensorial effect whatsoever and whose effects were totally unknown to the users. This is an example of how the ritual function of drug taking can override any actual physio- or psychological aspect of it.

The ritual of smoking a joint could probably be used as an archetypal example of a mutual display of transgression and male bonding, symbolized by the *joint* traveling from hand to hand and mouth to mouth. People rarely smoked joints on their own. For the equivalent of US $13, it was possible to provide for the whole group for a night. Sometimes they collected money to buy it together. Once acquired, however, people would not mention the cost anymore or ask for contributions to people who had turned up later. Somehow, people avoided focusing on the economic aspect of the activity, probably because it was felt it would contaminate its ritual value. Hence the significance of some common gestures, such as "passing it" to someone *first*, or giving it to someone to light it, as a sign of friendliness and as a welcoming gesture.

Drug-taking caused a kind of inversion in the way people normally judged behavior. Because a high degree of intoxication and loss of control was seen as a merit, breakdowns, accidents and awkwardnesses could be used to reinforce the status of participants rather than undermining it. In this context, women were prepared to enjoy incidents and produce relevant narratives as well, but not to participate very actively and centrally in the game. My guess is that, for women, drunkenness entailed a risk to elements of self image which were central to femininity, such as orderly management of gestures and bodies. The picture of a woman vomiting on a street corner, for example, does not have quite the same impact as for a man. In addition, the danger of suffering sexual harassment probably increases. I once went with a girlfriend to a disco in Barcelona where we did not know anybody. After she started dancing in quite a conspicuous style, she was approached by at least four men in about ten minutes. This may explain why women only got intoxicated on special occasions in the groups I studied. For instance, on a trip organized by the training school outside of Barcelona, there was a party where everybody was known and could be more or less trusted. There I saw a few Trepas women "letting themselves go". In addition to this, one must bear in mind that drug taking was not strictly necessary within the forms of interaction organized by women. True enough, smoking cigarettes was common amongst women, but the role of smoking tobacco in the management of appearances seems to be generally quite different to that of alcohol and other drugs (except, maybe, for the surreptitious smoking practiced by early teenagers). I have seen in many contexts that women and men who prefer not to smoke cannabis often take the initiative of rolling the joints. Thus, by participating in the organization of the activity, they can safely avoid smoking because their complicity has already been displayed.

More often than not, the women spoke about drug abuse in a disparaging manner, although usually very diplomatically. Silvia, for instance, pressed her boyfriend not to drink heavily and smoke joints on the same night because he got too far out of control and he would not be good for anything. However, she told him this in a jokingly good-humored tone, so that it did not sound like downright moralizing. In the first months of my fieldwork, I did not drink alcohol because I suffered from a stomach condition. Once I felt better, I switched to beer or *Cuba libres*. Paula, from the Rambleros, teased me that "I had fallen into vice". Clara, from the Trepas, said I was "making her suffer" with a twitch of real concern. One of the women confessed to feeling that she drank too much, and that she was worried about that. She was trying to reduce the number of beers but she said that she felt "as if she could not be with the people without drinking". I never heard of guilty feelings of this sort from men. Irene, from the Rambleros, said the following:

Extract 27 [Rambleros]

Irene: Well, I drink as well, right? now and then. · But, boy! I · once felt sick, · and no more! I have already decided it: never again. And, on top of all with tequila [...] Many times I have spoken with [the men], yeah? · With Ricardo for example I have spoken, but: "Why do you drink and this and that", "I don't know, and what can you do otherwise?". · And "What can you do? Well, have a good time; listen, you don't have a good time if you drink; I have a hard time". Because if I drink, then I'm down on the ground. · [If I'm gonna] be down on the ground, then I don't drink, right? · You have a hard time drinking. They are having a good time, · and they look as if they were not there, listen, but when they drink, they look as if they are not there. Th- they get stupid.

The reader again might get an impression that the men were absolutely wild and out of bounds. I must balance this view by saying that the Rambleros, for instance, took illegal drugs only very exceptionally, even though they were widely available. Apparently, they had taken them much more in the past, before they started going out regularly with the women. In a group that was very much oriented to doing things together, joint smoking was probably complicated to organize, because it was potentially segregative (see below). Additionally, on the short occasions when they met and talked in the middle of the week, drinking was very moderate. Amongst the Trepas, joints were almost always present when the whole group gathered. I also saw, or heard about, cocaine, LSD and stimulant pills on a few occasions. I never saw or heard about murderous stuff such as heroin or crack. The following extract from Jaume's interview will help to understand the social value of drug-taking practices:

Extract 28 [Trepas]

Jaume: I've always been on the streets since I was a kid, right? I've always (been) with the people in the streets, right? Until a period came when · because I saw that · that the people in the streets · were · · coming up with nasty stuff, with

drugs and so on, right? nasty. So · then I left the people of the streets and went ·
to the *esplai* [A typical Catalan organization where young people organize the
leisure of children for pedagogic purposes] [...] The people I could see that, ·
they did it to- ·· to appear bigger [or "more grown up"], right? And to me this
was rubbish because I didn't- · I didn't understand why the people wanted to
feel superior to others right? · No, because (xxx) For example, if I smoke joints,
I do not see myself as bigger than the others, I do not see myself as superior to
her [his girlfriend, who was present], who doesn't smoke, right? I mean, I
smoke because I like it and that's it, right? ·· And the people started to do
things like that, to feel superior to people, yeah?, sometimes. · And they chan-
the people changed the way they were as well. And then it was when I left
them, right? I mean, I didn't like the way they were and · I left these people ··
who were · more or less like me some of them, right? At the end it all came to a
bad end, [for] the ones who stayed in the group.

My interpretation is that Jaume rejected the meaning of drug-taking as
seen from the inner-city group he used to belong to when he was much
younger. This group had taken to exploiting the potential (and usually very
real) risks entailed by hard drug taking, a common theme in the construction of masculinity amongst lower class gangs. Jaume clearly repudiated a
form of masculinity expressed in terms of superiority. Ricardo, of the Rambleros, told me a story of a young conscript who smoked so much that he
was not good for anything anymore and made a fool of himself. He used
this story to make the point that one had to be careful. Ricardo did not engage in a critique of the ideas behind drug taking in the way that Jaume did.
He did complain, though, that going out and always doing the same things
was getting too monotonous and that he now liked to go out and just chat
and relax, even if he did not drink. It is also interesting that Jaume decided
to join the *esplai* as he left his previous gang. The *esplai* clearly provided
him with an alternative space where he could develop other aspects of his
identity. In another interview, Guille, from the Trepas, complained that in
Barcelona there was little else to do other than getting a "big piss". True
enough, the infrastructures of Barcelona, with a few youth clubs that open
at odd hours, do not provide for many alternatives to going to a pub and
consuming. I will come back to this issue later.

Smoking joints also created problems amongst the Trepas. Because it
was not allowed to smoke them in pubs and bars, the men used to stay outdoors for long periods thus leaving the women on their own indoors. The
women felt increasingly annoyed about this and the group discussion was
used to air heated arguments. The arguments were actual evidence of an-

other clash between men's and women's different agendas. As Natalia put it: "*well, have I come to have fun just with Silvia or have I come to have fun with everybody? I mean, because I come to have fun with everyone*". Pepe, in his interview, which was done later, said that men had grown more circumspect about the issue and that they would try to reduce the time they spent outside or that they would seek to explicitly invite women to join them.

1.2. The politics of rock music

The political ideas of some of the Trepas men had a considerable bearing on the way they constructed the world of popular music, particularly with regard to their favorite style: hard-core. Hard-core is one of the many developments of hard-rock music. It originated in the late eighties and incorporated punk's political lyrics and its somewhat sober musical layout combined with some characteristic instrumental effects from heavy metal.

When it comes to discussing the musical tastes and inclinations of the Trepas, some qualifications have to be made. What I will discuss below is based on the views expressed by the politicized male members of the group. Some non-politicized men shared their musical tastes but were not so actively involved in politics. It could be argued that these non-politicized members, one of whom was a member of the group's own rock band, may have experienced the meanings constructed by hard-core groups in different ways. Nevertheless, the socially oppositional meanings of hard-core were often quite transparent, as I show below. In chapter 4 (section 2), I also give additional evidence that non-politicized members shared a form of political "common sense" which coincided in a number of ways with the ideas of the politicized ones. It is from this perspective that I claim that the meanings they associated with hard-core were roughly equivalent.

The role of popular music in the construction of identities amongst present-day young people can hardly be overstressed. It is by far the most widespread form of art young people seem to associate with (see Jones 1990) and it often becomes the one explicit criterion that young people use to classify types of cliques and to identify themselves (Heller 1999). Frith (1987) considers the construction of identity as popular music's first function:

> The first reason, then, we enjoy popular music is because of its use
> in answering questions of identity: we use pop songs to create for
> ourselves a particular sort of self-definition, a particular place in so-
> ciety. The pleasure that pop music produces is a pleasure of identifi-
> cation – with the music we like, with the performers of that music,
> with the other people who like it. And it is important to note that the
> production of identity is also a production of non-identity – it is a
> process of inclusion and exclusion. (ibid.: 140)

The connection between the Trepas men's political ideas and their musical allegiances was relatively clear: Basque revolutionary rock was fine,
and punk, hard-core, ska and trash as well. Heavy metal, for them, was
something else. According to Pepe and Salva, heavy metal presented itself
as a challenge to the "system"; but this was more of a staged challenge
rather than a real one: it was a pose. Heavy metal was rhythmically more
monotonous, and "they [the artists] dress to give an aggressive impression
but they are little turtledoves", Pepe said. The rejection of the form of masculinity constructed through heavy metal is interestingly congruent with the
Trepas' rejection of simplified masculinity (this rejection is further discussed in chapter 4, section 2). Punk and hard-core was seen as allowing
much more creativity in ways of dressing and rhythmic patterns and as presenting a more authentic challenge to the establishment.

The musical expertise of the men in both groups surpassed mine by far
and it also surpassed the available literature on popular music within the
academic field of cultural studies, which is quite reduced and fragmented.
Nevertheless, I found a corroboration of Pepe and Salva's view on the significance of heavy metal:

> Any "rebel" or non-conformist imagery in heavy metal may be seen
> as a function of its masculine, "hard" stances, rather than as a con-
> scious participation in rock's growing self-reflexivity. (Straw 1990:
> 103)

Breen (1991) also coincides with the Trepas in characterizing the heavy
metal of the nineties as a product of marketing and big commercial initiatives which revived an early seventies' trend that seemed to have died out.
In my fieldwork, I had the impression that the Trepas men were sensitive to

the history and meanings of heavy metal, even those who were not ostensibly politicized. The heavy metal world comes across with the support of powerful media, specialized magazines and satellite television channels. Once Pepe and I were watching a show on a satellite channel in the summer of 1992, and I remember translating interviews for him: a row of flashy heavy metal musicians were insisting now and again that they were doing music just for fun, and that they did not feel they had to support any political idea or environmental cause.

On the contrary, participation in the punk and hard-core worlds required a much more active involvement in building one's own information channels, getting to know which establishments would usually organize concerts, which shops specialized in the style, which events were on, which new bands were coming out and so on. Roman, in her ethnographic study of women's position vis-à-vis punk slam dance in an English town, reports that hard-core people saw other rock audiences as "passive consumers rather than active producers of music" and that this came across in the relationship established between public and performers (1988: 152). She also says that some working class women saw punk slam dance as a trendy form of colonization by middle class punks who tried to associate with the aesthetics and experience of the working class: "they refer to the middle class youths who now slam dance as 'those rich' or 'spoiled kids', who have not yet been introduced to 'the real world'" (ibid.: 166—167).

The literature stresses the predominantly masculine character of the rock music world (Shepherd 1987), and especially of heavy metal, punk and hard-core (Roman 1988; Straw 1990; Breen 1991). Frith and McRobbie (1978/9, quoted in Frith 1987: 146), for instance, propose the "distinction between 'cock' rock and teenybop narratives, each working to define masculinity and femininity but for different audiences along different contours of feeling". Pablo of the Rambleros said that women liked more "immature", "simplistic" or "fifteen-year-old" types of music. The Rambleros women did not even want to go to heavy metal pubs. In a hard-core concert I went to with the Trepas, the women distanced themselves from the concert and just chatted as they were waiting for it to finish. This conflict of preferences caused organizational problems, which came out in the group discussions. Women involved in mainstream feminine identities avoided the "hardest" genres and tended to enjoy slower rhythms and "romantic" lyrics more than men did. This suggests that people went for music styles that had a kind of continuity with the identities they were constructing in the peer-group (rough masculinities=heavy metal, political contestation=hard-core, mainstream femininity=romantic themes that stress relationships and connection).

However, such generalizations can distort the picture a bit and obscure the varied modes of participation that women organize around popular culture. There may be some truth in these very general lines of preference according to gender, but the fact was that women liked a wide variety of styles. In both groups, there seemed to be an ample space of coincidence with regard to Spanish rock, which is actually very diverse, and that, for instance, allowed the Rambleros to find some pubs they all were happy with. Amongst the Trepas, women generally saw hard-core as too "hard," but they generally enjoyed other genres such as ska, punk, reggae, some types of Flamenco rock and Spanish rock. In both groups there seemed to be a veto on Catalan rock and on pure techno or disco music, usually called *Música máquina* 'Machine Music', except for some Rambleros women who did like these styles. I could not exactly make out what the problem with Catalan rock was: my own intuition is that it was seen as commercial and too associated with very young teenagers. Together with disco music, Catalan rock seems to be seen as lacking authenticity and a convincing rebelliousness. Finally, the Trepas men generally disliked salsa, which the women liked.

To understand forms of participation around popular music, it is also necessary to take into account the multiplicity of meaning potentials of musical genres and their possibilities of hybridization. Heavy metal, for instance, has established ballads as a subgenre; the ballads use a slower rhythm and display of "soft feeling," which some Rambleros women liked. I once asked Ayats (from the Trepas) how one could ascribe a particular group to a genre, and he said that it was far from straightforward. It was a matter of finding out what they were about, especially how they behaved in live concerts. It is likely that this difficulty came in part from the fact that many groups sang in English, even Catalan ones. Consequently, people found it more difficult to assess what they meant, although understanding the language was by no means essential. It is also my impression that Spanish rock is much more hybridized than mainstream Anglo-American rock:

Extract 29 [Trepas]

Pepe: For example, from · listeniing · · to what is punky, · if you listen to · punky, then · · you get to "Potato", right? "Potato" play reggae, Vitorian reggae,9 And if you listen to "Potato" as well, because you listen to · "Kortatu" they make a version from the "Specials" and you start listening to ska. And because you listen to skaa, well, you end up · listening to soul and, and to mod music as well. And because you listen to punky you end up listening to hard-core. And if you listen to rough hard-core, you end up listening to · · greencore and you end up listening to trash metal. And if you listen to · hard-core, you also end up listening to more melodious hard-core, · of course · · · ·

Joan: it is like a family with punk, to >put it like that

Pepe: <No · no no no · ska came before · punky, · and heavy came before that. · hard-core did come later but, it is not a matter of family but that · that, of course the- · they combine, right?

Joan: they · · interweave (xx) · · ·.[flamenco guitar chords are heard from the guitar Pepe is fiddling with]

Pepe: ah and the story of Celtic music Celtic music, of course, we like it a hell of a lot all of us, all of us.

Within this frame, there was quite a wide scope for young people to negotiate their tastes in many different ways. What really distinguished men and women's approach to music, and which singled out heavy metal and hard-core genres, was the role of these genres in the establishment of masculine relationships. Most men in both groups regularly organized events especially dedicated to music (going to concerts, reading magazines together, exchanging records, shopping expeditions, etc.). It was in this sense that music played a key role in the construction of masculine identities, as it provided opportunities for men to develop their ties. Clara, for instance, who declared that she liked a few hard-core groups, did not participate in the frequent conversations, exchanges of records, shopping expeditions that men organized around music; neither did she participate in the rock band.[10]

The Trepas men's allegiance to hard-core was linked to their sense of belonging to and constructing a cultural space which was opposed to dominant culture. Hard-core music fostered aesthetic values usually opposed to what one might see as a more conventional aesthetics: harsh and very loud sound with high speed rhythm and aggressive drum work, lyrics and voice. The voice sounds, at first impression, as if shouting was the main point of it. *"If noise is what you do not want, you are going to have it anyway"* are the words of a song of Salva's own making which refer to the mainstream-ish point of view about hard-core. I interpreted the shouting, the incredible loudness and the thickness of the sound as a symbolic challenge to a society that silences the views and the experiences of working class young people. The lyrics of one of the groups went "Don't say what you think, [just] think what they say" (original in English) portraying a conformist person. Once I ventured a comment about a Catalan band that sung in English because (I guessed) it made more sense commercially; Pepe denied that a hard-core group could be driven by such an interest, and said that it probably was because the style had not yet been adapted to Spanish. Finally, I reproduce below the translation of one of the lyrics of their own band, where the oppositional meanings were expressed through a rejection of the harassment suffered from the police:

Extract 30 [Trepas]

In the streets and in the bars,
harassing non-stop.
We must finish with this war,
(struggle) till the end.

As we go out of the door
on the way back: how are you?
I do not know (xxx)
to apply martial law

We are all suspects!
We are all dangerous!

They are entering the premises,
accusing us of dealing.
And if they have not found "it",
then they cannot charge us.

You see how you have to live,
If you do not want to die.
Have you thought (xxx)
(xxx) to resist.

We are all suspects!
We are all dangerous!

Fight, fight, fight, fight, fight, fight, fight, fight, fight, fight, fight,

2. Politicized identities

Because of the way in which I have carried out my description, I may have fostered the impression that the forms of gender presented by the groups I studied were very traditional, particularly in relation to the Rambleros. In this respect, it is worth pointing out that the idea of gender equality was universally espoused in both groups. In the group discussion, the Rambleros had a debate on household duties that provided clear evidence of this. Nevertheless, this same discussion showed that subscribing to a general and superficial idea of equality does not change the world. The women claimed that the men showed little readiness to do household chores; the men were at pains to maintain that this was not a gender issue; but a matter of personal preferences. On the other hand, in the Rambleros group, the women always played a key role in decisions about what to do and where to go. The men had actually given up many of the activities they liked to do when they used to go out by themselves in earlier years. On the other hand, as I suggested in section earlier and as I will show with more detail in chapter 4, there is a case for arguing that the Rambleros were a group presenting very traditional patterns of gender identity.

Amongst the Trepas, there was a core group of five members who, following their political agendas, were seeking to change these traditional forms of gender relations. Their commitment to leftist revolutionary ideas led to significant efforts to organize a change in practices and discourses that challenged hegemonic views of masculinity and femininity. Two women were actively involved in a feminist group. They had experience in organizing talks and discussions in schools. Their awareness about issues on women's rights was very elaborate, and many of the insights I may offer are due to them. The three politicized men of the group also had access to feminist discourses, probably from their own political activities and from the two women themselves. There is evidence that these men sought to redefine their masculinity as well.

Again, because traditional gender identities are typically defined in oppositional terms, the first way of challenging them seemed to be for individuals to adopt features associated with the other sex. I will begin with men's endeavors to redefine their masculinities. After this, I will deal with the issues involved in redefining femininity.

2.1. Redefining masculinity

I have already said that some of the forms of masculine displays found amongst the Rambleros, such as keyed verbal and physical aggression, were not practiced by the Trepas men. This alone gave the group a distinctly different atmosphere, even when politicized members were not around. Additionally, it is worth pointing out that all the men who were not politicized were speakers of Catalan. In my data, there are various indications that speakers of Catalan also seemed less ready to subscribe to the most simplified, risk-oriented, forms of masculinity. An experienced youth worker pointed out to me that Catalan-speaking working class young people were less prone to taking heavy drugs. Jaume's position, expressed in extract 28, may be an indication of why this happened. On one occasion when the Spanish speakers of the group had all gone, I was struck by the way the tone of the conversation changed. They suddenly began to make moves so that I could participate in the talk and they showed friendliness in explicit ways. On the basis of my data, it is not possible to explore whether these differences of interactional style between speakers of the two languages had anything to do with differing communicative traditions between locals and "immigrants". My impression is that they do, but this issue has never been researched. Whatever factors had a bearing on these sociolinguistic processes, the contrast between politicized and non-politicized forms of masculinity amongst the Trepas men was not very conspicuous (except for one case which I discuss below).

One of the inroads that the politicized men seemed to explore into forms of femininity was through *intimations*. When I negotiated my integration into the group with a Trepas woman, she assured me that the men were used to making conscious efforts to help new members to settle in. I very clearly perceived that one of the men did so. He used to come to my flat, where we talked at length about ourselves: tastes, projects, political allegiances and so on. He also helped by inviting me when members of the group met and by encouraging me to talk in some situations. He once did it by simply inviting me to talk about England and my experience at Lancaster University in front of other people. I must say that I found the situation a bit embarrassing. Women were generally better at making me talk. I think that the problem here was that I was also a man, and therefore we felt we had to display mutual interest in a more indirect way. In her interview, Clara also claimed that the politicized men sought to monitor people's emotions and states of feeling in the same way as women did:

Extract 31 [Trepas]
Clara: It's that · the guys from there, the ones I know are: Salva, · and Salva does that, and e-· I mean in a different way but he does, Salva shows a lot of concern, right? · A lot, a lot, he's very much of a sissy in this respect. · And then Pepe, and Pepe s- shows a lot of concern...

Because this group was less integrated than the Rambleros, it was common for it to be divided into small and separate groups attending to different focuses of activity. In this context, it was very common for men to actually develop one-to-one conversations. The group of seven men actually contained three "couples" who had strong ties based on long-lasting friendships. Some of these conversations, as far as I could make out, worked in some ways like women's events: catching up on news, commenting on problems and worries, sometimes developing very focused topics of conversation. I would not claim that these men intimated in the way women did, but I do think that these events provided the interactional infrastructure that made it possible for identities to be negotiated, a point I will come back to in chapter 4.

There were other subtle elements that pointed towards a transformed masculinity. The Rambleros men were always oriented to protect and save their own face in their interactions. This is not surprising if we think that a genre like verbal aggression requires that the participants mobilize themselves to assert their position. In contrast, amongst the politicized Trepas, self-mocking, or laughing at oneself, was common. I once heard Salva saying half-jokingly that his jokes were very bad. In one of the rehearsals of the rock band, he proposed trying a song again, and he added: "*after the cock-up done by the one who made the song*", meaning himself. Later in chapter 4, I argue that the possibility to accept and exploit self-exposure may have played an important role in allowing men to explore new identities.

2.2. Gender switching

The most spectacular case of transformation of gender identity was that of Aleix, a Trepas man. It could almost be said that he had performed a *gender switch* rather than a redefinition of masculinity. For most practical purposes, Aleix 'was' a woman (not in terms of sexual relationships, as far as I know). Most of the time, he participated in women's conversations and his strongest ties were with women. Unfortunately, my recording equipment developed a fault during his interview, so I cannot quote him directly. The most important point was that he claimed to have wilfully and consciously worked out this 'switch' a couple of years before. He remembered making conscious efforts to talk like a woman and that his political commitments played a very important role in motivating him to do so. At the time of the interview, he could not quite explain this process in detail, though. This probably means that he learned how to do it by doing it rather than by seeking to explicitly establish what women's relationships were about. Clara once told me that Aleix had behaved in a funny way for a while: "idealistic and 'flowers are wonderful' kind-of-thing" she had (more or less) said. In the interview, she also said that Aleix was still having many problems because of this gender switch, but we did not go into detail on this either. It might be that, in his first inroads into the other gender, Aleix adopted some stereotypical feminine stances that were seen as odd by Clara.

This process of transformation must have gone really deep, as he had created amongst women the expectation that he could be counted upon in practically any context. Clara's anecdote can illustrate how far this went. In an excursion, as the women proceeded to occupy one of the bedrooms for themselves, the one who distributed the beds took for granted that Aleix was going to sleep with them:

Extract 32 [Trepas]

Clara: and · Natalia said: "Well, we are so, and so, and so, and so, and so and Aleix". And I [go]: · "Natalia, Aleix is a guy". She says "Yeah, but · he is different" · · · and this Natalia Garcia "(x) he is different. No, I wouldn't m- · No, I wouldn't mind if-". · And you know how Natalia is, well, nobody is gonna have a glimpse of even · even · even· even her ankle, right?

Aleix's switching seemed to be the ultimate subversion of hegemonic masculinity. He did not seem to be much interested in men's conversations and tastes. I remember I once patted his back in a typical male friendly gesture and I got a feeling that I had not quite done the right thing. Although I never heard in the group any explicit comment on Aleix's special inclinations, he found himself in some situations that he experienced as an embarrassment. Once, as he came out of a bar, he found that the women and the men had spontaneously formed two separate groups outside. Because the choice was too visible, he could not decide what to do and finally chose to go back inside and join a woman who had stayed behind.

2.3. Redefining femininity

One of the ways in which the politicized Trepas women sought to challenge mainstream femininity was by adopting features of masculine performance and appearances. Their ways of dressing and their gestural patterns (take, for instance, their way of sitting: laid back, relaxed) was practically the same as that of the men. The same happened with their language: they used argot and strong swearing. Sometimes their swearing was actually stronger than the men's and they occasionally practiced verbal aggression. Salva said that he was normally circumspect with the language he used with the women, although sometimes the women might use very strong language. One of their lines, for instance, was "*eat my cunt*", the female equivalent to the Rambleros men's phrase. Nevertheless, its function was not the same as with the Rambleros: it was used precisely as a way of making simplified masculinity face itself. Because verbal aggression was not a legitimate activity in the group, its use could only be exceptional. It could only be understood not as playing the game but as playing *with* the game. Nevertheless, this did not rule out the possibility of using it to tell somebody off (especially, a man), and of showing that one may not be prepared to do the face-work that is usually expected of women. Aleix, who had been doing a great deal of effort to avoid sexist swearing, was dismayed to see his feminist friends not setting the right example.

If identities are constructed in social situations, that is, in our interactions with others and in the positions we take in everyday talk, then we shall need to coordinate whatever transformations we want to make with other people. Friendship relationships are thus one of the spaces where there is a possibility of organizing social change. This necessarily means that people will make an effort to control which potential meanings of utterances and acts are taken up and which are not. I will take the development of swearing amongst women as an example of the negotiation of these meanings:

Extract 33 [Trepas]
Clara, Natalia and Silvia were sitting on the terrace of a cafeteria at midday.

Clara: yo soy muy <u>malparlada</u> *eh?*
   I am a very <u>foul mouthed</u> *person, yeah?*

Natalia: (x) porque no me has oído hablar · (xxx eja)
   (x) because you haven't heard me speaking (xxxxx)

Silvia: [riu] ·· y (esta) hablaba por teléfono y empieza · "(en mi mesita no) las pendonas estas que están aquí no sé qué" y yo "hala Natalia por favor qué se van a pensar?" [riures]
   [laughs] ·· *And (she) was talking on the phone and starts: "(not in my desk) these bitches down there and so on". And I go: "Gee Natalia, please, what are they going to think?"*
   [laughters]

Natalia and Silvia were non-politicized women. Clara started by producing a kind of self-confession, in a serious voice. Nevertheless, her switch to Catalan to say "foul mouthed" suggests that she was introducing the voice of some external authority with which she might not identify at all, i.e., she might be implicitly rejecting what she appeared to say. Whether Natalia and Silvia interpreted this voice in this way, it is not clear. But, knowing Clara, it was clear that she was not trying to self-inflict any punishment. However, as I see it, the understanding of her utterance does not really depend on solving this ambivalence (whether she was confessing her "bad behavior" or she was rejecting those who would consider it to be so). I believe that the ambivalence is the actual point she is making. On the one hand, she acknowledged that she was flouting established standards of "good language". On the other, she was not giving any sign of being willing to do anything about it. The second participant, Natalia, came to the rescue by declaring: we are both swearers, we are on an equal footing.

Natalia had created a relationship of collusion. In the following turn, Silvia produced a narrative which sought to illustrate Natalia's point. She gave an example of Natalia using bad language in the wrong situation. Natalia had been talking on the phone in her capacity as secretary of the training school and made, as in a passing comment, a disparaging observation about her workmates. Silvia was now portraying herself within the story as reminding Natalia that such actions could damage the reputation of the training school because they were being heard by an outsider (the person on the phone).

Now the point I want to argue is that this extract provides evidence of women negotiating the meaning of swearing from a woman's standpoint. They did not seem to adopt this language simply by participating in masculine events or in conversations with men. A similar case is the one reported by Patricia, for instance, who said that she had got accustomed to using argot because she and Clara had "stuck it to each other".

In order to argue this point, I will compare this event with a hypothetical one conducted by men. First of all, in a masculine arena, the ambivalence expressed towards swearing would not really exist. Men's established orientation towards displaying transgression would leave no doubts about what was being claimed. In the interviews, men sometimes used the same expressions (Cat.: *malparlat*, Sp.: *malhablado*) but accompanied by laughter and conveying a kind of complicity with the male interviewer. The women, on the contrary, conveyed ambivalence. Silvia, for instance, claimed to be a user of bad language in her interview and said that she tried to avoid it but could not; Patricia said the same with respect to sexist language. In the extract, Natalia's response and Silvia's illustrative narrative built on this ambivalence of swearing as both fun and demeaning (Besides, the insult *pendona* 'bitch' would have a much more diminished effect amongst males, not being felt to be strong at all). Silvia's story presented Natalia in a situation where her status as a worthy person was accidentally threatened due to the use of improper language at the wrong time. The humorous potential came from Natalia's momentary loss of reputation (the loss being, of course, repairable). Amongst men, the fun of the story would have come from the undermining of the training school's reputation. Even if participants might have made judgments implicitly about the worthiness of the speaker, they would have focused on acknowledging his ability to perform a transgression.

The meaning of swearing negotiated within women's events was therefore not the same as in men's talk, as women were more sensitive to its demeaning character. They had to organize a collusive relationship where the connotations of swearing were temporarily suspended. In this way, they preserved within the space of the relationship the mutual recognition of worthiness. I think that this is an important point, because our friends are to an extent an extension of our image and we may implicitly seek guarantees that they will "behave themselves" in other situations, such as in the presence of outsiders. In contrast, I once saw how Clara refused to go along with the swearing of an older relative of hers. Apart from the fact that people naturally contradict themselves at times, the only explanation I can think of is that Clara's relative was an *outsider* to the group. As such, she had not participated in defining what swearing meant to them and therefore it was potentially demeaning.

I believe that the ambivalences felt by these women with respect to identity reflected the necessary paradoxes and contradictions of feminism, some of which are reflected in the difference versus dominance debate. On the one hand, feminism prompts women to participate in social spaces previously (and largely still) controlled by men. In doing so, the defining features of femininity become problematic. But then, problematizing femininity amounts to accepting masculinity as the universal norm. Thus, at some points, I perceived that Clara felt ambivalent about engaging in some types of small talk that are usually associated with women. Her tone in some instances of "gossip" sometimes came across as particularly theatrical or distant. I remember once she turned up with a smart new dress. Because she usually dressed very plainly, it was clear that there were going to be comments about it. So she displayed it to her friends by dramatizing some fashion-show steps with obvious exaggeration, thus distancing herself from the feminine-dress-appreciation ritual. Nevertheless, the occasion allowed her friends to show consideration for her dress.

If anything, the balance seemed to be tilting towards rediscovering femininity and developing it from within, rather than judging it against masculine standards. In the group discussion, Clara had made her position very clear. The group had been discussing the problems that women encountered in traditional male manual jobs (such as builder or garbage collector): the working conditions were not adapted to the needs of women and the male workers harassed them with verbal aggression or treated them as "weaklings". On the basis of these considerations, Clara argued that men were hardly an example of anything, that after all women "don't rape" and that, therefore, men had to "contemplate" women as women "contemplate" men.

Politics played an empowering role for politicized women. At least the ability with which they (and the politicized men as well) handled some subtle conceptual issues was not matched by any other person within the groups. Actually, my own university credentials did not ensure that I always understood at once the full implications of what they were saying. In the group discussion, their experience of speaking up in such situations was very visible. They held long turns and developed complex arguments. The group as a whole produced a remarkably orderly debate: the participants' right to speak was normally respected and everybody's views were taken up and shown consideration. The Rambleros' group discussion, on the contrary, was constructed more as fun, and it developed many playful confrontations where the more committed members dominated and the others, mostly women, remained on the sidelines.

Politics constituted a legitimate topic of conversation in the Trepas group, particularly amongst those who were active, and it contributed to the creation of cross-gender friendships. However, it seemed to me that the impact of the politicization of gender on the organization of the group was to actually reinforce the separation between the genders and this despite many members' reported efforts to overcome it. The politicized women had contributed to legitimizing feminine agendas so that, with time, women-only meetings had become a routine, almost as usual as the mixed ones. I attended some of these. The women would basically chat in the way they liked. Once they experimented on me, to see how I reacted to jokes that ridiculed men. It could be said that such events were no different from the chatting found amongst non-politicized women. Probably, the starkest difference was not in the forms of display pursued in the talk itself, but on the bearing that the issues discussed had outside of it. In the group discussion, the women brought in the complaint that men spent most of the time outdoors smoking their joints and left them alone. On that occasion, and in some others, the men were clearly forced to consider the implications of what they did from the women's point of view. The women's agenda had thus began to play a part in building an understanding of the activities of the peer-group.

2.4. The open couple

Another aspect of gender relations that the politicized Trepas were involved in transforming was the concept of the *couple*. They subscribed to the idea of the *open couple*, which seemed to consist of seeing the terms of couple relationships as open to negotiation. The politicized members of the group, either male or female, would, for instance, defend the non-exclusivity of the couple with respect to sexual relationships and this would come across implicitly in narratives and in people's reactions to events. In the group discussions, they seemed to imply that a couple relationship was to be seen as an extension of a friendship. This is consistent with many things I saw happening. For instance, a couple moved together to a flat at the same time that they decided to terminate their relationship as a couple, while keeping their friendship (they had been a couple for 3 years). This also created a situation where people could develop cross-gender friendships much more easily than in the Rambleros group, where a heterosexual pair might be subject to insistent teasing if they were seen as being too close. Termination of couple relationships amongst members of the group did not seem to create much tension within the whole group as far as I could see, whereas amongst the Rambleros it put those involved in a delicate position. The Rambleros would often joke about extra-partner relationships, whereas some of the Trepas actually practiced them. Nevertheless, due to the forced circumspection in which I had to conduct my inquiries, I cannot be too specific about how exactly people managed these situations. What was clear is that members treated them as normal, as if they were not even worth commenting on.

Concluding remarks

As we have seen, gender constitutes the leading thread through which we can understand how the Rambleros and the Trepas constructed their own social reality. The case of the Trepas also shows how some cliques may be quite diverse, particularly when they are held together by a leading group like the politicized Trepas, who were prepared to accept this diversity (although probably with some limits; had there been men associated with simplified masculinity, I guess there would have been tensions). It also shows that people are able, under certain circumstances, to resist the predominant patterns of gender and to introduce innovative elements with a degree of success. In this sense, the politicized Trepas had been able to reconstitute the value of drug-taking, rock music and couple relationships within this group in a way that permeated into the practices of some non-politicized members. These transformations, however, take a great deal of work, as people have to renegotiate the value of their practices to ensure that they are taken up or interpreted correctly, as is shown by the efforts of some women to redefine the value of swearing or by Aleix's fears that the others might see him as too close to the women. In chapter 4, we will see more of such strategies and struggles to legitimize contrasting patterns of gender identity.

Chapter 3

The polyvalence of talk

By describing the activities and speech genres of the Rambleros and the Trepas in terms of gender, I may have fostered a distorted impression of how the groups worked. In particular, my description may have over-stressed the divergent patterns of behavior and participation of individuals according to gender, so that the reader may feel that gender subgroupings were leading almost independent lives in the context of each particular group. It is worth taking some time to set the record straight in relation to this. This chapter will be dedicated to complementing and hence to balancing the picture given so far. I will do so basically by concentrating on the analysis of events that had a gender-*mixed* character.

There were many situations in which people ascribable to different gender groupings were together and engaged in the same activities, mostly talk. In the two previous chapters, I have shown that, in some gender mixed situations, women and men participated in different ways. The literature on women's talk in gender mixed groups has also provided ample evidence of this. Other aspects of these differences can be mentioned: dancing could be a case in point. On the dance-floors of discos, it seemed as if women displayed more involvement by producing more varied gesture sequences and more marked movements, whereas men would produce more sober movements or else engage in pretend play (a male crosser who had stepped out of line in this respect was subject to teasing). In hard-core, for instance, which is highly male dominated, men who did not do the violent slam dance would restrict their dance to shaking their head and sometimes their shoulders. It seems that elaborate dancing is at odds with the masculine tendency to claim spontaneity or naturalness. Amongst the Trepas, men would only reluctantly attend salsa parties. Salsa is a music-style which is very particularly centered on elaborate and expressive dancing patterns.

But in the argument I want to make here I would like to go beyond observable surface features of people's performance in particular situations. The framework and the categories I have proposed in chapters 1 and 2 would be of little interest if they could be applied only to events where the features described appeared in a pure and unequivocal form. The categories would be relevant to a very restricted set of situations and I would implicitly foster the fallacy that men and women form independent, self-contained subcultures. I want to conclude this first part of the book by providing some insights on how both differences and similarities, both separateness and togetherness, existed in the social situations of the groups. I will base my argument on the principle that *utterances have a multiplicity of meaning potentials* (a principle which can be extended to any action, either linguistic or non-linguistic). On this basis, many speech events can be seen as *polyvalent* in terms of their meanings and the identities they contribute to constructing. This is also why identities can in turn be developed through the exploitation of this polyvalence, as people's actions may point in different, sometimes contradictory directions.

I will begin by summarizing some general features of the groups' organization with respect to the separation of the genders. Then I will move on to describe how polyvalence was exploited in particular social situations.

1. The organization of the groups

The Rambleros formed a group that was very much oriented to doing everything together. If they sat in a bar, for instance, they would see to it that everybody was at a reasonable range so that they were integrated in the talk. It was possible that there were various lines of conversation at a time, but not extended disconnections from the whole group. When walking in the street, small groupings could be formed but they were not taken as excluding others, and people joined, shouted from a distance and interrupted conversations as a matter of course. Even if some people separated, say, to go and dance, there always remained a kind of a symbolic space where the group was and where people returned to. The activities of the Rambleros seemed to be always publicly available and I never felt I disrupted any established arrangement by joining a gathering. This means that, within the Rambleros, men and women were together for a very significant amount of time.

The Trepas group functioned quite differently. It was held together (if at all) by a core group formed basically by the politicized members. The other members usually had some ties with one or two members of the core, but a relatively superficial relationship with the others. This was probably because the group had originated in the training school, where people were acquainted with everybody but not necessarily close. The relationships that articulated the group sometimes functioned autonomously. Smaller sub-groups could meet in a variety of situations on their own: go to the movies, meet at somebody's place, go shopping for records, go for some drinks, etc. Even when the whole group was together, it reflected this underlying looseness. As a rule, it took the shape of many stable smaller groupings, one of the usual forms of subgrouping being based on gender, with the women organizing their chatting and the men their smoking. However, gender-mixed subgroups were also common.

The problem of the separation between the genders that the Trepas experienced was largely a product of this looseness in its organization. Interestingly enough, this separation was experienced as a problem when it became too visible or too apparent. This only happened when they went out at night at weekends. Most of my recordings were made in the café where they met every day after they finished their work at the training school and their conversations were largely gender-mixed, like most conversations amongst the Rambleros. They consisted primarily of narratives of events that had taken place during working hours. In the training school, genders were considerably separated (most men doing building work, most women management and design). Nevertheless, many of the narratives could catch the interests of everybody, as they usually contained humorous elements related to people they all knew or issues they shared as trainees.

2. Gender-mixed events and hybrid events

There were events which presupposed the participation of people belonging to two genders, such as *cross-gender talk*, or situations which contributed to the establishment of a couple. However, the point of these events is not that they superseded gender boundaries and differences, but that they allowed for gender to be manipulated and exploited in particular ways (see Thorne 1993 regarding cross-gender talk).

If we leave aside those events which seem to be geared towards performing particular types of gender displays, it is easy to see that people often got involved in interactional projects where gender was of little or no relevance. For instance, when people discussed issues of coordination (where to meet, where to go, what to do, where has so and so gone) or circumstances that had to do with it (weather, the atmosphere of a bar), there was no perceivable contrast in the modes of participation of men and women. There was a tacit understanding that everybody's preferences were, in principle, equally valid. In these situations, people could bring in elements related to their gender identities, such as their tastes or ways of talking. But a discussion about what film to see or what bar to visit was not in itself organized to produce any particular gender display: the preferences shown might have been. These events would belong to what Goffman (1974) calls *out-of-frame activity*, as they were oriented to preparing and sustaining the line of activity people intended to engage in, but were not the thing itself. They were the *rim* of the frame, as it would not be acceptable to discuss what to do all the time and end up not doing anything else. Extract 34 is an example of this type of event. The Rambleros were discussing which discos to visit that night. Notice how the discussion got polarized along gender lines, as women wished to visit more elegant discos (which were generally more expensive, hence the discussion on the cost of drinks).

Extract 34 [Rambleros]

All the Rambleros have turned up at the customary meeting place of their neighborhood on a Saturday night. While they were waiting for everybody to come, they have been chatting and joking. Tere has got a bit excited about the jokes they make about her and has tried to strike back by teasing some of the boys. She has ended up raising her voice so much that Pablo and Andrés have begun to be concerned about disturbing the neighbors. So they decide to move on to discuss what to do tonight.

Andrés: vamonoh va
   Come on! Let's go.

Luis: noh vamoh[?]
   Let's move on?

Paula: ei donde vamos[?]
   Hey! Where are we going then?

Luis: al sinvergüenza a tomar doh por una[?]
   To the "Sinvergüenza" [A disco] to take two for one? [pay one, drink two]

Paula: riqui [crida l'atenció a Ricardo]
   Riqui! [She tries to get Ricardo to listen]

Pablo: riquini[!]
   Riquini!

Luis: y luego no vamoooa · · [se senten veus] · · · al bóveda · o >al cutreh [altres discoteques]
   And then we can go to · · [several voices mix] · · · to the "Bóveda" · or >to the "Cutres" [other discos]

Noi 1: <(al cutres) no[?]
   <(To the "Cutres"), right?

Paula: >al merlin [una altra discoteca]
   >To the "Merlin" [another disco]

Noia a: <(ai no) · · ·
   <(oh no) · · ·

Pablo: al merlín
   To the "Merlin".

Paula: al- al
   To the- To the-

Luis: al merlín dehpuéé · · però primero al cutre · · a tomaar otra pero ·
   Afterwards to the "Merlin" · · but first to the "Cutres" · · · to drink another one, but ·

   sin pagar [veus de fons; el Ricardo parla] · porque al
   without paying [voices in the background; Ricardo's voice is heard] · because at the

   merlín (creo que) hacen pagar · ·
   "Merlin" (I think that) you've got to pay [a ticket] · ·

Paula: no · no hay que pagar entrada >eh[?]
   No · you don't have to pay a ticket >right?

Raquel?: <en donde en donde[?]
   Where? Where?

Andrés?: a donde[?]
   Where?

Ricardo?: en dónde[?]
   Where?

Paula: y cuesta trescientas cincuenta pelas una cerveza
   and one beer costs three hundred and fifty pesetas [about 2.5 US$]

Ricardo: en donde
   Where?

Paula: en merlín
   At "Merlin's"

Pablo: y una coacola? · · · ·
   And [how much is] a coke?

Tere: [veu molt forta] oye >y la irene y la alicia[?]
   [Very loud voice] Listen > and what about Irene and Alicia?

Luis: <bueno · · vamo haciendo (xx)
   <Well. · · Let's keep (xx)

Paula: >(xxxx)
   >(xxxx)

Ricardo: [alçant la veu] <no · yo te digo una cosa
[raising his voice] <No. Let me tell you something.

Tere: >(xxxxxxx)
>(xxxxxx)

Ricardo: [veu ben alta] <que yo · al velvet no vuelvo ·
[Very loud voice] <that I am not- · To "Velvet" [another disco] I am not going back,

porque te cueste> · ocho libras · un cubata
cause there you got to pay> · eight bucks · for a Cuba Libre drink

Pablo: <quien ha dicho naa[!?]
<Who's said anything about that!?

Andrés: siete setent- y cinco
Seven seventy-five

Noia 2: seiscientas >(veinti) [moltes veus discuteixen i parlen alhora]
Six hundred >(twenty) [Lots of voices arguing and talking at the same time]

Paula: espera riqui · [sobre el soroll] riqui · · quien ha dicho de >ir a velvet [?]
Wait Riqui · [shouting over the background noise], Riqui · · Who's mentioned
>"Velvet" anyway?

Laura?: <(xxx) una cocacola
<(xxx) and a coke.

Ricardo: por si acaso · porque lah muhere soi >(xx)
Just in case. Because you women are >(xx)

Paula: [veu alta] no · estamos diciendo=
[loud voice] No, we are saying=

Luis: =ei · ei
=Okay! Okay!

Andrés?: [veu molt afectada de pijo] =porque lo mimmo · >lo mimmo quereis i' a
[exaggerated, snobbish voice] =because you may well · > you may well want to go and

conocer otro gruppo
meet another group...[meaning: "to 'pick up' some other boys", a reference to a
previous conversation]

Luis: riqui · riqui
Riqui! Riqui!

Joan: [entre altres crides a escolta] ha ha ha ha ha
[amongst voices calling to order] Ha ha ha ha!

The status of this interaction as a "negotiation" is quite clear. however, many social situations do not normally allow for such an easy demarcation. In the previous chapters, I have proposed a few categories of speech genres that were associated with people who constructed particular gender forms. It is not difficult to find clear examples of these genres in some social contexts. However, it is much more common to find them combined or hybridized with other genres. Indeed, these categories are relevant to my analysis in as much as I can show that they are present outside these archetypal situations, embodied in particular words, in particular tones of voice, in the choices of topic, in the displays of features of character *and* in the responses that they trigger on more diffuse, polyvalent, occasions. In my recordings, I have samples of these negotiations that are full of dirty jokes and teasing inserted by participants that seemed to indulge in stepping out of the main line, sometimes causing long diversions from it. In the previous extract, for example, Andrés' last intervention turns the discussion into teasing. The group discussions provided plenty of similar examples.

In the same way, an informal chat could become temporarily focused on the problems of organizing some future activity. If it was an excursion, everybody could have something to say. If it was a five-a-side football match, the men could hold the upper hand. If the women came to watch it, then it affected everybody again, although the women did not have to worry about getting the necessary gear. In some situations, there was no reason to keep frame and rim separate. After all, it is good that a discussion can sometimes be given some entertainment value, and a momentary interruption of the fun can be acceptable in certain conditions. In the group discussions, on the contrary, there were numerous calls to order, as some people considered that it was important to stick to the point. The opposite example of this can be found in Extract 1, where the verbal aggression game and the negotiation about where to go were inextricably welded together. This kind of *hybrid* event, as I showed, relied on the multiple meaning potentials of utterances. And these various meaning potentials created polyvalences that could "travel" across the subsequent utterances. It is therefore worth considering what these polyvalences mean for the analysis of social interaction and the conceptualization of identity.

3. Polyvalent situations

If we follow the implications of Bakhtin's principle of dialogism, we should see speakers as always drawing upon speech genres available in their culture. In this sense, any situation refers back to previous situations at multiple levels, and no instance of speech can be seen as simply drawing upon itself, cannot be looked at as if it was a separate, independent event. The audience will bear in mind what a person says against the background of all the experiences that constitute their relationship with this person, who in turn will also bear in mind that the others are reading more than what she or he is strictly saying. Now it is not difficult to understand how men and women are often interpreted in divergent ways even when they may appear to be doing very similar things. Nobody can start the world afresh. In the following extract, we can see an example of how polyvalent interventions are exploited and responded to according to people's assessment of the speaker's intention:

Extract 35 [Trepas]

The Trepas group were sitting around two tables on the terrace of a café in the early afternoon. Pepe touched a bottle of beer that was standing on the table. It was not the type of beer they usually drank.

Pepe: cogí una cogorza con esa mierda el otro día tío
   Got drunk like hell with this shit the other day, mate.

Mauro: ah es cerveza no[?].
   Ah. It's beer, isn't it?

Ayats: [Veu] Ah · sí sí · et fots un parell i a (x).
   [Voice] Ah! Yes Yes. Drink a couple and (x).

Pepe: [Veu] sí nen · posa molt
   [Voice] Yes boy. It really gets you.

Pepe started by announcing that he had got drunk with the beer he was pointing at. Why did he say so? First of all, the audience contained some of his friends. They usually drank together and liked to play with the effects of heavy drinking. As such, he expected that his friends would be interested. The choice of strong language and the term of address *tío* 'mate' was a clear indication that he was speaking in his capacity as the person with whom they engaged in such activities. Now the audience also perceived that Pepe's point was that he had been taken by surprise by that particular beer, as they knew it was rare to get heavily intoxicated with beer. In the third turn, Ayats engaged in a dramatization. He reproduced a character speaking Catalan and expressing surprise. In the fourth turn, Pepe drama-tized, in the same way, another imaginary character responding to the first. These Catalan voices conveyed, through a higher pitch, some kind of in-genuous characters who were non-experienced drinkers taken aback by the alcoholic level of the beer. The idea that some conventional people could discredit themselves through unintended intoxication was humorous within their world of experienced drinkers (see chapter 5, section 2 for a detailed discussion on the connotations of Catalan).

It is clear that this narration and the dramatization was drawing upon the displays of masculinity I have typified. But I will also show how Silvia, a woman who was not particularly interested in drinking or drug taking, managed to participate in this conversation. This was because she found the opportunity to exploit a particular source of polyvalence whereby she did not need to show active involvement in this type of masculine display. Pepe had continued his story by describing the circumstances in which he had got drunk. He had found a brewery where they had dozens of types of beers in stock, with bottles of all possible shapes. Here Silvia pointed out that she had been in a similar establishment, where beers of all kinds were offered:

Extract 36 [Trepas]

Pepe: es que había una carta
  And there was a "menu".

Silvia: (xx) a la frambuesa aquello es · un menú ( ) de · a la sabor bueno a
  (xx) with raspberry. That was a menu ( ) with flavour, well, with

  frambuesa a la fresa · >alemanas (min) holandesas no se qué · belgas
  raspberry, strawberry · >German (xxx), Dutch, whatever, Belgian...

Pepe: <sí · · o sea de cada sí sí porque es que increíble >porque
  <Yes... That is, each... Yes yes, 'cause it's incredible >because...

Silvia: <negra marron amarilla hay unas que son
  <black, brown, yellow [Interrupting with very loud shrill voice] There are some that are

  · · (xxx) que pone afrodisíaca =o algo así también
  · · (xxx) it says "aphrodisiac" or something like that too

Pepe: =sí · esta también estaba en la carta · en este bar · había una (xx)
  =Yes. This one too. It was in the menu. In this bar. There was a (xx)

  afrodisíac no sé qué (xx)
  [Cat.] "aphrodisiac" so and so (xx).

Because the narrative focused on the exotic value of the brewery – the properties of form, taste, color of the beers – rather than on the level of alcohol, Silvia felt that she could make a valuable contribution that could be of interest to the men that were talking. It is significant that the reference to aphrodisiac beer did not trigger any special comment. The Rambleros men, with their ongoing sex-lines, would not have missed the opportunity. The conversation started with a typical male theme, getting drunk, but Silvia carved out a space for herself by exploiting the existing polyvalences.

By the time Silvia and Pepe had got really involved in the conversation, though, the other men appeared to have moved their attention away from them. This illustrates how the choice of identity simultaneously opened and closed possibilities for participation in particular social activities. In this case, Silvia's intervention was interpreted as having a different quality from that of the men. And, in spite of the fact that at least Pepe accepted her contribution, it did not substantially change her position in the group. Later, Pepe started a conversation about a concert, where the men got involved again, but where Silvia apparently did not find a way of participating actively. An example of a man finding himself in an equivalent situation is shown in the following extract from the Rambleros:

Extract 37 [Rambleros]

Irene turned up with a letter from a male friend she had met during her summer holiday. Ricardo was curious and wanted to examine the style of handwriting. Irene was suspicious that he was just planning to tease her. In this transcript, I have eliminated fragments of overlapping conversations.

Ricardo: (no te) quiereh ponerte a mi lao eh?
    (You don't) want to sit by my side, do you?

Paula: eh[?]
    Eh?

Irene: es un amigo
    It's a friend. [Probably meaning: "not a <u>boyfriend</u>"]

Alguna: es un amigo que (xxx x xx joder)
Woman: It is a friend who (xxx, xxx, damn!)

Paula: el josé?
    [Is it] José?

Irene: no el josé no.
    No, not José.

Pablo: el josé no el (julio) ·· [rep gest de confirmació] Ah!
    Not José but (Julio) ·· [he receives a confirmation gesture] Ah!

Ricardo: yo no te- yo no te- yo no te (ehplico) [······] a ver a ver · solo la- ·
    I'm not gonna- I'm not gonna- I'm not gonna (tell) [······] Let me see, let me see. Just the-

solo la (letra) ·· a ver tía · que te la leo todavía como te pongas
    just the (handwriting) ·· Let me see, girl, [Or else] I can still read it [aloud] if you take it

así ··· joder · qué desconfiada ·
    like this ··· Damn. How distrustful!

Paula: te ha mandao una foto[!?]
   He's sent you a photograph [!?]

Ricardo: no confías en mi[?]
   Don't you trust me?

Paula: a verlaa
   Can I have a look?

Ricardo: es una foto[?] ·· Irene[?] · es una foto[?]
   Is that a photograph? ·· Irene? Is that a photograph?

Ricardo proceeded to read aloud the address, pretending that he intended to read the letter aloud, but moved on to comment on the handwriting.

What is significant in this episode is how differently Irene reacted to Ricardo's request to see the letter in comparison with Paula's. Even though much visual information is lacking, it is clear that Irene perceived that Paula was looking at the letter in the same way as she was. She answered Paula's questions in a straight way with calm voice (*No, not José*) and probably handed her the photograph straight away. On the contrary, she resisted Ricardo's requests, as she took it that he might use the letter to make fun of her. Indeed, the tone in which Pablo and Ricardo were speaking in this event and in previous moments of the conversation seemed to anticipate some teasing, so that Irene was seeking to keep the letter within the reach of women only. After this, and at Ricardo's initiative, both men and women made some comments about the handwriting (a topic which was probably not quite central to the interests of the women with respect to the letter). Clearly, the approach of each participant to this event had been judged by others on the basis of the forms of participation and display they routinely constructed within the group, which precluded in principle the possibility that the men had approached the letter in the same way as women had.

This episode illustrates the extent to which the choice of a particular form of identity has important implications. It can also help to understand why crossers and people who redefined their gender identities for political reasons were treading very delicate ground. Because gender identities were often defined in terms of oppositions, actors were continually issuing signals as to the forms of participation in which they could be counted upon. Hence the polyvalences that were exploited in extract 33 when one of the women "confessed" that she was "foul mouthed".

One common resource for handling delicate interactional material was *keying*. I have explained above how one of the women showed her dress as if she was in a fashion show. The following episode contains a much more sophisticated pretend game:

Extract 38 [Trepas]

Pepe: oye q- q- qué ha pasado en el labavo
  Listen w- w- what happened in the toilets?

Silvia: e yo te lo cuento
  Er, I'm telling you.

Someone: (qué ha pasado allá)
  (What happened there).

Silvia: yo te lo cuento [Veu]
  I'm telling you [Mimicking voice].

Pepe: tú me lo cuentas [Silvia riu]
  You're telling me [Silvia laughs].

Silvia: eee=
  eeer=

Clara: =pues resulta [Veu molt alta exagerada, riures]
  =Well, it so happened [Exaggerated mimicking voice, very loud, with laughters]

Silvia: estaba la María
  There was María.

Clara: y entonces [Ella riu]
  And then [Laughing, loud]

Silvia: pintando un caballito que ha hecho de barro no?
  She was painting this horse she had made with clay right?

Clara: pero que aún no >(xxxxxx)
  But which she hadn't yet>(xxxxx)

Pepe: <déjala >el micro [Ell riu]
  <give her >the mike [He laughs]

Silvia: <y tal no? , y entonces, de vez en cuanto, eee, se iba al (xxx) a quitar la
  <And all that right? And then, now and then, eeer, she went to the (xxx) to clean out the

  pintura, y estaba en delineación y con un pincel ha empezado "que te tiro"...
  paint. And she was in the design section and with that brush she started "I'm gonna sprinkle you!"...

There could be various reasons why the narrated story was delivered in this form of pretend game. It may have been because it was the first day I recorded the Trepas, and they were making jokes about the microphone. This would explain the unnecessary metalanguage, i.e. the references to what is going on which are normally not voiced ("I'm telling you, you're telling me"). This event was very similar to the pretend games of children, who usually make explicit a great deal of what is going on so that the participants can appreciate how the activity is developing. On the other hand, Clara and Silvia might have been trying to dispel threatening implications of the act of "gossiping" by claiming that they were playing at it. This is probably why they were drawing upon stereotypical elements of the "women gossiping" genre: Clara's stylized *resulta* and *y entonces* 'and then'evoked women catching up on news about neighbors or acquaintances, a form of talk which is a common target for mockery. On the basis of this multiple embedding of voices, they were effectively distancing themselves from some features of their performance. For instance, on the basis of this event, we could not have concluded that the participants were "gossipers" because they were just pretending. Nevertheless, the narrative itself was a true story where the women explained to Pepe something he was supposedly interested in hearing. Pepe himself participated actively in the pretend game and also in a way which was not threatening to his identity. Of course, Silvia might have told the story in a more serious way. After all, there were plenty of situations within the group that could have been described as 'real' gossip. This is why I believe that this particular episode was organized in this way as a response to the microphone, which allowed them to play with the enjoyable possibilities of fostering ostensibly distorted impressions about themselves to the researcher.

Concluding remarks

Thus the construction of social identities in interaction does not necessarily take place by means of people participating in events that can be clearly typified and demarcated. The multiplicity of the meaning potentials of utterances creates the possibility for actors to produce and exploit polyvalent situations and hybrid speech genres which allow them to pursue different interactional agendas. In this way, gender identities can inform any type of interaction and it is perfectly possible that different people organize their involvement in one particular speech event to construct differing, even contradictory, forms of identity. In fact, as some forms of cross-gender talk clearly indicate, the *contrast* between diverging identity agendas may well constitute the essential component of some social situations.

Conclusions to part 1

Politicized identities: what difference do they make?

After this description of the different forms of gender identity constructed by the Rambleros and the Trepas, I hope it has become clear that there were markedly different discourses of gender amongst the groups I studied. Gender was actively and creatively constructed by individuals in everyday interaction so that a variety of forms of masculinity and femininity were possible. Individuals negotiated their participation in social events as well as the meanings or meaning potentials of utterances and actions. In these processes, it was thus possible for some people to change, redefine or transform the dominant patterns of gender behavior in various ways. There were, however, limitations on people's possibilities of introducing changes in gender patterns. The first limitation was that any meanings constructed in interaction must be produced and recognized through the concerted and coordinated action of various individuals (hence the meaning of conversations such as the one about the meaning of swearing amongst women). Individuals were also constrained by their own choices in the sense that others expected them to act in a consistent manner from one situation to another, as Goffman pointedly argues (1959, 1967). In chapter 3, I have shown how this type of constraint operated in particular situations. As masculinity and femininity are often defined in terms of opposed features (say, dirty language versus appropriate language), people who challenged the stereotypes or the dominant discourse could be seen as presenting a contradictory or inappropriate identity, as happened with the gender crossers within the Rambleros group. Thus, the dominant patterns or stereotypes on masculinity and femininity seemed to operate as a background against which individuals must position themselves, as a discourse they had to respond to, either accepting it or rejecting it.

Now the question would be to what extent the gender crossers and the politicized people contributed to challenging the hegemonic gender discourse. In my view, as I pointed out in chapter 1, I do not see gender crossing as a challenge to dominant forms of gender identity. Firstly, the gender crossers never sought to problematize the existing gender status quo, or to problematize the practices of their peers or of other people. On the contrary, they sought to participate in events, or project identities, associated

with the other sex without challenging the gender division and often by de-
ploying strategies of polyvalence that would allow them to deny that they
were doing any crossing whatsoever. For instance, sometimes the adoption
of "other-sex" traits was ostensibly exploited to produce particular dramatic
or hilarious effects, thus inviting other participants to treat it as a joke. Secondly, crossing behavior was perceived and explained (by self and others)
in terms of personal inclinations and idiosyncratic tastes. Hence all crossers
are somewhat "original" in their patterns of behavior, each person deploy-
ing their crossing strategies in a unique way, as Thorne (1993) also suggests when she points out that crossing should be seen as a continuum.
Therefore it makes more sense to treat them as rule-breakers, rather than as
creators of new rules and or patterns of gender relations.

However, this does not preclude the possibility that gender crossers reinterpret their experience in political terms in some circumstances. At least,
in a context where the dominant gender patterns are being problematized
(as happened in the Trepas group), we can imagine that crossing may play a
significant political role. The politicized Trepas women and women crossers may have used swearing or argot for different reasons, but the fact remains that this happy coincidence enhanced the possibilities of exploiting
alternative forms of identity in conversations and games. Certainly, the difference between crossers and feminists was in many situations of no practical relevance: their speech patterns, interactional style and political ideas
were very similar in many respects. But, in my view, the fact remains that
the politicized people did not simply seek to develop their identities in
original ways. They also sought to legitimate these initiatives. They endeavored to establish and sustain activities and relationships based on their
new principles. And, in doing so, they created new spaces where the traditional identities were not necessarily the reference point. In a way, they
created an alternative "normality" within the boundaries of the peer-group.
As a result, there tended to be a convergence in the patterns of self-display
which created a collective model of gender as opposed to the individualistic
character of crossing. Thus the endeavors of the feminist women of the
Trepas had contributed to creating the conditions that allowed other people
(such as crossers) to develop new identities more freely and this would not
have been done by people who were simply involved in crossing.

Nonetheless, the situation of the Trepas group allows for another line of
interpretation if we take into account other aspects of gender identity. As I
mentioned earlier, it is commonly accepted in the literature that girls' events
are generally organized to display mutual interest, intimacy and sympathy.

Hence the (sometimes equivocal) impression that girls or women are more supportive and caring. On the other hand, competition, hierarchy and maybe aggressivity are seen as the defining features of masculine events. However, in my view, this conceptual dichotomy overlooks a much more general one. The opposite of *mutually displaying personal interest* is actually *displaying interest in something other*, i.e. some common, external or impersonal source of interest, whatever it may be. In this sense, strength, competitiveness and self-sufficiency are but possible options, amongst many others, for the displaying of masculine character. Therefore, I would argue that, in my data, in contrast to many all-women's activities which provided opportunities for the participants to show clear interest in each other, *men's activities were generally organized to display interest in a focus of activity which could be treated as external to the participants.* I would argue that this basic organizational principle constitutes a common thread across remarkably different modes of display of masculinity. For instance, in my data, some correlations can be found, as I mentioned, between gender and musical tastes, level of drug taking (alcohol, hashish), participation in playful fighting or verbal aggression. However, these correlations often hide much more subtle differences that cannot be reduced to a simple question such as "what types of music do you like?" As I explained in chapter 3, it could be argued that most men and women shared most musical tastes. The difference was that, for the men, music was one of their legitimate foci of interest which contributed to organizing social interaction and establishing and sustaining relationships. It was, in this sense, much more important for them. The development of ties between men was clearly dependent on the possibility of organizing activities around popular music, drug-taking and talk about all these issues. Hence the need that men also had to produce funny or exaggerated narratives that could be treated as interesting or exciting in themselves.

The strategies I had to deploy to integrate myself within the Rambleros group provide another example of this dichotomy. In the first weeks of my fieldwork, I found that the Rambleros women had no trouble in approaching me, asking me questions and chatting about anything. I soon learned about most of their lives and they learnt about mine. With the men, although they also were kind and considerate, I did not manage to communicate with them until after a while, when I had found out what they did and how they talked and I had managed to find opportunities to participate in their games. Because men's events were ritually arranged around these external objects of common interest, their activities were necessarily oriented to produce, assert, enhance and recognize this interest. This is why it was probably more difficult for them to find a masculine way of accommodating a male stranger.

Thus in men's chats and games, one had to create involvement in objects (events, themes, games) external to the self. Concentration on somebody's personal circumstances was, in this sense, in direct contradiction to whatever they sought to do there. It is from this perspective that we can understand why men rejected women's tendency to segregate themselves from the main group to organize "private" chats. This rejection amounted to an imposition of the masculine logic as to what constitutes fun; a logic which they imposed first of all upon themselves.

I would also like to direct attention to the way men's intimation was framed by Luis (see chapter 1, section 2.3): the notion of "letting off steam" conveys a sense of distance between the person and the object. It suggests that the person is dealing with matters that are beyond his voluntary control: the cause of disclosure is constructed as external to the self. A comparative study of the organization of intimacy displays between women and men would probably yield fundamental differences as to how such situations are handled.

From this perspective, it is quite a different matter to consider to what extent people were being friendly, sympathetic, caring, competitive, aggressive and so on in particular social interactions. The fact that women display mutual interest and men display interest in something external has more to do, in my view, with what Goffman calls the "official line" individuals take in interaction (1974). This is why we can find events where men can get round to displaying intimacy through banter (Easthope 1986) or girls can be competitive by appearing caring (Hughes 1988). Many men, therefore, can show interest in each other through coordinated engagement in what they treat as something else.[11] This dichotomy, and the implications of it, plays a key role in the way people tacitly understand other people's actions and expect theirs to be understood.

From this perspective, the patterns of social interaction amongst the Trepas were not so innovative (except for the unique case of the gender "switcher"). Women were predominantly engaged in the typical intimations and chats I have described, whereas men would generally organize their typical drug-taking, music-loving and story-telling events. Precisely because women were not prepared to simply follow the men's initiatives, it was in this group where the segregation between the sexes was more noticeable. The conflict that arose because men used to stay outside the bars to smoke their joints was a result of this fact. Additionally, during my fieldwork, women-only get-togethers (often including the gender switcher and myself) were becoming increasingly common. In this context, the politicized women's adoption of masculine patterns of appearance and behavior was not done via participation in men's activities (as is typical for people who do crossing), but via renegotiation of social meanings within the space of women's relations (as is shown by the fact that Patricia got used to swearing due to her relationship with Clara). From this standpoint, it is difficult to ponder to what extent the Trepas were really challenging gender divisions in a fundamental way.

In the following chapters, I explore other aspects of the groups' social practices that will also serve to point at limitations in the participants' ability to introduce changes in their patterns of behavior. One important aspect I will analyze from this perspective will be their patterns of use of Catalan and Spanish, where the Rambleros and the Trepas also presented fundamental differences. These issues connect, as I will show in chapter 7, with the ways in which individuals and groups are constrained in their choices by their socioeconomic position and their access to socioeconomic resources.

Part 2

Languages and ideologies

Extract 39 [Trepas]

In this episode, Pepe is narrating something that happened at a concert. A member of the public who had been playing music with a kazoo was invited to perform on the stage. In his account, Pepe produces various languages and speech styles to represent the characters involved in the scene. Spanish is in bold italics and Catalan in normal bold. The underlined stretch is in an accent that reproduces the Southern Spanish Andalusian dialect.

Pepe: *sonó mogollón el concierto cuando salió el Ricardo.*
  The concert sounded damm good when Ricardo came in.

Chimo: *ha - (xx) que cantara benny hill (y empezó) a bailar*
  ha - (xx) him to sing "Benny Hill" (and he started) dancing.

Pepe: *(xxx) veinticuatro ideas no[?] allá el · Ricardo y entre canción y canción*
  (xxx) twenty four ideas, right? That guy, Ricardo, between song and song

  (con la tralla) pusieron se le oye a él no[?] con el pitorro de estos · y
  (with the cazoo?). They go and they hear him, right? With this whistle. And

  va el cantante y dice · [veu d'encantat] **buenu si hi ha algú que vol ajudar aquí**
  the singer goes and says: [silly voice] "Well if somebody wants to lend a hand here,

  alg- algú del públic · que vulgui pujar y no sé què *y la peña*
  som- somebody from the public · wants to come up and all that" *and the 'penya'*

  [veu gutural] <u>*vengaa*</u> [pica de mans] <u>*subee*</u> · *sube el notas al*
  [throaty voice] <u>come on</u> [clapping]. <u>Go up there</u>. *He goes up, the fool*

  escenario se pone con el micro ahí · se pone a tocar con eso (xx)
  climbs up to the stage, gets the mike, starts playing with this (xx).

Joan: ha-ha

Pepe: *y todo el mundo le aplaude eeh* [pica de mans] · *qué risa · i* **molt bé molt bé**
  And everybody clapping at him: <u>eeh!</u> [clap] ·*What a laugh · and* "very good very good"

In this lively episode, the most relevant elements of the linguistic repertoire of young people in Barcelona are present. The narrative is basically in the Spanish language and it incorporates elements of youth slang and inner city argot such as *mogollón* 'a lot', *peña* 'crowd' and *notas* 'foolish person'. It also depicts a character, the singer, as speaking in Catalan, while the crowd is dramatized as speaking in an Andalusian accent. The crowd was mocking a singer who was a bit too polite or too nice, and a member of the public who was seeking notoriety. Pepe had enjoyed the situation because of the crowd's capacity to react by encouraging the kazoo player and by sustaining the fun through feigned cheering. This initiative of the crowd had subverted the meanings that were constructed on the public stage. The singer is depicted in a kind of stupid tone, as if he was being a bit too formal, while the crowd is portrayed as capable of jointly producing a subtle and ironical situation. The episode can be used to anticipate my argument that the Rambleros and Trepas saw each language and language variety as associated with particular situations, social groups and ways of thinking and acting. This is why they identified more with the Andalusian-like style or with argot than with Catalan. However, this statement needs to be properly contextualized and qualified.

In this second part of the book (that is, in chapters 4, 5 and 6) I will explore the ways in which linguistic styles and languages were linked to the social situations in which they were used and, as a consequence, to the social relationships, identities and views of the world constructed in these situations. I intend to argue (through the examples provided by the Rambleros and the Trepas) that the use of linguistic varieties is ideologically invested, i.e. inextricably tied to the forms of culture constructed by particular social groups. As I indicated in the introduction, my analysis will draw upon the writings of the Russian theorist Mikhail Bakhtin and particularly upon his ideas about the link between speech genres and heteroglossia. The notion of heteroglossia refers to the fact that any language is always *stratified* into the forms and meanings constructed by the various regional, social, professional or generational groups that use it (1981). This stratification is attained through the ways in which language is used in particular social contexts. As Bakhtin puts it:

> This stratification is accomplished first of all by the specific organisms called *genres*. Certain features of language (lexicological, semantic, syntactic) will knit together with the intentional aim, and with the overall accentual system inherent in one or another genre: oratorical, publicistic, newspaper and journalistic genres, the genres of low literature (penny dreadfuls, for instance) or, finally, the various genres of high literature. Certain features of language take on the specific flavor of a given genre: they knit together with specific points of view, specific approaches, forms of thinking, nuances and accents characteristic of the given genre. (ibid.: 288–289)

Thus Bakhtin sees linguistic varieties not as mere "codes" that can be described in formal terms, but as linguistic-ideological entities. Speech genres are here the material form in which linguistic varieties appear. The use of particular varieties is therefore not simply dependent on context, but constitutive of the contexts and meanings where they are used.

For the analysis of conversational data from this perspective, the notion of *appropriation* is, as I will show, also useful. Heteroglossia shows up in people's talk as they integrate a variety of voices in their discourse. However, speakers do not incorporate the various speech forms of their society in their talk in the same ways. Some forms of speech are treated as closer to one's identity than others. I will therefore analyze in detail how the linguistic repertoire of Barcelona was appropriated by the Rambleros and the Trepas. In this way, I will explore how they identified with or alienated themselves from the particular modes of expression conveyed by each linguistic variety. The approach taken here is slightly different from some traditional approaches inspired on structural-functional thinking and which see linguistic varieties as conveying social meanings whose origin is to be found in the social or cultural system (see Williams 1992). Here meaning originates in the social use of the language, in the particular genres shaped in the social events of particular groups. In constructing their utterances, people *appropriate* the modes of expression that are available in their society and *transform* (or *reaccentuate*) them according to their own expressive intention. In this sense, the linguistic varieties and their associated meanings do not originate in some shared sociolinguistic competence, but are actively produced through these processes of appropriation and reaccentuation. This means that the way of speaking of a group of people can be analyzed in terms of the social-ideological linguistic repertoire existing in their society. The polyphonic organization of discourse will somehow reflect the way in which speakers see their own identity and their relationships vis-à-vis other social groups and identities. The description of a particular way of speaking and its ideological aspects thus entails the representation of a social space constituted by a particular set of social practices *and of its relation with other social spaces* as manifested in the polyphony and interdiscursivity of the text.

In chapter 4 I will analyze the use of two slightly different forms of youth slang: *stylized Spanish* (a variety spoken by the Rambleros which integrated traits from the Southern Andalusian dialects) and *inner city argot* (which was most noticeably spoken by the Trepas). From a methodological perspective, it was not easy to identify and define these two linguistic forms. They were not discrete varieties or linguistic subsystems that could be unequivocally defined on a yes/no basis in each utterance with the help of some set of formal features. As happens with young people in London, who use a variable set of resources from Jamaican creole (Hewitt 1986; Sebba 1993; Rampton 1991, 1995), stylized Spanish and inner city argot could be used in different degrees or with different emphases. They consisted of a set of expressive resources that could involve phonological, lexical, intonational, proxemic or simply thematic or semantic traits in ways that were difficult to predict or characterize in detail. It is probably more appropriate to refer to these phenomena as *speech styles* rather than as *varieties*, because the latter term seems to call forth the existence of some internally coherent system or subsystem that can be defined in purely formal terms. As Hill and Hill (1986) argue in their study of Nahuatl speakers in Mexico, people do not simply adopt discrete linguistic varieties when they speak. Rather, they manipulate and combine their linguistic resources in complex and creative ways. This is probably why the way people speak, particularly in informal arenas, is only superficially amenable to systematic formal description. Sociolinguists' interest in phenomena like linguistic variation, codeswitching and borrowing is usually based on the assumption that they are dealing with some form of cohabitation between linguistic systems which should be describable in terms of formal features, structures and rules. In my view, codeswitching, code-mixing or linguistic interference, rather than being exceptional linguistic curiosities, are but the most obvious and visible manifestations of multivoicedness. They originate in the essential dialogism of language and in the processes of appropriation of voices.

I will thus try to show how the speech styles that the Rambleros and the Trepas used contributed to establishing the relationships between members of the groups and their own perception of their position in society. These speech styles helped to create and sustain the *local orders of discourse* (Fairclough 1992), i.e. the set of discursive practices, social subjects and relationships that were seen as legitimate in those contexts. As such, the choice of speech styles was also significant from the perspective of the struggles and conflicts of interest that existed within the groups. As we will see, some group members imposed a particular implicit logic on social events which regulated what was seen as appropriate to do and say and how it should be done and said. By analyzing several aspects of the use of these styles within the groups, I hope I will provide a meaningful account of how the groups functioned and how they constructed their values and interests through their speech.

In chapter 5 I will look into the social meanings constructed through the use of Catalan and Spanish. My analysis will be based on the study of codeswitching practices. I will describe the ideological worlds that were called forth when people chose to use one language or the other. However, in such an analysis, it would be easy to fall into the trap of treating each language as a unitary entity, encouraged by the fact that it is much easier to tell which one is being used at any particular moment. The notions of "Catalan" and "Spanish" need to be deconstructed here. It is important not to confuse what these languages are with their legitimized standard forms. The standard is but one of their possible forms, the product of the forces of linguistic unification imposed on the heteroglossia that exists in all linguistic communities (Bakhtin 1981). What I will seek to do, therefore, is to analyze *the different types of voices* that are animated through the use of each language. Through the findings resulting from this analysis of codeswitching, I intend to shed light on the location of peer-group identities as one aspect of the interplay between language and social class in Catalonia. This analysis will be complemented first in chapter 6, where I will investigate the social and symbolic factors associated with the conventions of language choice between Catalan and Spanish that existed in the groups, and finally in chapter 7, where the relations between language and social stratification will be further elaborated.

Chapter 4

Speech styles and orders of discourse

As is typical in all large cities, the linguistic repertoire of Barcelona is rich and varied, and the talk of the Rambleros and the Trepas reflected this richness. Unfortunately, this repertoire has not been studied in a systematic and extensive manner comparable to the territorial dialects of both Catalan and Spanish. A notable exception is the study carried out by Amparo Tusón (1985a, 1985b), where she identifies a number of speech varieties of both languages and describes the social meanings or connotations associated with each variety (see also Ballart 1996 and Pla Fulquet 1995, who have studied the *Xava*, a Catalan urban variety). Her classification is mainly based on phonological criteria and on speakers' own perceptions of city accents. This is probably why she does not include youth slang or inner city argot in her list, as these speech styles seem to function quite independently from accents or even languages, while lay people do not perceive them as a locally characteristic (see section 2 below). My intention here is not to propose alternative criteria to identify the speech forms of Barcelona. I will simply describe the forms of speech that I managed to identify in the discourse of the groups I studied and I will explore the *ideological features* of these forms of speech, i.e. what values, ideas, practices and identities were associated with them. In this chapter, I will focus on two styles of speaking: *stylized Spanish* (spoken by most of the Rambleros men) and *inner city argot* (spoken by most of the Trepas). My emphasis on these styles stems from the fact that they contributed in a significant way to constituting the *local orders of discourse*, i.e. they played an essential part in the processes whereby particular activities, meanings, self-displays, were legitimated; in the processes whereby members regulated what was seen as valid interventions and truthful statements. I will therefore look into the various *truths* that these speech styles helped to create.

1. The "simple" truth of the Rambleros

The Rambleros spoke exclusively Spanish within the peer-group. This was the language they all spoke at home as well, even though three of them had a Catalan-speaking mother. Generally, the Ramberlos' speech was similar to that of the Spanish-speaking Trepas in that it contained the most widespread features of colloquial speech used by young Spanish speakers in Barcelona: a) use of the most popular forms of youth slang, b) phonologically, deletion of [ð] in intervocalic position or of [d] at the end of a word; that is: [aβláo] instead of [aβláðo] for *hablado* 'spoken', or [berðá] instead of [berðá̱ḏ] for *verdad* 'truth',[12] c) use of words or expressions of wider currency and typical of colloquial styles. It is not easy to find clear and systematic ways to ascribe particular expressions to the notion of "colloquial style" or "popular speech." Current dictionaries often identify some entries as *fam.*, *pop.*, *col.* and so on. However, the criteria used to classify these expressions as such are often left unclear.

In actual social situations, the distinction formal/colloquial is often dependent on how the participants assess the significance of the forms used in relation to the narrative context. For example, in discussing some news item from a newspaper, it may make sense to bring in elements of journalistic jargon. To be able to make empirical claims about the register-ascription of a form, we should find evidence of people recognizing it as belonging to this register or reacting to it in some visible way. And this is not easy, as people normally speak in the way they are supposed to do, and their linguistic performances are therefore implicitly accepted, taken for granted. However, I managed to detect some significant events in my data which provided evidence of people's sensitivity to registers. These consisted mainly of troubles and problems caused by particular linguistic choices. A few of them appeared in the group discussions. The group discussions were a half-formal/half-informal context. For both groups, they constituted at least an unusual situation where the expectations with regard to speech style became unclear and problematic. Although these activities were conducted by all in a relaxed and familiar way, there is plenty of evidence that the participants sensed such situations somehow as a public performance, particularly the Rambleros. The exploitation of forms of swearing as a transgression (illustrated in extract 2) is evidence that the group discussions were seen as formal situations which could be discredited with humorous inserts of dirty language. Another interesting episode was the reaction caused by Raquel's style of delivery as illustrated in extract 40. Raquel was explaining a problem she was experiencing at work. She was speaking against a background of unusual silence, with a soft voice, well-kept rhythm and "tidy" language. There was not a single word that one could potentially classify as too formal, but the situation came across as quite solemn. This is what allowed for Andrés' humorous reframing:

Extract 40 [Rambleros]

Andrés: [dos aplaudeixen] *bravo* · · *>bravo*
   [two people clap] *Bravo,* · *bravo!*

Raquel: *<no es que me da mucha rabia es verdá*
   No, it drives me mad. It's true!

Andrés: [fort] *esa es mi niña* · *mi raquel*
   [loud] *That's my girl, my Raquel!*

Andrés reacted (jokingly) as if Raquel had been giving a speech on a public stage. He pretended that he was Raquel's mother displaying her pride at her daughter's performance. This example is evidence that these Rambleros men felt that Raquel's delivery pointed at a class of events which did not belong naturally to them, as if their friend had claimed a character or an identity different from the Raquel they knew. This is interesting, as it means that Raquel had (potentially) crossed a symbolic line which was of importance. The following episode provides more revealing evidence of this boundary. Luis was here recalling a conflict that had taken place within the group in the past and which had resulted in some members abandoning the clique. He was trying to explain that these people had not shown respect and consideration for everybody's preferences when the whole group used to negotiate where to go and what to do. The sensitive wordings he used are underlined:

Extract 41 [Rambleros]

Two instances of simultaneous speech are bracketed within other people's turns.

Luis: posiblemente · *porque es- siempre vamos juntos y llega un momento que*
   Possibly, because we always go together, and then a moment comes when

   "donde vamos" · · *[Ricardo?: no sé] la gente n- se calla*
   [somebody says]: · *"where are we going?"* · *[Ricardo?: I don't know]. People... keep silent*

   normalmente no[?] · *pues llega una- <u>unn</u> · <u>sujeto determinado</u> quien sea* ·
   normally, right? Well, there comes [fem-]a- [masc-]aa · <u>given subject</u>, *whoever it may be-*

Pablo: un sujeto [veu greu escarnidora; noies riuen]
   "A subject"! [low, mimicking voice; women laugh]

Andrés: un sujeto · y un predicado de >(xx) [veus de noies]
  "A subject, and a predicate of... >(xx)" [women's voices]

Luis: <y dice · dice "vamos a tal sitio" · [*algú: no; Andrés: no*] *sitio*
  and says, and says: "we are going to such place." · [*somebody: no! Andrés: no*] *A place*

que pues · que es secundado *pues · por sus amigas por ·*
  which, well, which is endorsed, *well, by her friends, by...*

[Noies riuen; veus de fons]
  [Women laugh; background chatter]

Pablo: [ben alt] *que ha ensayado ehta noche ·* [noies riuen] *(xxxx) tío tío · tú hah*
  [very loud] *He's been rehearsing last night* [women laugh] *(xxxx). Boy, boy, you have*

estao ensayando hombre [Ell riu] · *oye qué hacías cuando (llegamos)*
  been rehearsing, man [laughing]. *Hey, what were you doing when we (came?)*

[noies van rient].
  [women keep laughing]

Irene: va callaros
  Hey, keep silent!

Luis: vale ya me callo
  Okay, I shut up.

Noia: no
Woman: no.

Laura: [fort] *di di di di*
  [loud] *Go on! Go on!*

Luis: pues eso pues ·
  Well, that's it, well...

Andrés: una vez que habla bien ya.
  For once he speaks properly now.

Luis: y el grupitoo · tres o cuatro [...]
  The little group · three or four [...]

Luis was trying to describe the facts without naming anybody. The need
to mention people indirectly led him to use the word *sujeto* 'subject'. The
word belongs to very specialized registers, such as linguistics (as Andrés'
remark suggests) or journalistic genres. Luis' particular use of the term
probably comes from the jargon of the police, that is, from the way they
name unidentified suspects. I remember one of my teachers at school saying to a misbehaving student: *eres un sujeto* 'you are a [bad] subject'. Later
on, the word *secundado* 'endorsed', more proper of written or media styles
and pronounced with maybe too much solemnity ([sekundáðo] instead of

[sekundáo]) created another humorous situation. Luis was treating the situation and his own self-presentation too formally. Pablo even asked him (again jokingly) if he had been *rehearsing*, as if he was giving a speech. The amusement generated by Pablo's contribution almost ruined Luis' intervention.

Thus, the exploitation of this boundary between, what we might call, the formal and the informal, or the high and the low, could be made in three ways. First, when popular discourses were used to discredit or subvert the more public ones (use of low instead of high register), as in the above-mentioned extract 2 (swearing in front of the tape recorder) or in the Trepas' group discussion, where they were unable to discuss courting because, as they mimmicked the voices of popular rituals of courting or "picking-up," they got carried away by hilarity. Second, when the use of popular language was taken as a false (identity) claim on the part of people who would not be expected to use it. This is what happened to a Trepas woman who usually dressed and spoke more formally than her friends, as she was closer to mainstream forms of femininity. On one occasion where she used a distinctive slang expression, her friends laughed at her because they felt it was at odds with her usual way of speaking. Thirdly, when formal language was taken as a claim to an identity inconsistent with the speaker's character as was usually projected and accepted within the group (the last two extracts are examples of this case). The fourth conceptual possibility (that a formal discourse was used to discredit an informal one) was not a legitimate option, as this would have been in contradiction to the transgressive ethos found in the groups and with their own identification with the rough, the low and the popular.

There is therefore a high-versus-low symbolic dichotomy here and it has an asymmetrical character. This dichotomy can also be found in the writings of Bakhtin and Bourdieu. Bakhtin (1981) claims that popular genres often exploit their relationship with more authoritative ones and acquire their meaning out of this dialogical relationship. Bourdieu points out that "'popular speech' is one of the products of application of dualistic taxonomies which structure the social world" (1991c: 93–94). Later, Bourdieu adds that this taxonomy is produced by "the pursuit of expressiveness based on the transgression of dominant censorships" and as a form of expression of particular forms of masculinity (ibid.). Indeed, as I have shown in the extracts, it is significant that this virtual "policing" of the forms of expression was exerted by the men. In the last two episodes, the role of the women was limited to the production of reactions to the central scene rather than participating in it (which was generally the rule in this group discussion). It is significant that, in the scene depicted in extract 40, Raquel had gained access to the floor thanks to the insistence of her boyfriend, who had convinced the others to pay attention.

My contention is, therefore, that these examples are evidence of the symbolic relationship that the Rambleros group established between their world and the voices of authority incorporated in mainstream public discourses (the media, the school, the administration). Although I have indicated that this opposition was constructed (at least more actively so) by the men, in this section I am actually arguing that it affected the whole group, as it was an essential element of the order of discourse, the symbolic regime, that men managed to impose on the whole group. Additionally, the Rambleros men did not *only* seek the transgression of authoritative forms of expression. They also expressed and constructed a separation, a remarkably wide divide, between these voices and their own. The distinction is important inasmuch as the exploitation of transgression also occurred amongst the Trepas, while this symbolic separation was more characteristic of the Rambleros. The Trepas were much more ambivalent with regard to formal discourses, which means that there was an important difference in the way both groups constructed their position in society (and hence their talk). In this section, I will begin by describing the most salient formal traits of the style of speaking of the Rambleros together with the types of people and activities with which it was associated. Then I will move on to describe in what way this particular speech style was used by the Rambleros men in their ideological struggles to legitimate their own views on social relations and their position in society.

1.1. Stylized Spanish

The Rambleros men spoke in a type of accent associated with an ideological space of considerable weight and tradition in Spanish culture. This accent was produced by incorporating many elements of the southern Andalusian dialect, although it would not be accurate to say that they actually spoke in the Andalusian dialect. In fact, only one female member came from an Andalusian family and only two brothers had one Andalusian parent. The rest of the members' parents (except two Catalan speakers and one Galician speaker) came from the North of the Spanish Meseta, where dialect forms are closest to standard Spanish. One of these two brothers, Luis, singled himself out in the group discussion as having an Andalusian accent. It is true that his speech generally presented more Andalusian features than that of the other men; but, in any case, it was a particular form of appropriation of a limited set of Andalusian features that he shared with his friends, who all used them to construct their particular form of masculinity. This partial appropriation of Andalusian is comparable to the appropriation of London Jamaican features or features of South Asian English or Panjabi by British adolescents of various ethnic backgrounds as described by Hewitt (1986), Sebba (1993) and Rampton (1991, 1995). Thus, the degree to which men used Andalusian features did not seem to have much to do with their family background but with their commitment to particular masculine values, as I will seek to argue in the present and next chapters. This is why I will call this accent *stylized Spanish*, that is, so that it remains clear that I refer to a form of colloquial Castilian which was different from what dialectologists call *Andalusian*. The term "stylized" (Rampton 1995) suggests that speakers may incorporate into their speech features of a particular speech variety in various degrees and according to the expressive potential of this variety.

This stylized variety did not include the typical elimination of the /θ/ versus /s/ distinction, known as *seseo*, which is the most perceptible and stigmatized feature of the Andalusian dialect: for instance [sená] instead of [θenár] for *cenar* 'to have supper'. The Andalusian features that the Rambleros men produced with considerable frequency were: a) deletion or aspiration of implosive [s], which according to dialectologists is replaced by variations in vowel quality in the formation of plurals ([líβrɔ:] instead of [líβros] for *libros* 'books'), for a marked vowel lengthening (of which I found many examples), and for an aspirated [h] in medial position ([ehkwéla] instead of [eskwéla] for *escuela* 'school'); occasionally they would also aspirate [θ] ([i̱hkjérða] instead of [iθkjérða] for *izquierda* 'left side'); b) there were some instances of the aspiration of the velar fricative [x], together with deletion of final [r] ([muhé̱] instead of [muxér] for *mujer* 'woman'); and elimination of the /ʎ/ versus /j/ distinction, which produces palatals ranging from [ʒ] to [j] (Tusón 1985b). The intonation patterns, vocal quality (with a marked pharyngealization) and pitch (particularly loud) of this way of speaking are also very characteristic.

The Andalusian dialect is commonly associated with peasants or with the lower classes. For centuries, the predominantly rural region of Andalusia in southern Spain has supplied a workforce to industrial centers such as Madrid, Barcelona, the Basque Country and other European areas. In Catalonia, the term *andalús* is often synonymous to *immigrant* (Rodríguez-Gómez 1993). Flamenco singing is usually performed in this variety. The associations of the dialect come from the social extraction of its speakers and, of course, from the way middle and upper class people have chosen to represent them. In fiction and in popular comedies, Andalusian is used to impersonate characters such as servants, peasants, prostitutes, pimps, drunkards, workers and the like. It may help to represent witty and funny individuals or, conversely, dumb and aggressive ones, depending on the needs of the narrative; but it always indicates low social origins. Some common "compliments" to women shouted by men across the street (and often perceived as sexist) are usually uttered in an Andalusian voice. Tusón points out that this dialect is often referred to as "funny", "incorrect" or "colorful" (1985a: 102).

Amongst the Rambleros, this accent was used almost exclusively by the Rambleros men plus some women crossers. I have said above that some features of Andalusian were very widespread, at least in the Spanish spoken by young working-class people, including women. Nevertheless, the differences of accent between the Rambleros men and women were almost categorically demarcated by the elimination or aspiration of implosive [s] as described above. This was accompanied by features of intonation, which are more difficult to define, or by other consonantal features such as aspiration of [x] (which men produced very irregularly). The elimination/aspiration of [s] in particular contexts was the most noticeable feature: I twice observed women scolding their male friends for "eating their esses".

However, the Rambleros men did not make a steady use of this accent. There were interesting patterns of variation. Andalusian features became more frequent when the men got particularly playful or wanted to stress the meanings conveyed through this type of voice. This is why in most extracts shown so far, men are depicted as presenting these features. However, they did not speak that way all the time. In the following extract, I present a relatively long episode in which the Rambleros men got lost in their car and decided to stop and discuss the situation calmly. In this context, they produced significantly fewer features of Andalusian than in more playful occasions.

Extract 42 [Rambleros]

Pablo was driving the car, the music had just stopped and Pablo and Luis were whispering as they were trying to find a way of reversing the direction of the car in the maze of Barcelona's one-way streets. In this extract, I have underlined the positions where aspiration or deletion of [s] occurred or could have occurred according to the phonetic context. Luis was probably the one who "dropped" [s] more consistently and Andrés the one who did it the least. However, in this episode, Luis' pronunciation came very close to that of standard Spanish as he concentrated on trying to assist Pablo (the driver) to make out where they were and what street they had to take.

Andrés: tumbas ostia [Probablement escollint cassettes] · · *la la la*
   "Tombs", christ! [Probably reading names of songs from a tape] · · *la la la*

Luis: (encima has) de tirar p'abajo donde puedas giras · · · *adonde la plaza de*
   (up there you have) to turn down, where you can you turn, · · *where the square of*

   (tiana) esa es almogávares pues la de abajo
   (tiana) this one is "almogávares" street, then the one below...

Ricardo: pallars
   "Pallars" *street.*

Luis: ahí pallars *no[?] eso es*
   This one's "Pallars", *isn't it? That's it.*

Pablo: (··) p'abajo
   Downwards.

Luis: dando vuelta a la plaza
   Driving round the square.

Ricardo: da la vuelta=
   Turn round?=

Andrés: =oye pero al zoo[?]=
   −Listen but, to the zoo?=

Ricardo: =no da la vu- aquella de allá [tustant la finestra "tap tap tap"]
   =No. Turn rou- that one there [poking the window glass "tap tap tap"]

Andrés: mira por aquí se va al zoo
   Look. This way you get to the zoo.

*Ricardo: porque esa que esa e_ almogávare_*
   'Cause this one is "Almogávares".

Luis: pues no pues tampoco puedes · sigue recto Pablo porque no puedes
   Well no then you can't either · go straight on Pablo, 'cause you can't do it.

Ricardo: esa es almogávareh.
   This one is "Almogávares".

Luis: qué e eso
   What is that?

Pablo: (··) la plaza (mohcu)
   (Moscow) square.

Ricardo: no no no tiene que dar la vuelta y pillarlo a aquella
  No no no. He's got to turn round and get it in that one.

Pablo: no · no >no

Andrés: <adonde vamos
  <Where are we going?

Pablo: no puedo
  I can't.

Luis: no quiere decir pues aquella recta y luego la próxima a la ihquierda
  No. He means, well, that one straight on and then the next one to the left

  y luego otra vez a la izquierda
  and then left again.

Andrés: adónde vamos
  Where are we going?

Ricardo: si es la de abajo si esa no es
  No, it's the one below, not this one.

Luis: no no · · ·

Ricardo: eso es almogávares
  This is "Almogávares".

Andrés: por aquí se va al zoo
  This way you get to the zoo.

In this episode, both Luis and Ricardo had their own ideas about what Pablo, the driver, had to do. Luis appeared to be putting on a very low, calm, serious voice, so that Pablo would take him seriously and follow his indications rather than Ricardo's ones. He also had an easier access to Pablo because he sat by his side on the front seat, whereas Ricardo and Andrés had to shout from behind.

It appears as if the adoption of such a serious voice involved adopting a more standard pronunciation. In contrast, there is an episode (presented in extract 9) where I recorded *women* "dropping" esses as they teased one of the men. This may well be due to the particular voices they adopted for teasing on that occasion. These two examples suggest that the use of this speech style was associated with particular activities (or genres) rather than imprinted on individuals by virtue of their sex. Its association with gender thus came from the role that particular speech genres played in the construction of gender identities and of simplified masculinity in particular. It was these speech genres that were therefore associated with stylized Spanish.

1.2. The "simple" truth

When Foucault (1972) wrote that discourses could be seen as having particular rules of formation which determined the types of statements that could be made in particular domains of life, he was probably not thinking at all of the kinds of social milieus that I am analyzing here. Foucault was ostensibly much more interested in the workings of dominant discourses associated with the exercise of power by leading social groups and institutions. However, I would argue that rules and constraints on discourse operate within any social grouping. With regard to the Rambleros, it is possible to give a sense of the "rules" that underlay the production of statements and the forms of participation open to group members. Of course, such rules were seldom made explicit. Extracts 40 and 41 constitute the closest we can get to positive evidence of implicit rules. I use the term *rule* to convey the idea that, by talking and acting within the Rambleros group, one developed a sense of what was and was not acceptable, funny or interesting to say or do. A certain political order or regime was established which helped to produce and recognize particular practices and representations of reality while ignoring or denying the possibility of others. I have called this order the order of the "simple truth". Here the term "simple" seeks to evoke the intimate connection that existed between this order and the principles of simplified masculinity described in chapter 1. The term "truth" is taken to mean those statements and practices that are seen as legitimate in a particular social context. The order of the simple truth thus constituted a kind of legitimation of simplicity and of the Rambleros men's interests as to what peer-group activities were about. I will try to explain a bit more what I mean by "simplicity" in this context.

The order of the simple truth constrained the form of linguistic performances and hence of social performances. It meant that the language generated by the members of the group had to be, as seen in extracts 40 and 41, a "simple" language. This simplicity does not necessarily concern structural simplicity of grammar or vocabulary. An early second language learner of Spanish would clearly not understand the Rambleros if just acquainted with the basics of the language. Simplicity here refers to the way statements and thoughts were produced and presented and to the rejection of forms of expression which conveyed formality, tightness, sophistication or distinction. Simple truth also meant that speakers should present themselves (and generally others as well) as "simple people", as displaying simplicity and naturalness. It did not mean that these people *were* actually simple, unintelligent or boring. This simplicity could be administered in very complex ways. In the case of the Rambleros, displays of simplicity were congruent with a form of organization which provided fun, affection and security and which coped with the complex demands of modern life on the person. In the case of the men, it is important to bear in mind how knowledgeable some were in relation to anything to do with rock music (the different styles, groups, new records available at home or abroad) or with their preferred sports. When I went with them to a basketball match for handicapped people in the Olympics, Mateo knew all the rules of the game and capabilities of the different players by heart. They also had an impressive knowledge of the goings-on of the football league. These forms of knowledge may not be socially valued ones, but they were evidence – in my view – of their capabilities of developing knowledge in the areas they were interested in.

It is not easy to represent this "simple" way of thinking. As I browsed through the data in search for the "telling" example, I had the feeling that the key was everywhere but hardly visible at any particular moment. The following short extract is a fleeting anecdote; but it contains some of the key elements of the regime of the simple truth, particularly of the way in which the Rambleros men developed subtle strategies to avoid situations that might discredit their masculine pose.

Extract 43 [Rambleros]

The Rambleros men have played a five-a-side football match in a sports centre. After the match, they have had a shower, they have changed and they have moved out of the dressing room and into the entrance hall of the centre, where all the women were waiting for them. Then they began chatting and having soft drinks. The following is just one of a myriad of short interactions that takes place at that particular moment.

Irene?: [veu molt alta] qué pelo llevas pablo tío[!!]
  [very loud voice] What happens with your hair, Pablo, man!!

Pablo: el mío. [fent veure que interpreta l'exclamació com una pregunta]
  Mine! [As the Spanish construction is ambiguous, Pablo pretends to take the exclamation as the question "which hair are you wearing?"]

Laura?: mira · mira como lo lleva[!]
  Look! Look at the shape it takes!

Irene?: >ya
  >Yeah.

Pablo: <mira · mira pasa la mano · 'ta ahpirao · · ten cuidado que (xxx) hta ahpirao
  <Look. Look! Feel it with the hand. · · · It's like vacuum-cleaned. · · ·Be careful 'cause (xxx) it's like vacuum-cleaned.

In the first exchange, Pablo avoided giving a straight response to Irene's comment by giving an obvious answer to an unintended second interpretation of her comment. This was a usual trick to create humorous effects in these situations. Although nobody actually reacted to its humorous intention, it served Pablo's purpose not to get involved in a (probably too feminine) discussion about his looks and thus in a situation where the women's frame had precedence. In this way, he later managed to reframe the situation as one in which his hair had taken an interestingly exotic shape and texture, and as if it had been treated in a rather surrealistic manner with a vacuum cleaner. Hence Pablo used the rhetorical device of the obvious answer and the rather poetic device of evoking aspects and objects removed from the (mainstream feminine) discourse of looks maintenance in order to keep a safe definition of the situation.

The trick of treating as obvious what is not so obvious was one of the most important devices used by the men to maintain the order of the simple truth. The group discussions provided some interesting examples of this strategy, as participants often struggled to establish their particular views on some contentious issue. But again, the order of discourse operated not in particular statements, but in the way the discussions were developed; and often my interest was not caught by what they said, but by what remained unsaid. I will seek to illustrate my point by commenting on various extracts from the argument on household chores that took place in the Rambleros' group discussion:

Extract 44 [Rambleros]
Paula was reproaching the men for not being involved enough with household duties in their homes.

Paula: por qué tú no tienes que hacer la cama · igual que tú- tú tampoco la haces
   Because you don't have to make your bed. Just like you- you don't make it either.

Andrés: y por qué- y por qué hay que hacerla?
   What f- what should we do it for?

Paula: cómo que por qué hay que hacerla?
   What do you mean "what should we do it for?"

Ricardo: por qué hay que hacer la cama si luego la vas a desacer?
   "What's the point of making the bed if you are going to undo it later?"

[veus de fons]
[background voices]

Paula: para qué comes si luego tienes que volver a comer · > · no comas
   Why do you eat if you have to eat again later. · >Don't eat!

Irene: <la otra, tía
   <There's the other [silly] one. Girl!

Here we can see again how Ricardo resorts again to the rhetorical device of the falsely obvious. The simple truth consisted to a great extent in a devotion to the obvious, the glaring, the natural, that which appeared as most transparent (and which often is not). Ricardo was clearly teasing Paula, seeking to subvert her seriousness, and also avoiding the possibility of having to acknowledge that he should work more at home. Although his argument was not really an argument, he could count on the other men recognizing his point rather than hers. His intervention is reminiscent of the characters of many comedies and Spanish Music Hall genres, where the grave and complicated problems of middle or upper class characters are rendered simple, somewhat hilarious and mundane by the cook or servant (often an Andalusian speaker, though not in this case), who sees things with a unique clarity, a penetrating authenticity. In British drama, similar voices are commonly expressed through speakers of Northern dialects or Cockney. An example is the famous concluding remark in the film *Life of Brian*: "you cum from nothin', you go to nothin'; what have you lost? Nothin'!". Such a position also allowed Ricardo to display a typical masculine detachedness and self-sufficiency, while the possibility of exploring the matter further was avoided.

It may be argued that Ricardo was "only joking," and that he would listen to reason in another situation. True enough. But it is precisely about situations that we are talking here. The significance of his move cannot obviously be inferred from this situation alone, but from its position within the whole set of activities and statements found in the group. To put it another way: maybe the right situation to listen to reason never came. My argument here is that Ricardo's stance was part of a subtle, implicit drive on the part of the Rambleros men to protect their form of masculinity by rejecting or ignoring any view that would call aspects of their identity into question. This was largely possible because the activities of the peer-group were oriented towards having fun, which made this type of intervention more likely to gain recognition. Nevertheless, in the following extract there is evidence of another type of strategy:

Extract 45 [Rambleros]

Paula: No, but you don't say to me that it is not so, because it's true. I have been in your place and you have just sat down [and not helped your mother to tidy up the table, etc.]

Pablo: Okay

Paula: What do you mean "Okay"? And why do you >have to just sit down in your place?

Pablo: <Yeah, · · (of course).

Ricardo: Because this is what they have got him accustomed to doing=

Andrés: =Because it's his home.

Paula: No- Well, alright, I will also do it next time · · and let your mother do everything. Do you think this is alright?

Pablo: I have never told you [to do] anything!

Irene: [laughs] >Christ!

Pablo: <Have I ever said anything to you?=

Paula: =Bu- but do you think it would be right, Pablo, if I went >to your place, and I just sat down?

Pablo:<I have never told you [to do] anything [Irene laughs]

Luis: You- you- one moment! You certainly-

Mateo: You have already- you are >getting the topic out of >proportion

Luis: <Shut up, Mateo, wait a minute.

Pablo: <Everything happened- everything happened as we were eating in my >plot [holiday home] and you

Mateo: <>she's already getting the topic out of proportion

Pablo: <went and said: "Gosh, I haven't done anything today. What will your mother say?" and I say "What is she gonna say? Nothing!"

Paula: But this has happened to me very seldom.

In this case, Pablo did engage in a serious discussion, but he did it by *not* acknowledging Paula's presupposition that people had to do the cleaning on their own initiative. For him, the question was simple: she had done the cleaning because she had chosen to do so. His argument was presented as if it was so plain and obvious that it was not worth discussing. Because she had not been *told* to clean, she could not claim that she received any unequal treatment, neither could she expect others to feel obliged. Again, this does not mean that Pablo had not got the point, but that he was not prepared to recognize that he was at fault. The men (including crossers) teamed up against Paula's allegations and colluded with Ricardo and Pablo; but there is later evidence that they obviously understood and recognized what Paula meant. Mateo pointed out later that, after all, such duties had always been done predominantly by women. Luis responded with a very interesting ad-hoc questionnaire of hypothetical masculine duties and asked the women if they would be prepared to do them in the way the men were. His point was directed towards showing that men's inadequacies (never explicitly acknowledged) were matched by other inadequacies on the part of the women.

Another common strategy of the men was to refer to particular examples or cases that allegedly denied the validity of a general statement. For instance, in this discussion, they could always point to some exceptional duty or job they usually did or had done. Seemingly, the debate on whether women generally got lower wages was centered by the men on cases they knew of women getting very good wages.

Now, the functioning of this order of discourse must be understood within the context of the peer-group, where most activities were oriented to having fun. The group discussion was not an exception in this case, as the Rambleros adopted an attitude similar to the one they adopted when they were on their own. This means that the participants managed to maintain their usual positions and ways of speaking. Informal conversations in pubs and discos were not aimed at clarifying any particular issue, unless it affected the organization of the group or the relationships between the members. I have also shown in chapter 1 that the ritual aspects of many masculine events consisted of threats to and defenses of face. This aggressive–defensive ethos was somehow transported to the group discussion. Rather than discussing Paula's point, they were responding to her interventions as an attack on their face needs. This is why they felt they had to subvert her views in some way or other. Some of the situations in this discussion also had parallelisms with the way men disrupted women's conversations by introducing trivial remarks or dirty jokes (see extract 19 in chapter 1). These types of stance also imposed a certain way of talking and doing things when the whole group was together and even more when the men dominated the central scene with their jokes and games.

In principle, the *simple truth* did not mean that some particular issues could not be discussed; but it very much determined the way they were discussed. Favorite topics of conversation were those having to do with the fun world of young people as described in chapters 1 and 2; but the Rambleros could also focus on other topics. One example was the argument they had once had (before I met them) over the right to abortion. There had been such entrenched and irreconcilable arguments that the whole group had decided not to raise the issue again. In practice, however, some types of topics were only rarely mentioned: these were politics (economy, taxation, Spanish and Catalan nationalism, environment, international relations, feminism, etc.), and "culture" in its more colloquial sense as meaning "high culture" (literature, theatre, history, art). If such topics came up for some exceptional reason, they were developed little: Laura reported once on a ludicrous tax increase which had affected their parents' family business. At that moment, I made a couple of comments regarding the reasons why the Barcelona city council had raised taxes (to cover the debt resulting from some investments made for the 1992 Olympic Games) and the possible electoral consequences of this. My bid to discuss the topic further was, nevertheless, unsuccessful. My repeated comments did not meet the minimum expression of response of any kind, as if they had not been said. The conversation moved to a discussion about the exact name of the tax and the heavy taxation upon the self-employed. The episode might not be of significance in itself; only if we bear in mind that this was the situation where I got closest to discussing any political issue whatsoever during my fieldwork, in stark contrast with the Trepas. In the interviews, all the Rambleros made it clear that they were not interested in politics. Two of the men had joined trade unions in their workplaces, but they did not appear to be significantly involved in them. In the group discussion, they talked about politics only because I asked them to. It became clear that they were only vaguely acquainted with the political opinions of their friends and had little common ground. The only thing they had in common was that they were staunch non-voters. They distrusted politicians and anything that had to do with party politics, which they seemed to regard as a mere power game in which politicians pursued only their own personal interests.

Another important feature of this *truth* was, as I perceived it, the *discourse of personal preference*: this consisted of framing opinions, sympathies and attitudes in terms of personal taste, of "liking". This discourse was adopted, in my view, to present personal decisions and manifestations of character in irrational terms, as a product of non-voluntary personal tendencies and inclinations. Given the meaning of *to like* and *taste* in our culture, this discourse relieved subjects of personal responsibility for their options and preferences, thus avoiding the need for debating or giving justifications or explanations. It played an important role in the struggles to legitimize particular agendas within the group, and particularly to legitimize those of the men. Thus, they would claim that they did what they did or talked as they talked because this was the way they were.

Further evidence is provided by people's declared attitudes towards the Catalan language. Three of the men said that they did not speak Catalan because they "did not like it" or because they "hated" everything Catalan.

None of their friends considered this as an opinion worth debating. Ricardo, for instance, simply said that he felt different about Catalan, that he "liked" it. On the other hand, this discourse of spontaneity and personal taste allows the group to accommodate diversity in some aspects without it being perceived as a threat. It was used quite successfully by Andrés in the group discussion to defend his miscellaneous tastes and hobbies, which were quite different from those of the rest of the men and involved some gender crossing. Another interesting example was soccer allegiances. Most women were supporters of the Barcelona Football Club, while the men seemed to entertain an anti-Barcelona consensus. In Barcelona, the main local soccer team is one of the city's institutions that carries most symbolic weight. It is generally perceived to be a symbol of Catalan identity. Thus it was not by chance that, amongst the Rambleros, football allegiances correlated with linguistic attitudes. However, the discourse of personal preference freed individuals from acknowledging that their sympathies and opinions might be changed through reflection or discussion. This particular anti-polemical orientation and their disassociation from public political debates led them to hold very contradictory political beliefs, at least in terms of traditional politics: combinations of leftist ideas (socialism, communism, civil rights, trade unionism, anarchism) with openly racist stances against black people, *moros* 'Northern African people' or Catalans, or even with sympathy for some of the tough policies of the Franco regime. Probably, these contradictions were also caused by the fact that they never discussed these matters in depth and therefore had little chance of building a coherent understanding of political issues or at least of creating some form of common ground within the group.

1.3. Identity and order of discourse

My contention here is that the order of discourse of the *simple truth* served to produce and sustain the form of masculinity constructed by the Rambleros men, what I have called *simplified masculinity*. It contributed toward reproducing this conservative form of masculinity because it helped them to prevent getting involved in situations where their androcentric and patriarchal ideology might be put in question. As they claimed to have simple, unsophisticated and spontaneous personalities, they avoided discussing issues such as homophobia and sexism beyond very superficial terms. Extract 45 shows how difficult it was for Paula to denounce the sexistbase of the men's attitudes without incorporating the more formal alternative discourses of feminism. As the men claimed that their tastes and preferences responded to "natural" drives, it was very difficult to question the validity of practices involving displays of homophobia, sexual prowess, physical strength and so on. The ways of talking and playing of the Rambleros men contributed to the *production* of these different aspects of masculinity displays and to the *protection* of the validity of their claims. The use of stylized Spanish served to contextualize interventions in terms of the characters, ideologies and practices associated with this accent. In this way, participants were able to deploy strategies to reject, deny or discredit any discourses, practices or statements that might pose a threat to their masculinity. This was one of the ways in which they managed to control the meaning potentials available within the peer-group.

The effect of this "order" on the construction of other types of identities was, I believe, very noticeable. In chapter 1 (section 3) I already argued that people involved in crossing were subject to teasing or scorn. In this sense, beneath a discourse that paid lip service to the freedom of individuals, any form of identity other than the dominant one became problematic, thus limiting the possibility for people to explore new identities. For women, this order was equally problematic. Women wished to cultivate more sophisticated personalities than men. This showed in many ways. They were much more involved in efforts to get good qualifications to enhance their job opportunities. All the men had left school because, as they declared, they found it boring and did not study, while four of the women had either obtained their secondary school qualifications or were working hard to get them. Three of the women were doing a clerical job and one of them was studying at the same time. The women were also prepared to show and acknowledge concern about their physical appearance and to dress in more elegant styles than the men. It is worth noticing that good looks were also a requirement of the types of jobs they targeted. In the group discussion, one of the men accused them of aiming at an easy life, hoping to marry a boyfriend with money, instead of getting "real jobs" like them. In chapter 1 (particularly, in extract 11) I already indicated that it was common for men to tease the women if they dressed too elegantly, to the point that women played down their dressing style within the group. On one occasion, one of the women arranged to go out with a work mate and took the opportunity to dress up by putting on more elegant clothing and more conspicuous make-up. Women were, as I have also said, more ready to handle topics of conversation in more depth and seriousness. The games of dirty jokes and verbal aggression that men played on women often acquired their transgressive potential (their "fun," from the men's perspective) precisely because they subverted the forms of display that women sought to sustain. It is also significant that some women, as Laura and Paula explained in the group discussion, did talk about politics with some female friends of theirs, that is, *outside* the group. The Rambleros women's adoption of a more formal way of speaking than the men's also indicates their desire to identify with common standards of appearance and demeanor. This led them to use stylized Spanish only rarely. Their willingness to learn and speak Catalan was also significant in this sense. They sometimes addressed comments in Catalan to me or used it with outsiders (which was also the subject of scorn and criticism by some of the men).

Probably because the group was so much oriented to doing things together, the Rambleros women had a limited space where they could develop their identities according to their own agendas. It is therefore not surprising that I did not detect substantial differences in their knowledge about the topics mentioned above, which were outside the scope of the group. Paula's interventions in the group discussions sought to challenge the men, but she herself moved beyond the boundaries of a mode of expression which kept the ball in the men's court and which could therefore be turned against her. The occasional reading of a feminist book, the wish to study at the university in order to "have more culture", the chat about politics with friends, seemed to speak more of exceptional inroads by women in worlds that had no bearing on the group's activities and little bearing on their own lives. Maybe these inroads were no different from the initiatives of the men who said that they read a lot or had a fondness for watching these "arts cinema" movies with subtitles on late night television sessions.

In a way, the order of the discourse of the Rambleros constituted a monological discourse which, as Bakhtin (1981) defines it, recognizes no other voice than itself. Nevertheless, in so far as it consisted of exploiting transgressions, its meanings were actually dependent on the discourses of authority that it sought to discredit. Just as in Bourdieu's (1991b) analysis of the discourse of Heidegger, the Rambleros' discourse lay a claim to autonomy; but it was only understandable in relation to what it sought to conceal. In actual fact, these forms of transgression, as has been often argued (Willis 1977; Bourdieu 1991b), often express a deep identification with authority in a negative way; because transgression is more easily available when there is an established norm. The Rambleros men's fondness for the military service, for instance, though expressed in an ambivalent way, was an indication of this dependency (see 6.2.), which was in stark contrast to the insubmissive pacifist ideas that the Trepas defended and which the Rambleros chose to ignore.

2. The politics of *la penya*

Young people in Barcelona use the term *la penya* to refer to themselves. The term is used to designate the young fun-loving population that fills pubs, discos and concert halls. It can also be used to designate a particular clique, often one's own clique. In this section, I intend to explore what *la penya* was and how it talked as seen from the particular perspective of the Trepas.

In its phonological features, the speech of the Trepas was closer than stylized Spanish to the standard forms of Catalan and Spanish (that is, for those who were native speakers of each language). The Spanish-speaking Trepas spoke similarly to the Rambleros women. What gave the speech of the Trepas group a distinctive tone was their marked use of the inner city argot of Barcelona. To a greater or lesser extent, argot was used by all the men, by the politicized women and by the women crossers, i.e. practically everybody. The Trepas used as much argot when they spoke Catalan as when they spoke Spanish. The argot vocabulary was generally common to both languages, although there could be phonological differences in the way some terms were pronounced in either language.

In this section, I will first seek to define what I mean by argot. Then I will show how argot was appropriated by the Trepas and how it was constructed as the voice of *la penya*. I will concentrate on arguing that both argot and the idea of *la penya* were reinterpreted within the political frame of thinking of the politicized Trepas. Finally, by focusing mainly on the group discussions, I will analyze their speech style in order to show how they transformed formal discourses to fit their expressive needs and values. Here I will argue that the narratives of the Trepas were manifestly polyphonic. From this perspective, their discursive practices were in stark contrast to those of the "monologic" Rambleros. This polyphony served to constitute and sustain an order of discourse that acknowledged a diversity of standpoints and the relative character of experience, thus emphasizing the search for common ground with others rather than the imposition of a particular view.

2.1. Argot, slang, popular speech

Argots and slangs belong to the category of language varieties that Halliday (1978) called *antilanguages*, that is, particular linguistic codes that are associated with social groups that are somehow set apart from, or in opposition to, mainstream society (see also Martín Rojo 1996). As such, antilanguages serve the function of producing alternative meanings and relations or, as Halliday puts it, their use involves "the acting out of a distinct social structure" (Halliday 1978: 167). However, while I agree with Halliday and Martín Rojo's insights on argots, their origins and uses by the underworld and other social groupings, in this subsection I wish to raise attention to some other subtle social uses of these varieties. It is common knowledge that expressions belonging to slangs and argots are not only used by thiefs, prisoners and the like. They can also be incorporated by other social groups who can transform their meaning according to their own expressive interests. This poses some obvious methodological problems as to the identification of expressions belonging to argot, slang or other unconventional speech forms. It is not easy to justify why a particular expression belongs to one category or the other.[13] The difficulties have often been compounded by the fact that lexicographers have traditionally relied upon written texts to do their dictionaries, thus producing a representation of these styles which is removed from the actual spoken situations in which they are primarily used and developed (Bourdieu 1991c). Bourdieu has called for researchers to determine from the speakers' perspective "whether a word is part of slang or part of the legitimate language" (ibid.: 265). Some dictionaries, such as Thorne (1990) or León (1992) for English and Spanish slang respectively, have used ethnographic data together with written sources. Nevertheless, they acknowledge that the criteria for ascribing particular expressions to colloquial speech, slang, argot or specialized jargons is largely based on their own intuitions.

In my view, to simply describe the language of particular speakers or to analyze their natural conversations would not necessarily give us the key to forms of universal classification of linguistic items. Chapman (1986) produces a list of the various social groups that contribute to the production of slang in the United States: truck drivers, jazz musicians, gamblers, criminals, yuppies, homosexuals, airline personnel, adolescents, students, etc. He indicates that argot expressions of these various groups become part of the slang when they are incorporated by other groups, but that this is not necessarily done in a uniform way. Speech styles (and probably registers, as traditionally conceived in linguistics) are not amenable to the kind of formal description that linguists and philologists are accustomed to perform (see Payrato 1996). These problems come from the way language has been conceived in mainstream linguistics, i.e. as a set of forms associated to meanings, this association having a general (not local, not context-specific) validity, even if these forms are used in a restricted set of situations or by particular social groups. Dictionaries are commonly built on the basis of this assumption of universal validity of form-meaning relations. However, this universalism clashes with the intrinsic situatedness and the dialogical character of the various colloquial forms of language. This means that we cannot really establish a criterion of general validity to classify linguistic forms in terms of their register ascription. What speakers do is to incorporate in their utterances the discourse of some social group (according to their own perception about the actual group and its discourse) in order to evoke, in some way or the other, the modes of thinking and the values, worldviews, identities and practices associated with this group. Thus, when somebody uses the word *boozed* instead of *drunk*, s/he is likely to refer to the way drunkenness is valued or judged amongst a group of "buddies" rather than between two people who are entitled to test a driver in their capacity as policemen. What is therefore relevant to questions of identity is to study the various ways in which people adopt or appropriate linguistic expressions within particular social domains. This will help to understand how linguistic expressions are drawn upon, transformed and reinterpreted to constitute social relationships and identities. A consequence of this situated character of language is that, even for slang or argot speakers, it does not make much sense to speak these styles outside of the activities and relationships where they are used. When I was a teenager, a friend of mine told me an anecdote he had experienced with a council official "with a grey suit" from the Department of Youth Policy. The man had stood up from his desk, patted my friend's shoulder and said *"hola, tiu!"* 'hi, man!'. We both found it hilarious. A member of the Trepas told me that she found some survey questionnaires that used slang as somewhat insulting or, at least, inappropriate.

In my analysis, I will keep the common distinction between *slang* and *argot*. The former is normally used to refer to the most widespread forms of unconventional speech and the latter to the forms of speech of the lowest social strata, petty delinquents and prison population.[14] Both the Rambleros and the Trepas used linguistic items that could be classified as belonging to the common youth slang of Barcelona. I provide below two token examples of Catalan slang expressions that can be used in both Catalan and Spanish with equivalent meanings. In the gloss, I explain how these expressions connected with some features of the types of masculine identities I have described. The words were used by members of both groups. The latter may be more distinctively "slangy" than the former, which is very widely used nowadays[15]:

Passada (Spanish *pasada*): n.f.: nominalization of the verb *passar-se* 'to go beyond the limit, over the top'. It speaks of an action where a risk has been taken or a rule has been broken. Therefore, in peer-group activities, it acquires the positive connotations of transgression, and its meaning has been extended to anything that appears exciting or surprising: *quina passada!* 'How cool! great! wonderful!'. It can also have a negative connotation depending on the tone of voice, when a particular action has really gone beyond the desirable limits

molar: to like something or to feel like doing something: *això (em) mola* (literally, 'this pleases (me)'). This expression is a key element of the order of discourse that pays tribute to tastes and impulses, where one's own actions are justifiable on the grounds of feeling or non-rational disposition.

From early on in my fieldwork, I noticed that the Trepas' speech was closer to argot. In the interviews, the Trepas confirmed their fondness for argot, while the Rambleros acknowledged that they made very limited use of this style. The following extract is from one of the Rambleros men:

Extract 46 [Rambleros]
Ricardo: ...el tipo de gente que vamos · siempree · habl- o sea hablamos así
  ... *the type of people we are, I believe, speak like this, in a*

normal · · aunque a veces · (no) a veces sí que decimos · (x) · me debes un
normal way, · although sometimes · (no) sometimes we do say:· (x) · "you owe me a

talego o me debes yo qué sé una libra oo · o lo que sea (pero-) · · ·
talego" [1.000 ptes.] or "you owe me" I don't know "a pound" [100 ptes.], or- · or
whatever, (but) · ·

normalmente (x) y eh que además si esta- según donde trabajes · [...]
normally (x) and it is also that if you ar- depending on where you are working · [...]

en un bar (x) · oye damee · da- · dame una libra · · que queda mal.
In a bar (x) · "Listen, give- · gi- · give me one pound" · It sounds bad.

Mateo said that they (the Rambleros) used argot "maybe now and then", but that they did not speak "like that". Luis said that they used it, but *sin costumbre* 'without regularity', and said that his more Andalusian or

"Gypsy" friends used it more. Pablo said that he did not "like" some slang words. The Rambleros women stated much more clearly that they did not use such expressions, which were, according to Irene, a bit *garrulo* 'rough' or *lolaila* (an expression that refers to a type of Rumba music associated with lower class people). Or, if they did use them, it was because the men had "stuck them to us", according to Paula. Alicia, finally, said that "they may say that, but not often". My impression is that the Rambleros were implying that they might use argot playfully, for special effects or to bring in an outsider's voice, but not as their main voice in the way that the Trepas did. The Rambleros seemed to want to distance themselves from the lowest strata of society, the drug dealers and petty criminals that they had seen in their neighborhood, the people who they identified as the producers of argot.

Different social groups thus appropriate forms of argot and slang in different ways. One of the main factors that sets apart youth slang or argot from stylized Spanish is that the former contains expressions that are clearly associated with the younger generations, such as the ones related to drug taking. In a vocabulary list I constructed on the basis of my data, 33 out of 174 items were related to drugs. Jaume Funes (1982) writes about the fundamental changes that drug-taking practices underwent during the sixties amongst young people of working-class extraction in the Barcelona metropolitan area. He says that the new drugs(cannabis derivatives, LSD, heroine as opposed to the "old" wine, spirits and tobacco) were introduced by the predominantly middle-class hippie movement and that working-class gangs adopted them later. Apparently, working class gangs also got involved in the drug trade, as they discovered that this could be a significant source of income. It is possible that the time Funes is describing, the 1960s, coincides with the time when youth slang was formed as we know it nowadays. At least, the oldest people I know who use or have used slang in a significant way were born in the 1950s and therefore were in their teens during the 1960s. This means that some of the parents of the members of the groups could have been speakers of slang. Nevertheless, I did not glean any evidence of this; and some of the Trepas reported that they did not speak much slang with their parents.

The expression *privar* 'to booze' is an example of a word that originated in argot and is now part of the general repertoire of slang employed by young people. Funes (1982) reports that it was used by the new lower working-class gangs at the time he carried out his study. In my student life in Barcelona, I did not come into contact with this word until about 1986, by which time it had probably come into general use, as it has now. These linguistic resources clearly catered for the ritual need to construct drug taking as positive. Even if they really originated in the world of drug pushers, car breakers and junkies described by Funes, it is not surprising that they were quickly taken up and popularized by teenagers and youngsters who sought to produce similar, though less extreme, forms of display. The perception that argot is mostly spoken by men (Chapman 1986; León 1992) probably comes from the association between argot and these types of activities, which are central to the construction of some masculine identities. Nevertheless, some Trepas women were also prominent in their use of argot in tune with their endeavors to redefine their femininities. In the next chapter, I comment further on the masculine overtones of argot with respect to the relationship between argot and the Catalan and Spanish languages.

A set of words could be isolated, as in the examples given by Ricardo above, as evidence that the Trepas spoke more argot than the Rambleros. Words used to name the police or security personnel (*maderos*, *monos*, *seguretas*), words referring to more mundane things, such as 'sleep' (*sobar*), 'money' (*la guita*), 'gums' (*la piñata*), 'home' (*el queo*) were used by the Rambleros only exceptionally if at all. Nevertheless, the real difference lay more in the fact that argot expressions were constantly made present in the speech of the Trepas, whereas with the Rambleros this was not the case. On the other hand, because the Trepas did not practice verbal aggression, they did not use much dirty language. As a result, the speaking style of the two groups was very noticeably different.

One aspect of the relationship that the Trepas had with argot was quite clearly expressed by Jaume in his interview. In the extract below, I have also underlined the slang or argot terms:

Extract 47 [Trepas]

Jaume: *yo · considero quee · · la gente estamos · estamos muy atrasados en*
    I · believe thaat · · we people are · we are very much lagging behind with

    el argot eh? porque · al- algun dia que veig gent que anava abans
    the argot, yeah? Because · wh- when some day I meet the people I used to go round with before,

    no? que ara estan me- amb · rollos chungos no? de camellos y tal ·
    right? who are now involved er- in · nasty businesses, right? pushers and all that.

    comença a parlar que no sé qué del bronx · que voy a pillar el bronx
    He starts talking about "I-don't-know-what the 'bronx'": "I am gonna pick up some 'bronx'."

o voy no sé cuantos · i <u>flipo</u> no[?] por- la forma que tenen de parlar
or I'm gonna so on and so forth." And I <u>feel amazed</u>, right? because- of the way of
speaking that they have.

jo és que · molt- · · sé lo que és perquè · · eer no sé lo que diuen però
To me is that · very- · · I know what it is because- · · I don't know what they say but

m'imagino lo que és no[?] i és allò no[?] però · · és <u>una passada</u> yo al·lucino
I imagine what it is, right? And it is that, right? But · · it's <u>incredible</u>, I'm <u>amazed</u>.

estic molt atrassat eh? o sigui [...]
I am really behind, yeah? I mean [...]

Jaume's testimony was that of a person who had spent his early teens with people who later drifted to hard drugs and to drug dealing. A chance meeting with his old acquaintances had served to remind him that he was no longer in touch with new developments, both linguistically and culturally. He had also learned about the meaning of the well-known graffiti signatures (*taques*) now present all over the world. Later in the interview, he stated that his argot (and Salva's too) was "antiquated". Silvia also reported on new coinages of argot which were not used by the Trepas.

The Trepas' relationship with argot was, therefore, similar to the Rambleros' men's connection with Andalusian. They adopted and reinterpreted argot together with the values constructed amongst inner city gangs. I will now seek to define the way in which this appropriation was accomplished by the Trepas.

2.2. *The voices of* la penya

In the following extract, we have a good example of the types of characters and contexts that the Trepas associated with inner city argot. It is a narrative intended to cause laughter, a kind of joke. A citizen who represents mainstream values calls a taxi while he watches a punkie passing by. The vision of the punkie reminds him of the "drug problem" and he makes a comment to the taxi driver. The taxi driver, however, responds in an unexpected way. In the narrative, the voice of authority was confronted with the voice of argot to present two contrasting views about drug taking. Notice that the narrative voice of the joke was in argot as well. Argot words are underlined:

Extract 48 [Trepas]

Salva: ...con la del taxi no? que e- el _pavo_ va a parar un taxi un taxi y hay
    the one of the taxi, right? That th- the _guy_ is about to call a taxi: "a taxi!" and there's

un _punki_ delante · · y pasa el _punki_ y dice · _pilla_ el _pavo_ no? · · que
    *a _punkie_ at the front · · and the _punkie_ walks away and he says · the taxi _picks_ the _guy_*
    right? ·· who

va con la gavardina y con gorrito y tal · pues yo no (xx) el taxi porque
    is wearing his trench coat and his little cap and all: "Well I don't (xx) the taxi because,

ahora con los problemas que hay con la droga y estos problemas ·
    nowadays, with all these problems you get about drugs and all these problems...".

pues yo vengo de _pillar_ tres gramos de _caballo_ y sin problemas [rialles]
    [And the driver answers:] "Well, I just _picked up_ three grams of _junk_, and no problems."
    [laughters]

Here the logic of the voice in argot (of the taxi driver) subverts the logic of
the person representing mainstreamish concerns about drugs. The joke can
be best understood if the reader imagines the client speaking Standard English and the taxi driver speaking a strong Cockney, London Jamaican or any
American inner city vernacular. Salva (and the audience) was siding with
the punkie and the taxi driver, even though they were not into heroin themselves, as far as I know. This form of subversion was roughly equivalent to
the strategies of the Rambleros men to impose the *simple truth*. In this case,
the voice in argot subverted the predominant discourse on drugs by pretending to ignore the problematic reading of drug addiction and by recasting it as a simple matter of drug availability.

Nevertheless, the Trepas endorsed this truth from a significantly different perspective, namely a political one. To understand these subtle processes, it is useful to explore the meaning of the notion of *la penya*. *La
penya* was a slang expression that designated the young people of Barcelona, particularly with reference to peer-group leisure activities, such as the
ones described in this book. However, the word could also be used to designate the audience of a concert, the clientele of a disco or a youth club, the
gang one was usually going round with or any particular gang or informal
grouping of young people which was seen as a meaningful unit for narrative purposes. *La penya* was, therefore, the term young people used to refer
to themselves.[16] In order to illustrate the functioning of the Trepas' local
order of discourse, I will seek to describe the way they reconstructed the
meaning of this expression and I will argue that the *penya* was given a po-

litical significance within the framework of the leftist or revolutionary ideas of the politicized members.

As with the Rambleros, it is difficult to find particular speech events that can be used as unequivocal evidence of the existence of a given ideological configuration. The evidence I give below about the politicization of the term *penya* may seem to support my argument in a relative way. But if I pulled out the examples one by one and analyzed them in isolation, maybe there would not be a single one which unmistakably indicated a political frame of reference. Other interpretations are always possible. It is against the background of other events and in the logic of their interrelation that the significance of particular episodes can be detected. It was after hearing the Trepas talk about politics, after understanding how politics impregnated their experience of hard-core music and how it impinged on their interpersonal relationships, that I began hearing a special "ring" in words like *penya* (I will from now on use the expression "the penya" without italics).

The Trepas' political outlook was akin to Marxist views of society, which construct the working class as the potentially liberating class. From this viewpoint, working-class forms of culture were seen as invested with oppositional value. For instance, Jaume, who was not particularly politicized, referred to graffiti as "an art", thus claiming legitimacy for these forms of expression. He particularly valued the most elaborate mural paintings. Often, the transgressive, boisterous, sometimes riotous actions of the penya were also presented in narratives as invested with authenticity and spontaneity and as free from calculated interest, like a truth that was pushed through the fictions of the hegemonic public domain. Sometimes, this truth was, as I said, akin to the *simple truth* of the Rambleros. Even stylized Spanish could be used to represent the voice of the penya in some cases. Pepe once narrated an episode in a concert, where the penya (the voice of the public) was represented as speaking in stylized Spanish (see extract 39).

It was also expected that members of the penya would show mutual solidarity. Jaume, for instance, commented with annoyance on how some members of the penya had been sabotaging graffiti of "other penyas", thus breaching this expectation of solidarity. To Magda, Catalan speakers belonging to the penya would kindly switch to Spanish to talk with her as opposed to the "people" who did not.

These examples are not taken from the interviews with politicized members. What the politicized members were doing was to give this solidarity a political flavor that was reminiscent of traditional slogans for working-class solidarity. This political reconstruction of the penya was also un-

dertaken by political groups in Barcelona, which used its language and imagery in their propaganda and in their activities. The powerful antimilitary
groups that promoted conscientious objection and sometimes opposition to
any kind of conscription had popularized phrases such as the ambilingual
(or *bivalent*, see Woolard 1999) slogan *la mili no mola* 'the military service
does not "please"' (see the definition of *molar* above). The name of a
prominent grass-roots organization was *Mili-KK* (KK=caca 'crap' in baby
talk). In this way, pacifist or anti-militaristic ideas were filtered through the
discourse of the penya, thus putting the discourse of personal preference at
the front (by using the verb *molar*). As the slogans of these political groups
were commonly addressed to people in their late teens and early twenties,
they usually included drawings from comic artists popular amongst the
young. For instance, a campaign against heroin conducted by an anarchist
group included designs from a well-known underground comic artist. Another common activity of these groups was to organize rock concerts for
the penya. Three Trepas people, including one woman, were ordinarily engaged in the neighborhood branch of one antimilitary group, and sometimes
attended national conferences or meetings at the central coordinating committee in Barcelona. It is therefore not surprising that the discourse of the
Trepas, and particularly their use of argot, acquired some political overtones in some contexts.

The types of population that the word *penya* might refer to in actual talk
were very varied and context dependent. Its meaning potentials could be
expanded in a similar way to the terms "people" and "popular", as discussed by Bourdieu (1991c 90–91):

> Like elastic concepts such as 'the working classes', 'the people' or 'the
> workers', which owe their political virtues to the fact that one can ex-
> tend the referent at will to include (during election time, for instance)
> peasants, managers and small businessmen, or, conversely, limit it to
> industrial workers only, or even just steel workers (and their ap-
> pointed representatives), the indeterminately extensive notion of
> 'working-class areas' owes its mystifying virtues, in the sphere of
> scholarly production, to the fact that, as in psychological projection,
> everyone can unconsciously manipulate its extension in order to ad-
> just it to their interests, prejudices or social fantasies.

These semantic manipulations are thus not exclusive to the discourse of
politicians and academics. Pepe used the term *penya* to refer to the peasant

population of his family's village of origin. Once, Chimo asked me what "social work" was about. I answered that it had to do with assistance to the poor, the elderly, drug-addicts, services to the young and so on. Later in the conversation he referred to those categories as "la penya". On another occasion, as Pepe was watching one of the private television channels which offered cheap quiz and competition programs combined with relentless sexist references, he said "*Quina penya més xunga*" 'What a disgusting lot'. This particular usage to refer to a team of television producers or the whole television corporation should not be seen as an exceptional case, but probably as a way of expressing that these people were also to be judged with regard to the meanings and expectations accorded to any penya.

For a politicized member like Pepe, his loyalty to the penya seemed to go beyond his allegiances to particular political organizations. He explained to me that he had left his Marxist-Leninist party because it did not connect with the experience of the people of the neighborhoods. However, Clara once made an interesting remark with regard to this romantic view of the lower classes. As she was reflecting on her own economic hardships, she said: "there is nothing glamorous about being poor."

The penya were, therefore, at one and the same time, the penniless, the needy, those bonded by suffering and exploitation, as well as the groups of drunk youngsters and boisterous rock fans. The politicized Trepas had produced this two-sidedness of the words. This ambivalence or polysemy was the very foundation upon which their perspective was possible. Peer-group activities were not seen as an appropriate ground for straight political debate and mobilization, as most of the members of the group were not directly involved in politics. The ambivalence of the term *penya* made it possible to maintain a balance, whereby peer-group activities were subtly invested with political meaning, but without being totally colonized by it. This created a situation where people could participate in the group without necessarily having to display political awareness, while the possibility remained open for developing a political sensitivity. In any case, since the politicized members were very sensitive to the political implications of what people said and since they constituted the core group that held the clique together, it is possible that political ideology had already played an important role in the establishment of relations leading to the formation of the group. Certainly, it was difficult to participate in many discussions without getting impregnated with the political meanings that were made available. Non-politicized members should have noticed, as I did, that in addition to the double-voicing present in the cultivation of transgression (with its hidden voice of authority, as I argued in the previous section), there was a third voice attached to it, the revolutionary voice that sought to recruit these transgressions to its own cause. As a result, non-politicized members shared many of the political attitudes of the politicized ones. These shared attitudes clearly emerged in the group discussion and in the interviews, in contrast with what happened with the Rambleros.

2.3. The relative truth

The way in which the order of discourse of the Trepas was created and established can be best illustrated through an analysis of the group discussion. For them, the group discussion was a special occasion and it developed quite differently from that of the Rambleros. The Trepas were relatively diverse and disperse due to the fact that the group had just been formed at the training school. There were people with relatively different characters and backgrounds. It included all the types of gender identities I have described (except simplified masculinity) and also speakers of both Catalan and Spanish. Additionally, there were people who had closer ties with some members than with others. The group was able to accommodate this diversity partly because it operated in a very fragmented way, as was described in the previous chapter. Nevertheless, in the group discussion, all members present were facing each other and were involved in a unitary course of action where issues about their relationships were discussed openly and explicitly. Such an activity was clearly central to the interests of the politicized members in particular. For them, their previous experience in discussing and theorizing about identity was a clear advantage. Nevertheless, they did not use their resources to try to bluntly dismiss or supersede the views of other members. The discussion actually became a considerably formal and orderly debate, with most participants taking long turns and presenting sophisticated argumentations. The views of everybody were normally listened to and responded to in such a way that, I believe, nobody felt pushed aside. Additionally, the politicized Trepas had no qualms about using a style of language that was more formal than that of the Rambleros. Of course, they did not produce a purely political discourse, as this might have alienated non-politicized participants and might have generally been felt as inappropriate. What they did was to speak in a hybrid style which combined features that we usually would associate with different discourses.

Let us look into the following abstract, where Aleix was talking about the "problem" of cross-gender friendships:

Extract 49 [Trepas]

Aleix: es que a vegades crec que no és només que noo · t'entenguis igual sí
It's that sometimes, I don't think it is only that you don't · understand each other, you might well be able to

t'entendríes no? lo que passa es que no et surt (*o sea*) · tu has
do it, right? What happens is that it does not come naturally to you, (*that is*): · you have

creat un tipus de relació a partir de · a partir d'unes coincidències tu
created a form of relationship on the basis of- on the basis of some coincidences. You

tens · ah exacte un [...]
have... That's it! You have [...] [continued below]

Up to here, Aleix's style coincided more or less with a standard register and his words had a very generalizing and conceptual tone. The vocabulary choices could well be used in any formal text and his lengthy turn was listened to with silence and attention. Later in his intervention, he said the following:

Extract 50 [Trepas]

Aleix: [...] entre · o sia · una amistat entre un tiu i una tia no? o siga · jo crec
[...] between, I mean, a friendship between a boy and a girl, right? I mean, I believe

que és · super possible no? · ara crec que es curro i crec que és molt de
it is · very possible, right? Now, I believe that it's hard work and I believe that it is very

curro no? · per això de les afinitats · [...] llavors jo
hard work, right? And this is precisely because of these affinities. [...] Therefore I

crec que aquest és un tope superfort · i és el més bèstia que trobem no?
believe that this is a very strong barrier, the biggest you can find, right?

· o siga · mm · això pues mirant al grup · o sia · *hay amigos y hay*
· I- I mean... Mm. And this, looking at the group, I mean: "*there are [masc-] friends and there are*

amigas · yy entre la (xx) crec que tenim molts · · vui dir que sí que
[fem-] friends · aand between..." (xx) I believe that we have a lot of- · I mean that we do

ens entenem i jo tinc · bueno crec que sóc amic de totes i · i tots
communicate and I have, well, I believe that I am a friend of [fem-]them all and, and [masc-]we all

som amics de les <u>ties</u> i (totes les) · pero · sí que hi han coses com · tu ets d'un
are friends of the <u>girls</u> and ([fem-] all the-); but it remains true that there are things like
this: you are at a

institut que surten dues noies · de la mà d'un institut
[secondary] school where two young women come out · from the school holding hands,

no? · perquè són amigues i s'estimen i s'ho expliquen tot no?
right? · because they are friends and they care for each other and tell each other
everything, right?

I have underlined the items which are somehow special: *tia, curro, super, tope,* are common youth slang; *bèstia,* 'wild' or 'big', is very colloquial;
bueno, a Spanish borrowing, would not be used by a speaker of standard
Catalan in a formal situation. After his framing of the question in formal
terms, Aleix had come back to the voice of the penya. This indicated that
he was clearly seeking to connect this argument with the everyday experience of their own relationships with their *col.legues* 'buddies'. To make this
clearer, there was a switch to Spanish (underlined phrase) used to impersonate an imaginary member of the group uttering a view that treated cross-
gender relations as unproblematic. He used this rhetorical device to take
issue with this view.

Another feature which I would like to highlight from this episode is the
fact that Aleix spoke in the first person plural. In doing so, he was including himself amongst the people criticized for not having cross-gender
friendships. Pepe had started off the argument on a similar line, by saying
that he acknowledged that there were barriers for cross-gender friendships
and that he had not solved the problem, although he was working on it.
This is in stark contrast with the group discussion of the Rambleros, which
was often centered on defending one's position and undermining that of
others. Aleix, who was particularly close to many of the women, could
have easily disassociated himself from the others and accused them of per-
petuating gender boundaries. But this was not what the discussion was
about for them. They were more interested in integrating the views of others and in showing how these connected to theirs.

Later in the discussion, a woman manifested her disagreement with regard to what other people understood by friendship. The others were arguing that men had more things in common with men and women with
women. They were giving examples of particular activities (such as playing
in the musical band). They said that the differences in tastes and preferences between men and women contributed to people having a tendency to

mix with people of their own sex. The woman, though, was arguing that a
real friendship did not depend on those things, because a real friend was the
one with whom everything could be shared. The bulk of the group then
tried to convince her that it was not possible to expect to have "everything"
in common with somebody. But she would not give in. At a point, Pepe
came up with this interesting contribution:

Extract 51 [Trepas]

Pepe: I- I believe Magda is quite right. And even more · · I am not happy · with the
· with the explanation we give that, well, "it is normal · if so and so the topic,
the topic that is worrying me, I see that Salva · is going to understand me better
· than Jaume" [<Silvia: of course, you'll tell him] <No, no. Then, I am not
happy with this. Because because · · at least, on my part [...] Maybe, maybe this
is what Magda means, what Magda is aiming at. But my experience is · that
sometimes · I am not going to mention to her, to Magda, this [particular] thing,
not because she · cannot have this issue in common with me, but because I feel
embarrassed and I say: "Ugh! Who knows if talking about this with Magda · I
will not be- · I will not be · talking too much!", right? · Then, I think there is an
additional problem here.

I must say that Magda was not entirely satisfied that her point really had
been taken up by Pepe; but the move is nevertheless significant. Again, in
this narrative, Pepe was depicting himself as being at fault in a hypothetical
episode, which he had invented to try to connect the issue discussed with
actual experience. This rhetorical device of dramatizing situations and
characters expressing different views was common amongst the Trepas.
Interestingly enough, stylized Spanish appeared in some of the voices
dramatized. These voices reproduced precisely stereotyped speech genres
of verbal aggression associated with this speech style. Additionally, the
Trepas used these voices to represent ignorant or sexist characters, a fact
which throws a new light on the potential significations of this type of
voice and the way they Trepas perceived it. For instance, in the group discussion, Pepe and Clara characterized, through this voice, the wrong way
for a man to "propose" to a woman, expressed through stereotyped genres
such as "*Eh̲ta noche qué hase̲, reina?*" 'What are you doing tonight, sweet-
heart?' (the first [s] is aspirated, the [θ] has changed to [s] and the second
[s] has been dropped) or "*háseme tuyo!*" 'Make me yours' or 'take me'
(again the [θ] of "*haceme*" has changed to [s]).

From this perspective, the Rambleros and the Trepas contrasted with
each other symbolically: one's *own* speech style was often the other's *alien*

voice and vice-versa. The meanings of these voices were not fixed. The Trepas, for instance, were relatively ambivalent about stylized Spanish, as this variety was also associated with the penya. Pepe and Salva were particularly fond of a famous Spanish actor who spoke in this way. An advert in a television channel featuring a voice singing [meɣúhtarfúrβo] from "*me gusta el fútbol*" 'I like soccer' was Pepe's favorite jingle for a while. Shouting in the streets, an action meant to be playfully disruptive and rebellious, was often done in this voice as well.

With regard to the use of dramatized dialogues to present opinions and reflections, the following extract shows how Clara explained why she did not struggle to get some male dominated jobs after suffering from harassment and poor working conditions:

Extract 52 [Trepas]

Clara: And it is, it is a contradiction I still feel right? · That, shit! "because society would work so much better and so on and so forth, · right? And as a woman I think this and that, right? And therefore I am going to struggle about this and that". · · *But,* "Uugh! Well, as a woman, my name is Clara and therefore I have my limitations and I can do without er er · · · punishing myself, right? What the hell! I have to go on living and · I want to live as well as possible, right? And to have · a good quality of life. · And I can do without fighting and · I can't-" · · *and · and I do worry about it, right? · But...*

This transformation of feminist discourse into a voice of a simple working-class woman (the underlined fragment) was clearly more than a rhetorical device to convince followers. It was part and parcel of the worldview they were constructing and really believed in. For them, feminist ideas had to be relevant to their experience and therefore had to be expressed from the voice of this experience and shared with others. This was partly the reason why the feminist militants had considered that the chats they organized in secondary schools were becoming problematic because they had grown older and their experience was less akin to that of the students with which they wanted to engage in dialogue.

The truth of the politicized Trepas was, therefore, not a truth that sought to impose any particular statement. It was a truth based on the establishment of a dialogue, a truth based on the legitimization of the experience of the other and which sought to strike a relationship with this other rather than to impose a particular view. Hence the *subject positions* that the politicized Trepas created in their discourse made it possible to undertake conceptual explorations that were impossible within the Rambleros. The discussion on cross-gender friendship amongst the Rambleros focused on who preferred whom to be intimate with, whether one risked being scorned and what examples the group's history provided of such relationships. The revelation of anecdotes, contrasting experiences and differing preferences never led them to discuss how friendships arose and why things were as they were. With regard to the question of gender in the job market, the Rambleros concentrated on enumerating different cases and situations they had experienced. In contrast, the Trepas studied their experiences to discuss what they could do to fight sexism at work, which again contributed to the creation of a sense of common enterprise amongst members rather than of confrontation.

A final qualification must be made with regard to my argument that the relative truth was constructed as collaborative and non-confrontational. If I analyze the various debates that took place in the Trepas' group discussion, it is also possible to find instances of people challenging somebody's views very directly. Again, I would argue that there is a case for stressing that formal features do not necessarily contain a direct link with particular meanings, subject positions or relationships. At one point, I asked the group to discuss whether men and women played different roles in courting or "picking up" (when people sought some kind of sexual relation with somebody). At that point, Pepe complained that men always had to take the most risky and explicit steps to disclose sexual interest. The women proceeded to argue that they also experienced fear of exposure. But Pepe would not have it: he argued that the masculine fear was much more acute and that women should also honor their feminist principles in this field. Some situations were created where statements were flatly refused in formal terms: "this is false", "this is not true". Nevertheless, a close look at how arguments were presented and developed makes it clear that the way people took these statements had nothing to do with an entrenched defense of the self. Their relationships, the subject positions created throughout the discussion and in their previous experiences maintained the collaborative frame of understanding that selected the appropriate potential meanings and dispelled others. This is comparable to the Rambleros in that the closeness of their relationships allowed them to play aggressive games without endangering their relations. Nevertheless, the differences in the meanings, rituals, subject positions and relationships that these confrontations contributed to construct was, from one group to the other, very great indeed.

Concluding remarks

To conclude, the Rambleros and the Trepas used various colloquial varieties of Catalan and Spanish in ways which were intimately connected with the patterns of gender identity, and hence, with the most essential components of youth culture in these particular contexts. These speech styles were thus ideologically invested, not simply because they conveyed given meanings of allegiance and solidarity, but because they served to produce particular presentations of self, to evoke particular social relations and to legitimize particular views about the world. Stylized Spanish served to construct and evoke the most typical elements of working-class masculine culture (transgression, aggression, naturalness, unsophistication) and it was also strategically used by most Rambleros men to protect their identities and to discredit more sophisticated discourses. Inner city argot could also be used in this way, as it was associated with the values of transgression and toughness. However the Trepas also associated it with their idealization of the oppressed classes, such that it acquired connotations of political resistance. In this way, the Trepas did not so much reject formal discourses (as the Rambleros men did), but constructed mixed genres that combined formal discourses (mainly those available in the field of politics) with argot. This was a way of claiming legitimacy for their political views by suggesting that their preferred political discourses connected with the everyday experience of working-class young people. For them, it was possible to co-opt the most popular and marginal discourses for the causes of class and gender emancipation. This is partly why their attitude towards differing views and forms of expression was much more open-minded than that of the Rambleros.

Chapter 5

Catalan and Spanish voices

Up to now, I have made only passing reference to the fact that the Rambleros and the Trepas operated, to a greater or lesser extent, in two languages: Catalan and Spanish. Now I will focus on this issue in the light of the findings and reflections presented in the previous chapters. We have seen that gender identities were very important to understanding the meanings of the most typical features of youth culture in the contexts studied. We have also seen how the two cliques developed particular speech styles that served to construct their relationships and ideologies. Now it is time to see how bilingualism fitted into their picture. For the sake of orderly exposition, I have divided the analysis of bilingual discourse into two aspects. The first aspect, the one dealt with in this chapter, involves simply "saying something" in a particular language as some kind of exceptional episode, a joke, a quotation or any form of dramatization which is *bracketed off* from our main performance. The interlocutors may have adopted one particular language for their conversation, but, at particular moments, another language comes up. This type of short departure occurs very often in bilingual communities. They have been studied under the label of "codeswitching", although the term usually covers a wider range of phenomena, that is, any form of linguistic alternation (Gumperz 1982). The second aspect refers to the fact of speaking a particular language as we usually understand it, that is, of using it as our main narrative voice. It entails a decision, a *choice* such as "I am going to speak Catalan to communicate with this particular person". This aspect, usually studied under the label of *language choice*, will be dealt with in the next chapter. These two aspects coincide with Rampton's (1995, 1998) newly refined and redefined distinction between metaphorical and situational codeswitching, which he took from Blom and Gumperz' (1972) earlier work.

Code-switching studies have long sought to develop an adequate framework to understand the significance of communicative phenomena such as the linguistic alternations studied in this chapter. The conceptual and methodological framework developed here has significant connections, as I see it, with the work of Scotton (1988), who considers that people switch codes to redefine social situations and relationships, and that of

Auer (1988), who sees codeswitching as playing a key role in the sequential organization of conversations. It has perhaps a closer connection with the work of Heller (1994) and Rampton (1995), who see codeswitching as an interactional component of the processes of definition of relations between social groups. What I will do is to focus on the processes whereby the Rambleros and the Trepas appropriated the two languages in their discourse and I will conceptualize these processes basically by drawing upon ideas from Bakhtin and Goffman. I will actually show that Catalan and Spanish were used to construct and convey significantly different ideologies and identities, such that a certain *symbolic specialization* was created, as happened with the use of stylized Spanish and inner-city argot. However, I need to make an important qualification before stating my argument in a more specific way.

I have already shown that two particular speech styles can be taken, reworked or manipulated to construct different and contradictory meanings. We can therefore imagine that whole languages should also be amenable to such symbolic manipulations. In fact, languages should involve a much wider range of potential significations, as they must incorporate a multiplicity of (already polyvalent) speech styles. Indeed, languages such as Catalan, Spanish, French or English do not exist in an abstract, context-free way. They are always spoken in particular situations, by particular people, with particular purposes, and therefore, through the varied styles that are available to their speakers. Of course, different languages may incorporate styles that can be treated as equivalent, as is probably the case for most languages which possess a standard written form. On the other hand, each single language may be seen as encompassing a unique range of speech styles. This means that, when speakers incorporate elements of more than one language in an utterance, it is not enough to identify them as instances of, say, Catalan/French or Spanish/English codeswitching. It is also necessary to find out what types of discourse are being integrated or responded to in this utterance. If we do so, we will be able to understand the processes whereby the social meanings of linguistic varieties are acquired, maintained or transformed.

I will not try to be exhaustive as to the range of meanings that the use of Catalan or Spanish can convey. What I will do in this chapter is to construct a modest *inventory* of what I managed to obtain in my fieldwork amongst the Rambleros and the Trepas. Through this inventory, I will show that many voices articulated through Catalan and Spanish were similar, but that many others were not; and that a close analysis of these voices provided evidence that the Spanish ones were clearly more central to the construction of the identities of the peer-group.

This analysis is based on the observation of subtle, tiny details and passing moments of people's talk that are usually not given much attention. Before presenting this inventory of voices, I wish to explain in a detailed and practical way how I carried out this type of analysis. In the first section, I will thus explain how I developed the ideas of Bakhtin (1981, 1986) and Goffman (1974) for the analysis of linguistic alternation. In section two I will then move on to describe the various types of voices that were associated with either language.

1. Towards a dialogical analysis of codeswitching: methodological considerations

The distinction presented above between using a language as one's own voice and using it in an exceptional, figurative manner has been much debated within sociolinguistics (see Gumperz 1982; Auer 1984, 1988). The two aspects coincide roughly with Blom and Gumperz' distinction between situational and metaphorical codeswitching (1972), and with the traditional sociolinguistic distinction between *language choice* and *linguistic alternation* (or simply *codeswitching* in a restricted sense). In his later work, Gumperz (1982) argues that situational and metaphorical switching should be seen as different aspects of the same phenomenon, i.e. the use of linguistic alternation as a device for *contextualization*. From this viewpoint, switching is treated as a rhetorical resource that can be used to achieve particular communicative effects: to signal how speakers wish to define the interaction they are in, or how their utterances, or bits of utterances, should be interpreted.

I do not really disagree with this view. However, it is also true that the distinction is often useful at a descriptive level because it coincides with culturally relevant, *emic*, distinctions that can be found in many bilingual contexts. Woolard (1989) observed, for instance, that both Catalan and Spanish speakers treated the two types of switching very differently. Situational codeswitching was associated with (and used to infer) speakers' ethnic ascription, whereas metaphorical codeswitching was treated as inconsequential in terms of social categorization. Hence speakers could practice metaphorical switching with fewer restrictions, while situational choices were much constrained by established conventions. In his inspiring analysis of switching practices in inter-ethnic arenas, Rampton (1998) argues that the distinction between situational and metaphorical switching is analytically relevant if reinterpreted in terms of Bakhtin's notion of *double-voicing*. He also observes that metaphorical codeswitching often appears associated with changes of *key* (Goffman 1974). Rampton acknowledges that it is not always easy to decide whether a particular instance of talk constitutes a metaphorical or a situational switch; but he argues that this difficulty applies to any analysis based on the distinction between literal and figurative meaning (Rampton 1998: 303–304).

Indeed, it is not always easy to decide whether a particular utterance is keyed or not, whether it is a joke or a threat, a bluff or a warning. My analysis does not rest on the assumption that it is always clear or that it should be. Rather, the distinction between situational and metaphorical codeswitching is relevant precisely because it can be exploited to produce ambiguities, as I will show below. From a Bakhtinian perspective, the alternation between linguistic varieties or languages can be seen as one particular aspect of the polyphony of utterances. In this way, bilingual speakers can be seen as *appropriating* the two languages in different ways, in different degrees of *our-ownness* and *otherness*, as Bakhtin puts it (1986: 89). Language choice would involve seeing one linguistic variety as being fully appropriated by the speaker on a given occasion, whereas codeswitching would refer to voices treated in a more distant manner. At some points, it may well be that some social actors have an interest in not being clear as to where they actually stand. This schema would again get close to Gumperz' distinction between *we-codes* and *they-codes*. However, as I will show below, an us/them or a self/other dichotomy is not the only way in which we can look into the meanings of linguistic alternation. In conclusion, the use of various linguistic varieties provides evidence about the social groups with which these varieties are associated, as well as about the relationships between the speaker and these groups. As one particular manifestation of heteroglossia, codeswitching can be used to investigate the dialogical relationships that the Trepas and the Rambleros constructed in their discourses in relation to the Catalan and Spanish languages and in relation to the people and situations they associated with these languages.

Although this chapter is based primarily on the analysis of instances of codeswitching, I have not restricted my discussion to instances of *manifest* codeswitching, i.e. utterances combining two languages. The *absence* of codeswitching may sometimes help to appreciate interesting relationships when comparing different texts and situations. On the other hand, it is common for people to produce short interventions in one single language when making jokes or dramatizing funny characters (i.e. in *keyings*). I have considered these as instances of codeswitching if they were done with special voices and in a language different from the one we should expect in that context.

It is also important to bear in mind that many of the transcripts are not taken from spontaneous peer-group activities, but from research oriented activities such as interviews and group discussions. Such situations provided (quite unexpectedly) a large amount of bilingual data that helped to raise interesting issues despite the fact of not being situations spontaneously generated by the young people studied. For instance, I have considered that instances of switching to Spanish in interviews held in Catalan were highly significant, because they could not have been encouraged by me, as I was seen as distinctly and unmistakably a Catalan-speaking person.

My analysis thus incorporates some basic ideas of Goffman's (1974) proposal for a frame analysis of talk and articulates it with Bakhtin's notion of polyphony (Bakhtin 1981, 1984a, 1986) for the analysis of conversational data. In a way, Goffman's *frames* and *figures* have helped me to hear Bakhtin's *voices*. Goffman (ibid.) proposes that we should see people's speech performances as structured narratives. He considers that these narratives have an intrinsically theatrical character, because speakers always seek, in one way or another, to construct a scene. As a result, our speech is populated with characters and props that the speaker has arranged to appear within the sequential organisation of the narrative. The speaker herself, according to Goffman, is split within this narrative into the different characters and roles she animates through different voices and gestural indications. The application of this approach to the analysis of codeswitching is partly inspired by the work of Sebba (1993) amongst speakers of London Jamaican, and Rampton (1991, 1995) on the uses of Punjabi, South Asian English and Creole in interracial groups of British adolescents. As Sebba (1993: 124–137) suggests, an analysis of what types of narrative voices are adopted for what purposes, of what types of characters each linguistic variety is used to evoke, can provide important clues as to the social identities of the people studied. Each choice of a language is evidence of how this language is used to signify things. Instead of asking subjects to foreground a particular (linguistic) object and to produce a description of what it means to them, one can examine what roles this object plays in their narratives, what use they make of it. Such an approach may provide unique insights that may not be accessible by just asking fuzzy or untactful questions to informants on attitudes and perceived connotations.

1.1. The logistics of staging

The construction of a narrative requires a certain coordination and skill, and it is always vulnerable to failures, false starts, and lapses. In the following episode, Guille (from the Trepas group) was constructing a hypothetical scene where a Spanish speaker was negotiating the language of the interaction:

Extract 53 [Trepas]
Reminder of transcription conventions: Catalan is represented in normal font and Spanish in italics.

Guille: si · si et ve de guai et diu escolta'm · o *escuchame · háblame el castellano*
If, if he asks nicely and says: "listen to me", or *"listen to me, speak* Castilian,

que te entiendo mejor no? · doncs · li parlaràs però · si va
as I will understand better", right? Then, you'll speak [it]. But, if he comes

en plan borde està clar que no · que es foti
with a stupid air, there's clearly no way. To hell with him!

Guille considered it to be more congruent to represent the voice of a Spanish total monolingual in Spanish. So he re-ran the "listen" in Spanish. This example suggests that our narratives are arranged in a manner related to the way we organize and understand actual social situations, i.e. they are populated by people and objects associated with particular qualities, capacities and actions: a Spanish speaker, then, should be depicted as speaking in Spanish.

Nevertheless, what seemed clear to Guille was not replicated by other members of his group. Whether or not it is necessary to adopt the *original* language as a feature of the dramatization is optional. Patrícia animated a similar situation in Catalan. Pepe once quoted in Spanish something I had said in Catalan. In this last case, Pepe probably considered that the abstract meaning was more important than the form of the utterance.[17]

The logistics of staging sometimes produces the need for a special narrative figure that appears at particular junctures. This figure represents the person who *organizes*, in a manner of speaking, the dramatic action from "behind the scenes". It corresponds to what Goffman calls interactional *out-*

of-frame activity. Sebba (1993: 114–116) identifies a type of language switch which is used to produce *asides* to the main narration and which is aimed at, for instance, requesting information which is seen as necessary for the interaction to continue. There were examples of this in my data as well, such as the typical *o siga* or *o sea* 'I mean'.

1.2. What is being quoted

In the previous extract, Guille was reproducing an imaginary scene; not something that had really happened, but a hypothetical situation which had a kind of categorical value as an example of a Spanish speaker with good manners. In the following extract, in contrast, Pepe was seeking to reproduce a scene which had some historical status:

Extract 54 [Trepas]

Pepe: estàvem tothom allà · dinant · · i la meva germana · parlava del tema tabú ·
We were all there having lunch. · And my sister · used to come up with the taboo topic,

però súper tabú no[?] · que teníem a casa que era · *porque sí sí* ·
but the really taboo one, right? that we had at home, which was: *"Because, yes yes,*

porque yo soy independentista ep! · totes les cares blanques no[?] la- la del meu
because I am an 'independentista' [i.e. in favour of Catalan independence] ". Hey! All
faces white, right? M- my

pare · i les- · i les nostres també no[?] el meu pare indignant- · indignat el pavo ·
father's face and- · ours as well, right? My father anger-, the guy really [got] angry:

pero pero como · se tendría que saber · que en mi casa eso no se puede
"But- but how [can this be]? It should be very clear · that in my home such things cannot

decir · no? i jo i la clara pensant · *no estoy de acuerdo · no estoy de acuerdo*
be said", right? And Clara and I [were] thinking: *"I do not agree, I do not agree,*

porque yo soy anarquista · porque ·ni españa ni cataluña · porque yo soy
because I am an anarchist.· Because neither Spain nor Catalonia, because I am an

anarquista no? · dèiem · *que no que no · qué coñoo · hombree · no- nos estan*
anarchist", right? we used to say, *"No way, no way. Damn it, man! W- we are being*

ehplotando los españoles noh van a explotar también loh catalane ·
exploited by the Spaniards and we are going to be exploited by the Catalans as well".

d'aquest pal no? · · peroò ja · a primer de buup · fins
This type of thinking, right? · ·Buut already, at the beginning of secondary school, up

a vu- no · vuitè d'egebé i primer de bup ja · començava a
to eig- no, eight form and in the first year already, I was (already) beginning to

pensar que (ja) bueno · mira va ser el mateix moment que vaig decidir que
think that "well". Look, it was at the same moment that I decided that-

quee · que bakunin no · que no · quan vai començar a ser marxista
thaat · that Bakunin didn't- that it didn't [work], when I started being a Marxist.

This is a very skilful and lively dramatization. We can almost see Pepe's family sitting around the table, with his father, who had strong feelings against Catalans, reacting to his daughter's defiant announcement of her pro-Catalan feelings. In contrast to the Catalan narrative voice, the characters of this story were speaking Spanish as they clearly had done in the actual event that was being relived. This contrast of languages allowed Pepe to forego the connectives, such as "she said" or "he answered".

Later on, though, the narrative drifted into describing the thoughts of Pepe himself and his other sister as they were witnessing the scene. Here a connective was needed ("thinking:"), otherwise the audience may have thought that Pepe and his sister had participated in the family argument. Curiously enough, these thoughts were articulated with an assertive, almost angry tone, colored with reiterations and interjections, as if they had indeed been spoken in the scene. Now, even accepting that thoughts can be thought with some emphasis, if we take Pepe's account at face value, we should conclude that he had some form of mysterious privileged access to Clara's thoughts, and even that the thoughts of the two siblings had been literally identical at the time.

Of course, there is no mystery, because Pepe did not expect his narrative to be taken literally. Quotations are rarely accurate in a strict sense. Pepe was explaining how he and his sister had developed their political ideas in their early teens. He did so by showing first the voices to which they were responding (represented by members of his family: father and older sister); after this, as I understand it, he reproduced his own thoughts in the light of the discussions he had had with Clara about these matters. To present these thoughts as a contemporary response to the spoken dialogue at the dinner table was clearly a dramatic device that made it possible to give a brilliantly situated account of what his political thinking was at the time.

We can also imagine that the real spoken dialogue between father and daughter might have gone quite differently. Indeed, the defiant tone that Pepe put in his older sister's voice was probably geared to create a dramatic effect. It is hard to believe that she could have been so boldly provocative. Pepe's quotes, therefore, represented these dialogues and reflections; but they did not reproduce them accurately. The quotes had a categorical value, not a descriptive one. The categorical value was explicitly indicated through the expression "of this sort, right?", a clause that does not belong to the staged scene, but to the narrator.

1.3. Past and present in the utterance

It is clear that, when reporting *past* events, people manipulate them to fit the particular expressive intention of the *present* speech situation. In some cases, this adaptation can go quite far without raising issues of sincerity. In the following episode, Pablo was telling an anecdote of how he had hid himself under the table when he was little in order to catch a glimpse of the Three Magic Kings as they came to bring their presents during the night of January the 6th:

Extract 55 [Rambleros]

Pablo: cuando tenía cuatro o cinco año ya te digo me meto bajo la mesa del
    I was four or five, as I'm telling you, I hide under the table in the

comedor y (xx) un pie (xx) son lah zapatillah del viejo · y este qué
    dining room and (I see) a foot. (xx) they are the old man's slippers! And: "What's this
    one

hace aquí · · [riures] que hace aquí ehte, (x) subo allí y veo (xx) y
    doing here?" · · [his companions laugh] "What's this one doing here?" (x) I come up
    there and I see (him) and

digo vete a la mierda hombre [rient]
    say: "Go to hell, man!" [laughters].

The scenic austerity of this narrative is remarkable. Pablo used no formal connectives, as he used his voice to establish the contrast between the narrative voice and the animated voices. The image of the father's slipper was enough to give the audience a sense of what was happening, namely his father was entering the room with the presents. Pablo's first dramatized exclamations expressed the surprise he had felt when he saw his father instead of the Three Kings. The exclamations probably do not correspond to what he had really said at the time. Additionally, the final telling-off was clearly not something that five-year-olds say to their parents. It expressed the disappointment he had felt, expressed in the type of language he spoke in the present: in the language and style in which the Rambleros men constructed their identities.

Pablo was thus playing with various narrative levels: he was portraying himself as a child who talked as he did in the present. This ambiguity was not created for people to investigate or to find out what "really" happened, but to produce a relevant narrative and identity display in the context. The participants appreciated his contribution by laughing and never sought to sort out what was fiction from what was accurate reproduction. The question of the non-accuracy of quotations has also been commented upon by Gumperz (1982: 82–83), Hill and Hill, (1986: 394) Romaine (1989: 148–149) and Auer (1990), who note that it is common for speakers not to quote in the language actually used on the reported occasion. As Sebba (1993: 117–122) and Auer (1990) rightly point out, this is a matter that has to do with the narrative organisation of talk. Extracts 57 and 60 below provide further evidence of this.

1.4. Ambivalent characters

Up to now, I have presented retellings of real or imagined scenes where the (present) voice of the narrator and the (past or hypothetical) voice of the animated characters were clearly separable. In the following extract, this is not so. In the rehearsal of the Trepas' band, Salva was trying to coordinate the group to play a song called *cabrones* 'bastards':

Extract 56 [Trepas]

Salva: va · cabrones otra vez · · pero qué paranoya suéltalo · · qué punto tío [Ell riu]
   Come on. [Let's play] "Bastards" again. But, what a nuisance, drop this! What a pest, man [He laughs].

Somebody: (· vamos de nuevo)
   (Let's try again).

Salva: [cridant amb veu gutural] *'enga cabrone ·*
   [Shouting with a guttural voice] *"Come on, bastards!"*

Someone: oye (no vamos) a empezar com la nueva
   Listen! (Are we not gonna) start with the new one?

Salva: seamoh cabrones tío que ara que [comença la música]
   Let's be bastards, man, 'cause now [The music starts]

The second time Salva said "*cabrones!*", he changed to a voice akin to Andalusian or stylized Spanish. Because it was not his own voice, stylized

Spanish indicated that the insult was uttered not by himself but by an impersonated character which was somehow *other* than himself. Of course, this device served to indicate that the insult had been uttered in jest; it was a *keyed* insult. However, the shouting (the calling to order) had been effectively done. The utterance had therefore two potential meanings: a) Salva might be shouting the name of the song (and thus probably asking his companions to start playing it), b) he might be playfully insulting the audience (and thus prompting the group to stop making disorderly noises and start doing serious work). The introduction of the stylized voice served to convey Salva's intention to dissociate himself from the insulting voice and from a voice which claimed rights to direct the group, while still insisting that he wished the group to start playing.

The character he had animated was, therefore, not entirely himself, but not entirely an *other* either. The speaking subject was symbolically split due to the various potential significations of what he said. It was Salva himself putting on the character of an *other* which was somehow speaking for him. The exploitation of the ambivalence of ironical, mocking or cynical voices is very common in interaction. I will show below how codeswitching was one of the formal devices used to construct them. Sebba (1993: 106–108, 132) identifies similar voices amongst speakers of London Jamaican, in the form of "one-liner" and "punch lines" aimed to create humorous effects. Sebba shows how London Jamaican is used to signal to the audience that potentially face threatening statements should be taken in jest. This probably indicates that there are parallels between the speech genres associated with London Jamaican and stylized Spanish. Similar uses of Punjabi amongst British adolescents are reported by Rampton (1995).

1.5. Codeswitching and speech genres

The example quoted above is the ideal illustration of how our speech incorporates the speech genres available in our culture: not only accents or languages, but also characters and situations. Although the notion of *genre* may be sometimes difficult to operationalize in a systematic way, it does help to understand how meanings are created beyond the structural properties of language. In the example given above, the meaning of the utterance was not based on the simple fact that it happened to be colored by the accent or the tone of Andalusian. It had come in the shape of a common type of utterance used to perform a particular action and to create a particular situation. As genres originate in the real life of the language, where they are appropriated, reaccentuated and hybridized in various ways, we cannot expect them to appear in fixed forms. Neither can we expect these communicative processes to be respectful of grammatical boundaries. In the example below, the switch from Spanish back to Catalan splits a prepositional phrase:

Extract 57 [Trepas]

Patrícia: ens parlàvem en castellà hasta que un dia em diu escolta tu i jo
   We used to speak to each other in Castilian, until one day he says: "Listen, you and I

   parlem català *pero a qué viene eso de* [Ella riu] · parlar tot el dia en castellà.
   speak Catalan. Why- *What is this thing of* [She laughs] speaking all day in Castilian!

Patrícia was retelling an episode where she had inadvertently been talking in Castilian to a Catalan speaker, which is something that people generally consider either unnatural, unnecessary or undesirable (see Woolard 1989; Pujolar 1991b). Her reason for using a Spanish phrase was probably to clarify which of these potential interpretations she wished to offer. As I see it, such a statement, in Catalan, could have sounded nationalistic, i.e. as saying "why are we Catalans, who should be loyal to our language, betraying our roots and speaking Castilian?". As it was actually said, it implies "what a funny silly thing we found ourselves doing!". It is not impossible to convey this tone in Catalan, but it should be accompanied with clear cues expressing amusement. The switch to Spanish, accompanied by a lively tone of surprise and a laughter, brought in the tone and the intention of the *penya*. Because, in Spanish, the phrasing "*a qué viene eso de* + nominalized verb phrase" is common, Patrícia had taken the first part as a fixed unit even though it splits a syntactic unit. It is probable that people tend to stop and think (or laugh) after "*de*" rather that at any other point of this phrase, thus allowing for variations to happen afterwards, such as changing languages.

1.6. Translucent speaking subjects

In the previous examples, we have seen many cases of embedding. The voices of animated characters were somehow inserted in utterances controlled by a main narrative voice. These ephemeral subjects were, in a way, speaking *their own words*, i.e. they were represented as the fictitious animators of reported utterances. However, we can find other types of speaking subjects who are not really given a life of their own on the narrative stage. They appear in a much less "transparent" way. In extract 58 below, I give an example of this type of phenomenon, which I have labeled as the portrayal of *translucent* characters.

Extract 58 [Trepas]

Magda: bueno yo estaba en un centro excursionista y ahí todo dios era catalán · ·
Well, I was in this hiking society. And there everybody was Catalan.

y yo bueno yo <u>sul-</u> soltaba mi di- <u>el meu discurset</u> · pero bueno cuando me tenía
And I, well, I <u>del-</u> delivered my <u>my little speech</u>, but, well, when I had

que introducir más en el tema y hablar
to get more into the topic and speak...

Magda was explaining her experience of having to speak Catalan in a predominantly Catalan-speaking environment. Her switch to Catalan, accompanied with a change of voice quality, expressed the effort she had to make in those situations. Nevertheless, this dramatization was done without her own narrative voice yielding control. The Magda of the past made just a passing appearance in the shape of a voice coloring a direct object belonging to a wider syntactic unit.

The forms in which these *translucent* speaking subjects can be presented are probably unlimited. Their ambivalence constitutes their *double-voicing*, as two different perspectives become embedded within the same utterance or part of an utterance. An equivalent example is found in Virginia Woolf's novel *To the Lighthouse* (1927). In this novel, the narrative voice rarely relinquishes control of the text, and the characters often speak in the third person in face-to face conversation (i.e. they use *she, he, her, him,* instead of *I, me, you,* etc.).

As we interpret texts, we seek to identify the genres and voices upon which they draw, and the types of speakers and situations these are associated with. If we do not identify the voices with particular speakers, we will nevertheless understand that they belong to somebody (an individual or a type of individuals) who owns these voices in some way. And if we do not identify the genre with a particular intention or situation, we will nevertheless interpret that there is one, be it real or invented, in the past or in the future, possible or imaginary. So Aleix's switch in extract 50 ("*hay amigos y hay amigas*") was not attributable to any particular speaker, but was understood as if it had been uttered by a character representing a particular perspective on things, a perspective which did not perceive the important qualitative differences between same- and cross-gender friendships.

The world of our talk is therefore populated with the objects and persons that we encounter in our experience. By analyzing the way we treat these objects and persons, it is possible to get a glimpse at the way we interpret the world.

2. An inventory of voices

As we have seen, people produce a variety of voices when they speak. Voices, like the sounds of modern synthetizers, can be manipulated to convey particular expressive intentions. In this section, we will see that the young people studied used Catalan and Spanish to *synthesize* distinctly different types of voices. I have shown above that talk can be analyzed in terms of narratives that present particular sequential dramatizations of events for conversational audiences. Just as in any literary narrative or theatrical performance, people's utterances do not merely provide denotative meanings. People's discourse is always impregnated by the expressive intention of the author. It also becomes populated by the voices of various characters, although sometimes the presence of these characters may be only faintly perceivable. As Goffman (1974) points out, even the equivalents of décors and props of stage plays can appear in spoken narratives. Here I will try to recount what characters or voices appeared as speaking Spanish and Catalan in the narratives of the Rambleros and the Trepas. In this way, I intend to explore the way in which these two languages connected with the ideological world in which the Trepas and the Rambleros were living.

What I will argue is that Spanish was generally experienced as a fully functional language, while Catalan was seen as limited in its expressive potential. This was because the Rambleros and the Trepas were either familiar with or capable of using both the formal and informal registers of Spanish, while they only had access to the formal variety of Catalan used at school and in some middle-class contexts. As a result, Spanish had become the language in which they constructed the values and identities that were fostered within the groups, while Catalan was seen as representing more distant social worlds.

I will begin by analyzing voices associated with authority and with formal domains. Usually, these were the voices I had less difficulty in identifying. It was relatively easy to identify the *sources*, i.e. the characters and situations they evoked. In addition to this, I will analyze the population of stereotyped characters that appeared to be meaningful to the participants and appeared in narratives (peasants, hippies, and so on). Finally, I will analyze a set of voices which I perceived to be closely related to the meanings constructed within the peer-group. These were also voices whose characteristics, qualities and *sources* were much more difficult to characterize and identify. Therefore, the analysis of these voices will be done in greater detail. We will see that both Spanish and Catalan could be used to animate the types of voices that could be seen as formal or authoritative, whereas there were very significant differences between the types of voices that affected key aspects of the construction of identities within the peer-group.

Finally, in this section, I will not deal separately with the Rambleros and the Trepas. The main reason for this is that I did not perceive significant differences from one group to the other in relation to the particular phenomena analyzed here. It is also necessary to acknowledge that most of the data comes from the Trepas, as the Rambleros made little use of Catalan and did not provide so much evidence from which the meanings of both languages could be contrasted. However, the few examples of codeswitching provided by the Rambleros do support the argument I am putting forward.

2.1. Formal voices and discourses of authority

Both the Trepas and the Rambleros produced voices which evoked their experiences at school. These were usually voices of teachers, normally in Catalan, particularly amongst the Trepas, who were still attending classes at the training-school. Pepe had a favorite phrase: "*Ep! una mica de respecte!*" 'Hey, let us show some respect!'. It had the familiar ring of a teacher calling the pupils to order. When I asked Paula, a Ramblero woman, about her childhood experiences with the Catalan language, her first recollection was the lesson about "*les os obertes i les os tancades*" 'open and closed *os*', a phonological distinction which does not exist in Spanish. Ricardo remembered himself learning "*cargol treu banya*", a children's song, at the kindergarten. The following extract reproduces, as I understand it, the voice of a teacher:

Extract 59 [Rambleros]

Laura was tying to convince the people in the Rambleros group to get inside the cars, as everybody was distracted and chatting away.

Joan: *bueno os habéis divertido al menos*
  Well. At least you've had a good time.

Alguna: [sense connexió amb l'anterior] *las fiestas (··)*
  [unconnected with the previous turn] *The parties (··)*

Laura: va tíos va · hombre ·· [picant de mans i fent veu de mestra
  Come on folks, come on. Gee! [Clapping and putting on a schoolteacher's

  d'escola] va vinga va · vinga va · dintre dintre
  voice] Come on, come on. Get inside, Get inside.

Alguna: *(xx) un poco cansado no[?]*
  (xx) a bit tired, aren't you?

Laura's voice performed a similar function to that of Salva in extract 56 above. After having asked once for people to get inside the cars, further insistence might have been felt as tiresome or as if she was claiming to have some authority. With the switch, she could turn the event into a kind of pretend game. Similar examples are presented in girl's pretend play in Goodwin (1990).

Nevertheless, teachers could also be represented as speaking in Spanish, as Clara did, and also Patrícia, who performed a switch to Spanish in a Catalan narrative to represent the school authority. Clara once produced an imaginary stretch of my research report by switching to Spanish as well (the original language was English). In the following extract, Patrícia was explaining the activities of a course on filming that she was attending. The final assignment of the course was to produce a big video with all the students working as a production team:

Extract 60 [Trepas]

Patrícia: i l'aleix estava fent el guió del- del vídeoo ·· del video del curset ·
  And Aleix was writing the script of the- of the videoo ·· for the course ·

  vamos del vídeo *importante*.
  that is, of the *important* video.

Here Patrícia (from the Trepas) adopted a Spanish voice to represent a change of speaking subject, i.e. a change of perspective which conveyed that the course's final video was not important from *her* point of view, but from the course's viewpoint and that of those who ran it. This does not necessarily mean that the school staff spoke Spanish or that the course was in Spanish. The switch might have been used simply to convey this transposed perspective, not the language actually used in the context (see Auer 1990).

As both Catalan and Spanish enjoy official status in Catalonia, they are commonly used in politics, in the administration and in the media. The voices and modes of expression of these public domains enter the private sphere in various ways. Carlos, for instance, who spoke Spanish only, proposed that the group should meet beside the "*Informació olímpica*" (one of the Olympics' information booths), pronouncing the Catalan words with a particularly flat voice. One event was of particular significance to me during my fieldwork. After having been with the groups for some months, I accompanied the Trepas to a kind of graduation ceremony, where a few hundred trainees of employment schemes in Barcelona had to listen to a number of officials making formal speeches. After having submerged myself in the predominantly Spanish-speaking world of the Trepas, it was very revealing for me to attend an event which was carried out fully in Catalan, quite naturally and by speakers who wore suits and ties and produced unmistakable native-Catalan accents. Not surprisingly, the playful, disruptive (and therefore, out of frame) initiatives of some of the students were generally conducted in Spanish, including those of a Catalan speaker who was a bit drunk and who was shouting while hiding behind his companions. It is probably not surprising either that one of the trainees sought to exploit the potential meanings of the situation by shouting "*In Castilian!*". He turned round smiling, although his companions did not show appreciation of his joke. The climax of the event came when a technician, dressed in his overalls, who had been trying to get the microphones working, turned up on the stage and tested one of the microphones by shouting "*hola! hola!*" 'hello!' in Spanish. Suddenly, the audience pretended to react as if his *out-of-frame* intervention belonged to the *official line* and engaged in unprecedented clapping and cheering and laughing. The break of frame was remarkably well understood by the authorities, who produced a circumstantial smile.

I had a similar impression on another occasion with regard to the association between language and class. The Trepas and I met in a square where a big crowd was coming out of a park after watching the town's annual fireworks. We were suddenly submerged in a world of older, middle class people who were almost exclusively speakers of Catalan.

It is in the light of these telling events that I came to understand an episode I had not quite understood at the time. We were celebrating Clara's birthday around a big long table in a restaurant. People started shouting *"unas palabras!"* 'give us a speech!'. Clara stood up obligingly and said, in Catalan, "I am very thankful to you, you are all very nice and so on; that is all!". At that moment, I thought that the "speech" had been delivered more or less seriously. Later I understood that Clara had gone through the embarrassment of the situation by putting on a pretend-character similar to those up-tight authority figures. The subsequent smiles produced by the audience had been an acknowledgment of the game played.

The world of politics is another space shared by both languages. Voices associated with the Spanish central government would commonly appear in Spanish. Policemen, for instance, were most usually animated in Spanish, as happened in a Catalan narrative produced by Pepe. On the other hand, Catalan politicians are predominantly middle and upper class. Most of the leaders of the parties belong to the Barcelonian bourgeoisie, with friendships and family ties that cross deep ideological boundaries (see Antich 1994). During the sixties, all parties adopted nationalist claims for self-government (see Woolard 1989). It is not a surprise, then, that Catalan politics is a predominantly Catalan-speaking domain, probably with the exception of some trade unions which recruit most of their members amongst the Spanish-speaking working-classes. Nevertheless, political events get reported by a predominantly Spanish-speaking media which is usually more interested in developments concerning the Spanish government in Madrid. Catalan politics rides between these two domains (amongst others), and politicians are used to the dilemma of being surrounded by microphones that are connected with different linguistic communities.

The politicized members of the Trepas reported that Catalan was used and encouraged in the political organizations where they worked. Some of these issued their propaganda exclusively in this language. In the group discussion, Catalan speakers used their language in situations in which they normally did not, such as when responding to somebody who had spoken in Spanish or with whom they usually spoke Spanish. This is one of the ways in which it was noticeable that they had framed the group discussion as a kind of political event.

Ideas related to Catalanism, Catalan nationalism or, beyond that, Catalan racism could be represented in Catalan. Irene of the Rambleros mentioned a rather dated popular saying that referred to immigrants from Murcia, a Spanish region close to Andalusia: *"Murcianos, toca ferro!"* 'Murcians, touch iron!', i.e. 'be careful!'. Magda's switch in the following example is interesting. The politicized members of the Trepas were trying to convince her that an independent Catalonia would be a good thing because

cause it would prevent overcentralisation. Magda strongly opposed this idea:

Extract 61 [Trepas]

Magda: pero tú puedes hacerlo sin decir · [veu greu] *cataluña es una*
  But you can do it without saying [low voice]: "Catalonia is one

historia · y todo lo demás otra · escolta'm
  story and all the rest is another [story]. Listen!"

The switch "*escolta'm*" 'listen to me' reproduced a speech genre stereo-typically used in Spain to mimic Catalans. Magda was arguing that to claim a Catalan state was an extremist option; to her, it meant a culturally uni-form state, which she represented through the hypothetical assertion of a nationalist (*Catalonia is one thing and all the rest is another*). The ironical "listen" had the additional meaning potential of emphatically calling the audience to pay attention to her and to display a readiness to argue. Magda was also exploiting the humorous potential of impersonating a Catalan with a funny voice: the stereotyped Catalan was like the living (talking) image of what the Catalan state would be.

Catalan could also be identified with things "inextricably Catalan". Clara was talking in Castilian once about the "*San Esteban*" day 'boxing day' and said, laughing, "how bad it sounds in Castilian!". In the Ramble-ros' group discussion, various members took to explaining their Christmas dishes mimicking Catalan voices, probably the voices they had heard amongst their Catalan speaking relatives. Other examples, more clearly belonging to informal arenas, were whole phrases and popular sayings, in particular those that can be used in fun-making activities: "*Salut i força al canut*", (a toast to male sexual strength), or the popular "*Sant Hilari Sant Hilari...*" (a toast inviting people to empty their glasses). There were also Catalan phrases referring to the feasting activities of a small village in Catalonia where some of the Rambleros regularly went on holiday.

Conversely, Spanish nationalist, extremist or anti-Catalan views were usually conveyed by a switch to Spanish in Catalan narratives. One exam-ple was provided by Jaume:

Extract 62 [Trepas]

Jaume: però hi ha gent que sap parlar català però no el vol · parlar
  But there are people who can speak Catalan, but they do not want to speak it

perquè · *son · españoles y como soy español pues · mi idioma es el*
because · *"They are Spaniards and, because I am Spanish, well, my language is*

castellano y el catalán para los cerdos no[?] · hi ha gent que pensa no[?]
Castilian and Catalan [is] for pigs", right? Some people think like this, right?

Another perspective conveyed through Spanish was that of young anarchists as reported in extract 54 by Pepe; and by Clara when she switched once to Spanish to say "I do not have a culture, I am universal" to summarize her earlier identity conflict as a "daughter of an immigrant". This type of anarchist is one of Barcelona's stereotypical figures of young second-generation immigrants. In the following extract, this voice helps to understand Clara's switches as she explained how Salva started to speak Catalan:

Extract 63 [Trepas]

Clara: perquè el salva ha fet un · · u- un *acto de militancia* · · vui dir el salva abans
Because Salva performed an · · a- an *act of militancy.* · *I mean* Salva before

no parlava mai el cas- mai mai el cast- · català · mai · mai · *era ·*
never used to speak Cas- never never Cast- · Catalan · never · never · *He was an*

anarquista · ·i · *si eres anarquista pues · tu hablas en castellano* · ·
anarchist · · and · *If you are an anarchist, well, you speak in Castilian.* ·

pero mm · va conèiixer l'aleix · · · *hizo un acto de militancia*
But mm · he met Aleix · · [and] *performed an act of militancy*

The narrative voice is clearly in Catalan, but the principles and actions which had to do with anarchism were in Spanish, surely as a way of conveying the voices and modes of expression in which this perspective had been constructed by these young people. On other occasions, Pepe quoted with a switch to Spanish a news item in a Basque nationalist publication. Clara also explained that, in demonstrations, they used to begin shouting slogans in Catalan; but that people drifted into Spanish spontaneously as they became more involved or more creative with slogans. It is also interesting that Patrícia represented with stylized Spanish what she considered a kind of clumsy or untactful feminism, from which she wished to distance herself. Again, stylized Spanish was used to animate a character with a poor understanding of the subtleties of life.

The media constituted a rich and diverse source of voices. First, there were the serious, factual voices of the news presenters, which could appear in both languages. Pepe once took my microphone and impersonated the television weatherman in Catalan. Salva, in his interview, jokingly approached my microphone and asked, in Catalan, whether this would be reported to a famous Spanish gossip magazine. In a video filmed by members of the group on an outing of the training school, Chimo impersonated, in Spanish, a news correspondent. In the group discussions, I provided cards with different questions people could address, and Magda took pleasure reading them aloud while impersonating (in both languages) a television presenter of a competition show.

The media also provided less official kinds of voices associated with different programs and audiences: cartoon or soap opera characters, music groups, humor programs and so on. Here both Catalan and Spanish could be used to evoke formal and informal voices. However, none of the Catalan voices came really close to evoking characters with whom the Rambleros or the Trepas might identify. In Catalan, I witnessed Silvia and Pepe singing the song of a famous Japanese cartoon series for very young children. A Spanish speaking youth worker once dropped a "*no passa res*" 'nothing happens', 'that's all right' after I apologized in Spanish. Magda said once "*aquí hi ha marro*" 'something stinks here'. The last two phrases had been popularized by the humorous musical group *la Trinca* during the eighties. Another Catalan program, *Força Barça*, a kind of *Spitting Image* exclusively dedicated to the affairs of the Barcelona Football Club, was very popular amongst the Rambleros. Some of them reproduced with impressive skill its Catalan voices and also Spanish voices with Catalan accents (which were used, incidentally, to ridicule the characters that were being mimicked). In Spanish, one humor program provided the Rambleros with other sources for the impersonation of ridiculous characters. The phrase "*qué mala suerte!*" 'tough luck', evoked a puppet which reproduced a well-known singer. Salva once tried to describe to me a cookery program with the cook's usual phrase "*rico rico*" 'delicious'. Voices from advertisements also appeared, such as Magda's "*repetimos, natillas*" 'let's get another pudding'. At the end of the group discussion, Magda and Pepe engaged in a dramatization of a television chat program where the presenter and many of the guests were usually very presumptuous and made implicit claims about their depth of intellectual insight. Such voices were dramatized in a very lively way in their original Spanish form, sometimes ridiculed by a touch of Andalusian stylization. In the codeswitching of the following extract, Patrícia was clearly drawing upon the language of advertising as she was telling me about the financial arrangements that a drama school offered for one of its courses:

Extract 64 [Trepas]

Patrícia: es una escola de pago · i el curs val unaa- · tot el any · són unes
  It is a private school. And the course costs a-, for the whole year, it's about

  cent mi- · quasi doscentes mil peles · *lo pagas a codo- cómodos*
  a hundred th- almost two hundred thousand ptes. *You pay in cof- comfortable*

  plazos dee ochoo o diez mil pelas al mes però · · però són deu bitllets [pica a la
  taula, somriu]
  instalments oof eeight or ten thousand ptas. per month but, · but it's ten papers! [knocks
  the table and smiles].

In an analysis of codeswithing in a radio show in Barcelona, Woolard (1995) found very similar Spanish voices. In the switch below, Pepe reproduced an imaginary literacy event where he was allegedly reading the label of a cassette case in the home of a friend who had music of all types:

Extract 65 [Trepas]

Pepe: tinc un amic · que té tot · a casa seva tot ple de cintes · ii agafes
  I've got a friend · who's got all · his home all full of tapes. Aand you take any one

  qualsevol ii *grupo del kurdistan* no? · pum o · o també tinc un altre
  aand: "*group from Kurdistan*", right? There! or · or I have also got another one ...

This switch is an indication of the fact that commercial products, especially of transnational origin, are generally labeled in Spanish when not in English. Only tapes, CDs and records produced by Catalan artists sometimes appear in Catalan.

2.2. Popular characters

I have based my analysis on the assumption that our talk is an amalgamation of different voices which we ascribe to characters of various qualities and statuses, a principle which is essential to our understanding of how we make sense of real-life utterances. Many of these characters are what we usually call *stereotypes*, i.e. relatively fixed or typified images of social groups and their associated qualities. They usually have their own names as a class of individuals, and they are part and parcel of our views about our society and ourselves. One very salient example is the *Catalans* versus *Castilians* dichotomy as discussed by Woolard (1989), which corresponds to many native Catalans' view that non-speakers of Catalan are not really Catalan. In a previous study I conducted amongst university students (Pujolar 1991b), I found that people used other categories (for instance: Catalan-speaker) when they tried to avoid this ideological implication. Amongst the groups I studied, the most common expression was "people who speak Catalan", although I sometimes heard the word "Catalan" in this sense as well. Nevertheless, speakers of Spanish referred to themselves as "Catalan" on numerous occasions, even those who sometimes said that they did not feel Catalan. It seemed as if the word sometimes had a geographical meaning, sometimes an ethnolinguistic one, sometimes both, depending on the situation. What was clear is that the difference was still perceived, although it appeared that people were circumspect about the matter and sought not to make it salient. This also coincides with Boix' (1989, 1993) findings amongst a group of youth club leaders in Barcelona.

Nevertheless, in spite of this effort to play down ethnolinguistic boundaries that were politically sensitive, there was evidence that they were still quite important. The repertoire of stereotyped characters I found very often contained an underlying ethnolinguistic dimension. One of these interesting characters was the *maria* (a 'mary'), a proper noun transformed to designate a type of person, commonly a middle-aged or older Catalan-speaking woman who, according to Patrícia, lives in some neighborhoods "sitting in the street in front of her door and chatting" with neighbors. According to Luis, the *marías* constituted a significant part of the clients of the supermarket where he worked. They were "very Catalan" and were unrepentant about using Catalan with him. A Spanish-speaking equivalent of such women seemed to be the *marujas* (which is actually a Spanish diminutive for *María*). For Lola, her fellow workers in the factory were *marujas* and she did not get along well with them.

Peasants were amongst the people usually impersonated as speaking Catalan. Pepe, for instance, had picked up an expression he had reportedly heard from a farmer probably seeking to curse a trespasser: *mussol de rec* (literally 'ditch owl').[18] Silvia said that most fellow students spoke Catalan in her school because they came from "small villages". In Clara's interview, when I commented that Chimo's Catalan sounded much more native than that of most members of the Trepas, she said that he was from a very rural Catalan district (which was in truth his parents' birthplace, as he had always lived in Barcelona). Amongst some members of the Trepas group, Catalan speakers from outside Barcelona (a category which also included me) were jokingly referred to as being *de Vic* 'from Vic' (an inland town which is known to be "very Catalan"). Of course, it was also possible to reproduce rural voices through Spanish. Stylized Spanish often served this purpose. In my data, I also have Pepe telling an anecdote in which a speaker of a Spanish northern dialect from a small village was represented.

The tone of rurality could be used as much to convey traditional authenticity or, on the contrary, strangeness, distance or weirdness. Clara confessed that Catalans who were *from Vic* gave her a bad first impression. She also said that such people, like myself, made her feel obliged to speak Catalan. This strangeness was also expressed in the way the Trepas (including native speakers of Catalan) distanced themselves from the Catalan expressions that were different from theirs. I was usually teased for my accent and for the use of colloquial forms they did not know (although some of them were common amongst Catalan-speaking Barcelonians). They clearly did not show the interest I have found in some Catalan speakers in Barcelona, who seek to learn and use inland expressions to construct a kind of popular register or to appropriate its perceived authenticity. Sometimes, inland Catalan was portrayed as obscure. On one occasion, Pepe produced an invented unintelligible utterance which sounded phonetically Catalan. He was impersonating an imaginary speaker of inland Catalan whose speech was not understandable.

A rich source of popular characters was provided by the cultural fashions and musical movements of pop and rock music: heavies, punks, hippies, rockers, mods, rastas, skins, rappers, *lolailos*. As is generally known, these cultural and musical movements are usually accompanied by a philosophy of life, political ideas, ways of dressing and ways of speaking.[19] The term *lolailos* is taken from the typical jingle of the Rumba music and was associated generally with the lower classes and the Spanish language (although many Romany Rumba singers are speakers of Catalan). Other movements were probably less linguistically marked. Nevertheless, in so far as they were seen as part of the penya, such groups could be represented as speaking Spanish or stylized Spanish, as I have shown above. A possible exception could be the *hippies*. In the following extract, Salva counterposed the young people of his neighborhood with people of other Catalan-speaking neighborhoods in this way:

Extract 66 [Trepas]

Salva: In the coordinating committee, we generally speak Catalan, right? But the people from Santa Coloma · · they all speak Castilian. · The people from Sants all speak Catalan. · I don't know. It depends, right? · I believe that it also depends on the neighbourhood. · Because in Santa Coloma, they are all quite rough. ·· And in Sants, well, they are all · very much like that, [higher, singing tone] *very hippie, very Catalanist and* [...].

In this episode, the character of the "Catalanist hippies" was expressed through a higher pitched, ironizing voice. In contrast, the adjective *garrulones* 'rough people' applied to the people of his Spanish-speaking neighborhood and had a kind of affectionate tone (also as opposed to the undiminished *garrulo* 'rough').

Similar kinds of ironizing voices were used to impersonate different types of Catalan speakers, as I will show below. There seemed to be a common thread amongst the population of stereotyped characters I encountered in people's talk. Catalan-speaking characters rarely appeared in a positive light. They were rarely the "good guys". Further evidence is provided by the significance of words like *kumbas* or *esplai*. These words were derogatorily used to refer to boy scouts and voluntary youth workers respectively or to persons seen as similar in character, that is, as somewhat dim-witted. The Scout and the *Esplai* movements have been of enormous importance in recent Catalan history. Because they were organized by the Catalan bourgeoisie or by the church (which was predominantly pro-Catalan), these institutions provided pedagogical spaces where particular forms of children and youth cultures were developed independently from the structures of the Spanish state. They are clearly associated with the Catalan culture and language (see Boix 1989, 1993). Below, Jaume was explaining how he had abandoned his previous gang and joined an *esplai*:

Extract 67 [Trepas]
Jaume: When I was fourteen years old, I made my own penya, right? from the penya who was in ·· in the 'esplai'. Then, well, my · vocabulary probably changed a bit, more ·· At first it was more *street-like*, right? It changed a bit, · and it because like... not 'kumba' but · like · I mean: *typical 'esplai'*, right? I mean [Putting on a Catalan urban accent] "a bit like this (xxx)" ·· But that was a short- a short time and · afterwards, with the people I have always got along well, it has been with guys · more or less · who are not- who are like me, right? and · this is why · my speech is not very ··· it's simple it is not something refined or anything, right?

In this extract, Jaume dramatized the voice of a speaker of an urban variety of Catalan. This variety, commonly called *xava*, is highly stigmatized because it is perceived as daft, very castilianized and (probably) as working-class (see Tusón 1985b; Ballart 1996). It is quite significant that the one

Catalan variety that could be associated with informal contexts was also used to impersonate characters that present some form of inadequacy, however vague, and that expressions meant to convey the experience or the point of view of the penya, such as *callejero* 'street-like' or *típico esplai* 'typical *esplai*', were voiced in Spanish.

2.3. Other types of voice

In this section, I have so far analyzed voices featuring characters who were somehow easy to identify: stereotyped speakers of Catalan or Spanish, teachers, anarchists, cartoon and popular figures and so on. I have already indicated that Catalan hardly appeared in any voice or character which represented the values and identities of the group (the couple of popular sayings associated with drinking and sexual prowess mentioned above are the only exceptions I found to this general rule). The political discourse of anarchism, which some politicized Trepas connected with the oppositional values of the penya, was also conveyed through Spanish.

In addition to the more or less recognizable set of popular characters associated with the two languages, I also found other voices whose origin and meaning were much more difficult to trace. In some cases, this could be due to the fact that the Rambleros and the Trepas might have been evoking aspects of their experience which were unknown to me. However, I believe that it is common for people to possess a repertoire of more fuzzy and ambivalent voices whose meanings can only be described through detailed and properly contextualized analyzes. Some of these voices can actually have a close relation to people's own sense of self, as opposed to the voices I have analyzed so far, most of which were quotations from *other* characters.

The evidence I found in my data of these more imprecise voices also supports the argument that the Catalan language had a problematic relationship with peer-group values and identities. One set of such Catalan voices seemed to point primarily to *non-masculine* characters, i.e. animated figures who presented features opposed to hegemonic masculinity: non-drinkers, non-swearers, non-slang speakers, non-rough people, naive or plainly stupid characters, people close to mainstream values, with proper manners and so on. For instance, on one occasion, three Rambleros men found themselves queuing in a fast food establishment where the menu-board was in Catalan. They engaged in a playful reading of the menu with funny voices accompanied by laughter. A similar episode appeared in the group discussions. When I asked what they felt about Catalan, some commented on phonemes they found difficult to articulate and some produced examples of words or phrases accompanied by mimickings and laughter. In such exercises of mimicry, they generally put great effort into producing a good performance, such that the accent and vocal quality of the utterances sounded much more authentic or native to me than the actual normal speech of many Catalan speakers in Barcelona.

The representation of inadequate characters through a Catalan voice appeared in a similar genre: the *staged faulty performances*. They consisted, in this case, of producing Spanish words that had been transformed to appear as if they were Catalan. They were funny because they evoked a character trying to speak Catalan and failing to produce the right expression. Woolard describes such cases as parodic performances that exaggerate and highlight "the unintentional hybrids of 'obscure people'" (1995: 242). In the Trepas' hard-core group rehearsals, for instance, they played a song called *otro golpe* 'another blow'. After shouting the name of the song to prompt the group to start, Salva had to insist a second time, and he rephrased his prompting as *"un altre golp"* (instead of *"un altre cop"*) in order to achieve a humorous effect (notice that this switch accomplishes a similar function to the switch into stylized Spanish quoted in extract 56). Amongst the Rambleros, Laura was very fond of playing this game and produced words such as *cachuperru* 'dog', *xoriço fritu* (instead of *xoriço fregit* 'fried chorizo') or *les tualles* (instead of *les tovalloles* 'the towels'). Heller (1994) found similar types of linguistic games amongst bilingual children and adolescents in Toronto.

According to my experience, these linguistic games are also common in predominantly Catalan-speaking areas. Their meaning is not easy to pin down. I have heard Catalan speakers producing staged faulty Spanish, particularly when dramatizing dialogues where a Catalan speaker confronts Spanish-speaking policemen or other authorities. In these cases, the fun seems to consist of the fact that the Catalan speaker fails to produce the appropriate performance that the authorities would expect. It seems to me that these linguistic games are a way of expressing disidentification: Catalan-speakers towards Spanish and vice versa.

On the other hand, amongst the Rambleros and the Trepas, staged faulty Spanish seemed to serve to ridicule Catalan speakers who had a strong accent or inadequate knowledge of Spanish, as when some Trepas used to mimic my own accent. I am not aware of having heard the opposite case in

Catalan-speaking milieus. Catalan speakers do produce staged faulty Catalan; but these seem to be done to ridicule some Catalan speakers who wish to avoid Castilian loan-words but who produce inappropriate literal translations or impossible expressions. There is probably a significance in this subtle asymmetry.

Another form of linguistic mockery was expressed by changing a Spanish word for its Catalan equivalent, such as *xinès* instead of *chino* 'Chinese restaurant'. In this case, the humorous effect came from the fact that the voice represented an excessively purist Catalan speaker.

Extract 35 in chapter 3 shows a dramatization performed through Catalan voices amongst two Trepas men. These voices expressed surprise at the high alcoholic level of a particular type of beer. The characters they impersonated were therefore unlike "real" men who are expected to withstand large doses of alcohol. In the episode extracted below, Catalan characters were used to impersonate similarly childish persons:

Extract 68 [Trepas]

Ayats was wearing a T-shirt featuring some hard rock group. Pepe initiated the sequence by telling Ayats that his shirt was ugly. He was probably representing a teacher censoring Ayats for being improperly dressed. Ayats, though, turned it into a pretend squabble amongst kids.

Pepe: [amb èmfasi] quina samarreta <u>més ll- ll- lletja</u> que portes nen
    [With emphasis] What an <u>u- u- ugly</u> T-shirt you are wearing, kid.

Ayats: [Amb pronúncia exageradament acurada] la teva és una [Èmfasi]
    [With exaggerated accuracy in pronunciation] yours is a [Emphasis]

    <u>merda · aixi de >clar</u>
    <u>shit! That's >plain</u>

Pepe: <sí · sí · ja ho sé
    <Yeah yeah, I know.

Ayats: aixi de clar · no no <u>josep</u> aixi de clar
    That's plain. No, no Josep. That's plain.

Pepe: sí sí · ja ho sé · però jo no dic que no
    Yeah yeah. I know. But I am not saying otherwise.

Ayats: [Veu molt baixa] <u>li diré al marcel</u> que m'ho has dit això eh[?] ·
    [Low voice] <u>I will tell Marcel</u> that you said that to me, right? >(xxxx)

Pepe: [Cridant] <marcel · mira què m'ha dit de la samarreta=
    [Shouting] <Marcel. Look what he said to me about the T-shirt=

Ayats: [Cridant]=marcel · <u>no potser no si aquí mano jo home</u>
    [Shouting] =Marcel. "<u>Oh no, that cannot be. I am the one in charge here, man!</u>"

This episode is a pretend game featuring two kids fighting over a T-shirt. The expression *lletja* 'ugly' sounded childish in this context, as well as *merda* 'shit', pronounced and treated as if it was a very strong word ("That's plain!"), which it was not (at least for Ayats and Pepe). Additionally, to name Pepe with his full name and in Catalan *josep* suggests that the school context was being evoked. Additionally, the line "I will tell Marcel" reminds us of schoolboys betraying their companions to the teacher. The underlined stretch in the last line was probably the voice of a teacher.

These naive characters who did not speak in argot and did not drink were played out in a characteristic tone of voice, as if pronounced in the front of the mouth.[20] It was the same voice used by Pepe and Ayats to produce the exclamation *Ospa!*, which was a euphemized form (and therefore not tough enough) of the swearword *hòstia*, which is of religious origin. On one occasion, Pepe said that the name of the hard-core group would not sound good if it was translated into Catalan, meaning it would not sound hard, tough enough. In order to illustrate this point, he produced the actual translation *with this same voice* as evidence that Catalan would not have provided the right tone. On another occasion, Pepe dramatized a Catalan singer of a concert with this voice, while he used stylized Spanish in the same narrative to animate the voices of the public.

Such voices point to a stereotype about the Catalans that was used in a similar way to the stylized Spanish characters, i e. to dramatize figures who should be seen as *other*, to convey irony, distance or lack of seriousness. The Rambleros used plenty of these voices. For instance, after I explained to Irene and Alicia that I walked to the tube-station every day after I saw them, Alicia said to Irene "*és molt esportista*" 'he is quite a sportsman'. Although the voice was plain and the statement might have been taken as serious, the switch to Catalan indicated that she was exaggerating, that is, teasing. On another occasion, Irene, had an acute need to pass water and expressed it through a Catalan phrase. This allowed her to distance herself from what she was saying, thus diminishing the demeaning potential of using scatological expressions. With one of the Rambleros men, I had several short conversations in Catalan. This happened late at night and the point of it was that speaking Catalan was "a laugh". One of the couples in the Rambleros decided one day to have a conversation in Catalan, half to practice and half to have fun. The event was presented to others as great fun. Isolated harmless exclamations, some of which have already been shown, were often produced in Catalan, such as "*renoi!*" 'gosh'. Such voices were also used in genres connected with out-of-frame activity or frame maintenance. These were interventions which had to do with the organisation of the groups, but not with the fun making: for instance, coordination work and greetings. Thus it was not uncommon amongst the Rambleros to produce moves in Catalan such as *"què fan?"* 'what are they doing', *"on anem?"* 'where are we going?', or *"nem?"* 'let's go?'. Such proposals for the group to take a course of action could be taken as mitigated (in Brown and Levinson's sense) if they were done in Catalan, as they could be understood potentially as a joke. This use of codeswitching to soften a proposal, a request or an order also appears in extracts 56 and 59. Goodwin (1990) also reports on girls diminishing the force of commands through dramatizations of characters. In my fieldwork, it was not unusual for me to be greeted in Catalan, particularly by Spanish speakers, although this did not imply that the person wanted to engage in a lengthy conversation in this language. In greetings, it is also very typical to adopt a half serious half joking stance (i.e. a keyed frame), as if our showing concern for other people should not be carried too far or taken too seriously in the present situation. This is probably why we find abundant examples of codeswitching in the so-called conversational openings and closings in the literature (see Heller 1988; Codó 1998; Torras 1999).

If, instead of analyzing switches into Catalan, we focus on switches into Spanish in Catalan narratives, the asymmetrical position of the two languages amongst the Trepas becomes much clearer (it is not possible to explore this point with regard to the Rambleros, as they never spoke Catalan with each other). Spanish was the actual voice of the (Trepas) group. It was the voice in which their world was experienced and their views were constructed. The switches into Spanish were a constant reminder that the world outside the narrative was in this language:

Extract 69 [Trepas]
Jaume: ya · pero tu te'n recordes que · aquell dia que va haver aquell
Yeah, but you remember that · that day when there was that

pique no[?] dee · · *que si los porros a fuera si los porros ad-* · pues
row, right? oveer: *"Whether joints outside or joints insid-"*.

elles fan lo mateix · · i no es donen compte no? · y nosatros [...]
Well, they [the women] do the same. · And they do not realise it, right? and we [men] [...]

Here Jaume referred to a conflict experienced by the group, whereby women had complained that men spent most of their time outside the premises of bars and left the women inside on their own (see chapter 2). The switch did not actually reproduce anybody's intervention (additionally, part of the discussion had been in Catalan), but a particular representation of what the argument was about. A similar example was provided by Pepe when he described people's general reaction to the working conditions of the training school. There is also an equivalent example from Patrícia in the group discussion, as she was talking about the separation between the genders:

Extract 70 [Trepas]

Patrícia: ... també fumo · · i sí que ho veig el rotllo- no ho veig pel rotllo de
... I also smoke. · And I do see it. The issue, I don't see it as a question of

gustos · ho veig pel rotllo de · *el corrillo de chicos el corrillo de chicas*
tastes, I see is as a question of · *the little ring of boys the little ring of girls*

Patrícia chose to depict a typical image of the group in Spanish. Congruently with this image, the *view* or *opinion* of the group or the penya was usually animated in this language (see also extracts 50 and 69). Therefore it is not a surprise that Jaume represented his thoughts in Spanish, although he considered himself to be a full bilingual and many saw him as a Catalan speaker:

Extract 71 [Trepas]

Jaume: vull llegir però · · me costa un montón d'agafar un llibre i és que
I want to read, but · · I its awfully difficult for me to pick up a book and it's that

es un- · si tingués molt més temps no[?] però és que · · quan tinc
is a- ·if I had much more time, right? But it is like this · · When I can

algo que fer · penso · *me leo un libro · o me voy a la calle con los*
do something, I think: *"do I read a book... or do I go out in the street with my*

colegas · prefereixo estar amb la gent no[?] la veritat · prefereixò
mates?" I prefer to be with these people, right? The truth is: I prefer

estar amb la gent que estar amb un llibre
to be with these people than to be with a book.

In extract 54, Pepe also quoted his thoughts in Spanish. In thinking aloud in this way, the impression was that people were animating their inner selves, or the persons they normally were as opposed to their current selves as interviewees.

Additionally, many switches to Spanish appeared to be done simply to add dramatic effectiveness and liveliness to a narrative. In these cases, the Spanish voice took over parts of the narrative mode itself. It became a voice meant to display more involvement, accompanied by gestures and vocal effects. In a very long narrative produced by Aleix in which he was arguing that some young people also had sexist attitudes in the workplace, he would present the conceptual principles of his argument in Catalan while the examples he gave were in the form of scenes dramatized in Spanish. In these scenes, not only were the voices of the characters dramatized in Spanish: the narrative voice was in Spanish too. A simpler example came up in Patrícia's interview. She compared a debate on feminism given in a secondary school, where people were a bit passive, with one given at the university, where "*t'empiezan con elucubraciones*" 'they start with long-winded theoretizations'. Here the switch to Spanish is accompanied with a mimicking voice expressing scorn for such pretentious speculations. Of course, it is arguable that I could have counted this episode as a Spanish voice with a negative overtone. Nevertheless, I believe that Spanish was used here as a device to produce a more dramatic effect.

Other Spanish voices were of an even more subtle quality. Up to now I have presented switches which one would probably represent in written language between quotation marks, even though the exact meaning of some voices might be difficult to assess. Other types of voice, however, seem to have a much more ambivalent, skewed status. Clara's switches are a case in point. Her family language was Spanish and she could speak Catalan fluently. Nevertheless, she rarely spoke *only* in Catalan. When speaking with me, she would switch languages very often. Sometimes it was not clear to me whether there was actually a main or matrix language in her speech. Often, she would switch to Spanish for a quote, a dramatization, a joke, irony, and not come back when the purpose of the switch seemed to have ended. So I found myself, across several turns, responding in Catalan to her Spanish interventions and wondering if I should not accommodate to her. Sometimes I did so, but then she would often switch back to Catalan, which was all the more disorientating.

To interpret Clara's switching practices, more than just stylistic effects should be taken into consideration. Because of her political beliefs, Clara felt that she had to speak Catalan with me, or at least avoid prompting a switch to Spanish on my part. Thus, while her switches into Spanish generally followed the need to produce particular expressive effects, her switches into Catalan were done so that I would not feel obliged to speak in Spanish myself.

In her interview, she declared that she had some difficulties of expression in Catalan, which she solved by simply switching to Spanish. But, what could these 'difficulties of expression' consist of? I have located some examples which illustrate the difference between Clara's Catalan and Spanish voices:

Extract 72 [Trepas]

Clara: no siempree [Ella riu] · *te invito a comer · qué[?]*
  Not always [She laughs]. *I invite you to eat. What?*

Joan: *brazo de gitano* [i li ensenyo el braç, ella riu fort]
  A 'Gypsy's arm' [I show her my arm; it is a pun, because a 'Gypsy's arm' is a type of cake; she laughs loudly].

Clara: ei pues el dimarts vens a casa ·[assenteixo] · *qué te ha parecido mi*
  Hey, then you come Tuesday to my place. [I nod] *How did you find my*

  casa bonita >o fea [riu]
  house: beautiful >or ugly?

Joan: <*sí · noo*
  <*yes · noo.*

After many turns of jokes, Clara switched to Catalan (underlined) probably to ensure that I took her invitation seriously. Her voice was now serious and flat. After a pause where I shyly accepted her invitation, Clara switched back to Spanish to ask my opinion about her flat, which I had already seen. This time, her voice (a soft, higher pitch) was half ironic and opened the possibility of joking again. Additionally, putting her question in terms of "beautiful" or "ugly" evoked the childish language analyzed in extract 68 above. The proper slang words would be *guai, chachi* 'great' or *cutre* 'crap'. As I see it, her ironic tone was meant to express role distance and was probably geared to avoid an embarrassing situation had I not liked her house.

So this ironic voice could have a very important role in managing relationships and communication. In my first nights out with the Trepas, Clara said to me various times things such as "you will turn yourself into a cynical person" or "you are very witty" through switches to Spanish. These were some of the skilful moves she performed so that we could get to know each other by talking half seriously and half jokingly about our personalities.

The importance of the expressive contrast between her Catalan and Spanish voices can be shown in the following extract, where she was explaining to me how she convinced a friend to start her studies again:

Extract 73 [Trepas]

Clara: estava al centre cívic · · *comiendole la cabeza a la · a la natalia* · ·
I was in the Civic Centre · · "*nagging · Natalia*

para que se matriculara [...] · *matriculaté · porque no sé qué ·*
so that she would register [...]: "*Do register, because I don't know,*

porque con (xx) llegarás muy lejos
because with (xx) you'll get very far"

The idea of *convincing Natalia* was expressed through the slang or colloquial phrase *comer la cabeza* (literally 'to eat someone's head'). Had this been expressed in a flat, standard voice, it might have sounded paternalistic of Clara to do this with a friend. Additionally, the cliché line "you'll get very far" also conveyed irony.

Now it could be said that this was a Spanish *funny voice* comparable to the Catalan ones mentioned above. Nevertheless, it was a voice *of hers*, not a voice of *someone else*. This ironic tone was very common in peer-group talk. Probably everybody had such a register. Catalan voices tended to become a flat, dry, matter of fact, radio-weather-forecast kind of voice. Spanish could be used to produce teasing, affection, fun, lively tones, i.e. the tones of the everyday talk of the group. Spanish thus provided some symbolic means through which relationships were established and developed within the group. Because having fun was the main frame of activity, some otherwise serious issues could be talked about in the form of jokes. This voice was therefore fundamental to the identities of the group and this explains why Clara could not be brought to maintain Catalan throughout a whole conversation.

Concluding remarks

It is an established notion in sociolinguistics that the variety spoken by a given social group often becomes a symbol of the values and identities of the group, and that it may also be shaped and used in a way that conforms with the group's idea of itself. As such, speakers are encouraged to show loyalty to their own group's culture and way of speaking. This allegedly explains why peripheral or lower class communities often maintain their local varieties in the face of competition from more powerful linguistic forms such as standard or dominant languages. This is usually referred to as the status/solidarity dichotomy. According to this view, many speakers seek to find a balance between their desire for social advancement and the pressures to display solidarity towards their local variety (Woolard 1985b). For the study of language choice and codeswitching, Gumperz (1982: 66, 73) proposes the categories of *we-code*, as "associated with in-group and informal activities" (such as relationships with kin and friends) versus *they-code*, "associated with the more formal, stiffer and less personal out-group relations." He argues that speakers effectively interpret code-switches on the basis of this dichotomous association in combination with the subtle contextualizing functions that linguistic alternations perform in talk (ibid.: 91–95). In a way, this dichotomy can also be portrayed as an inside/outside, in-group/out-group symbolic contrast.

I think that something of this kind is happening to an extent in my data, although the complexities of the situation I studied require a more elaborated explanatory framework. What emerges from the analysis of the code-switching practices of the Rambleros and the Trepas is that the function of we-code was associated with Spanish, whereas Catalan was generally treated as a they-code. Spanish occupied most of the conversational space within the groups and it was the language in which the expressive recources (speech genres and styles) associated with peer-group values and identities were being developed. Spanish, to summarize, sounded tougher and cooler, and it was more appropriate to evoke transgressive characters and most of the groups' shared experiences. Catalan, on the other hand, was a language not mastered by everybody and only used in a restricted set of situations. The only shared experience of significance with Catalan had been at school and in other public domains, which means that it often evoked formal and submissive characters and situations.

However, some important qualifications need to be made in relation to how the we/they dichotomy is commonly portrayed in the literature. First, I believe that Catalan cannot really be portrayed as a dominant language or as a language of wider communication than Spanish even in that particular context. Spanish is, after all, the language of the state, the overwhelmingly predominant language of advertising and the media, and the main language spoken in the community. What we have here is that some of the processes of sociolinguistic identification that normally contribute to the maintenance of local varieties operate in favour of the dominant language precisely because the population of immigrant origin has been able to establish the use of its we-code at the local level and to benefit from its status as a dominant language within Spain.

Secondly, I do not really subscribe to the notion that the we/they dichotomy is somehow at the root of the interpretive devices that people use to produce and understand utterances. I have already argued that the production and interpretation of an utterance operate on the basis of the dialogical processes that connect the utterance with previous utterances and actions, and which rely on people's ability to identify the genres and voices that are being used. This means that the symbolic spaces associated with each language emerge as a *product* of these processes. They do not originate in a pre-determined identity or competence. I see the we/they dichotomy as a *social construct*, a product of the processes whereby groups establish dialogical relationships between different discourses and languages. This is why we can find situations such as this one, where Spanish was not only the we-code for Spanish speakers, but also for people who had Catalan as the family language.

Chapter 6

Language choices

So far we have explored the figurative or metaphorical uses of Catalan and Spanish and other speech styles in the discourse of the Rambleros and the Trepas. Extract 74 illustrates a case of linguistic alternation that is driven by other communicative needs. Ayats and Pepe of the Trepas group used to speak Catalan to each other. This is why, in this episode, they start speaking in Catalan (with elements of youth slang), but later switch to Spanish to address Mauro, an acquaintance of theirs.

Extract 74 [Trepas]
The following conversation took place on the terrace of a café. A few Trepas men, Ayats, Pepe and Mauro were recalling an occasion where they encountered a rock group playing in the street. Silvia, a Trepas woman, also intervened now and then. Chimo appeared to be making comments probably to Jaume, whose voice cannot be distinctively identified in the recording. Catalan is in bold type and Spanish in bold italics.

Ayats: **i aquells tius de la guitarra tiu[?]**
    And what about those guys with the guitar, man?

Chimo?: *ala [expressa sorpresa per un incident no relacionat amb la conversa]*
    Jesus! [expressing surprise for some incident unrelated to the conversation]

Pepe: **osti sí com tiraven els cabrons eh[?]**
    Christ! Yeah! That was some nice playing those bastards did, huh?

Ayats *[a Mauro]: dos tíos en la calle tocando · (x) un (letritis) · te lo juro que*
    [to Mauro]: Two guys, playing in the street · (x) one (xxx) · I swear that

    en el pal- me pegaba unos sudores tío · solo tío entrar allí
    in the (x), I was sweating like hell, man, the minute I got in there

Pepe: *hacía unos punteaos que eran increíbles · a más too*
    He was doing these really incredible solo plucks . Moreover, everything,

    too era improvisao todo
    everything, everything was improvised, everything.

Ayats: *sí · un · era un ritmo así na na-na na-na eh no me*
    Yeah, a- the rhythm was something like that: na-na na-na. Er, I can't

    acuerdo el ritmo no[?] [to arrastrat baixet] · y el tío iba
    remember the rhythm, right? [low dragging voice] · and the guy was

dando caña iba dando caña sabes[?]
keeping up the beat keeping up the beat, you know?

Chimo?: aaa sueño tío
Aah. I feel sleepy, man.

Ayats: (xx) el gusanillo · toqué y la peña · coros coros · tío
(xx) the craving · I started playing and the penya: "chorus, chorus", man

Mauro: (xxx) santa coloma ahí te podías pillar la guitarra allí
(xxx) in Santa Coloma. There there were guitars available, there

en la ventanilla y ( )
at the window and ( )

Sílvia: donde[?]
Where?

Mauro: donde estaba el chiringuito
Where that booth was.

Thus, Ayats and Pepe started the conversation in Catalan, the language they normally talked between themselves. This did not exclude any of their conversation partners, as amongst the Trepas both languages could be used freely. However, to adress Mauro, they switched to Spanish because this was the language they both used with him, although Mauro had no problems in understanding Catalan. This is a very common situation in Barcelona. People adopt one particular language to address each person, such that people alternate the use of the two languages as a matter of course in many conversations. However, what are the processes that lead people to adopt one particular language of communication with one particular person?

This is what I am going to explore in this chapter. In the previous one, I argued that the Catalan and Spanish languages were linked to particular types of performance or character display, to particular games or interactional patterns, to particular conceptions of the world and of social relations. However, my analysis has been restricted to exploring what Rampton (1995) calls the more *figurative* uses of code alternation, i.e. how Catalan and Spanish voices were appropriated and reaccentuated to evoke particular contexts, characters or ideological perspectives. There is one more question to address: what led people to assume one language as their main narrative voice in particular situations and what were the consequences of these choices?

The analysis provided so far may have fostered the impression that linguistic choices depended on the cultural associations that each language appeared to convey. From this perspective, one might be led to believe, because of its unmasculine overtones, that Catalan would be very little used in the peer-group context, and least of all by men. Of course, this would be a very simplistic and overstretched conclusion. One did not appear feminine because one spoke Catalan. There were many ways of speaking it and many different and even contradictory meanings that could be constructed and conveyed in a conversation in Catalan. Moreover, amongst the Trepas, most native speakers and users of Catalan were men, while the Rambleros women did not speak Catalan in the peer-group, no matter how conventionally feminine they were and how positive they felt about the language. People were also aware that there were Catalan music groups of all styles and that Catalan could also be spoken while appropriating many elements of argot or youth slang, as happens in extract 74 above (see Saladrigas 1997).

I will therefore explain the processes of language choice amongst the Rambleros and the Trepas (mainly the Trepas, as the Rambleros had much less room for choice, as I will show), that is, the procedures they used to decide what language to speak with whom and when. I will also try to explain the origins of what we might call "conventions of language choice" in Barcelona. I will argue that the social meanings of Catalan and Spanish as described earlier can influence the way in which people applied, interpreted and negotiated these conventions. Conversely, I will also try to show that these conventions had an important (probably more important, as I see it) bearing on the social values attached to each language; that is, because the general conventions of language choice discouraged the effective use of Catalan in the peer-group context, it was through Spanish that people eventually developed the expressive resources, genres and voices that fitted the values and meanings associated with youth culture. Therefore, my hypothesis is that there is a dialectical process here (or a vicious circle, from the perspective of people involved in promoting the Catalan language) that tends to centrifugate the social spaces and symbolic resources of the Catalan language.

Language choice is also an interesting issue to explore because it is an aspect of social behavior that is subject to serious constraints and hence it will be relevant to the discussion in chapter 7 about the relation between social action and social structures. Here I will analyze how the Rambleros and the Trepas organized their language choices in their everyday lives. I will compare their declared choices with their actual ones, and I will also analyze the types of explanations and justifications they gave for their linguistic behavior. We will see that there was a significant degree of diversity in all these aspects.

This chapter is divided into two sections. In the first section, I will briefly summarize the political and academic debates that have taken place in Catalonia in relation to language choice. This summary will also help to understand the wider context in which the linguistic practices of the Rambleros and the Trepas were inserted, which will be analyzed in the second section.

1. Language choice in Catalonia: a political issue

The way in which language choice has been treated by Catalan sociolinguists owes much to the early works of Lluís Aracil (1965, 1979), who developed, together will Lafont (1977) and others the so-called *language conflict* perspective (see Martin-Jones 1989). Aracil's proposals emerged as a critique of the *diglossia* perspective (Ferguson 1959; Fishman 1964, 1967) and its excessively consensual and static view of societal bilingualism. The *diglossia* perspective viewed language choice as the reflection of common and relatively stable norms that ascribed linguistic varieties to particular social domains (such as formal and informal domains). In contrast, Aracil argued that the norms and ideologies associated with language choice were the product of historical and political struggles (see also Vallverdú 1980). From his perspective, bilingualism was always unstable because the two languages underwent continuous displacements as to the social domains (*àmbits d'ús*) where they were spoken, thus causing language shift (when the local variety eventually lost all the social spaces where it was used) or language normalization (when the local variety managed to recover lost ground).

In Catalonia, Aracil's model made much more sense to local activists, sociolinguists and language planners in the 1970s and 1980s than the politically aseptic *diglossia* perspective. This is why most Catalan sociolinguistics oriented their work towards the identification of existing and shifting trends in the patterns of language choice. In this section, I will review some of the most widely known studies. This will serve two purposes: a) to give the reader a detailed picture of the sociolinguistic situation of Barcelona and its latest developments with regard to language choice in face-to-face interaction, and b) to provide a critique to some of the approaches which, in my view, present conceptual and methodological problems that I have tried to solve in my work.

In the early seventies, the political persecution of the Catalan language had made Spanish the only language used in public arenas. This factor, coupled with the large numbers of Spanish-speaking immigrants, had turned Catalan into an almost private language only used amongst native speakers, most of whom could not even write it. For instance, Calsamiglia and Tusón (1980, 1984) and Turell (1984) found that the use of Spanish predominated among linguistically mixed groups of teenagers and amongst a group of shopfloor workers in Barcelona respectively. The main reason for this was the Catalan speakers' tendency to accommodate. This is why, after Catalan was reestablished as an official language, the Catalan government and other voluntary organizations launched public campaigns to promote so-called *passive bilingualism*. Passive bilingualism consisted of doing bilingual conversations (instead of accommodating to Spanish) when interacting with Spanish speakers who understood Catalan but did not feel confident enough to speak it (which was the most usual case at the time).[21]

In this context, many sociolinguists sought to assess whether the new language policies launched in the 1980s effectively led to changes in the conventions of language choice in face-to-face interaction. Tusón (1985a, 1990) observed the linguistic behavior of small children and university students in classroom contexts where Catalan was used as a medium of instruction. She found that many Spanish speakers were beginning to use Catalan, although Spanish still predominated in the informal domains. During the eighties, it became clear that Spanish speaking children were learning and using Catalan at school so that many of them were able to use it in the peer-group context as well. However, this was by no means the common trend. The quantitative studies done by Bastardas (1985, 1986) and by Erill et al. (1992) in a number of secondary schools confirmed that Catalan speakers still tended to accommodate to a much greater extent than Spanish speakers. Only a tiny minority of them declared that they practiced passive bilingualism. Subsequent studies carried out by Boix (1989) amongst a group of youth club trainees, Pujolar (1991b, 1993) amongst a group of university students and Vila (1996) amongst small children attending an immersion school, confirmed these findings.

By 1989 a debate emerged in the Catalan media on whether bilingual conversations were desirable or even possible. In an electronic call-in survey on a television program, 26% of the callers said they agreed with passive bilingualism, whereas 20% said they disagreed. The remaining expressed neither agreement nor disagreement. (Vallverdú 1989; callers did not have the opportunity to justify their vote). The program triggered a debate in which various politicians, journalists, writers and sociolinguists engaged in a public discussion sometimes involving accounts of personal experiences. Vallverdú (ibid.) declared that he did conduct bilingual conversations, but that they were not "real" conversations, that is, they were service encounters with taxi drivers, waiters, shop assistants and the like. Bastardas (1991), in a paper written for an international sociolinguistic symposium, considered that this was the general trend amongst Catalan speakers and that people tended to give up bilingual conversations in the so-called private domain, with friends or relatives (see also Marí 1989).[22] However, other commentators claimed that they practiced passive bilingualism to a full extent and argued that it was both possible and desirable (Moll 1989; Rahola 1989).

Many Catalan sociolinguists and language planners feel despondent about the matter and tend to acknowledge defeat in this struggle to promote the colloquial use of Catalan. However, beyond these considerations, it is also useful to discuss the interpretive frameworks that have been used to study the phenomenon of language choice. Most influential in this respect has been the study done by Woolard (1989) on language and ethnicity in Barcelona. Woolard pointed out that language was the main criterion for ethnic classification or ethnic boundary marking in everyday life. The norms of language choice served to distinguish the *Catalans* from the *Castilians* or *immigrants*, an ethnic distinction which also carried an underlying class division. From this perspective, Catalan identity was associated with the use of Catalan in *in-group arenas,* whereas Spanish could be used in *inter-group* communication. Language use was thus associated with loyalty to one's own group. In a matched-guise experiment, Woolard also showed that, in a group formed by Catalan-speaking and Spanish-speaking students, individuals developed negative attitudes not so much against people belonging to the other ethnolinguistic group, but against people of one's own linguistic group who used *the other* language. Woolard also observed that this situation created interesting contradictions in many contexts:

> The bilingual faced with a Castilian monolingual is confronted with a quandary. To speak different languages would be to give the appearance of conflict or distance in the immediate interchange; to speak Catalan with those who are less proficient is to force them to demonstrate incompetence and to be in a "one down" position; but to speak Castilian is to exclude the Castilian speaker from the inner cir-

cle of the solidary –and economically dominant– Catalan group. (Woolard 1989: 82)

This is why, as Woolard also noticed, the conventions of language choice were often challenged by people associated with pro-Catalan leftist groups, where many Spanish speakers sought to learn and use Catalan and where bilingual conversations were also encouraged.

Woolard's idea that language choice served to construct and maintain ethnic boundaries and loyalties was later taken up by Emili Boix, who published a book with the suggestive title *Triar no és Trair* 'to choose is not to betray' (1989, 1993). Boix observed the linguistic behavior of young people who were involved in a training course for youth club leaders. Such courses are normally organized by institutions with a strong commitment to promoting the Catalan language. In this context, Boix found many Spanish speakers using Catalan, although Catalan speakers still tended to accommodate more often than Spanish speakers. He concluded that language choice had become much less problematic in this new generation of young people: "In informal interactions, young people in Barcelona may want to be categorized in terms of interpersonal relations rather than in terms of inter-group relations" (Boix 1990: 218).

Boix argued that the strong feelings of ethnolinguistic loyalty found by Woolard had diminished. Young people had generally developed linguistically mixed networks of friends, so that they avoided a politicization of linguistic issues. In this context, bilingual conversations were avoided precisely because they were interpreted as a form of political struggle and as a way of making ethnolinguistic identities visible in social interaction. In my own study amongst university students, it emerged that many people perceived passive bilingualism as a form of confrontation (Pujolar 1991b). Most people assumed as natural that conversations should be monolingual, whereby bilingual conversations were interpreted as a disagreement or as a strategy to pressurize Spanish speakers.

Additionally, Boix pointed out that Catalan was ceasing to be a mark of group membership because it was used by Spanish speakers as well (1989, 1993). Another matched-guise experiment conducted by Woolard and Gahng (1990) also supported these findings. However, it was clear that Spanish still predominated in ethnolinguistically mixed contexts, which meant that the campaigns had not worked and that the process of language shift had not been stopped. Bastardas (1991) considered that three main factors limited people's ability to change linguistic conventions: 1) the fact that linguistic behavior is unconscious to a great extent; 2) the fact that it concerns practical issues of communication such as dealing with limited language abilities, ease of expression and accidental misunderstandings; and 3) the fact that people worry about the way their behavior will be interpreted and judged by the interlocutors.

At this point, it seems that Catalan sociolinguists have come to a dead end. The policies do not work and there does not seem to be a way forward. It is thus time to take stock and to consider whether some important issues have been left out and whether we can develop a more sophisticated understanding of language choice. One of the issues that have been somehow lost on the way is Woolard's point that ethnolinguistic struggles reflected and contributed to class struggles. This is part of a general tendency to approach the field as if it consisted of Spanish-speakers and Catalan speakers only and as if social actors were not involved in struggles that had to do with other aspects of their social identity, such as class, gender, age and so on. A second problem has to do with how conclusions are phrased in many studies, particularly with the way in which some research results are presented as reflecting general trends. The quote below is representative of these theoretical and methodological problems. It comes from a survey amongst secondary students in the town of Sabadell (similar problems can be found in more "qualitative" studies, however). Erill et al. found that *only* 6 % of students reportedly maintained Catalan in interactions with Spanish-speaking peers (1992: 80). They concluded the following:

> We face, therefore, a usual practice that drives many to an obvious betrayal in linguistic terms –according to some authors– although to many it may be rooted in an unconscious practice that has been appropriated in tune with the requirements termed as *good manners* by a given society; these good manners not concealing anything else but a socializing strategy deployed in order to coerce language choice in actual communication. (ibid.: 101)

Now this somewhat baroque explanation (it may be useful to consult the original text in the appendix) assumes that language choice is fundamentally a question of ethnolinguistic loyalty (a *betrayal* in this case, even when it is hidden under other considerations, such as politeness or interactional routine) and also that the importance of a particular linguistic practice can be reduced to its numbers or percentages. Thus, the authors do not take into account the interesting fact that, in Sabadell, Catalan is the family language of only 31.6 % of the students (plus 4.7 % who come from bilingual families; ibid.: 74). This raises the percentage of "maintainers" to 16.5 % of those who have Catalan as a family language. Still, of course, a minority. However, Erill et al. do not consider the impact that this minority produces by openly flouting common conventions of "proper" demeanor. In my study amongst university students (Pujolar 1991b), one participant told me that, although they were a minority, Catalanist people had played a key role in establishing Catalan as the predominant language in that context. This was because, by always speaking Catalan, they had caused other people to reassess the linguistic backgrounds and preferences of others at the time when they were making first contacts and early acquaintances. For instance, if somebody had the opportunity of witnessing a given individual speaking Catalan to someone else, this somebody would then be able to establish whether the individual in question could or should be addressed in Catalan in future encounters. On the other hand, the explanation given above does not consider that teenagers may operate, in their daily lives, with forms of classification other than ethnolinguistic membership to organize and make sense of their linguistic behavior.

To consider that predominant patterns are the only significant patterns prevents us from appreciating that conventions of language choice are subject to *struggles* and that it is in these struggles, in their stakes and connections with other social struggles, that we will find what is of interest both to the language planner and the social scientist. The problem is similar to the one identified by researchers on gender in relation to the practice of generalizing out of the hegemonic forms of masculinity (see the introduction to Part 1). Thus it may well be that for many young people it is more important to make friends than to be "Catalan" or "Castilian". It may well be that concerns about politeness are used as an excuse or a strategy to hide other issues. However, what is of interest is to explore in what way the meaning of linguistic practices is negotiated and legitimized in particular social contexts; to explore to what extent and in what ways social actors can effectively perform these negotiations; to consider whether these practices reflect struggles in terms of class, gender and ethnic relations. Only from this perspective will we be able to find out how alternative practices are made possible, whether these practices may or may not lead to social changes and, finally, whether policies can be developed that are really sensitive to the conditions in which social actors lead their lives.

In this chapter, I will therefore seek to address the issue of language choice from this perspective, that is, by focusing on the diversity of practices and discourses that existed in the context studied. This means that I will basically deal with the local experience of language choice amongst the Rambleros and the Trepas. Later on, in chapter 7, I will discuss the ways in which the practices analyzed were connected with wider processes of struggle in terms of class, ethnicity and gender.

2. Language choice amongst the Rambleros and the Trepas

In this section, I will try to map out how the members of the groups made use of the Catalan and Spanish languages in their daily lives. In order to trace the workings of the processes of language choice, I have had to rely extensively on people's accounts. There is probably no other alternative for a researcher joining an already settled group where communicative practices are more or less well established. The Rambleros and the Trepas had already established which language they spoke to whom, so that the processes of negotiation involved in these choices were no longer visible. The strength of Boix' (1989) research lies precisely in the fact that he conducted research with a group of young people who had just met for a training course. Some researchers have stressed that people's reports about their language choices do not necessarily coincide with their actual behavior (Bourhis 1984). This happens very often in Catalonia as well. Therefore, in my analysis, I have had to consider very carefully how particular statements and accounts should be interpreted. In any case, I also possessed a wealth of data from my direct experience as a participant observer that helped a lot to interpret people's declared behaviour.

It is often said that language choice is difficult to study because many people come to switch languages in a fairly unreflective way. In my earlier study, many respondents declared that linguistic accommodation had simply become an automatic habit devoid of any meaningful intention. While I would not deny this idea, I will obviously resist any move to treat it as an explanation, as it is precisely what needs explaining. As Bastardas (and some of my respondents) pointed out, these linguistic habits can, after all, be modified at greater or lesser cost (Bastardas 1996; Pujolar 1991b). The questions still remain about the assumptions and conditions under which such habits are established and maintained.

I have divided this section into three parts. The first is devoted to a discussion of the issue of linguistic competence, in particular how it contributes to the framing of language choice as a question of face saving. In the second part, I analyze the established convention that people must be consistent in the language they speak with each person. In these first subsections, I will describe the main patterns of language choice in Catalonia as a whole, and I will draw comparisons with the forms of language choice I found in the groups when I did my fieldwork. In the third subsection, I will consider how different forms of gender, as analyzed in part 1, gave rise to significantly different patterns of language choice amongst the people I studied.

2.1. Who had the choice?

All the Rambleros (11) had Spanish as their family language, although 3 of them had one parent who was a native speaker of Catalan. From what I gathered from various sources, 7 group members (including the previous three) were able to speak Catalan if they needed to. The rest generally stressed the fact that they spoke it with difficulty or awkwardness. Amongst the relatively regular members of the Trepas, half (7) had Spanish, 5 Catalan and 2 both languages as their family language, although the latter two were treated by others as speakers of Catalan. Two Trepas had a Catalan-speaking parent who did not normally use Catalan within the family and were thus treated as Spanish speakers. All the Trepas could speak Spanish fluently. Catalan was spoken with fluency by at least 11 of them, whom I saw having long conversations in this language. Another member of the group was reportedly able to speak it if she needed to. The remaining two claimed that they had significant difficulties when they spoke it. Nevertheless, I often felt that some people underestimated their linguistic competence. My impressions gathered at hearing them switching, quoting and dramatizing voices led me to believe that they would probably have spoken it quite well (considering that it was not their first language), had they not been very sensitive to producing hesitations and mistakes. In any case, everybody could understand Catalan and could participate in conversations where Catalan was used.

Be that as it may, the use of Catalan and Spanish was not directly determined by any variable such as fluency, family background, social class, gender, schooling, setting, etc. The spaces occupied by both languages, the meanings conveyed by them or expressed through them, were the product of complex processes embedded in the social situations where they were used, and which included both issues of fluency and of the ritual implications of language choice.

2.1.1. Linguistic competence and embarrassment

When I inquired about how they managed with Catalan, most Spanish speakers pointed out that their competence in the language was unsatisfactory, or at least significantly inferior to their Spanish. This was said both by people who rarely used Catalan and by people who used it occasionally or even often. Participants pointed to their inadequate competence as the main rationale behind their linguistic choices. Here it is particularly important to bear in mind that, when facing the questions of a 'conspicuously Catalan' interviewer, interviewees were particularly interested in dispelling any political reading of their views. And this in spite of the fact that I formatted the questions very carefully not to invite interviewees to take it in this way.[23] Silvia's explanations illustrate this very clearly:

Extract 75 [Trepas]

Silvia: Well I speak Castilian, almost always · · I have no problems about C- about speaking Catalan, but sometimes it's difficult, right? Depending on which words because I am not used to speaking it, right? Well, not used · · If I- If I have to speak it, I do, I mean. It is not that I prefer to be spoken to in Castilian. Not at all, it makes no difference to me, right? Buut since I was little I have always spoken in Castilian at home, right? My mother, my father is from Girona right? My mother is from, from Málaga, right? Therefore my mother always spoke in Castilian and the same to us. And nevertheless with my uncles and aunts, then we speak Catalan, right? My (father) well (is) the same. And · then, with other people, it depends. If I speak Catalan, then I speak Catalan. If I speak Castilian, then · in Castilian but · I feel much more comfortable speaking in Castilian, right? Because · I can express myself better · · But · it's not- not for any other reason.

Joan: and at school, did it not pose a problem, >when it was introduced?

Silvia: <(when-) · not at all, never. Since I was little already, when I started having classes of Catalan, well, in primary school, right?

Silvia was clearly insisting that she had no prejudices against the Catalan language. Additionally, she was grounding her justifications in factors which were beyond her personal control and responsibility, i.e. her linguistic competence which was a product of her family and social environment. It is worth bearing in mind that some Catalanist people do not accept this as a justification. One recurrent line within this frame was that speaking Catalan involved the need for laborious, tiresome, ad hoc translation:

Extract 76 [Trepas]

Magda: It is not that I cannot speak it, because I do, I can speak it. But it so happens that I think in Castilian, because I am speaking in Catalan and I am thinking in Castilian, because I keep translating and I say words that, because I do not know how to translate them, I [have to] change them? No. I want to say the word I am thinking of · And it is not because I do not want them to speak Catalan to me.

Similar views were expressed by others. It is significant that Silvia (in extract 75 above) had a bilingual family background, similar to four others who were considered to be Spanish speakers. Jaume, on the other hand, with a bilingual family background as well, was usually identified as a Catalan speaker, but insisted that he did not have any linguistic preferences:

Extract 77 [Trepas]

Jaume: *with her* · with her I speak in Castilian, right? With Chimo I speak Catalan, with you Catalan and sometimes if anyone begins in Castilian, [then] in Castilian. I haven't got a language · of my own, right? to speak, I mean · · I can express myself as I wish in Castilian and in Catalan

This asymmetry is also reflected in the fact that people of Catalan-only background did not express any qualms about speaking Spanish. They simply indicated what language they spoke with whom. Three speakers of Catalan actually pointed out that they had more difficulties writing Catalan than writing Spanish. In their peer-group activities, I felt that they spoke Spanish more than Catalan.

From the point of view of face-to-face interaction, insufficient linguistic competence can cause what we might call logistical or processing difficulties. If we compare speaking a second language with learning how to drive, or with driving a new car, we are faced with a situation of procedural awkwardness. We have to pay unusual attention to mechanisms and moves which we usually take for granted. We are bound to produce false starts, hesitations and unwanted moves. Given the particularly rich character of peer-group talk, where one is supposed to produce skilled jokes, ironies, keyings, dramatizations, voice re-accentuations, and so on, it is understandable that people want to exploit their linguistic abilities to the limit. Additionally, a faulty performance can be face-threatening, that is, it can make the actor be seen as somehow inadequate, morally inferior, not up to the requirements of participation in everyday social intercourse. Natalia, in her interview, revealed that she spoke Spanish when addressed in Catalan by a teacher "because this is my way of defending myself". The Spanish speakers in my study often said that speaking Catalan made them feel anxious and embarrassed. Some had vivid memories of their experience at school, when a teacher singled them out to answer a question in the classroom before their schoolmates. Mateo's story is probably the most telling:

Extract 78 [Rambleros]

Mateo: Oh Christ! What ridicule, when they made me speak it. · I did not want to, on most of the occasions the situation was that (xx) that I would avoid coming out to- · and sometimes · whatever exercise, like this, I used to say: "No, no, I haven't done it", just for the sole reason of not coming out there · to make a fool of myself.

Pablo, for instance, claimed that, because there was no punitive enforcement, that he simply ignored the teacher and spoke Spanish, like Natalia above. Natalia also reported the deep anxiety she felt in the presentation phase of a training course, where all the participants introduced themselves in Catalan. After she managed to muddle through the situation, she found out that most of the other trainees were Spanish speakers like her. Paula reported feeling embarrassed in some situations at work, where she sometimes decided to remain silent. Irene said that she liked to say things in Catalan (probably isolated phrases or expression), but she said that she only did it when she knew that there was no Catalan speaker around. Clara went as far as to say that she had embraced anarchism as a teenager partly because it freed her from feeling any obligation to speak Catalan. The idea of this well known sector of Spanish-speaking anarchists in Barcelona is that anarchism proposes the constitution of a universal culture based on working-class interests and which supersedes national and regional cultural allegiances. Thus,· as anarchist subjects renounce their culture of origin, they are under no obligation to show loyalty or to integrate into any other. In linguistic terms, this meant that one could keep on speaking Spanish and not feel guilty about it.

Extract 79 [Trepas]

*Clara: I realised that- right? that what I was doing was · was to use, well · well, a
story-line just because of the embarrassment, · right? well, about speaking a
language I have never spoken. (So what I did) was to get the embarrassment
out, and that was it (I mean, it is not) · it's not throwing the idea out. I was very
aware · of the reason why I used the (story) why I was an anarchist, yeah? [...]
If it's for embarrassment, well, either you say it is embarrassment · · or just kick
out the embarrassment · · · I mean that I didn't "see the light".*

Just as with any other kind of failure, linguistic stumbles could be used
as a pretext for mockery and public amusement. Particularly amongst the
Rambleros, where face-threats were a common sport, anecdotes of this type
abounded in the group's narratives. Paula said that she felt very closely
monitored by her boyfriend as she ventured to speak Catalan to a waiter,
which she interpreted as him waiting for an exploitable mistake. When
people sought opportunities to speak Catalan, they took care to choose the
appropriate context to do so. Natalia and Magda (both Spanish speakers of
the Trepas) had a short private conversation in Catalan because Natalia
wished to practice the language. Salva said that he spoke Catalan with
Ayats, amongst other things, because "he is not going to laugh at me" if he
made linguistic mistakes.

2.1 2. Who sets the standards?

Salva's comment raises the important issue that the expected standards of
(linguistic) competence are socially negotiable. Indeed, when people judge
the appropriacy of a performance, they do it by reference to some kind of
ideal model. There is evidence (see below) that the predominant model of
competence for these young people was that of the "correct", standard, unitary language. Bakhtin (1981), Grillo (1989) and Bourdieu (1991a) have
already argued that the standard language is used as an instrument of ideological and political unification and centralization. Of particular interest
here is Bourdieu's observation that the establishment of the "legitimate"
standard language after the French revolution reconstituted the way dialects, local varieties and particular styles were perceived, namely that anything different from the standard language was seen as a corrupted, faulty
version of it. He stresses the role of the school in imposing this linguistic
regime, which is also enforced by the requirements of the (national) labor
market.

This official or traditional conception of language use emerged in the explanations provided by many: Chimo, a Catalan speaker, said that he felt safer writing in Spanish, because in Catalan he was more likely to misspell, and misspellings were penalized at school with lower marks. One member of the Rambleros who had once produced a wrong Catalan expression was teased that she was "kicking the dictionary". Catalan teachers and speakers in general have always insisted that the Catalan language should be clean from Spanish borrowings, which are called *barbarismes*. Silvia said that she used some "*barbarismos*" in job interviews, but not too many. Laura reported, quite resentfully, being scorned by a Catalan speaker at school because the latter had identified a fault in her speech. She added, quite rightly, that Catalan speakers said "barbarisms" as well and were not laughed at.

Interestingly enough, Laura commented on another occasion on which she did not speak proper Spanish either when she was with the group, although she could if she wished to. Clearly, their "bad" Spanish was locally legitimized by the group's practices, whereas "bad" Catalan was seen as problematic. Therefore, Spanish-speaking people seeking to speak Catalan were always evaluated (like at school) on the basis of what they failed to achieve, rather than on what they *did* achieve. A more process oriented approach to language learning, and public initiatives to legitimate learner's Catalan could ease the pressures people feel on this account.[24] Indeed, I will show below that the Trepas who managed to overcome such problems, did so by redefining their own standards of linguistic competence.[25]

2.1.3. Saving face

In this situation, it is not surprising that many Catalan speakers, when facing a Spanish speaker, proceed to quickly do some face-saving, namely to indicate that the encounter can be safely carried out in Spanish. Such negotiations are more often than not conducted in a circumspect, unspoken, way. If the Spanish-speaking interlocutor appears in danger of getting exposed, the participants deploy strategies to prevent this from happening. Therefore, Catalan speakers often seek to act as if the choice of language was simply out of the question and as if it was only natural that the conversation should be carried out in Spanish. Patrícia, for example, said that she spoke Catalan in the meetings of her political group, but "if someone speaks to me in Castilian, I respond in Castilian", and similar assertions can be found for the other Catalan speaking members of the group, except for Aleix.

An important assumption here is that *communicative exchanges must be monolingual*, a point which is also corroborated in my previous research, where many defended this position explicitly (Pujolar 1991b). In this light, the choice of a language conveys an implicit request for the interlocutor to follow suit. Consequently, a person who is not particularly good at or willing to speak Catalan may feel this as an imposition. Patrícia reported that, in formal meetings, some Spanish-speaking women made an effort to use Catalan, but sometimes gave up; she said she ended up mixing the two languages as she tried to adapt to the changing choices of others. My interpretation of this was that maintaining Catalan might have been understood as a form of pressurizing.

It is therefore common for people to talk about language choice in terms of manners, politeness, civility and so on. Magda, of the Trepas, claimed that she used Catalan with old people "for respect", because they usually had difficulties with Spanish. Lola also declared that she used Catalan with young children and old persons from villages only because of their inadequate skills in Spanish. In my research amongst university students, many affirmed that maintaining Catalan was rude, an impolite thing to do (Pujolar 1991b). Indeed, both Magda and Silvia, while affirming that they did not mind being addressed in Catalan, said they also felt annoyed in situations where people actually did so, which they attributed to people's nationalist agendas. Magda reported on a hiking club where everybody spoke Catalan at first, until some members of the "*penya*" saw that it was better to speak Spanish with her.

It is, therefore, within this ideological frame that the person who maintains Catalan can be seen as a "rude" person who does not care about the face needs of the addressee. Although not everybody shares these views about the matter, it is something which Catalanists have to deal with in day-to-day exchanges. In my previous research (Pujolar 1991b), I found plenty of examples of stigmatization of Catalanists, similar to the stances conveyed by Silvia and Magda, and reported by Patrícia:

Extract 80 [Trepas]

Patrícia: I can't be bothered because, additionally, I do not really feel like starting to fight about the importance of Catalan because they'll send me to hell. · If I go to the school and I start saying that · th- they have to speak in Catalan because of this and that, they'll throw a brick at my head [She laughs]. · It is as they used to say: "*because feminists* do this and that" and what they may do is to throw a bottle at you. It is the same. Therefore, you'd better do it in some other way. So if it is about speaking Cat- you spe- you speak Catalan to them now and then [...]

This creates a complicated situation for Catalan speakers who seek to maintain Catalan. It is typical of Spanish speakers to invite Catalan speakers to use their own language as a way of displaying kindness. Practically all Spanish speakers in both groups did this to me. Nevertheless, my impression was that I was offered a right with the expectation that I would not really exercise it, as Catalans who do so are severely criticized, probably because they provide an interactional "reminder" of cultural differences, and of the idea that Spanish speakers should "integrate" into Catalan society by learning the language.

Another phenomenon seems to contradict the monolingual principle, but actually does not. In a conversation involving more than two participants, with speakers of various languages, it is perfectly alright to speak Catalan. In this sense, it is common to witness many bilingual conversations in Barcelona. However, this is done as long as Spanish speakers are not addressed in a way that makes them feel that they should respond in Catalan. Thus the common phenomenon arises of people switching languages as they move their gaze from one participant to another, a strategy which may be subject to variation if there is a high degree of trust or, of course, if failures of coordination occur (see Woolard 1989: 64). This phenomenon was very usual amongst the Trepas and it was reported by Patrícia in her interview.

It seems that, in the groups, Catalan speakers were not prepared to take risks while seeking to establish bonds of empathy and collusion amongst people of their own generation. Of course, the predisposition of people to do face saving for the audience may not be equally distributed. We already know that many Catalan speakers feel safe to maintain Catalan in service encounters with waiters and taxi drivers. Maybe this means that Catalan speakers feel that it is not so necessary to perform face-saving strategies with these types of person. Maybe this is why the professionals affected often react as if they were being insulted or shown disrespect. Woolard (1989), for instance, reports on an episode where a group of Catalan speakers incensed a Spanish-speaking waiter by simply placing their orders in Catalan. After all, do waiters and taxi drivers not deserve to be treated with politeness as well?

2.2. *"Don't mess me up!" (Stick to your choice!)*

The traditionally narrow approach to language has it that speaking involves a simple transfer of information. This has usually driven attention away from the more social and ideological aspects of language choice. A youth worker of the Rambleros' neighborhood once commented to me that, when one uses another language, one becomes almost a different person: "your voice may change and even your posture". I have discussed how people associated Catalan and Spanish with particular types of people and activities. In chapter 2 I also indicated that conversations between Catalan speaking Trepas appeared to point towards different forms of display of masculinity. These facts suggest that the choice of a language for an interpersonal relationship may constitute an important decision with regard to how this relationship will be managed. It seems inevitable that, when people choose a language, they also choose to an extent how they have to be understood, judged, and what can be expected of them. The issue seems to be quite subtle. Although it is not possible for me to show what difference it made to speak either Catalan or Spanish in this sense, and whether there were differences between men and women, one clear principle seemed to be operating for the groups I studied: *people were expected to maintain the language that they had established in a particular relationship.* In Catalonia in general, in the first encounters with a new acquaintance, people usually choose to speak one language or another depending on how participants assess the linguistic backgrounds and preferences of the interlocutors. Circumstantial factors also count, such as the language spoken by the person who makes the introductions or the language used in that particular social environment. After the first encounters, where there may be changes and hesitations, people tend to use one of the languages consistently (see Woolard 1989; Pujolar 1991b).

Goffman (1967) reminds us that the audiences of our face-to-face performances will expect us to present a relatively coherent face at least with regard to what they consider as situationally salient. In my data, there was plenty of evidence that people were expected to stick to their choices, whatever these were:

Extract 81 [Trepas]
Clara: Well, with Ayats [Salva] has always spoken Catalan. And one day, he
started to speak [it] to me that: "*Ei! Shhhh, stop it!*" [We laugh] *"(I'll give you)*
a couple of blows! (You can be) as militant as you like, but don't mess up with

me". Of course, because, above all, you, <u>you speak</u>, · more or less right? well, <u>how you have begun to speak with a person</u>. *Look I, I used to have a boyfriend who was · half gypsy, but I m- I met him speaking · in Catalan* [...] and we always spoke Catalan, because it wasn't · (right? yeah), *and · and when we spoke in Castilian, well, we couldn't.*

On another occasion, when I was talking with Clara and Patrícia, the latter addressed the former in Catalan possibly because her utterance was somehow connected to something she had been saying to me; and Clara told her off amiably.

Sociolinguists have rarely addressed this issue, although it is an almost universal feature of the everyday experience of bilinguals. This is probably because of the descriptive character of most research perspectives: the phenomenon itself is not very visible. The problem of finding evidence about stylistic choices (discussed in chapter 4) is very similar. This is why Boix (1993: 180) sought to conduct his ethnographic study in a setting where people were meeting for the first time so that he could gather data on explicit or visible negotiations of language choice. Gal (1979: 101–108) noticed that she could predict most of the time the language that was going to be used if she knew the persons involved. Heller (1985) discusses an interesting case in Montréal where she was involved in a conversation in French with a colleague in the presence of a conversation partner who did not understand French and who knew her as an Anglophone and his colleague as a Francophone. She points out as an explanation the fact that they had met in a work environment where one had to show commitment to speaking French and that they would "not risk damaging our own face or each other's with respect to our colleagues" (ibid.: 75). What Heller seems to imply here is that the two colleagues were torn between the need to project their *francophonie* in a consistent way and the need to display solidarity with regard to the monolingual Anglophone. Bastardas (1991: 104) refers to language choice as a "consolidated habit". In my previous research (Pujolar 1991b: 48–49, 66), 7 out of 8 interviewees also revealed that they resisted changes of choice. One of the interviewees affirmed that language was inextricably associated with the idea one had about a person in a comparable way to that person's name. They felt changes of choice to be "odd", "unnatural", although one of the Catalanist interviewees pointed out that choices could be changed if one wanted (and, in some cases, they reportedly were).

Clara's examples above suggest that she sometimes felt the need to socially enforce this "habit". Bearing this in mind, Patrícia said that she sought to establish Catalan at the early stages of getting to know somebody. Chimo, a Catalan speaker, reported on cases where he spoke Spanish with Catalan speakers because they had initially not been aware of each other's backgrounds. He said that, often, they would not change languages even after the discovery of this perceived incongruency. Patrícia, in extract 57, described a similar situation, but there she appeared to imply that the initial choice had been "corrected". The assumption that Catalan speakers should speak Catalan amongst themselves also appeared in my previous study (Pujolar 1991b). Chimo's story suggests that this association of the language with Catalan identity still remained, but that it was much weaker than in the past, at least in that context. Patrícia made another interesting observation on the matter. Here it may be useful to remind the reader that Patrícia was a Catalan speaker and that the interview was being conducted in Catalan:

Extract 82 [Trepas]
Patrícia: Once you have a lot of contact with a person-, for instance: I -with Clara- I begin talking in Catalan with her and it sounds faked [em sona fals] · · to talk to her in Cat- to have a conversation with her in Catalan. And for her m- for her it's the same.

Patrícia implied that changing language was almost like putting on a fabricated or a fictional character. A Spanish-speaking friend of mine, who had been working as a receptionist, told me that she usually felt very tense when she spoke Catalan with visitors and callers. She reported being afraid of being "discovered" because of some mistake or slight accent. This looks like a somewhat extreme case, where speaking Catalan was experienced as a kind of passing. This raises the question of the extent to which one is seen as a different person when one speaks in a different language. One would imagine that this varies in different cultures, types of people and even in different situations. Bastardas (1991: 106) tells the anecdote of government ministers being seen to adapt to Spanish on Catalan television, a potential threat to their Catalanist credentials. The incongruency is clearly in people's perceptions of how the minister should behave in public and in his capacity as such, i.e. as an example for all Catalans. In the groups I studied (and I would say in Catalonia in general), the stakes did not seem to be so high. The differences between both groups were significant, as most of the Trepas did not see speaking Catalan as something exceptional, whereas for most of the Rambleros it was. However, although some Rambleros were actively unsympathetic towards Catalan, they found it normal for people to speak it, for instance, at work. The Trepas appeared to be little concerned about the language any one person spoke to another within the group and in their presence. However, in some cases, to be addressed in the wrong language by the wrong person was experienced as problematic, even when the interactants involved might well speak that same language to a third group member. Somehow, most Trepas perceived that the language was not so much attached to a given individual, but to their own relationship with this individual.

During my fieldwork, I had the impression that these feelings of congruence or incongruence did not work in the same way for Catalan and for Spanish. Once, for instance, as Pepe introduced me to his brother, he engaged in conversation with me in Spanish, which was the language he used with his brother but not with me. It also appeared that the possibilities of keying opened the door to a more relaxed linguistic policy in peer-group talk. It was common for Pepe to address me in Spanish in jokes and dramatizations, occasions where the status of the speaking subject was ambiguous. As I argued in chapter 5 (section 2), most keyed and ironic voices were performed in Spanish, unless these voices were used in dramatizations and mockeries featuring characters who failed to display the locally legitimized forms of masculinity. This asymmetry between Catalan and Spanish voices had important consequences because keyings were a constant resource in peer-group talk, as I have argued in chapters 3 and 5. Keyings introduced an element of ambiguity where people could effectively establish *precedents* of choices different than their established ones. This might explain why people perceived that their speech patterns were a bit "messy':

Extract 83 [Trepas]

Guille: I don't know, me, with Edu, for instance, who is a guy, right? with whom · ·
more or less, we get along, like, quite good, right? And I start to speak with him
in Catalan, and I end up speaking in Castilian [he laughs] and, at the beginning,
no. At the beginning it didn't happen to me. At the beginning: in Catalan, right?
But later, because we mix, right? with more people, well, or [because] you are
explaining something and, · you start with a person to speak in Castilian
because you are used to speaking to her in Castilian, and all of a sudden you
change into Catalan, right? But it is that, I am not even aware of it, right? · I
don't know. I think that we speak a bit of everything [i.e. both languages].

It was probably a result of this asymmetry of voices that I had the impression that Spanish was always taking more space than one would have expected, that is, taking into account only who was supposed to speak what to whom. There was also the interesting fact that Pepe and Ayats, who spoke Catalan when I met them, had somehow shifted to Spanish a year later. They did not provide a convincing explanation for this shift. My own impression was that it was caused by a combination of these factors: they engaged in keyings very often and also spoke most of the time when other Spanish speakers were present. As I witnessed the beginning of this process, I had the feeling that the Catalan speaker (Ayats) was consciously and subtly provoking it. To find the process concluded after a few months confirmed my earlier suspicions. Ayats may have felt out of place in many situations where he was the only person being spoken to in Catalan. It is interesting that an explicit renegotiaton of language choice was avoided. It could be claimed that this is just an isolated, unrepresentative case. But it is quite consistent with what I have been discussing so far. It is conceivable that two people might shift from Spanish to Catalan as well, but I would be surprised if this was done other than by making a conscious, explicit decision, as I illustrate below.

2.3. Language choice and identity

Apart from the very general principles explained so far, there were significant differences in the way people organized their use of the two languages. From the early stages of my fieldwork, I realised that gender seemed to have a very close relationship with people's linguistic attitudes and choices. This relationship was not easy to grasp, because the patterns did not really appear divided along sex lines, i.e. between men and women. It was after I managed to conceptualize gender in a more critical way that I became convinced that the relationship was analytically relevant. It is probably not surprising that the connection between linguistic attitudes and gender is so clear. Given that gender is such an important factor to understand key elements of youth culture, it is unavoidable that it constitutes to a great extent the way bilingualism is experienced in such contexts. This is why this subsection on the different patterns of bilingual practice has been divided according to the types of gender described in part 1.

2.3.1. Language choice and simplified masculinity

I have already indicated that the Rambleros made no use of Catalan other than in dramatizations and keyings (some of which, incidentally, could be quite long and extend across various turns). This state of affairs could be considered as simply natural and obvious, as they were all Spanish speakers and one would expect them to use the language they mastered best. Nevertheless, we should not overlook the various ways in which some members of this group contributed to maintaining or protecting this linguistic arrangement. Situations where Catalan could or should be used were common. Let us look at some examples:

Extract 84 [Rambleros]

One day, with the Rambleros, we entered a café and we started ordering some soft drinks and coffee. A couple of members of the group ordered their drinks first in Spanish to the waiter. The waiter answered back and asked for details in Catalan. Then two other members of the group, a man and a woman, switched to Catalan to make their orders thus accommodating to the language of the waiter. Then Luis turned to the woman and made a censoring comment for her use of Catalan. [From fieldnotes]

We could call this type of action *policing*. It has connections with the policing reported in chapter 4 with regard to the use of excessively formal language, and it has also connections with what Heller (1994) calls "border patrolling", as it served to set up and maintain a symbolic boundary that established the peer-group as a Spanish-only territory. It is worth pointing out, however, that only Luis and Pablo seemed to have an interest in creating and keeping this boundary. In their respective interviews, they made their anti-Catalan feelings very clear. Other group members, and particularly the women, went in the opposite direction. However, the strategy probably had the effect of discouraging group members to speak Catalan in some occasions. I witnessed a few episodes similar to the one reported above. On another occasion, a woman had decided to practice some Catalan because it was good for her job. She had the idea of offering a bite of her sandwich to her friends by saying "*vols?*" 'would you like some?' When she offered to Pablo, he responded with a visible scowl. Another similar incident happened in a bar where our room was full of people singing songs together. One of the women got told off for singing along with a Catalan pop song. Also, Andrés once told a joke in Catalan. When he saw that people did not laugh (probably because they did not see the joke (I didn't either)), he felt he had to justify why he had told it in Catalan by arguing that the joke had to be in Catalan because this was what made it funny.

These reactions towards the use of Catalan were always directed at "plain" uses of Catalan, never at keyings and dramatizations (funny voices, ironies, citations). In the group discussion, a couple announced that they had been talking in Catalan one night as they were having dinner together. The man, though, was very quick to point out that they had done it *"por cachondeo"* 'for fun'. This is an extract from the interview with one of the men who had"anti-Catalan "anti-Catalan"" beliefs:

Extract 85 [Rambleros]

Luis: It's that it's never gone down [meaning that it was difficult for him to learn Catalan at school], *and the more · difficult something gets for me, the more I detest it, right? [...] It has never pleased me, Catalan, nor- · · I- I understand it, sometimes I speak it, but I don't- · It can be said that I hate everything Catalan* [Naughty laughter], *in a few words. Some things. · Everything that has anything to do with fanatisms, like the Barcelona [football club], or, I mean, like-*

A waiter chipping in: (this has got nothing to do with it), you like "Catalanas" [Catalan women] more than Catalan.

Luis: That's also true [I laugh] · · · *Catalan women, yes.*

The two people who most strongly opposed Catalan were precisely the ones who presented the most visible features of simplified masculinity described in chapter 3: verbal aggression, displays of self-sufficiency, a stronger stylized accent. However, this connection between simplified masculinity and opposition to Catalan was not straightforward. First, a third person said that he disliked Catalan but did not match this description (although he did not express this attitude in an active way, as the others did). Secondly, not all people subscribing to simplified masculinity were unsympathetic towards Catalan (it was two out of four in my data).

The rejection of Catalan was commonly grounded on the argument that Catalan was "imposed" at school:

Extract 86 [Rambleros]

Pablo: I don't like Catalan. I don't know, · · I mean, you have to learn it because you are in Catalonia, but it's simply, I mean, as if they forced you to. · And because I don't like to be forced [to do anything] well, maybe this is why I don't like it. · Well just like Latin. I find Latin disgusting, · because they forced me, I mean...

Similar views were expressed by Luis. They might have originated in the political arguments of the early eighties, where some political groups argued that Catalan had to be just an optional subject, instead of being introduced as the medium of instruction. It is also interesting that this anti-Catalan stripe was never framed in political terms:

Extract 87 [Rambleros]

Luis: Teachers [who were] very obsessed [about it], who said the typical thing:
[Putting on a throaty voice] "because with Franco we had a hard time, now that
we can, then, now in Catalan, now in Catalan." · And (what) is our fault in all
this, man; just leave us alone!.

In the group discussion, Luis also rejected a political motivation by saying that he "did not feel Spanish".

In contrast to this position, there were also the Rambleros men who said they "feel Catalan" and who now and then presented evidence of positive feelings towards Catalan things, such as the Catalan television channel or some music groups. Simplified masculinity, therefore, seemed to *open the possibility* of adopting negative stances towards Catalan, but it did not necessarily lead to them:

Extract 88 [Rambleros]

Ricardo: It's what I [always] say. I I-, (I mean) if you were, I mean with- · with
people who speak Catalan all day, well, you would end up speaking Catalan. ·
(what happens here) okay, here we take the piss out of it · and all that, er- "this
word comes across funny eer-, and the rest of it". · (x) To me, it pleases me e- ·
and I think that I am one of the few whom Catalan pleases, I mean no- · I mean
I don't speak it for the fact that (it makes me-) · I don't know. But it pleases me,
it pleases me to hear a conversation in Catalan [...] Well and, like Pablo and I
don't know who else, who don't- it seems that it doesn't please them, Catalan.
To me it does please me. (x) It is so that it does noot- · Well, I do (x) with the
odd customer. It happens to me the same as with Andrés, because we are
waiters, well · well sometimes, well, you do speak Catalan, right? Even if you
put your foot in it, right?

Two interesting observations can be made on the basis of this extract. First, the issue is clearly presented in terms of personal preference, a constitutive feature of the Rambleros' local order of discourse (see 5.1). I also remember the Rambleros men spontaneously talking about whether they felt Catalan. Some did and some did not, but their different positions did not bring about any discussion, as it was seen as a personal matter. Secondly, Ricardo mentioned in his interview the Catalan *funny voices* I described in 6.2. He pointed out that he could participate in jokes about Catalan just for the fun of it, but that this did not imply that he did not feel positive about this language. This is a clear indication that such voices were always ambivalent in the way people perceived their significance, as happens with many sexist or racist practices. Ricardo was prepared to make fun of Catalan and of at least some types of Catalan characters, but he did not feel that these practices implied that he had some personal or political feelings against Catalan. This means that the legitimacy of these practices within the group could be sustained precisely because their implications with regard to political loyalties were unclear, even when some members might have had an interest in promoting these jokes because of their anti-Catalan feelings.

An additional illustration of this point was that the funny voices came perceptibly more often than not from people who claimed to feel positive about Catalan, including women. With Ricardo, for instance, I recorded a long keyed conversation in Catalan which was meant to be taken in jest. On the basis of my intuitive competence of the rules of the game, I also produced anecdotes, jokes and sayings originating in Catalan quarters and which were similar in character to theirs (sexual innuendo, ridiculing of public authority figures, often Catalan ones). These, often voiced in Catalan, were generally well understood and well received, and I felt they created a kind of complicity, as if the existence of a Catalan voice similar to their own overruled any anti-Catalan concern.

In terms of language choice, and as far as I could make out from my observations and from my informants' reports, good or bad feelings towards Catalan did not result in significantly different patterns of language use amongst those subscribing to simplified masculinities. People who worked as waiters or shop assistants said that they had to use Catalan now and then, but they apparently did so as little as possible because they felt very keenly the risk of exposure. The same can be said of women crossers. The two Trepas' women crossers reportedly avoided speaking Catalan as much as they could, sometimes even in work situations where it would clearly be much wiser to use it. In the interviews, these women asserted their right to speak Spanish. Another Trepas woman avoided using Catalan as well, though she presented no evidence of crossing. She justified herself on the basis of her absolute helplessness and her feeling of insecurity.

There are several good reasons to believe that the basic tenets of simplified masculinity played a very important role in matters of language choice. First of all, there was the question of coping with the sense of inadequacy and embarrassment involved in speaking a language with difficulty. I have said that the Rambleros men were especially protective of their faces, particularly because teasing and face threats were central to the interaction rituals of the group. Indeed, in the extract shown above, Luis was frank enough to trace his rejection of Catalan to the frustration experienced at school. While some members were prepared to acknowledge this, others appeared to have turned it into a symbol of defiance against injustice. They did not know Catalan because they did not want to.

Secondly, the logistics of speaking a second language might have imposed very important restrictions on the forms of self-presentation promoted in the group. These consisted of ways of handling oneself with emphasized naturalness, casualness, relaxedness. To speak Catalan would have meant to accept a certain artificiality and slowness. Slowness would have meant that much of the apparent "magic" of performances could be lost. To give an impression of artificiality would have been at odds with people who presented their way of speaking as something given, rather than something they had constructed.

Thirdly, another language is not simply another "code", i.e. an alternative way of conveying a message. All speech forms come with many associations, charged with meanings pointing in many directions, imposing gestures, a vocal style, a tone which needs to be appropriated, reaccentuated, reshaped. In this sense, all these verbal aggressions, the repertoire of swearing, the slang, the accent, would not be the same, would not evoke the same characters, would not respond to the same voices. To an extent, another language is another truth. Therefore, Catalan probably posed a threat to the alleged transparency of the meanings that the Rambleros sought to convey. Multilingualism was, from this point of view, the ultimate threat to monologism. The person who speaks another language is, in this sense, a person who must accept more than one perspective, more than one discourse. And this is at odds with a regime of truth that only accepts the plain statement, the foot on the ground, the obvious argument, the direct contact with "reality".

Finally, I believe that the Catalan language had a problematic fit with regard to the ambivalent relationship with the discourses of authority that the Rambleros men constructed. I already argued that this form of simplified masculinity contained an implicit, deep seated conformism dressed as transgression, a situation akin to Willis' (1977) working-class lads. In this context, Catalan could be treated as something to oppose (because of its institutional status) or something oppositional in itself, as it challenged the hegemony of the state's language. However, I found no evidence that the second option was ever considered. On the contrary, the very idea that studying Catalan could be seen as an imposition and studying Spanish as natural implies that the Catalan authority was seen as lacking legitimacy. This legitimacy seemed to rely exclusively on the Spanish state as representing a fundamentally unilingual nation. Pablo's argument that Catalan was taught just "because we are in Catalonia" clearly points to the wider political unit: Spain (not the Catalan speaking regions, not Europe, not the world). The state appeared as the basic point of reference from where things had to be judged. Other points of reference or sources of authority were subordinate or superfluous. The "Spanishness" of the Rambleros came across in many other ways: a) through their involvement with media sports, such as football and the Olympics, which are based on the state as a basic symbolic space; b) through the use of the category Spain as a way of situating and categorizing people and events in multiple ways (i.e. when I was "coming back to Spain", whether I was studying "the young in Spain", whether one had the right to expect bar attendants to speak Spanish –and not only English– in the Balearic tourist resorts –where the local language is, incidentally, Catalan–, whether there were Spaniards at Lancaster University, etc.). Additionally, at a time when thousands of young people in Barcelona were rejecting conscription, I was amazed that none of the Rambleros seemed to have even considered applying for conscientious objection. I think that this constitutes a sign that their forms of transgression were based on a deep identification with Spanish authority, to which they accorded legitimacy.[26]

The Rambleros' Spanishness contrasted with that of the Trepas, who were generally not interested in mass sports, rarely pronounced the word *Spain* or *Spanish*, sympathized with the idea of Catalonia's independence and were staunch anti-militarists. Of course, the state constituted for them (as for everybody) a fundamental criterion of implicit categorization, but less conspicuously so in their talk.

2.3.2. Femininity and language choice

As I said, from the early stages of fieldwork I noticed that the women, particularly the Rambleros women, seemed to express a very different feeling than men towards the Catalan language or towards issues associated with Catalan culture. One indirect –though highly significant– sign of this was their allegiance to the Barcelona Football Club, which put them in direct opposition to the men's soccer loyalties. Some of the Rambleros women were also fond of the newly emerging Catalan rock, which was generally ignored or despised by the others. I also perceived from the beginning subtle hints that they felt positive about speaking the language, sometimes in the form of ambivalent humorous switches or passing comments about "feeling Catalan". I also witnessed –and was told of– various cases in which women spoke Catalan in short exchanges with outsiders of the group: with a waiter, with pedestrians asking for a light, for directions and so on. I never saw such things amongst the Rambleros men.

In the interviews, these impressions were confirmed. One of the defining traits of mainstream femininity was commitment to education. It is therefore not surprising that the feelings of these women about Catalan at school were totally different from that of their male friends. To them, it was just "one more subject", and they said they usually liked it because they liked all language subjects. They all reported doing well in Catalan at primary school, although some had had some problems in secondary school. Those who experienced these problems always framed the question as a school problem (as they would judge problems with other subjects) rather than developing an oppositional spirit against Catalan. School exercises and interactions with teachers and other students seemed to provide most of the opportunities for speaking Catalan to the women who were studying, although one said that she spoke it with school mates only occasionally. Some of the women who were working or looking for jobs were regularly involved in training courses where Catalan was also taught.

It is important to bear in mind that the clerical, secretarial and semi-skilled jobs targeted by these women also required skills in Catalan, although this did not imply that the use of Catalan predominated in the workplace, as Paula's words illustrate:

Extract 89 [Rambleros]
Paula: The ones at the reception desk speak Catalan to each other. But I may be speaking with them, · and for instance, eh- · They · they may well be speaking in Catalan, right? and I come, and if they have to tell me something, they say it to me in Castilian. And I say it to them · that "it's not necessary for- · for you speak to me in Castilian now", but · it's a habit already.

This also caused frustration for one of the politicized Trepas women. When she was working as a waitress in a café, she found that she addressed Catalan-speaking clients in Catalan, but was usually responded to in Spanish. She felt insulted and claimed that it was a way of humiliating her by asserting her status as a servant, a clear class-related reading. In my hometown, which is overwhelmingly Catalan-speaking, a friend once gave me a sticker with the Catalan flag and a phrase printed on it which read "I am a Castilian, please speak to me in Catalan". It had been printed by a Spanish speaker who had been unsuccessful in making his acquaintances speak Catalan to him.

As a result of this, in spite of their favorable disposition towards using Catalan, these women used it only exceptionally. Of course, this disposition made all the difference with regard to their orientation towards study and semi-skilled jobs. Additionally, the use of Catalan was not in conflict with the form of femininity they were constructing. If they were prepared to show concern for their appearance and display greater sophistication by learning new skills, speaking more formally or dressing more elegantly, speaking Catalan was only a plus for them. In this sense, they could only fear the teasing of their male companions. As they were not really committed to the order of the *simple truth*, the Catalan voice could not be a threat to their identity. This is why Catalan could even become on some occasions an issue to exploit in cross gender talk: once, when I gave the Rambleros a first draft of my analysis to read, one of the women approached one of the men who sometimes told people off for speaking Catalan, and she defiantly told him that she had read the Catalan version of it.

2.3.3. Politicized choices

Amongst the Trepas, most Catalan speakers switched to Spanish when addressing Spanish speakers. As a result, Spanish was the language that dominated at least when a large number of people were together talking or playing. It was certainly the language symbolically associated with the group, not only because of the group's voices as analyzed in 6.2, but also because any utterance addressed to the group as a whole (a joke, an instruction, an announcement or an exclamation) was normally uttered in Spanish. Additionally, utterances and conversations in Catalan were characteristically pronounced in lower, almost "private" voices. This may also have been caused by the circumstance that Catalan was spoken by pairs of men who had closer and older relationships between them. I also saw many a time that a group conversing in Catalan would willingly interrupt their talk when Spanish speakers appeared, and change language and topic as if they had been talking private matters. Besides, the Spanish-speaking members of the group were commonly the most outspoken participants. Catalan, therefore, occupied a peripheralized space, a phenomenon similar to the status of women's rituals.[27] It is possible that this impression of Spanish predominance was partly caused by the fact that I was much closer to the Spanish speakers. In his interview, Pepe actually said that he was not so sure that Spanish predominated within the group. It is possible that he did not experience it as I did, as Pepe was a Spanish speaker who spoke Catalan with most Catalan-speaking members of the group. Nevertheless, when the whole group gathered together, there was little doubt about this matter. What is true is that the predominance of Spanish was not the product of any form of *policing* aimed at restricting the use of Catalan, as happened with the Rambleros. On the contrary, the members of the Trepas who were politically aware had been making conscious efforts to increase the use of Catalan. The three Spanish speakers who actually spoke Catalan with other members of the group were amongst the politicized Trepas. In the interviews, they confirmed that their use of Catalan was the product of a conscious decision grounded on political principles. This decision had been accompanied by considerable reflexive and practical work: reflexive work to build an understanding of what sense it made to speak Catalan, and the practical work necessary to find situations to make effective use of it.

Clara and Pepe declared that they had first used anarchist ideas to justify their exclusive use of Spanish (Salva had apparently done the same), the idea being that anarchism pleaded loyalty to a universal culture and not to local ones. Clara had finally decided to acknowledge that her stance was inconsistent (see extract 79). Pepe also pointed out that he had adopted Catalan to be "at peace with himself", because he did not want to be "a resented immigrant". Interestingly enough, he dated his first inroads into Catalan at the time when he switched to Marxism, although he acknowledged that the two ideologies did not provide a substantially different approach to this issue. His explanations suggest to me that the change from primary to secondary school (which was contemporary to the ideological change) might have played an important role as well, as it usually causes a renewal of friendship links. Salva, according to Clara, changed his position after discussing the matter with Aleix, who had argued that anarchist principles could also be used to defend the case of any oppressed people, such as the Catalan one. Clara described Salva's decision to use Catalan as an "act of militancy". The reasons they used to ground their position were quite similar. According to Pepe, it was because *convivència* 'living together in harmony'[28] meant that "respect has to go both ways", implying more or less that everyone should generally use the two languages as a matter of displaying respect. The same term, *convivència*, was also used by Clara, who had a vision of all cultures having the same value and deserving respect.

The political nature of these views about *convivència* may not be very visible if we do not take into account the wider context. Clara, Pepe, Aleix and Salva's views constituted not only a particular way of seeing Catalan society, but also a response to existing discourses on the matter. Clara and Pepe explicitly indicated that they responded to the anti-Catalan ideas they had experienced among members of their families. In his interview, Salva responded to the discourse of Catalanism:

Extract 90 [Trepas]

Salva: I don't know. Because if Catalan is the language of this place, · then: one should speak it right? · And not because I say "because this is Catalonia, we have to speak it", right? But · · it's to say: "damn, what a healthy thing it is · to know- to be able to speak two languages", right? · · And apart from this, well, that it is interesting for me.

In constructing their position vis-à-vis Catalan and Catalonia, the politicized Trepas distanced themselves both from anti-Catalan positions and from exclusivist Catalanist stances which deny all legitimacy to cultures other than Catalan. The Catalanist stances were typically associated with Catalonia's ruling coalition, and more particularly with its leader, Jordi Pujol. From early on, Pepe had told me that he loathed Pujol but that he was strongly in favor of the promotion of the Catalan language. In the group discussion, Clara answered arguments against Catalonia's independence by claiming that "I am not saying vote for an independent Catalonia and I am Jordi Pujol; I am Clara!" and proceeded to argue that she was in favor of Catalonia's freedom as a positive form of emancipation. Aleix's position below illustrates this view from the perspective of a Catalan speaker:

Extract 91 [Trepas]

Aleix: [In the political meetings] there is an effort to speak Catalan for political reasons, that is, to promote- too- what we were talking about · · (xxx you may be working) on a particular issue, but you seek (to work on a more global perspective), right? · I mean if there are some people working on a particular issue, you are not going to despise it, you want people to understand yours, you understand the meaning of the other. Then, · some of us, because we are in for the issue of promoting Catalan; others · because they say "Well, I am a

Castilian speaker, but here there are people here who had always spoken it." ·
And you (ask) them to like work on it, right? · Then at the level of [these
organizations], (everybody), (then), that's the idea.

It could be argued that the position of these politicized members was
very similar to that of three non-politicized Catalan speakers in the group
who used both languages and were also sympathetic to policies of catalani-
zation. Chimo said that he felt close to Esquerra Republicana de Catalunya
(Republican Left of Catalonia) in terms of its pro-Catalan policies, but not
in other aspects of the party's policies and practices. Jaume also said that he
was in favor of a free Catalonia, but was not a nationalist and did not really
feel he had a language of his own. He rejected anti-Catalan positions as
well, and so did Guille. However, although the views of Chimo, Jaume and
Guille might appear similar on the surface to those of his politicized companions, they presupposed different attitudes and gave rise to different linguistic practices. They may have used more Catalan than anybody, but they
never appeared to challenge the existing conventions which reduced much
of the space where Catalan could potentially be used:

Extract 92 [Trepas]
Guille: As a kid I used to have friends, for example these friends from my block
who were Castilian, right? · And, I don't know, I heard him speaking in
Castilian. And I felt it [would be] awkward to respond in Catalan, right? I do
not know the reason. So I ended up speaking in Castilian. · And maybe I wasn't
doing the right thing, right? Because the guy might well have wished to learn
Catalan, you know what I mean? But, · I don't know, · · I don't know why I did
it, but I did.

Later on, Guille said that he had never considered maintaining Catalan
in such situations. His reflections seemed more a product of the interview
rather than an issue he had been pondering about himself. Chimo even indicated that he had not made any significant effort to use Catalan when he
realized that he had been speaking Spanish with a Catalan speaker, contrary
to the case of Patrícia as quoted in extract 57. In contrast, the politicized
members' views were effectively reflected in their practices. Patrícia declared that she employed implicit strategies to establish Catalan with her
friends. Clara, who was a Spanish speaker, used to take all her school notes
and exams in Catalan. She also made the point of buying many Catalan
books in spite of the fact that they were usually more expensive. She had
also resolved to speak Catalan with shop-keepers and in other service en-

counters before she actually dared to speak it with friends. Salva and Pepe had managed to establish Catalan as the language of communication with some of their friends within the group. Both Pepe and Clara reported having difficulties in making Catalan speakers speak Catalan to them. Pepe explained in the interview how he had to overcome this resistance from Catalan speakers:

Extract 93 [Trepas]

Pepe: It is curious because, if I see a person whose language is Catalan, and I start speaking in Catalan- Now it does not happen to me as much as it used to before. But because before I used to speak it much worse[29] than now, so well, it seemed as if it was, well: "poor thing" right? And they always spoke to me in Castilian. And this is, well, very impolite. And it is- it seems to me that it shows a lack of respect, quite considerable, right? When I was a member of the [party], it used to happen [...] What happens, because of what I was just saying that they used to frustrate you, untiiil, until you, until you are stronger than the embarrassment, and you stop giving up, yourself, right? Then if you speak Catalan with somebody and this is a Catal-, this person always speaks Catalan, and he answers you in Castilian, you ignore it in the same way, you go on speaking Catalan, until the guy realizes, right? Or does not, or you say "Why are you responding to me in Castilian", right? [he plays a Flamenco chord with a guitar]

Indeed, this was how Pepe managed to make me speak Catalan at the beginning of the fieldwork, thus establishing it as the language which we always used. In addition to reformulating political discourses, the Trepas had naturally defined their own standards on what was to be seen as proper Catalan. Their speech contained numerous slang expressions, Spanish borrowings and syntactic or morphological interferences; but I never saw anybody making fun of anyone for that matter. Salva said that he spoke Catalan to Ayats because he knew he was not going to be laughed at. This challenge to common standards of linguistic propriety also affected the assumption that one-to-one interactions had to be monolingual. Aleix and Clara had developed a bilingual, *code-switched* style.

Extract 94 [Trepas]

Clara: Aleix's discourse is: · "Everyone · may speak as they like and this and that, but my cult-[ure is Catalan], I mean," right? "That's why I · always speak Catalan". (I mean) "If you wish, you can always speak · in Castilian. · Fine. Therefore I always speak Catalan"

Aleix said in his interview that, because Catalan was his family language and Spanish the predominant language in the street, that he was therefore of a mixed identity. He rejected explicitly uniformist views of identity and of language use and he affirmed that his way of talking was mixed in accordance with his daily experience. I did see Aleix in conversations with monolingual Spanish speakers with whom he spoke in a code-switched style, although in the group discussion he appeared to drift to Spanish-only when he got very engrossed in the conversation. Clara used a code-switched style with me and her interview is a fine example of this. She told me that, because I was such an obvious Catalan speaker, she felt obliged to speak Catalan to me. When I asked her whether her lesser competence in Catalan did not cause her problems for communicating with Catalan speakers, she simply answered that, when she had any difficulties, then she switched to Castilian. My interpretation is that her code-switching style was the result of a compromise between all these tensions, i.e. her desire to speak Catalan so that I would not be forced to speak Spanish and her desire to speak Spanish to convey the meanings she wished to get across.

Clara's and Aleix's code-switches were generally based on changes of narrative level or speaker alignment, such as the ones described in chapter 5. In this way, they produced bilingual narratives which came across as relatively natural and which did not force the audience to accommodate.

The transformations that the politicized Trepas performed on the dominant patterns of language choice had obviously been made possible by the particular order of discourse they had established in some of their peer-group relationships. They were able to question the assumptions behind their practices and to encourage each other to make the necessary efforts to introduce changes. Drawing upon their political consciousness and their participation in political activities, they had created new linguistic practices in a comparable way to their innovations in gender aspects. Their readiness to integrate various voices and to accept a variety of perspectives was probably important in allowing them to cope with the slightly different meanings that Catalan seemed to evoke. Because their truth was a relative one, and because they had a different sense of how their self should be protected (see chapter 4, section 2), they were probably more able to cope with the embarrassment and the unmasculine potential meanings that problematized the choice of Catalan.

Nevertheless, this did not really solve the symbolic asymmetries between the two languages. Neither did it create an environment where Catalan gained space in proportion with the number of its speakers. As in the case of gender identities, it made a difference, but not a revolution. On the basis of the following episode from the group discussion, I will make some final remarks on how the choice of language was managed amongst the politicized Trepas:

Extract 95 [Trepas]

Jaume: [...] i una altra gent no té aquest tipu de confiança no és perquè
... and with other people you may not have this level of trust. It is not because you

no confiïs sinó · · perquè no · · · sí · depèn · dee
don't trust them, but · · because it isn't- · · · Yeah, if it depends on-

Pepe: i la confiança passa per unes coses segons lo que lo que · a partir
And trust can involve a range of things depending on what what, on the basis

de què · haixi sortit aquesta amistat
of what this friendship has arisen.

Jaume: *claro*
      Of course.

Pepe: clar si-· *sii tú y yo somos amigos a partir de que un día · nos*
Of course, if- *iif you and I are friends from the day,*

encontramos con esta situación y
we met in this situation and...

Here Pepe, a Spanish speaker, responded in Catalan to a point Jaume had made in the same language (Jaume, in turn, was responding to a long turn made by Aleix, also in Catalan). It is significant that Pepe actually took up not only the language, but also the words (*confiança* 'trust') and the temporal dimension used by Jaume before (the present perfect, expressing a past moment included within the temporal span defined in the context). Although the word *confiança* is easily translatable (in Spanish: *confianza*), it could be argued that Pepe's choice of Catalan was due to the fact that he had appropriated most elements of Jaume's voice in his intervention. In a way, Pepe seemed to format his intervention as a mere continuation of Jaume's turn (by beginning it with "*i*" 'and'). However, once Pepe got the floor, other factors had to be taken into account with regard to language choice: Pepe and Jaume normally spoke Spanish to each other. This is why Jaume responded to him in Spanish ("*claro!*" 'of course') later, thus choosing interpersonal rather than textual coherence of language. After a fraction of a second, Pepe was responding to Jaume's response in Catalan, and using the equivalent word ("*clar!*"). Because Pepe was concentrating on constructing his argument, he had not considered taking into account what language Jaume expected him to speak; or if he had, he had chosen to over-look it. But as he managed to evaluate Jaume's response in the subsequent instants, he somehow decided to switch (a decision quite clearly located within the hesitation space after "*clar!*"). The switch to Spanish also coin-cided with a switch in the narrative mode: Pepe started an exemplification (after the statement of a general principle), where direct address terms were used (*tú y yo* 'you and I') and where the tense became the present. The nar-rative thus acquired a more dramatic tone and, in the lines just below this stretch, Pepe's animated characters began to talk in their own voice.

These ambiguities were very common in the talk of the Trepas. The choice of language was not always amenable to simple rules of who speaks what to whom. For instance, in situations where people joined a conversa-tion that was already running, bilinguals tended to use the language in which that conversation had been taking place, sometimes overruling their expected choices with particular persons. In these cases, they did not get a response in the language they had actually used, but in the language they *should* have used, thus re-establishing the "right" interpersonal language as the main norm. Thus it was common that a Spanish speaker entered a con-versation in Catalan and was responded to in Spanish by a Catalan speaker, or that a Catalan speaker entered in Spanish and was responded to in Cata-lan (this happened to me many times, as well as to others). This suggests that people did not wish to be seen as imposing their own preferred lan-guage, as they were still aware of the political sensitivity of the matter.

There were other sources of ambiguity of language choice that arose in conversations with more than two participants. Extract 74, for example, contains another type of potential ambiguity. Ayats and Pepe started speak-ing in Catalan to each other and later switched to Spanish to address Mauro. However, Ayats and Pepe accomplished five turns in Spanish be-fore Mauro intervened, such that their interventions actually appeared as responses to each other's interventions and not to Mauro's. Where can one draw the line between just responding to each other in Spanish (but speak-ing to another addressee) and effectively *speaking* to (and thus addressing) each other in Spanish? Only participants can decide whether the line is ef-fectively there and whether it is relevant for them.

The complexities of language choice were compounded by the com-plexities of the multivoiced, multilevelled character of utterances, with their dramatizations, ironizing voices, various narrative modes and so on. So sometimes, a remark I had interpreted as serious was taken up as a joke. Hence the linguistic "chaos" that Guille was referring to in extract 83, and the possibility that the language of particular pairs of people might shift, as in the case of Pepe and Ayats mentioned above. The most important asymmetry between the choice of Catalan and Spanish was, therefore, that the latter had the fundamental support of the forms of speaking and identities constructed within the group, whereas the former had to rely on conscious political determination and was dependent on self-discipline. For instance, in the group discussion, people used mainly Spanish. Aleix, however, made an effort to intervene mostly in Catalan, sometimes in direct response to interventions in Spanish. Nevertheless, in interventions where he got deeply involved in arguments with Spanish speakers, he somehow forgot his resolve. The same happened to Patrícia. Although it could be argued that this was because Aleix or Patrícia might be trying to develop a bilingual style, it is significant that most of the switches to Spanish came at points where behavior became less consciously monitored. This asymmetry probably added to the feeling that Catalan was not entirely of their world, the world they were constructing in their get-togethers.

Concluding remarks

I hope that by now I will have convinced the reader that the patterns of language choice in Barcelona are very diverse, that they are the object of on-going struggle as to what particular choices mean and, especially, that it makes sense to look at them in this way rather than focusing only on the most widespread forms of linguistic behaviour. Having said that, it is certainly the case that Spanish predominated amongst the groups studied. For the Rambleros, it was the family language and they did not find themselves in any situation in which speaking Catalan would have made any sense. Amongst the Trepas, Spanish predominated because of its status as a *lingua franca*, even though politicized members were making an effort to challenge the predominant conventions of language choice. The correlation between linguistic attitudes and gender was particularly interesting. Simplified masculinity seemed to encourage individuals to see Catalan as associated with the authority that is being continuously challenged (although in ambivalent and nuanced ways), while mainstream femininity encouraged individuals to display a readiness to use Catalan and a certain identification with Catalan symbols. These contrasts apparently involved differing patterns of language use in domains such as the workplace, which suggests that there may be connections between language use and class position, an issue which I will discuss at length in chapter 7.

Conclusions to part 2

The ideological investment of speech varieties

In chapter 4, I discussed the ideological world associated with stylized Spanish and with argot. I showed through various examples how these varieties were constructed as a response to and as a transgression of the discourses of authority and the mainstream values of society. As such, they contributed in a significant way to the construction of the various forms of masculinity described in part 1. In chapter 5, I compared the types of meanings and identities associated with the use of Catalan and Spanish. This comparison showed that both Catalan and Spanish voices were used to incorporate voices from authority figures (officials, teachers, media presenters), while a certain specialization appeared with regard to more informal voices. Catalan was used to evoke characters who were alien to the values and experiences of the groups (silly, naive, childish, unmasculine voices), whereas Spanish was used to represent their own experience and a range of ironizing and playful voices that were central to the patterns of talk within the peer-group. These findings connect with the intuitions voiced by some Catalan linguists, who claim that youth slang in Barcelona involves the appropriation of Spanish linguistic resources to a much larger extent than those of Catalan (Argente et al. 1979: 256). Thus, Catalan had an uneasy fit in the world of the Rambleros and the Trepas, and the language policies put forward during the eighties and nineties have not produced any significant change on that front. In chapter 6, I showed how the existing conventions of language choice contributed to establish Spanish as the dominant language amongst the Trepas. Some members of this group had managed to introduce some changes in their patterns of language choice by creating bilingual speech styles or by seeking to establish Catalan as the language of communication in some situations, but they had not managed to pull the Catalan language from its one-down position. On the contrary, the use of Spanish seemed to be on the increase due to its key symbolic functions within this group.

A number of important issues have emerged from this analysis of the linguistic repertoire of the Rambleros and the Trepas. The crucial point is that the use of particular speech styles and languages is ideologically invested in a fundamental way. This ideological investment does not consist of mere symbolic associations or connotations that somehow impregnate the normal, literal or denotative meanings of utterances. Rather, speech styles and languages play a constitutive role in the processes of meaning production, that is, in the processes whereby social situations are organized, relationships are established, identities are constructed, intentions are interpreted, topics are raised, objects and concepts are created. This does not really imply that language constitutes or determines our way of thinking or of perceiving reality in the way linguistic anthropologists have traditionally believed (see Gumperz and Levinson 1996). It is in social interaction, in situated practice, where meanings are produced and (re)shaped. The ideological investment of the linguistic repertoire originates in the way in which particular speech styles or languages are used to construct particular meanings, identities, relationships. My analysis provides some hints as to how this process takes place. First, it occurs through the appropriation of previously existing discourses or voices. This appropriation usually takes place by incorporating particular speech genres (linguistic expressions and textual configurations associated with particular contexts and their constellations of ideologies, social relations and identities). Secondly, it takes place through the adaptation and reaccentuation of these discourses and voices, which results in the creation of new meanings. From this perspective, language is in constant change as it is being adapted to new communicative needs. The frame analysis of talk is one of the ways in which we can discover how speakers incorporate and transform a multiplicity of voices. Thus we saw that stylized Spanish and argot were appropriated in significantly different ways by the Rambleros and the Trepas. This framework could also help to understand why Catalan was a relatively dry, one-sided, inexpressive, maybe mono-voiced language in the way they all used it. It had to do with the particular situations where they had had access to Catalan, and with the fact that the linguistic conventions of language choice prevented them from developing the symbolic potential of Catalan in a creative way.

Part 3

Situated practices and social structures

So far, I have provided a relatively detailed analysis of the social and linguistic practices of the Rambleros and the Trepas, and particularly of how gender identities constituted the key aspects of social identity within these cliques and how these identities were partly constructed through the appropriation of particular linguistic varieties. Now it is time to consider what these findings tell us about social problems and processes of wider relevance. Without this additional level of analysis, a piece of research runs the risk of remaining theoretically irrelevant and socially meaningless in the sense that a more or less accurate description of a number of social interactions does not necessarily help to answer important questions such as what makes a particular social practice sexist, or in what way some language choices contribute to the political subordination of the Catalan-speaking community. Without this additional level of analysis, it may not be possible to differentiate what constitutes simply "being nasty or rude to a woman" from "reproducing discriminatory practices", to distinguish between a reasonable, practical and polite language choice from a decision that effectively contributes to diminishing the communicative functions of the Catalan language. Of course, these distinctions do not speak of substantial properties of the practices themselves, which must be necessarily ambivalent. The distinctions arise from the need to consider the wider political significance of the social practices analyzed.

Therefore, what I seek to do is essentially to *extrapolate* my findings, that is, to situate the practices analyzed in terms of socially relevant processes that transcend the uniqueness of individuals and contexts. And to perform the extrapolations I draw basically upon Bourdieu's ideas about how society works. I acknowledge that this is not a fully satisfactory way of doing it. Bourdieu's speculations about fields, habitus and capitals were not quite devised to perform this type of operation. It is, however, the most satisfactory way I have found. In contrast with other sciences, the social sciences lack a basic operational consensus as to what samples and procedures are needed to perform valid extrapolations. This means that I will need to make explicit *how* I have incorporated Bourdieu's notions, including what I perceive as the limitations of his model. This will make this part of the book somewhat different from the previous ones, as it will necessarily combine data analysis with theoretical speculation. Chapter 7 will therefore combine two lines of discourse, that is, data analysis with some metalanguage about the limits of this same analysis. I will follow two main threads. First, I will explore what this analysis can tell us about the three questions mentioned in the introduction and which informed my research agenda (why young people do not heed linguistic policies, why is anti-social behavior so common, in what way youth cultures reinforce gender inequalities). Secondly, I will reflect on the theoretical significance of these findings, i.e. how they connect with conceptual debates in the fields of Discourse Analysis and Sociolinguistics.

Before "plunging" directly into the analysis, it is necessary to explain briefly how I have interpreted and incorporated Bourdieu's ideas for the purposes described. The work of Bourdieu and his associates is now widely known (Bourdieu et al. 1966; Bourdieu and Passeron 1970; Bourdieu 1972, 1979, 1984a). I will explain the three main reasons that led me to take an interest in his work and I will then give a brief outline of the aspects of his model I have found useful.

First, Bourdieu has developed an empirically-based model that addresses political issues. He has sought to uncover and denounce processes of social domination that inform policies. Secondly, this ethical approach is accompanied by a critical awareness of issues associated with the research process. The social position of the researcher plays an important role in the way she constitutes the research object. Bourdieu thus claims that the research process has to be *reflexive*, that is, it must include an analysis of the conditions of production of the sociological work itself (see Bourdieu and Wacquant 1992) and it must be very clear and explicit about the criteria and procedures of analysis. This makes it easier to take issue or to engage in dialogue with his views. Thirdly, in addition to this scrutiny of the relation between the researcher's discourse and oneself, one must also analyze very carefully the relationship between the conceptual framework developed and the actual experience of agents. Bourdieu has in mind the methods of some anthropologists who, he argues, try to capture the patterns or "the logic" behind a particular set of practices by laying out fixed sets of rules. A theory of practice must account for "the distance between the practical experience of agents... and the model which enables the mechanisms it describes to function" (ibid.: 70). I have assumed that this point can also be applied, in some cases, to the distance between local experience and wider social processes seen in more general terms. To describe these more abstract levels of practice, Bourdieu has developed the notions of *habitus* and *social field*, the latter being the notion that I will use to construct the extrapolations needed to locate the practices of the Rambleros and the Trepas within larger-scale spaces of social participation.

Bourdieu's framework revolves around three basic concepts: *field* (or *market*), *capital* and *habitus*. *Fields* are socially constituted (and constituting) spaces "of conflict and competition... in which participants vie to establish monopoly over the species of capital effective in it" (Wacquant 1992: 17). Examples of the fields he has researched are: education, politics, the media, sports, the academy, the arts. In my analysis, I will consider that this notion can also be applied to very small social contexts, such as a youth clique. Therefore, the Rambleros and the Trepas constituted tiny fields (in Fairclough's terms, local orders of discourse), which had a position within the wider field of youth culture. Capital is "accumulable social-symbolic resources" (Collins 1993: 116) or "properties which are active within the universe under study –those properties capable of conferring strength, power and consequently profit on their holder" (Bourdieu 1987: 3–4), i.e. what is seen as having an exchange value in a given field. Within the youth cliques studied, for instance, the particular features of character associated with masculinity constituted a form of capital that members (particularly men) sought to accumulate and whose value they sought to protect. Habitus is the set of skills and dispositions, both mental and physical, that people acquire by participating in particular social fields. The habitus constitutes the largely unconscious, routinized and unreflective practical sense that guides people's perceptions, actions and reactions in everyday life and which makes them sensitive to the forms of capital of each field. Hence the Rambleros and the Trepas had developed a whole range of skills and attitudes out of their participation in the world of youth culture which allowed them to act quite "spontaneously" as legitimate members of the groups.

Bourdieu's studies have mainly revolved around the question of domination, i.e. how power relations are established and reproduced in the various fields. He observes that, quite often, the dominated classes participate in active (though unconscious) ways in producing the conditions that constitute their position as dominated. Women investing in strands of education that lead to subordinated positions in the job market would be an example of this. This is an effect of what he calls *symbolic violence*, that is, of the process whereby the dominant classes succeed in imposing their own ideology as to what counts as capital in a given field and what individuals can expect in it. Bourdieu's studies are very much geared towards uncovering or denouncing these hidden agendas or reproductive effects of particular practices and discourses. He seeks to show how power relations are often established because they produce a *misrecognition* that conceals their own workings and effects, thus leading social actors to delude themselves as to the real significance of their practices.

Bourdieu sees each social field or market as having its own specific form of capital and its own dynamics of internal struggle, and as producing a range of "habituses" according to the positions and experiences of actors within it. He also affirms that all fields have a degree of autonomy, but that they are also closely linked to the political and socioeconomic fields, which play a central role in the social order. For instance, in Bourdieu and Passeron (1970), he has argued that the educational system contributes to reproducing class hierarchies while keeping the fiction that educational achievement depends exclusively on personal gifts or skills. He also observes that *social fields*, such as the arts, sports, literature, science, politics, the intelligentsia and the media, typically present internal divisions and struggles that are connected with divisions in the field of economic and class relations. For instance, tastes and preferences in arts, sports or literature oftenfol low class lines (Bourdieu et al. 1966; Bourdieu 1979, 1988a). Additionally, one can detect struggles within factions of each field that are aimed at defining what is of value within it (i.e. what counts as *capital*). In these struggles, the factions commonly correspond to particular socioeconomic groups, as when the field of sports was constituted around aristocratic and bourgeois values (disinterest, character, manliness) as a form of differentiation in relation to the values of the intellectual petite bourgeoisie (willpower, culture) (Bourdieu 1984b: 121–122).

We could define two main kinds of struggle: struggles for capital accumulation and struggles for capital (re)definition. The first one refers to people's strategies to acquire what is seen as valuable in a given context. The second can be exemplified through Bourdieu's discussion of the linguistic field, particularly of the significance of forms of variation. Bourdieu considers that traditional mainstream linguistics as based on Saussure's separation between the *internal* elements (language) and the *external* elements (language use). This he considers as an example of an *"intellectualist philosophy* which treats language as an object of contemplation rather than as an instrument of action and power" (Bourdieu 1991a: 37), thus contributing to concealing its role in reproducing social inequalities. The metaphor of language as a *treasure* accessible to the whole linguistic community conceals the fact that society holds a plurality of speech forms associated with different values, such that a linguistic hierarchy, i.e. a *linguistic field*, is created, a field with important connections with class hierarchies. What linguists call language is just a particular linguistic form (the standard or *legitimate* language) whose legitimacy is generally recognized, though access to it is unequally distributed (for instance, the children of peasants and workers characteristically have fewer opportunities for learning it). As the standard language is associated with participation in powerful institutions, access to prestigious employment and the dominant classes that control the state and the means of production, it serves as a gatekeeping device. This is how, Bourdieu observes, linguistic hierarchization plays a significant role in the processes of inclusion and (self)exclusion of people in particular social milieus. In this sense, he considers that the school plays a major role in the production and reproduction of class hierarchies, as it causes a high degree of failure amongst the working classes, but accomplishes the function of legitimizing the cultural and linguistic forms (i.e. the linguistic capital) of the dominant classes.

Bourdieu also considers that the "unceasing struggles between the different authorities" (1991a: 58) to legitimize particular forms of expression, such as is the case of writers advocating for "popular" forms of speech, are largely irrelevant. These struggles, he argues, do not constitute a challenge to the legitimate language, but simply correspond to the struggles between sections of the literary and academic fields that endeavor to impose particular principles of legitimization which rely on the legitimacy of their corresponding institutions to establish these principles. These struggles may therefore affect the market value of particular linguistic forms (and the power position of the different parties involved), but not the overall functioning of the linguistic market itself, which remains untouched. Strategies of *distinction* are another example of struggles to redefine what counts as capital. They can explain other types of shifts in the value of linguistic forms. *Distinction* is a value associated with social features that are unequally distributed and can therefore become symbolically charged as boundary markers. Thus, competence in the legitimate language is valued partly because it is possessed by a few. Hence, as "petit-bourgeois" people endeavor to discard "vulgar" forms of language so as to appear as natural speakers of standard forms, the upper classes and intellectuals can adopt new strategies of distinction as a form of social distancing. One typical strategy of distinction is what Bourdieu calls "controlled hypocorrection", which is when upper-class speakers make a point of using popular forms of expression because they can afford it, that is, because they possess enough symbolic capital to display "confident relaxation and lofty ignorance of pedantic rules" (1991a: 63).

Bourdieu's ideas have aroused considerable interest because they constitute an interesting way to rethink the old problematic dichotomies between structure and action, determination and creativity, the subjective and the objective, and so on. The notion of *habitus*, for instance, challenges the traditional and still largely commonsensical view that actors apply the principles of rational calculation to every one of their decisions. His view is that action is "reasonable without being the product of rational design" (Bourdieu 1980: 50), that is, the product of dispositions that subjects develop throughout their lives as a response to the conditions in which they live. This is particularly useful in a study such as this one, where it would have been obviously difficult to describe the social practices of the Trepas and the Rambleros as the product of a strictly rational weighing up of aims and means. None of his major studies has focused on the young or youth culture as the central issue. However, as we will see, his analyses of students' relation to "culture" (in the belletristic sense) and of the social significance of sports also contain some interesting points on this account (Bourdieu and Passeron 1964; Bourdieu 1984b, 1988a). In chapter 7, I will therefore examine the potential of Bourdieu's framework to accomplish the type of social analysis I am looking for. In particular, I will consider how the phenomena described in parts 1 and 2 connect with wider political processes that have to do with the problems associated with youth cultures in modern society, the redefinition of gender roles and identities, and the normalization of non-state languages such as Catalan. This means that data analysis, theoretical reflection and political implications will be discussed simultaneously at many points. To do so, I will consider that the Rambleros and the Trepas were operating from a particular position within the field of youth culture. From this viewpoint, I will explore (through their own experiences) how this field connected with other social fields (particularly the educational and economic fields) and what political implications can be derived from these considerations.

Chapter 7

Youth culture as a social field

The notions of *young* and *old* exist in all societies, both as a relative measure of people's age and as a way of identifying the social status of their members. In this last case, *youth* is opposed to *adulthood* in the sense that the young are seen as *not yet* full members of society. The rituals of coming of age that exist in many societies are used precisely to grant adult status to young members. Bourdieu suggests that the key to understanding the condition of being young is not biology, but the socially constructed opposition of *juniority* vs. *seniority*, which is treated differently in different societies (and often in different social fields within complex societies) in ways that serve to regulate access to resources and power.

In industrialized societies, the term *youth culture* has been used to designate a very varied set of social phenomena (practices, aesthetic and musical movements, ideologies) associated with young people, usually anything that has to do with forms of leisure and association outside adult-dominated milieus (the school, the family, workplace). What we call *youth culture* probably emerged after the socioeconomic changes of the post-war period, when the numbers of people who had access to secondary and even higher education increased dramatically. People's access to work and to adult responsibilities was thus delayed, such that the experience of the adolescent student became common to all social groups. Bourdieu defines youth metaphorically as a "half-way house between childhood and adulthood" (1984b: 96). Youth culture has therefore emerged in this time lag that modern society has created between puberty and adulthood, particularly within the considerable amount of free time that students and young unmarried workers enjoy.

As a social field, youth culture appears to be much more loosely integrated than other fields studied by Bourdieu and his associates. Patterns of behavior, dress, language, interactional style, and artistic tastes are varied and often strikingly dissimilar both between and within youth cliques or groupings. The significant differences between the Rambleros and the Trepas, whose social origins were practically identical, can serve as an illustration of this point. This diversity is probably due to the fact that the young are not an organized body subject to standard conditions of access and sanction procedures. However, despite these differences, we also see that some cultural forms, musical movements, rock groups, hairstyles, dance styles, fashions and so on mobilize millions of young people across the globe, thus showing that a certain common symbolic experience must be at work, something that gives some coherence to the field.

In this chapter, I will seek to explore some features of the internal dynamics of the field of youth culture. As I mentioned earlier, this will not be done on the basis of data of general relevance, such as statistical data. Rather, I will explore the field from the perspective of the findings presented in parts 1 and 2 and also with the help of my own personal experiences and other sources of information on the subject. This means that I will produce a partial reconstruction of the workings of this field out of the bits and pieces of a relatively and necessarily partial experience. However, thanks to this procedure I will be able to discuss how the practices analyzed were of significance beyond the particular social context where the data was gathered.

My discussion will revolve around two possible orientations of the social practices analyzed: the reproductive and the transformative. In the first section, I will deal with aspects of practice that can be seen as the product of social constraints (particularly, the social backgrounds of the people studied), as well as those practices that appeared to point towards the reproduction of the unequal relations of which they were, in a way, the product. In the second section, I will consider the ways in which some practices can be seen as transformative. This part entails a certain critique of some of Bourdieu's ideas and concepts that I find lean excessively towards the "reproductive" side of the scale, as well as a proposal to develop his framework in ways that serve to inform analyses of situated practice which can be amenable to the formulation of policies and practical applications. Beneath this rather technical framing of the problem lie the key questions of this research, namely why people adopt particular forms of behavior rather than others and in what conditions we can consider that social subjects have a choice as to the identities they may develop.

1. Reproduced and reproductive practices

One of the most repeated points put forward by Bourdieu in his writings is that the internal divisions within any social field often reproduce the class divisions of the socioeconomic field, though this correspondence is dis-

guised by practices and ideologies that appear to make each field autonomous. Precisely, it is the apparent autonomy of each field that actually allows it to perform its socially reproductive function more fully. It gives
advantages to the already advantaged and disadvantages to the already dis-
advantaged while it hides its true workings, principles and effects under
criteria and procedures that are apparently independent of class origins.
From this perspective, we should expect that the field of youth culture will
contain a) a set of positions for individuals active within it, b) its specific
forms of symbolic capital and c) struggles to accumulate its legitimate
forms of capital as well as to define and redefine what counts as legitimate
capital, all these elements (a, b and c) being in turn a reflection (though in
disguise) of positions, forms of capital and struggles in the socioeconomic
and political fields which largely lead to the reproduction of social inequalities.

On one of the few occasions on which he comments on issues related to
youth culture, Bourdieu (1984b) argues that the experience of those youngsters who drop out of school and seek to enter the labor market when they
are teenagers (thus entering the world of adults in many respects) must be
quite different from those who go on to higher education and live off the
financial support of their families or scholarships for a much longer period
of time (nowadays even into their thirties). He suggests that this is one aspect in which the field of socioeconomic relations bears upon the field of
youth culture, as early school leaving is typical of working-class sections
(see also Eckert 1989). This is, of course, one of the reproductive effects of
the educational field –which favors middle and upper class students– as
well as the result of widespread working-class perceptions about studying
as not really relevant to their expected occupations. From this perspective,
the young people I studied belonged to the section of the working class that
is over-represented amongst the population of early school leavers because
of these reproductive trends.[30] Although it is not possible to establish causal
links in individual cases, it is interesting to appreciate some of the effects of
putting people in such a position.

For instance, early school leaving was reinterpreted by the Ramblero
Luis as a sign of tough, "real world"-oriented masculinity. This was a way
of seeking to revalue his own position by denying the value of educational
qualifications. He was trying to establish a kind of *exchange rate* between
the forms of capital active in, on the one hand, education and the job market and, on the other, the values of the peer-group which were polarized
around the snob/rough (read also feminine/masculine) dichotomy. The class

overtones of the snob/rough dichotomy (which constituted the basis of the most typically masculine peer-group practices) were made explicit in Salva's interview, where he compared the "rough" guys of working class districts with the softer "catalanist" hippies of middle class neighborhoods (see extract 71 in chapter 5 and also chapter 2, subsection 1.2, on the meaning of slam dance). Hence when many male events revolve around who is tougher, slicker or funnier, we may see these occasions as instances of struggle to accumulate and legitimize the particular forms of capital active within this field in ways that have close connections with the actors' positions in other fields. As is suggested by these examples, the relationships between youth culture and other fields do not involve solely the socioeconomic or political spheres, but also a number of related and overlapping fields, such as education and the relations between the sexes and ethnic groups.[31]

Given these first indications that the field of youth culture "behaves" very much as expected from a Bourdieuan perspective, it is time to consider in detail how the field comes to be constituted as it is and to operate as it does. The two main questions are:

1. How is it that, in each social field, individuals generally come to assume in each social field the position that corresponds to their social origin?
2. Why do people come to act in ways that reproduce relations of domination in this context?

In relation to the first question, Bourdieu's view is that the answer lies in the processes of formation of the *habitus*. He considers that individual action is guided by a *practical sense* which is, to a great extent, unconscious and unreflexive, and which leads individuals to act in particular contexts according to an incorporated "feel" about their position and the rules of the game rather than according to an abstract knowledge of the relevant situational features. This practical sense is based on the incorporation and routinization of appropriate behavior, attitudes and systems of knowledge that result from (and help to guide) people's participation in particular fields. The dispositions of the habitus are largely determined by the experiences that fields and markets impose on it. In Bourdieu and Wacquant (1992: 132–137), he also points out that many of the basic dispositions are acquired during childhood. As a consequence, people's beliefs, values and forms of behavior reflect the social structures in which they live and which they themselves contribute toward creating, often unthinkingly. Bourdieu theorizes on the workings of the relations of domination from this perspective: habituses *are produced* by fields in ways that tend to push individuals to reproduce the structures which *produced* them as they are. He also observes that relations of domination are of an essentially symbolic character, as they are actualized in interactions or in "relations of communication implying cognition and recognition" (Bourdieu 1991a: 37). This means that "domination presupposes, on the part of those who submit to it, a form of complicity" (ibid.: 50–51), as it involves that they (the dominated) accept the categories of perception and interpretation (i.e. ideologies) that constitute them as such. This is what Bourdieu calls *symbolic violence*, the process of imposition of a relation of domination which is, essentially, of a symbolic kind, "a violence of which one is both the subject and the object" in the sense that one is actively (though inadvertently) involved in its production and reproduction (Bourdieu and Wacquant 1992: 165–166). Through this idea of *symbolic violence*, Bourdieu explores those practices and beliefs produced by the dominated and which contribute to sustaining their own domination because they are the result of the *doxic* (practical sense) acceptance of the mental structures and dispositions (i.e. habitus) that have been inculcated by virtue of the relation of domination.

From this perspective, one important aspect of symbolic domination is how particular social groups come to identify with and actively foster stigmatized features or forms of behavior (Bourdicu 1991a: 94–95). With the help of my data, I shall show how processes like these were at work amongst the people I studied, processes that contributed to reproducing inequalities in terms of class, ethnicity and gender.

1.1. The job market

With regard to the Rambleros and the Trepas' relationship to the job market, it is interesting to see how their own marginal position in this field fostered the attitudes and dispositions associated with such a position and hampered still further their possibilities of improvement. Their marginality was partially produced by their low educational qualifications, as all men (except one Trepa) and many women (particularly the Trepas women, except one) had dropped out of school halfway through their secondary studies. This situation obviously restricted their access to particular positions in the job market, such that they tended to remain in the low-income social strata. In turn, this fostered in them negative attitudes towards education, discipline, saving and good manners. Being in a way a product of their own condition, these attitudes were also actively produced and encouraged as symbols of identity and commitment to peer-group values, such that they contributed to diminishing even more people's chances of improving their low position. A vicious circle was thus created where the characteristic cultural patterns of the two cliques emerged as both effects and causes of their position. In this subsection, I will seek to explore how these circular relationships were created and experienced in the two groups.

1.2. Unemployment and job instability

During the nineties unemployment and job instability was very high amongst the young, as is shown in figure 5. Most Rambleros and Trepas were seeking employment against a background of depression in the job market. As a consequence, they not only got lesser-valued jobs; it was also totally impossible for them to become economically independent from their parents.

Especially from 1993 onwards, when the employment peak due to the Olympics was left behind, there were very few possibilities for young people to work in minimally acceptable conditions. Pepe said that one could find full-time black-market jobs for 30.000 ptes. monthly pay (approx. US$200), with no contract and no social security. One of the Trepas women was doing survey questionnaires at such a low commission per item that she could not afford any public transport to call on addresses spread all over Barcelona. Another woman found that some job advertisements she had pursued were covert invitations to prostitution. In 1992, the brother of one of the participants had been arrested for selling paper-tissues in the Rambles because the authorities wanted the Olympic summer clean from street dealers. Clara, at one point, declared that job-hunting was so depressing that she had decided to give it up altogether and others apparently took the same line. Only some members of the Rambleros, particularly women, seemed to feel positive about their clerical or semi-skilled jobs, though any idea of becoming independent was hampered by job insecurity and long periods of unemployment.

At the time, the contract system allowed temporary contracts for three years, after which workers had to be made permanent. The two people who

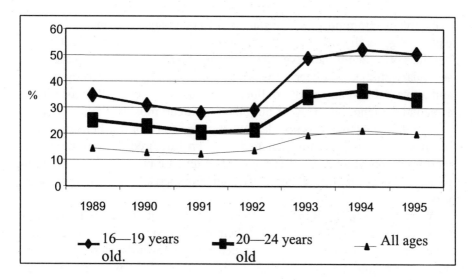

Figure 5: Unemployment rates in Catalonia. Sources: Institut d'Estadística de Catalunya (1992: 127; 1993: 129, 142–143), Departament de Treball (1995:
213; 1996: 297) and Instituto Nacional de Estadística (1998).[32]

had managed to stay three years in a job were fired so that the company did
not acquire any obligations. Other companies had two registered licenses
and alternated contracts from one company to the other so that people never
got permanent contracts.[33]

1.3. Attitudes towards education

Many Rambleros and Trepas entertained negative attitudes towards education that could be compared, in some aspects, to those found by Willis
(1977) amongst British working-class adolescent males. Amongst the
Rambleros, these attitudes were a source for important divisions along gender lines. While most Rambleros men gave little value to education, women
(and particularly the Rambleros women) valued it highly and invested considerably in it. The men explained that they had been unable to show interest in studying and could not bring themselves to do the homework. In contrast, assertive (and effective) commitments to study or to the idea of a career, of continuous improving and learning were only possible amongst the
Rambleros women and one woman and two men of the Trepas (i.e. all

mainstream femininity women plus two Catalan-speaking men). The Trepas were generally not very explicit about what they thought of education,
but the stories about their everyday routines showed that their experience of
secondary studies had been or was still generally characterized by truancy
and a total lack of any study routine. Some of them were still registering at
a secondary school every year but failed to attend most of the lectures and
did not do the exams. It is not clear what the reasons for this behavior were,
but it was consistent with their generally unstructured daily routines and
their rejection of anything that meant a systematic commitment and discipline. In this group, this situation affected both men and women in the same
way.

With regard to the Rambleros women, it was noticeable that they were
(or were on the way to being) much better qualified than the men, and also
sought access to training opportunities geared towards clerical employment: computing courses, English, Catalan. Two of the women were considering going to university and two others had achieved secondary school
qualifications but had not carried on. The following extract shows Irene's
attitude towards education. She had left a part-time job because schoolwork
was getting difficult and her marks had been going down:

Extract 96 [Rambleros]

Irene: Gosh! It cost me an effort. What do you want me to say? to get to fifth grade
[end of vocational training studies]. · Come on. Gosh! Years of studying and
studying, right? And now, er now I'm just not going to drop it. That's for sure.
And the job? Well, yeah, I do like it, right? I have learned many things. · But I
believe that, what I had to learn there, I have already learnt it. · Now it's
already always the same thing same thing same thing same thing. What I was
discussing with my mother is that I would like to go on working, but · in
another place, right?

The really interesting thing about this extract from Irene's interview is
that it is phrased as a kind of vindication, as if she felt the need to justify
her investment in her studies. It is actually noticeable that her argument is
addressed in some ambiguous way to somebody other than myself. In the
disclaimer *"what do you want me to say?"*, I very much doubt the "you"
refers to me, and the same happens with the questions or counter arguments
she anticipates (*"And the job? Well, yeah!"*). She was probably responding
to the discourse of the Rambleros men, a discourse that disapproved of a
deep commitment to study. She probably had in mind the scorn men had
shown for studying in the group discussion. Some men had argued that

women were studying just because they were hoping to get good boyfriends "with nice cars" (as Luis put it), whereas they constructed their leaving school as a kind of manly commitment to confronting the real world.

However, I believe that these more positive attitudes did not make a substantial difference to their social position and prospects. As women, they could only get the typically feminine low-paid posts (clerks, attendants) which, as they perceived quite clearly, are not seen as part of a professional career. As Goffman (1977: 317–318) has very pointedly observed, these posts are based on a male-centered notion of leadership in the workplace, which reserves some support roles for women (often young and sexually attractive ones). Thus, the educational and professional trajectories of most men and of the Rambleros women, despite their significant differences, were equally oriented towards occupying the lower echelons of the socioeconomic market. The marked differences in educational attitudes between men and women did not result in substantially different relative positions in professional terms, as the market value of their skills and qualifications was after all mediated by the logic of the relationship between the sexes in the labor market. From this point of view, it is also significant that the three Rambleros women who finished their secondary studies did not go on to university even when they had actually obtained the necessary qualifications to do so. Probably because their working-class families did not generally see studying as a priority, and probably because they saw it as even less of a priority for women, they had not found the encouragement and financial support needed to pursue a university degree.

Bourdieu observes that working-class women typically deploy strategies to improve socially through marriage, as this is their only possible avenue of upward social mobility, and hence seek to increase their symbolic capital by adopting more docile attitudes and more legitimate forms of speech, appearance and demeanor in order to appear worthier in the eyes of powerful men (see Bourdieu 1991a: 50, 97; Bourdieu and Wacquant 1992: 173). From this perspective, the Rambleros men's view that the women had a hidden agenda might not have been so off the mark as it appeared to be, not in the sense that women had such "plans" in mind, but in the sense that they adjusted their expectations and dispositions towards what was seen as a legitimate trajectory for a young woman in their social milieu, namely that of finding an appropriate partner rather than struggling for an independent career. This means that everybody was responding to the possibilities that the market offered, with unskilled jobs for many males and semi-skilled jobs for some women. From this perspective, the trajectory of the Rambleros women was just as reproductive as that of men, as it was oriented towards what the market offered to working-class women.

These attitudes were therefore the result of the subtle processes whereby individuals develop a sense of a) their place in society and b) the possibilities open to people of their social extraction. On the one hand, their experience in particular fields (family, school, friends) had inculcated into them the habits, attitudes, dispositions and expectations (i.e. the habitus) associated with working-class people and working-class professional trajectories. On the other hand, they had also adjusted their dispositions to respond to the particular demands of particular sections of the market. For instance, Luis' comment on "boyfriends with cars" showed that he had a sensitivity to the differential value of educational capital for men and women, as he knew that secondary-school qualifications would not grant him access to the types of professional and marital opportunities open to women. Indeed, from their perspective, it was true that educational qualifications were of limited value. First, the Trepas and the Rambleros were aware that educational achievement did not ensure direct and fast rewards in the job market, as even university graduates had difficulties in finding jobs due to the considerably high rates of unemployment amongst young people. And secondly, they aspired to occupations where qualifications were not necessary and where, as happened with Willis' lads, their own cultural practices and dispositions were well received and encouraged by fellow workers. From this perspective, it is interesting to appreciate that sensitivity to the demands of the socioeconomic market appeared to be much more developed amongst the Rambleros than amongst the Trepas, a fact which resulted in more stable patterns of employment for the former (see below for further discussion on this point).

However, even accepting the fact that these young people had a point in casting doubts on the value of educational qualifications, we still need to explain how counter-school attitudes emerged and why they seemed to take shape via the active rejection of the whole set of values and dispositions typically fostered by the school, such as ability to learn and display knowledge, discipline and good manners (as opposed to the simplicity, unsophistication, spontaneity and transgression fostered within the peer-group). Bourdieu suggests that it is typical of stigmatized groups to make a virtue out of necessity by claiming their stigma as the basis of their identity (Bourdieu 1991a: 95). The efforts of Luis to present his educational failure as a positive option might have to do with this phenomenon. Counter-school culture would therefore be a particular manifestation of symbolic violence, that is, a process whereby a dominated group incorporates the attributes and attitudes that define them as such. In this case, under the guise of resistance, these young people were accepting the schemata of perception of the dominant classes, although they adhered to the negative poles of them. They displayed their rejection of the mainstream (middle-class) values and dispositions that the school represented by adopting the opposite ones. In this way, they implicitly recognized the symbolic dichotomies that the school sought to inculcate and adopted the stigmatized features that contributed toward confirming their position within the educational and the socioeconomic fields. In this way, they were very actively working to take up the position society had prepared for them.

1.4. Discipline and personal investment in employment

The development of a certain self-discipline is an important feature of the habitus associated with those who invest heavily in education and in professional careers. Any wage earning occupation requires, in some way or other, an orderly management of time and body as well as a systematic availability and commitment in terms of time and effort. However, for the Rambleros and the Trepas, the development of appropriate working habits was hampered by the contradictions inherent in their position. First, their restricted access to employment and financial resources due to underqualification, high unemployment and job instability implied that heavy personal investment in improving their position in the job market had little chance of being rewarded by a substantial improvement (or the prospect of an improvement) in their standing. Secondly, their experience of employment was generally frustrating on various accounts. As happens within the family and the school, the workplace is a social space where young people have little control over the activities and participants involved. Workmates can be nice and fun, but also nasty, boring, mean, stupid, sexist, distant, old-fashioned, snobbish, etc. Similarly, a job could be long, repetitive, depressing and boring, as most jobs for unskilled workers are. For the Rambleros and Trepas, the frustrating experiences in the workplace were set against the experience of the peer-group, which was a real source of enjoyment and where they could develop their creativity and self-esteem. Mateo, for instance, commented that he went through the working hours just looking forward to the weekend fun. Finally, the peer-group often encouraged attitudes and dispositions that were the opposite of those expected in the job market, such that the contradictions between social expectations in the workplace and the peer-group became much more acute than is probably the case in people of other social groups.

In this regard, it was in the Trepas group where people were least attuned to the basic requirements employers set on employees. Significant differences between the Rambleros and the Trepas in relation to orderliness and discipline could be detected in the organization of the peer-group activities themselves. Even in their leisure activities, the Rambleros were used to a certain personal and interpersonal discipline. They were reasonably well coordinated: punctual (for Southern European standards), sticking together all night at weekends, always knowing where everybody was, nobody ever getting abandoned or forgotten. They also dressed in a fairly tidy way. Once, because they had decided to go to a locale where clients were selected on the basis of dress, Pablo scolded Luis for dressing too shabbily. More than once I found that I had dressed too casually myself when I went out with them. In his interview, Pablo insisted on putting across his point that his present life was very laid back because he was unemployed, but that this was not the usual state of affairs. This never happened amongst the Trepas. On the contrary, most Trepas had a certain cult of being laid back, of *doing just what you feel like now*, which also had a bearing on the way the group was organized. People arranged to meet with two or three close friends and it was not unusual for some to be forgotten and not informed about meeting points and times. Except when they arranged to meet for a concert or a band rehearsal, it was not uncommon for people to keep arriving up to more than an hour after the agreed time. Sometimes, when the group started to move, somebody had just gone to make a phone-call or was on some other business and the group had to wait again. Because people had to take different means of transport, they arrived at meeting points at different times, and it was usual for different subgroups in different places to lose track of each other. This attitude led to a situation where nobody seemed to be responsible towards anybody else. This is why some conflicts arose, such as when men spent lengthy periods of time smoking their joints outdoors and virtually forgetting about the women who were waiting for them inside a pub. Once Patricia got worked up and went home because three couples had started kissing and were completely ignoring other group members (in that case, she and I).

The tendency of many Trepas to lead more or less disorganized lives seemed to be accentuated when they faced long periods of unemployment and unsuccessful job hunting. In these periods, they had nothing else to do other than hang around with their friends all day, drink, smoke, attend concerts and so on. This situation led to a total disorganization of house chores (shopping, cooking, cleaning) as well as to irregular eating and sleeping hours. In any case, when they had to confront the "real world", the Trepas had a much more problematic experience in terms of job hunting and working. The impact of having to be disciplined at work was expressed by Salva in his interview, where he described his first job after leaving the training school:

Extract 97 [Trepas]

Salva: Yeah, a change like hell. · I don't know. It's that- · it's getting used to it, right? · Cause, of course (I went into) the job and- · It was- well · damn it: [up to now it was] *"Now we go to the square, a few joints, · a few beers and (a high) like hell" because, of course, you cannot go out. · And, you've got to re-situate yourself, right? To say: "now I'm in a serious job and where- where I can't go beyond the limit". And at the training school, well, I was like, like- like I wished right? · But it's, I don't know, to get used to it, right? Maybe it takes a bit of resignation...*

The training school had certainly been a relaxed experience for the Trepas. They had met new friends of their own age (it was precisely where the Trepas group itself had been born). Jaume said that he liked the training school because he was not pushed around and people showed him respect. Guille reported that he used to get drunk in working hours or simply did not turn up. Clara and Pepe also came to work very irregularly at the time I was there. They said this was because they felt bored and demoralized when it emerged that the school was going to close down. The politicized members of the group had even deployed some trade-union activity (more playful than serious, such as writing graffiti and sticking revolutionary propaganda in their lockers). They did it with the collusion of the staff, who were generally of left-wing orientation and considered that the Trepas were the best group, the most creative and most seriously committed to work (this was actually true, as the general profile of the other trainees was quite low in all respects, some of them having records of petty criminality).

I think that the Trepas' undisciplined and laid-back ethos was largely grounded on the fact that they had to commit themselves to jobs that were quite uninteresting and against which they wanted to show their rejection. However, it was also my impression that it had become a kind of aesthetic pose that prevented them from getting really involved even in things that might have been to their interest. From this perspective, it was another example of a feature that can be seen both as an effect and as a cause of marginalization from the job market and that can become, in certain conditions, a symbol of resistance that has the paradoxical effect of reproducing the structures that actors intend to resist. This means that the Trepas were actively working to give employers good grounds not to hire them and to reproduce conservative stereotypes about young working-class people. The pose was a manifestation of symbolic violence in that it brought them, in an ambivalent way, to take up the role that society had prepared for them as working-class people and to abandon any aspiration to the positions open to the economically advantaged.

1.5. Feminism and the job market

This lesser sensitivity or responsiveness of the Trepas to the requirements of the job market was particularly obvious in the case of the more politicized feminist women. The Trepas women who were involved in redefining femininity and in forms of crossing had not only adopted masculine forms ofself- presentation. They had also followed the path of many men in dropping out of school and going for heavy manual work. However, what they actually found was that the job market did not really have a place for them. As I mentioned earlier, the types of jobs available to these young people were considerably gender-differentiated. As Pepe said, "things come to us already given" and they could do very little about it no matter how politically aware they were. Women were more easily eligible for tough manual jobs if these could be seen to have a kind of continuity with household chores, such as cleaning personnel or some jobs in the textile industry (where Lola worked). Only poorly paid jobs such as delivering publicity leaflets, or passing poll questionnaires seemed to be available to both sexes. Recent political developments had timidly opened up some previously male-dominated domains to women. One Ramblero man worked in a well-known factory where women were being treated on equal terms. In this context, two women had managed to convince the training school staff that they wished to work as builders, although they stayed in the scheme a few weeks only. Clara had worked as a street cleaner for some time, but found that the company's commitment to equality did not necessarily translate into the necessary changes in the organization and relationships in the workplace. Working conditions and infrastructures (for instance, changing rooms) were not adapted to the needs of women. Additionally, women in male working-class jobs often suffered from verbal aggression from their male workmates. Patricia reported how, in some tough jobs, women were derided as "weaklings" by men.

In this context, it appeared as if the Trepas women had ended up having the worst options of all. Their lack of qualifications –and possibly their appearances– were cutting them off from access to the types of employment open to more mainstream forms of femininity, such as clerical and semi-skilled jobs, while masculine jobs remained largely closed to them. Now, at the end of the fieldwork, these women had made moves to go back to secondary school. Some had started attending classes but none was doing well. Their stories conveyed feelings of disengagement and demoralization, resulting in truancy, lack of study and failure to turn up at exams. The last time I visited them, one had given up and was waiting to turn 25 in order to be eligible for direct access to university. Another was looking for a drama school she could afford and where secondary studies were not required.

The case of the feminist Trepas women shows, on the one hand, that people can challenge the tendencies that push them towards reproducing gender divisions (by redefining what counts as legitimate capital for women within the clique), but also that there are serious risks involved in such initiatives, namely that the hidden links that exist between these divisions and well-trodden paths within the economic field are broken. In this context, the working-class women who adopted features of a working-class male habitus were effectively giving away any possible form of capital (qualifications, skills, looks, good manners, discipline) that might be useful either in the marital or the socioeconomic markets. This case thus points towards interesting avenues to understand why particular patterns of gender differentiation are maintained in working-class milieus.

1.6. Money

I have said that the Rambleros and the Trepas invested more heavily in the peer-group than in other areas of life in terms of time, effort and involvement. The same can be said in relation to money. Because most of them were not economically independent, their basic needs (particularly housing, dress and food) were provided for by their families. In Catalonia, it is quite common nowadays that young people have access to stable employment much later than the previous generations. One of the consequences of this is that most people tend to stay in their parents' homes up to their late twenties. This means that, for the Rambleros and the Trepas, the main source of expenditure was the peer-group (drinking, drug taking, music and other forms of non-basic consumption). In the group discussion, some Rambleros men acknowledged that some months they spent their whole full-time wage basically in *vicio* 'fun'. Although these were exceptional cases, the truth was that money to spend on fun was often cited as the main reason for work, as people did not expect their parents to subsidize their leisure expenses.

The Trepas sometimes experienced an acute scarcity of money. Some members of the group had to be bought drinks often and I noticed that some avoided eating for long periods even when they were very hungry. It was also usual to wait outdoors until late hours, when some locales allow free entrance.

It is not possible here to consider whether the attitudes of the Rambleros and Trepas with regard to spending and saving were more or less influenced by their class position, gender or age. The chances are that everything counted. Some indirect comments and jokes seemed to indicate that the Rambleros women tended to save more than the men did. However, such attitudes apparently changed, at least for some members, as they grew older. Five years after the fieldwork, two Ramblero couples had bought flats and were paying mortgages. This means that some of them gradually developed more long-term orientations. In any case, it is quite clear that low or unstable income levels did have a bearing on aspects of the functioning of both cliques. They generally attended the cheapest pubs and discos that were available. The Rambleros, who were somewhat better off, occasionally attended some locales that were selective on the looks and the dressing patterns of the clients (for instance, people were not allowed to enter in sports shoes).

The limited economic resources thus reinforced people's orientation towards the "rough" section of youth culture. From a purely economic viewpoint, their preferences were, if not a necessary outcome, a much more convenient option, given their economic position and given that they coincided with those of their working class milieus, probably for similar reasons. So if neither group liked snobbish people and snobbish places, this was a virtue which fortunately coincided with their necessities, as the alternative would have been to adopt a lifestyle which many of them could not afford. Therefore, the idealization of the "rough" was another feature of their conduct which, being determined or encouraged by economic conditions, was experienced and constructed as the product of free choice. It is

another instance of the special form of symbolic violence I have hypothe-
sized above: actors were actively incorporating the dispositions that were in
accordance with their place in society.

1.7. Speech, appearance and demeanor

Speech, appearance and demeanor are essential elements of people's
habitus. They are closely inter-related aspects of our personality which are
ever present in our day-to-day contacts with other persons. They constitute
the bases of communication and relation with others to the point that the
way we speak, dress and act is inseparable from what we actually say and
do and the way we relate to others. Here I will use the term *interactional
style* to encompass all these aspects of people's social performance. Bourdieu considers that variations in interactional style are connected with class
hierarchies, such that differing speech varieties and patterns of appearance
and demeanor are invested with differing values. The value of particular
features of the interactional style depends, to a large extent, on their convertibility with symbolic or economic capital in other fields. For instance,
competence in the legitimate language (the language used by the most
prestigious social groups and institutions) is associated with access to prestigious jobs, whereas dialects, urban vernaculars and slangs are not.

From this perspective, virtually all the Trepas and all the Rambleros
men tended to adopt the least valued interactional styles, which are constitutive of the "rough" pole of youth culture. For instance, the Andalusian
accent and the inner-city argot are clearly of low value, associated with un-
educatedworking- class milieus. Bearing in mind that the Rambleros were
overwhelmingly of non-Andalusian background, their Andalusian accent
can only be interpreted as a form of position-taking, an active commitment
to stigmatized features which are available in Barcelona probably due to the
fact that the majority of immigrants did come from Andalusia. Additionally, the fact that many Rambleros were functionally monolingual in Spanish constituted a further linguistic "deficit" in a social context where bilingualism is a common requirement for access to skilled jobs and for participation in middle and upper-class milieus. Other characteristic features of
interactional style of these young people (verbal and physical aggression,
foul language, laid-back appearances, drug taking) also matched many of
the common stereotypes associated with working-class males and whose
legitimacy is also problematic in many contexts. The "minimum effort"

style of the Trepas was also reflected in their gestural style, speech, dress and overall appearance.

There is evidence that all these features increased their difficulties of access to the job market, particularly in the case of the Trepas. Many employers consider the looks of their employees as part of the front the business is presenting to outsiders, sometimes even in posts which are quite hidden from view (see Goffman 1959), or simply as an indication of the character and reliability of the employee. This is why Pepe was once rejected from a job (after having been initially recruited) because of his hairstyle, and this in spite of the fact that he had had his hair cut short in the process. Probably to avoid similar problems, Salva had his hair cut short when he started a full-time job in a warehouse. Patricia indicated that, in job interviews, she had to be very careful not to use too much slang, and Lola said that she avoided the use of slang with clients in her workplace.

The relationship between interactional style and the job market was not so problematic for the Rambleros, who also showed a greater sensitivity to the expectations of employers in these matters. The clothes and hairstyle of the men were more formal and their accent was certainly played down when they were not having fun, such that they probably were able to project a more conventional impression when necessary. The women generally used little slang, controlled their swearing, did not adopt non-standard pronunciations, displayed readiness to speak Catalan and dressed as smartly as the men allowed them to without teasing them. Even these women's support for the Barcelona Football Club (which was loathed by the Rambleros men) was more in tune with the expectations that they were likely to find in many workplaces associated with middle-class milieus.

1.8. Gender relations and bilingualism

An analysis of gender relations and bilingual practice within the two groups can yield further insights as to the processes whereby domination is established, maintained or changed, particularly through the configuration of a habitus which embodies the dispositions inculcated by society. Although these two aspects of social practice are of a quite different nature, it is interesting to appreciate that they shared an important condition: patterns of division and inequality were maintained even when formal regulations or legal enforcements had disappeared and even when some individuals sought to actively challenge these divisions and inequalities. Let us consider each case separately.

1.8.1. *Gender relations*

The Rambleros and the Trepas had all grown up in a society where men and women are legally equal and where public schools have mixed-sex classrooms.[34] Another important difference with respect to previous generations was that young women enjoyed much more freedom of movement than their mothers' generation, who would not have been allowed to hang around with boys until late hours.

However, these quite substantial changes had not been enough to do away with traditional gender divisions and inequalities in many respects. Divisions were reflected in the substantial differences in conversational styles, music tastes, drug-consumption habits, speech, dress, attitudes towards studying and so on. Moreover, these differences contributed to reproducing the traditional oppositions between the masculine and the feminine within the boundaries of the peer-group and the workplace. From this perspective, the ongoing confrontations between the Rambleros men and women concerning speech and dress were the very sites where the forms of capital associated with simplified masculinity and mainstream femininity were accumulated and where their value was constantly reconfirmed. In these struggles, the men generally seemed to hold the upper hand as to what meanings and values were legitimate (what was seen as fun, as appropriate dress, and so on), particularly in activities which involved the whole group. Consequently, although the Rambleros women declared that they were in favor of equal rights between men and women, they assumed the traditional feminine stances in many aspects. One example was their ambivalent attitude towards transgressive practices ('I do not do it but I laugh about it'), which effectively yielded situational control to men in many situations. Another significant case happened during the group discussion, where the Rambleros women assumed a totally passive attitude, letting the men voice their opinions and compete for the floor while they kept their own views to themselves. Although this stance could be attributed to an understandable cautiousness, it is significant that the only woman who, exceptionally, managed to intervene as much as the men was also the one who most openly expressed feminist beliefs.

In relation to the Trepas, although women and men had effectively challenged male domination within the group by legitimizing feminine forms of leisure and by introducing cross-gender practices, the truth was that the basic elements of gender differentiation remained untouched. Men were still predominantly gathering around typically masculine rituals while women kept their patterns of intimation and chatting, though in a slightly "rougher" formal mode. Thus Aleix, the only man who had adopted a typically feminine communicative style, had achieved this by associating with the women and having no part in masculine events. The division between the masculine and feminine worlds was therefore reproduced. Despite the fact that this division was perceived as problematic, the politicized Trepas were unable to overcome it or at least fully comprehend it, as it emerged in the group discussion about sex-mixed friendships.

1.8.2. A bilingual market

As I explained in detail in chapter 6, the political conditions surrounding the use of Catalan and Spanish had changed substantially in the previous decade. Public language policies had switched from a repressive policy against Catalan to a bilingual policy that strongly encouraged it. However, just as in the case of gender relations, the everyday processes that restricted the use of Catalan were still operating at the local level. The case of the Trepas is the most significant because they had a wider room for choice. The Rambleros were after all using their own mother tongue. Had they been immigrants in a foreign country, and bearing in mind that three of them came from mixed couples, they might have used the local language to a greater extent, as happens with young people of Italian origin in Germany (Auer 1990). In any case, it is worth noting that, despite the almost non-existent use of Catalan within the group, the Rambleros were sensitive to the requirements of the job market in this matter as well. With the exception of Luis (who appeared to be radically opposed to its use) and Mateo (who claimed that he understood it but was totally unable to speak it), the rest said that they could use it when necessary. Even the anti-Catalanist Pablo pointed out that his knowledge of Catalan had been enough to pass the language exam of a public sector job.

In contrast with the Rambleros, the Trepas were a linguistically mixed group where some members actively sought to encourage the use of Catalan. But, despite their efforts, the Catalan language played only a marginal role within the group. Why was this so? First, they had not managed to displace Spanish from its position as dominant *lingua franca,* and even the more politically aware found it difficult to change the language they were accustomed to speak to particular friends. Secondly, there were the connotations of authority, snobbishness, infantility and unmasculinity that Catalan had acquired as a result of the local processes of appropriation of voices in the peer-group context. This symbolic devaluation of Catalan was performed by all the Trepas, regardless of their political commitments or family language. The politicized Trepas were therefore promoting Catalan with one hand and devaluing it with another. The decisions taken through explicit, conscious reflection were being undermined by behavior learned and produced in implicit form. There is evidence that this process was not taking place among the Trepas and the Rambleros only. I have heard the phrase that "Catalan is not fashionable amongst the young" many times in Barcelona and coming from very diverse people. It is thus likely that this phenomenon is significantly widespread (though we cannot know to what extent).

To seek an explanation for these patterns of behavior within Bourdieu's framework is relatively complex. They seem to respond to contradictory trends in the linguistic field and in its connections with the fields of politics and socioeconomic relations. In socioeconomic terms, Catalan was the language of those who had a better position in the market. In political terms, it was a subordinated language, although the new language policies were seeking to revalue it by promoting new linguistic practices and ideologies. The language policies were seeking to overturn the status of Catalan as a subordinated language at the institutional level and to make people feel that it belonged to all citizens, and not only to those who happened to speak it at home. This meant that some language practices had to be changed, such as the almost automatic accommodation of Catalan speakers to Spanish speakers. Apparently, these developments had had an uneven impact on different social groups and on communicative practices in different contexts. It seems that the old and new orders coexisted and interacted in complex ways, thus giving rise to contradictory *habituses,* which in turn resulted in different patterns of language choice, as we found amongst the Trepas.

The attitude of the Catalan-speaking Trepas reflected the older and still predominant pattern of language choice in Catalonia, which was the result of the subordinated position of Catalan society within Spain. It makes an interesting example of symbolic violence in the sense that these people assumed an active role in the devaluation and marginalization of Catalan within the group *even when* Castilian speakers encouraged them to use it. This old linguistic habitus was developed during the years when the Spanish state established a linguistic market where Castilian enjoyed something close to a monopoly. From 1714 onwards, Spanish had gradually become a kind of universal currency, whereby any Spanish speaker had the right (sanctioned by both official law and common sense) to speak her mother tongue anywhere in the country, was under no obligation to learn any other regional language and had the right to expect to be addressed in Spanish as a matter of course, in a good accent if possible and without incurring any reciprocal obligation. This is certainly why the Rambleros Luis and Pablo saw the obligation to learn Catalan at school as an arbitrary imposition, whereas the obligation to learn Spanish was seen as natural and commonsensical. From this perspective, Catalan speakers used the state's official language very much for the same reasons as Occitan speakers would have used French in Bearn, Bourdieu's native region (Bourdieu 1991a). The only difference was that, in contrast with what had happened in the French Midi, the Spanish ruling classes had not succeeded in their efforts to devalue Catalan to the status of a dialect or a corrupted patois. This is probably why *politeness* and *linguistic proficiency* were the only legitimate arguments available to justify linguistic choices in an open, explicit way. Of course, the asymmetrical linguistic abilities and face-saving duties were but the product of the power that the Spanish state had deployed to unify the linguistic market under the exclusive and excluding obligation to learn and use Spanish. The *lesser* linguistic ability of many young people, as well as its ideological justifications, had thus been actively produced by Spain's power structures: they were the result of the written and unwritten laws of the Spanish linguistic market, to which Catalan speakers had adapted reasonably well by becoming bilingual and by acquiring the skill to respond in Spanish when necessary. This is why, when Clara worked as a waitress, her customers answered back in Spanish when they noticed her Spanish accent.

However, the way in which Clara experienced this situation, i.e. as a form of implicit exclusion, responded to another feature of the complex configuration of sociopolitical relations in Catalonia. Because Catalan speakers dominate local economic resources, it is in the interest of many working-class Spanish speakers to speak Catalan, as this is one of the ways in which one can have access to the social milieus where important economic and symbolic resources are available. Now Catalan speakers seem to be generally unconcerned about the needs of these working-class people and about the consequences of a practice that effectively establishes a boundary between "Catalans" and "non-Catalans", a boundary that carries important economic implications. It is common amongst minority language speakers to resist letting others speak their language, maybe because they want to keep exclusive rights to define what their identity means, or maybe to protect whatever material advantage their identity brings. Whatever the reasons are, in this case Catalan speakers act both as dominated and as dominators, as the linguistic practices they developed as minority speakers are now serving to exclude many working-class people from the avenues of social advancement that most western societies offer.

On the other hand, there were indications that some people were responding to the new conditions of the linguistic market brought about by the emergence of a Catalan political power and its new linguistic policies. Catalan had gained value thanks to the power exerted by the local authorities and pressure groups, so that many Spanish speakers had begun to use some Catalan at school, at work or in official places. For instance, the Trepas and the Rambleros had found that many employers held job interviews in Catalan, probably because they wanted to see evidence of bilingual skills (competence in Spanish was normally taken for granted). Paula reported feeling anxious in an interview for this reason, although she got the job in the end. People who had to take examinations for jobs and courses also had to prove their knowledge of Catalan (which they always did, in the cases I knew about). Irene, a Spanish speaker, was not required to speak Catalan in her interview, but afterwards she was especially assigned the job of attending Catalan-speaking callers. All the people who had direct contact with the public in the workplace (waitresses, shop assistants, receptionists, secretaries) reported having to use some Catalan at work.

In addition to the new conditions leading to the introduction of Catalan in education and the job market, the politicized Trepas were also responding to the processes that had taken place in the political field. This is why it made sense for them to make conscious efforts to speak it in situations where in Bourdieu's Bearn it would have been virtually unthinkable (for instance, to speak Occitan with native-speakers of French). This means that, to an extent, their patterns of language use were sensitive to existing struggles and contradictions within the political field.

One important aspect in this regard was that the young people studied generally positioned themselves against any form of nationalism, whether it was Catalan or Spanish oriented. Because the promotion of Catalan was traditionally associated with the local nationalist tradition, people reacted to it in various ways. I have identified four main positions:

A: That of Luis, Pablo and Magda, who expressed the strongest anti-Catalanist feelings while pointing out that they were apolitical and that they were not Spanish nationalists. This position was associated with the unconscious assumption of the ideological principles of the old Spanish national market, whereby the promotion of Catalan was perceived as an imposition, a nuisance or a threat to the rights one could take for granted as Spanish speakers.

B: The politicized Trepas, who had sought to redefine the meaning of using Catalan by distancing themselves from Catalan nationalism and by arguing that their linguistic practices were an expression of a multiculturalist spirit.

C: The Rambleros women and other Spanish speakers, who more or less accepted the bilingual status quo (the predominance of Spanish and the need to learn Catalan) without elaborating on its political implications.

D: The Catalan speakers for whom the language issue was not particularly important, and who, in order to avoid being seen as nationalists, took great care not to be seen to force other people to speak Catalan to them. This is why Patricia spoke Spanish to her political colleagues who were trying to practice Catalan, lest she should be seen as pressurizing them.

Positions A and B represented positive or active stances, the first seeking to preserve the old order, the second trying to participate in the definition of a new paradigm. Positions C and D represented passive and ambivalent stances that still rested, basically, on attitudes and dispositions inherited from the old order.

From a more socioeconomic perspective, another avenue of interpretation is possible. If we presuppose that the Catalan bilingual market functions in a comparable way to a Bourdieuan linguistic market, then the *bilingual habitus* would have become the equivalent of the proficiency in the legitimate language in a monolingual context. In this case, bilingualism would have become for the Spanish-speaking working classes a proficiency which was seen as legitimate but which many did not acquire, thus giving the bilingual middle-classes (which were predominantly Catalan-speaking) the upper hand in a market which they already dominated (see Woolard 1989). From this perspective, the devaluation of Catalan that was taking place within the two groups would be equivalent to the devaluation of the standard language that takes place in most youth cliques of industrialized societies. It would be another manifestation of symbolic violence under the guise of resistance. Some Spanish-speaking working-class youths would be turning a consequence of their marginalization into a symbol to cherish and maintain. To be consistent with this "choice", they had to orient their professional careers towards sections of the job market where competence in Catalan was not needed, and precisely towards those sections that were occupied by people of the same social background. Thus, their beliefs and attitudes fitted perfectly with the social position they were supposed to take up.

Putting together all these different perspectives, we can see the workings of incorporated dispositions and attitudes towards language learning and using, dispositions that reflect the tensions between the political and the socioeconomic spheres as well as ongoing historical changes. The processes that lead people to incorporate these patterns of behavior are so subtle that they escape the control of their will and often their capacity to understand them and explain them with words. Thus Catalan speakers may switch to Spanish even when their interlocutors do not want them to, while they can also speak Catalan in the presence of people who cannot understand it, as Spanish cannot be spoken "between Catalans". Many Spanish-speakers may sincerely believe that their language choices follow their individual "tastes" or are simply a matter of language competence, but there are deeper political processes working under the surface. The politicized Trepas probably saw themselves as defenders of Catalan, but the subtle processes of appropriation of voices undid much of their work.

2. Social change and situated practice in Bourdieu's model

So far I have used Bourdieu's framework to identify and interpret the practices of the Rambleros and the Trepas in terms of their position within the field of youth culture and as a product of their relation with various other fields, especially the field of socioeconomic relations, but also the fields of education, gender relations, ethnolinguistic relations and politics. In so doing, I have stressed those aspects that appeared to lead these young people to acquire the dispositions (attitudes towards education, dress, language, manners, etc.) that are commonly associated with the lower classes, thus assuming a position within all these fields that was consistent with their own social origins. Amongst the processes leading to this intergenerational reproduction of class position, there was the fact that peer-group practices and identities often encouraged the adoption and active celebration of the cultural forms that were most devalued, particularly in the field of socio-economic relations.

Now it is time to qualify these interpretations and to consider the limits of the social forces that appeared to work so unrelentingly in section 1. To an extent, this exercise involves casting doubts on some interpretations proposed above, as well as on the model in which they are based, that is, Bourdieu's. At this point, I would like to make clear that I am not so much (at least not always) taking issue with Bourdieu's ideas as such but with the way in which they can be brought to bear upon my data and my research agenda. However, there is the inevitable implication that Bourdieu's present conception of fields, habitus and capitals is difficult to apply to the analysis of situated practice and to an understanding of processes of social change. My view of the basic problems of Bourdieu's works coincides very much with that of Aaron Cicourel, as he argues that it is not clear how the formation of habitus and the imposition of dominant values can be linked to "the moment to moment or locally managed and practiced activities" (1993: 98), i.e. how the "objective structures" described constitute and are constituted in situated social processes.

In this section, I will discuss three issues that Bourdieu's model does not seem to be able to address: a) Why did the Trepas have more difficulties in finding jobs? b) Why are transgressive practices associated with working-class sectors? c) In what way could we see the Trepas' practices as forms of resistance? Finally, I will also discuss the implications of these considerations for the development of positive policies to avoid social exclusion, sexism, racism and so on.

2.1. The differences between the two groups

In the previous section I explained that the Rambleros had access to jobs that were generally more stable than those of the Trepas. This finding was somewhat unexpected because, as many colleagues have pointed out to me, one would have thought that it was the Trepas who were endowed with more cultural capital (such as their knowledge about politics and history, their ability to talk in a conceptually rich way, their positive attitudes towards Catalan), so that they should have been more successful in the job market. Thus, the logical alternative interpretation was that the Trepas showed less *sensitivity* to the demands of the jobmarket , as they failed to appreciate that the market "rewards" the more conservative forms of identity, particularly in the lower occupational strata, where intellectual skills are not valued and where individuals are put under pressure to maintain the sexual division of labor and the more conventional types of appearance and demeanor. Bourdieu concedes that such differences of sensitivity can exist and that the value of cultural forms is not fixed. However, his writings do not indicate how these variations emerge and how they can be treated analytically. On the contrary, the dispositions of the habitus and the values of particular features are mentioned for explanatory purposes, but are not made the objects of explanation themselves. The habitus is simply treated as the product of objective structures, while values are treated as simply arbitrary. For instance, statements that particular social features or practices are of *low value*, because of their association with *lower class* people, appear together with observations that the class position of people is partially determined by the value of their practices. Although this apparent double bind is one of the bases of the model and is acceptable in the sense that social groups can be seen as caught in a kind of vicious circle of deprivation and devaluation of their attributes, it is nonetheless a dangerous hermeneutic device if used to interpret data, because it may lead the analyst to produce a tautological discourse that concentrates only on aspects of the data that fit in with the model and disregards as irrelevant those that do not.[35] Consequently, when we face a contradiction between common expectations and actual findings, such as this one, the model does not help us to acquire an understanding of the processes involved. The only way out is to observe that the Trepas were failing to convert their cultural capital into economic capital.

To break this hermeneutic circularity we may wish to consider the conditions that surrounded the experience of job hunting within the two groups. The Rambleros often found jobs through informal contacts rather than via newspaper ads. I once spoke with one of the parents and it became very clear to me that job searching was something that involved everybody, i.e. friends and relatives. Amongst the Trepas, on the contrary, it was experienced more individually, such that people became demoralized and often avoided talking about it altogether. This means that the personal attributes of the Rambleros might not have been so important in the job-hunting process. Their better position in the job market might have been due to their higher degree of integration within the family and the community. In turn, this higher integration might have helped them to acquire the necessary dispositions to ensure their eligibility.

Bourdieu believes very strongly that it is simply the social position of speakers that determines the value of their cultural features, which means that one is left with the impression that there is no need to scrutinize the processes whereby the various forms of capital acquire their value[36] (See Lipuma 1993 and Hasan 1998). Consequently, we just have to assume a direct connection between (value-arbitrary) cultural features and marginalization. This may easily lead researchers to develop rather aprioristic or circular arguments. In this way, we may overlook the important social processes through which cultural features are incorporated, acquire their particular values and contribute to integration and marginalization. This is why Bourdieu's writings do not provide ways to explore the differences between Rambleros and Trepas in terms of access to the job market.

2.2. The social location of peer-group practices

Another arguable point is the idea that transgressive, rough or deviant practices are characteristic of working class youths and can be used to partially explain, as I did above, their marginal position in the job market. This view is commonplace amongst researchers of youth culture. However, it is also true that the use of juvenile slang can be found amongst youth cliques of very diverse social origin, while dirty language is clearly present in most adult (especially male) informal milieus. The same can be said in relation to drug taking, rock music and other features. In fact, many of these practices are remarkably coincident with the type of behavior Goffman associates with *backstages*, i.e. "a place, relative to a given performance (i.e. the *frontstage*), where the impression fostered by the performance is knowingly contradicted as a matter of course" (Goffman 1959: 114). An example would be when shop attendants retire to a reserved room and relax, chat and engage in activities which would be inappropriate to carry on in front of customers. Backstages and backstage activities are, Goffman points out, present in all social settings and groups, and have come to be associated with characteristic forms of behavior, such as "profanity, open sexual remarks ..., rough informal dress, 'sloppy' sitting and standing posture, use of dialect or substandard speech, mumbling and shouting, playful aggression

and 'kidding'..." (ibid.: 129).The question thus arises of whether the pre-
sumed association between these features and the working classes is valid
or simply responds to social prejudices that "appear to resonate well with
(tacitly understood) personal experiences" of academics, as Cicourel (1993:
102) suggests in his critique of Bourdieu.

Bourdieu would probably associate transgressive practices with his "alternative markets", i.e. the "space provided by private life, among friends...
where the laws of price formation which apply to more formal markets are
suspended" (1991a: 71) or, alternatively, the "spaces that belong to the
dominated classes", particularly those based on the "transgression of the
fundamental principles of cultural legitimacy" and on the "will to distinguish oneself vis-à-vis ordinary forms of expression" such as the ones that
support the forms of slang of gangs of young people (ibid.: 94–99).
Bourdieu does not elaborate on the relationship between informal and marginal spaces. He points out that different markets can be classified according to their degree of autonomy "according to the degree of censorship
which they impose" (ibid.): from the most subjected (to dominant norms) to
the most inhibited. Hence working-class gangs can produce reversed for-
malities that create, in some contexts, a degree of tension similar to the one
found in very formal upper class milieus. Finally, the cases of upper-class
people adopting popular features of performance and speech should be
seen, following the logic of the model, as strategies of condescension and
distinction.

In my view, these observations are generally valid, but it is the task of
sociologists to be more specific about where and how transgressive practices originate, in what conditions they are interpreted and evaluated in differing ways, and how they come to play the reproductive role that we assume they play (if they do). Otherwise it will be very difficult to tackle social problems that arise in informal contexts. I will try to briefly explore
some of these issues here with respect to the Rambleros and the Trepas by
drawing upon Goffman's insights on the functioning of backstages.

Goffman observes that, in backstage spaces, individuals relax from,
comment about or prepare for the performances they have to carry on in the
frontstages of life. In these constexts, it becomes conventional to derogate
elements and individuals of the frontstage performance (Goffman 1959:
172–173), this derogation often being so conventionalized that it may have
nothing to do with people's actual feelings for whatever is being derogated.
Sometimes, Goffman claims, the backstage performance "may become an
obligation and a pose in itself" (ibid.: 161). The practices I have described

could be fitted in many ways within this framework. Some of the conversations analyzed referred to people's experience at school or in the workplace, and could be seen as typical instances of the kind of backstage chat mentioned by Goffman. Stretching a little the meaning of the term, we could see youth culture as a backstage space in relation to the performances that are expected from young people in adult life or in milieus controlled by adults. Certainly, the relationships of solidarity established between group members and with other acquaintances of the same age (and maybe class) were comparable to the examples given by Goffman of the relation of "colleagueship" that is established between members of the same sex, ethnic group or profession, a relationship which involves a certain complicity and camaraderie that excludes outgroup members from access to backstage regions and activities (ibid.: 158–161). In a way, the fact that most activities were carried out in dark and late hours and in physical spaces separated from all the others (school, workplace, family home) points to the fact that they are traditionally and generally treated as backstage and as requiring a limited access and visibility from non-members (ibid.: 116). Additionally, the derogatory (i.e. transgressive) character of peer-group practices was indeed conventional in the sense that it became obligatory or, better, constitutive of the social space itself. To participate in the groups meant to engage in such exercises, but to "play the game" did not mean to believe in it a hundred per cent. In the interviews, some participants provided interesting examples of discrepancies with elements of their performances within the groups. For instance, the Ramblero Ricardo declared that drinking was becoming boring and that their jokes about the Catalan language made sense as a form of fun but that his attitude towards the language was in truth positive (a position shared by all the women of this group). Finally, the naturalness claimed in many masculine performances also ties in with the frontstage-tense backstage-relaxed dichotomy. This naturalness, as both Goffman and Bourdieu point out, does not always come so naturally. The pressure exerted on the Rambleros women to play down their appearances could be seen as an example of the need to preserve the transgressive and unsophisticated ethos within the group.

Seeing youth culture as kind of "structural backstage" or a "backstage frontage" (i.e. in the sense that backstage performances become themselves conventional) may lead us to explore the ways in which the practices of youth cliques are dependent on and constituted around dominant discourses. Let us take the school as an example where a given institution actively inculcates the legitimacy of the dominant forms of capital. The process takes place through educational procedures which typically involve the whole classroom, a frontstage space where individuals are evaluated according to their performance and in the presence of their fellow students, such that an educational hierarchy is created between pupils, a hierarchy which sets apart the "good" and the "bad" students, that is, those who manage to acquire educational capital and those who do not. The logical outcome of such a process must be that any backstage activity will be oriented to evoke, call into question or deride, the forms of capital created and distributed in the frontstage. Because the school plays a major role in the creation of friendships and cliques, it is logical to think that it contributes significantly to the constitution of the social spaces where the forms of transgression typical of youth culture are created and developed. The school is the first social milieu that provides plenty of opportunities for individuals to organize backstage performances, particularly by (inconsequentially) threatening the established educational order. Backstage behavior together with colleagueship amongst pupils and against the teacher become conventional and an end in itself. Even highly motivated students often feel forced to display conventional disinterest in classroom activities, lest they should betray the pose of those of their own ranks. For some pupils, especially those who do not do well, backstage activities become the most important ones. The higher the deprivation the higher the need to display excellence in backstage spaces. Thus Willis' lads sought to humiliate and deride the pupils who did well at school probably to make up for the humiliation they themselves experienced when they were treated as low-achievers in the classroom. Indeed, in my childhood, I remember that many people with low marks would characteristically seek to gain control and notoriety in the playground, where they even resented competition from high achievers who also were, for instance, good at soccer. Thus people who do not get a good deal from one social space may seek to do better in another. Some individuals will therefore take a confrontative stance against the school, society, adults, anyone, and will try to excel in antisocial and risky practices which will never cease to constitute a kind of "compensation". The meaning of backstage practices will thus be highly dependent on the dominant practices and identities against which they are developed, as well as on the processes of appropriation and reaccentuation that take place in peergroup arenas. This is why some forms of behavior will appear as meaningless in themselves, ridiculous or gratuitously dangerous.

It follows that the association between the features and practices described and the social extraction of the Rambleros and the Trepas may not be so categorical and necessary. It may be that deprived groups simply tend to invest *relatively more* in backstage practices (and their corresponding identities) in terms of time, money, emotional attachment and so on. It may also be that they do not tend to keep frontstage and backstage performances as separated or insulated as better-off groups do and as many posts of responsibility in the job market require. Therefore, the ways in which these social features (speech, proxemics, dress, tastes) can come to operate as stigmas is probably highly subtle and varies greatly according to context.

Bourdieu's model does not provide the means to explore the details of these processes. This is, first, because these processes can only be detected through the close analysis of situated practice, which Bourdieu usually avoids because he associates this level of analysis with an uncritical interactionism. And secondly, because he claims that the values of forms of capital or cultural features are entirely arbitrary, i.e. the result of the arbitrary imposition of dominant values by dominant groups, so that there is no need to explore other processes or relationships that may bear upon the forms of capital active within a given field. The consequence of this is that the particular characteristics of each form of capital in terms of its connections with practices and individuals, and its relationship with forms of capital of other fields, are treated in a relatively vague way. In relation to the matter at hand, one should take into account that the dependence of transgressive practices upon dominant practices is quite different from the misrecognized relations that the fields of education, the arts or sports have with the field of socioeconomic relations. There are clear connections between these. A high position in any of the former fields provides symbolic capital that has exchange value in the latter. For instance, top academics may earn a lot of money and acquire powerful connections with politicians and entrepreneurs. This is why we can find that most of these fields are dominated by actors whose social origin is similar, i.e. the ruling classes, as they are the ones who can either invest more in acquiring the right forms of capital in whatever field they choose or in redefining what counts as capital in a way that fits their interests. Additionally, these fields are more autonomous in the sense that their actors (especially the powerful ones) can establish internal procedures and criteria to define and distribute sources of value that need not have a strictly direct relationship with those of other fields. On the contrary, transgressive practices are highly (though negatively) dependent on dominant divisions, i.e. on dominant forms of classification and evaluation. If dominant cultural patterns change, it makes no sense to transgress them anymore. Additionally, the capital accumulated in transgressive spaces is rarely convertible outside those spaces. This is why it is rare to find individuals of upper-class origin investing seriously in those spaces, except for some who (I would guess) suffer from forms of exclusion other than economic (family conflicts, mental or physical handicaps) or take it as a kind of temporary game from which they know that they can opt out at any time. In contrast, for those who are being excluded from meaningful participation in every other field, the peer-group may provide a space to gain some form of symbolic capital by whatever means; and the means that are left are basically one's body and one's readiness to play with risk. Thus, if these individuals define their values in opposition to the dominant ones, they find themselves investing in something which reinforces their exclusion from the rest of society and, in some cases, even puts their life at risk.

This avenue of interpretation might well help us to understand some of the problems posed at the beginning of this book concerning reckless driving and hard-drug taking: such behavior should characteristically be found in individuals who have trouble in carving out a position for themselves in the frontstages of life, as well as any individual who has an interest in accumulating the forms of capital that are valid in the peer-group context for whatever reason. In relation to the Trepas and the Rambleros, the implication of this is that the problem with their peer-group identities was not so much the identities in themselves, but the fact that their economic instability made them confer too much importance to the world constructed within the peer-group.

2.3. Relaxing, rebuffing or resisting

After considering the association that exists between transgressive practices and the lower classes, another question arises, namely that of their value as forms of resistance and/or as practices that can lead to social change. The issue of resistance is one of the most contentious points of Bourdieu's model. He has often been accused of determinism. Bourdieu is generally skeptical about the transformatory character of many forms of resistance or progressive policies (see also Hasan 1998). In this case, though, I also resist seeing the transgressive practices of the Rambleros and the Trepas as forms of resistance and as potentially revolutionary (this is, I believe, a dangerous form of self-deception, of which the Trepas were partly guilty). The two cliques constituted "autonomous" spaces that did not really challenge the hierarchical logic of the dominant market. As Bourdieu puts it:

> ...the formal law, which is thus provisionally suspended rather than truly transgressed, remains valid, and it re-imposes itself on dominated individuals once they leave the unregulated areas where they can be outspoken (and where they can spend all their lives). (Bourdieu 1991a: 71)

It is obviously hard to see any transformatory or revolutionary value in swearing, drug-taking, playful fighting and other such games. Willis (1977) also observed that his rough lads enjoyed breaking the rules of the school but never really challenged the authority of the staff. The attitudes of the Rambleros men towards the military service pointed in the same direction. The disappearance of religious swearing in this generation, now that the church plays a secondary role in the social and political spheres, also points towards the direct dependence on these markets of the dominant ones.

However, there was some potential for social change in peer-group practices. The Trepas' view that they had some sort of political or revolutionary flavor tied in with some cases (such as the Catalan anti-military movement or the Basque National Liberation Movement) where grass-roots oppositional movements seem to owe their (at least partial) successes to their ability to establish implicit and ambivalent connections between the codes of political resistance and the codes of transgressive youth culture. Peer-group practices were thus being reinterpreted as a form of mobilization that connected with other more politically visible forms of mobilization. Consequently, peer-group identities can become politically relevant if particular sectors manage to symbolically *co-opt* them in a way that is perceived as legitimate (see also Bourdieu 1991a: 130).

Transgressive practices appear, therefore, not as transformatory in themselves, but as open to the incorporation of new patterns of practice (as the politically correct initiatives of the Trepas show) as well as available for incorporation *into* processes of mobilization.

To consider a clearer example of successful resistance, we may draw upon, as Kathryn Woolard has pointed out (1985b, 1989), the case of Catalonia under the dictatorship of general Franco. Woolard has described how Catalan society was able to challenge the cultural hegemony of the Spanish state in spite of the latter's total control of official institutions. She points out that Franco's brutal methods might have failed to gain the appropriate legitimacy, and also that Catalans' control over the local economy might have played a very important role in maintaining the prestige of the Catalan culture (1985b: 742). She then argues that the Catalan example is evidence that one cannot assume, as Bourdieu does in his writings, that modern societies necessarily constitute an *integrated* linguistic market, as this automatically excludes the possibility of addressing the complex dynamics, phenomena and processes associated with the vulnerabilities of these markets.

Now it is not impossible to stretch Bourdieu's framework to account for some of the phenomena that Woolard investigated. One could argue that the Catalan language retained much of its linguistic value because it maintained its convertibility into economic capital, and particularly because it became a mark of distinction in the face of the massive immigration movements that brought uneducated Castilian speakers to fill the demand for unskilled labor. However, such explanations can only be arrived at via an *ex post facto* interpretation. Bourdieu does not deny the possibility of resistance, but his writings are clearly geared towards identifying (and denouncing) reproductive trends, as well as towards favoring one-sided interpretations of social practices. The result is an analysis that levels off ambivalence and precludes the consideration of other directions to which social practices may be pointing. It is thus difficult to use Bourdieu's ideas to explore the fine and fuzzy line between forms of "dummy" resistance, such as transgression, and other forms of social practice that could involve real resistance and an effective potential for social change.

The two examples studied here seem to suggest that the driving forces of change lies somewhere outside the peer-group, possibly in milieus associated with pressure groups and minorities that can create autonomous spaces where the formation of alternative cultural forms and ideologies is possible. This would mean that the difference between the alternative cultural practices of pressure or minority groups on the one hand, and those of youth gangs on the other, would lie on the fact that the former retain a certain constitutive power despite their subordinate position, while the latter are much more dependent on dominant discourses.

Concluding remarks

The differences between (and within) the Rambleros and the Trepas are an interesting source of questions as to the significance of peer-group practices, their causes and consequences. These differences certainly prevented

me from being tempted to put forward easy explanations and generalizations. They can help to understand where the limits of social determinants
lie and how social changes can be promoted through particular policies.
These limits are precisely what is of interest to policy makers, social workers, schoolteachers or parents in relation to the "problems" of youth culture.
They want to know the causes of problematic behavior and find out solu-
tions that can be applied to particular social contexts. How could we provide this type of knowledge from the perspective developed here?

Bourdieu suggests that the most extreme forms of typical youth-gang
misbehavior, "the cult of violence and quasi-suicidal games, of bikes, alcohol or hard drugs", are associated with the most deprived social groups because they can draw no benefit from morality and sensitivity (Bourdieu
1991a: 95–96). This negative causality could be technically reinterpreted in
the following way: socially deprived individuals develop strategies to accumulate alternative forms of capital in alternative markets. However, this
explanation leaves the above-mentioned interest groups relatively empty-
handed. After all, they see that not all young persons and cliques develop
the same patterns of behavior. There are not only differences across cultures, but also differences amongst people of equivalent social backgrounds
(the differences between Rambleros and Trepas being a good example of
this) and similarities amongst people of very different social backgrounds,
such as whennot-so- deprived people engage in games and practices similar
to those of lower-class gangs. If (as Bourdieu acknowledges) the market
does not have a direct, unmediated and undifferentiated effect on people's
practices, the parties concerned will naturally wish to know what other
relevant processes may be at work.

In chapter 2 extract 28, the Trepa Jaume was telling us a very interesting
story about his early adolescence in a previous clique. As he grew older, he
found that his friends were going for harder and harder drugs. They were
doing this, in his own words, to "feel superior". Because he did not want to
go down that road, he decided to leave the clique and enter a more mainstreamish youth club. His story shows that drug taking had become a form
of capital accumulation in his previous clique; it had become constitutive of
the identities produced within that group. Therefore, he had perceived that
he had only two choices left: either to stay and play the game or leave. Fortunately enough, he found (through his family contacts) an alternative social space with totally different forms of capital accumulation. Why he took
this chance and why the others did not is an interesting question. His connections with Catalan-speaking networks might have had something to do

with it. Jaume's father was a Catalan speaker who, having worked all his life in the management team of a big factory, had been made redundant and laid off recently. The youth club was connected with an important network of Catalan institutions created during the dictatorship (excursion societies, scout groups), and which was partly aimed at providing alternative leisure and pedagogical spaces at community level. These services were mainly used by middle-class Catalan-speaking families.

True, these social processes may have a degree of unpredictability and haphazardness. Bourdieu's assumption that the values of social features are arbitrary, together with his frequent use of statistics, contribute to the impression that the patterns of behavior that do not match the rule must be due to mere chance or to idiosyncratic differences between human beings. Jaume's story, however, may give us a clue as to where to look for an explanation of more substance. His story reminds us that identities need a social base, that is, a network of meaningful relationships with others where values, habits, meanings can be jointly developed. The youth club provided him with an alternative social space, where he could seek to accumulate its particular forms of capital and to develop an identity which was more acceptable to himself and to society in general.

The case of the politicized Trepas also reminds us that ideas and commitment to ideas need more than purely rational reflection and apprehension. The practices that we have identified as somewhat innovative in terms of gender relations and language use had been made possible because these people had participated in social spaces (political parties, grass-roots movements) that encouraged commitment to social change. That is, they had been *involved* in activities and personal relationships where these ideas had been part of the process of capital accumulation and identity formation. This is why it made sense for them to transfer the ideas to the peer-group and why they perceived them as important enough to take the trouble to do so.

It is probably true that tiny alternative markets, such as Jaume's youth club or some more or less marginal political groups, make little difference to the overall configuration of economic and political relations in industrialized societies. However, these findings give us an important clue as to how social changes can be supported at community level, namely by providing the infrastructures and encouraging the initiatives that would allow for the creation of new social spaces where individuals might actively develop new forms of identity. From the perspective of people worried about anti-social behavior, the question to ask would be to what extent young working-class people in Barcelona had alternative options to their typical leisure activities. Participation in political groups was clearly an option that some Trepas had taken up, although it was not widely seen as attractive. Other than this, there were almost no alternatives for these people to engage in meaningful relationships with others that involved active and creative participation. The lack of public spaces and services for leisure was one factor, with youth clubs and civic centers being open only on weekdays. The new fashionable sports or forms of tourism tend to be quite expensive. Why most of the Rambleros and Trepas did not feel attracted by voluntary associations, religious groups and the like would be a good question to ask, but these did not seem to be regarded as an option.

From the perspective of people concerned with gender relations or with the future of the Catalan language, the questions would be similar to those concerned with social integration in general: how could one create new social spaces or promote existing ones where the desired meanings, values and practices could be developed? How could one organize access to new social spaces in a way that would make sense for these people to participate in? It is clear that any "proposal" for these people should be attractive in the sense that they should see room for self-improvement probably in terms of integration within a local community or group which provided a certain prestige and support.

The term *participation* is therefore the pivotal point around which policy implications can be drawn from this approach. Identities, values, attitudes, abilities only grow in networks of relations where individuals can lead a meaningful existence and can contribute to the shaping of their relationships with others. The issue is therefore how we can create, help to create or allow others to create spaces of participation for those who must organize their lives at the fringes of the fields where wealth and other forms of capital of our society are produced and distributed.

I believe that Bourdieu's model contains many useful elements. His conceptualization of the dynamics of social fields, of the relationships between fields, of the relations between habitus, field and action open up new avenues of sociological exploration such as the one presented here. In my view, we need to explore how to balance the deterministic slant of his works with new conceptual proposals as to how fields can be created, maintained or transformed, thus opening for social actors the possibility to organize alternative practices, values and habituses, such as Jaume did.

Conclusions to part 3

Theoretical implications of this approach

In this final part of the book, I have discussed the significance of the practices described in parts 1 and 2 within the wider political processes of which they were a part. I tried to conceptualize these relations between practices and structures by drawing on ideas from Bourdieu. From this perspective, the cultural forms of the Trepas and the Rambleros were the products of the social structure in which they were inserted as well as the producers of new structures that they contributed toward shaping. There are various conclusions can that be drawn from my analyses from the two standpoints, that is, from a view of practices as reproductive and as productive. Bourdieu's framework is of considerable help in showing how local networks can be seen as located in wider social fields and how their internal dynamics are affected by the gravity (as he puts it) of these fields. There is a strong case for arguing that the cultural practices analyzed in this book were largely the product of the social position of the Rambleros and the Trepas as the children of low middle-class and working-class families. It is the people of these social groups that provide the highest rates of educational failure and who are likely to access the least valued kinds of employment. This situation leads many young people to join others who share their experience and who develop a rejection against the mainstream social values and institutions that have participated in their exclusion. The attitudes they develop in these groups are likely to increase their chances of marginalization unless they have a clear sense of what the limits are between the peer-group and the rest of society.

However, there are still many gaps to fill in this analysis, some of them having to do with the partial character of the data gathered, others having to do with theoretical problems in Bourdieu's model and others with both. With more data, we might be able to assess, for instance, whether politicized identities are treated differently in other sections of the job market (such as middle and upper-middle class jobs). This would mean that the market regulates the possibility of organizing particular projects of self in a partial way, that is, by putting pressure on the lower-classes to remain conservative. Were it possible to substantiate this hypothesis, the case of the Trepas would be a clear example of resistance to socioeconomic determinants, as well as an example of the relative value of particular forms of capital; the value being relative both in relation to a feature's position within the whole field and in relation to the processes that lead to the determination of value in particular contexts. And this is where we would find ourselves in the limits of what Bourdieu's model allows us to do. His writings do not indicate how we can conceptualize and explore the processes whereby particular social features (i.e given forms of capital) acquire their values and meanings. To explore these issues, we have to acknowledge that it is possible for individuals to act in creative and ambivalent ways in particular contexts, that is, we have to pay due attention to *situated practice*, to the local processes whereby individuals construct meanings and identities. The details of how fields work at the local level, and how they come to produce the results associated with their location (or not, i.e. how they can bring about social change) are difficult to investigate with Bourdieu's analytical tools. In turn, these limitations affect the applicability of the model, that is, the possibility of addressing political issues in ways that can inform social movements and policies.

Bourdieu's model has been criticized for being too deterministic, for laying excessive emphasis upon the reproductive aspects of social practice, as well as for his lack of attention to the interactional, situated dimension of practice. In my view, the limitations that many authors find in his work are due to one basic problem, that is, that his analyses are founded upon an inadequate theory of meaning. In his interpretations, he always assumes that the values of practices and discourses are totally arbitrary rather than produced in (situated) social practice. His belief in the absolute arbitrariness of meaning has already been criticized by Lipuma (1993) and Hasan (1998).

Bourdieu has responded to the frequent criticisms on the deterministic or mechanistic character of his model in various ways. He has observed that the habitus is not mechanically produced by social structures, but that it is an *open* system of dispositions that is sensitive to new experiences and hence to modifications. Individuals, he claims may adjust to their conditions of existence (i.e. react to their experiences) in different ways (see Bourdieu 1991c: 127–128; Bourdieu and Wacquant 1992: 130–133). Additionally, people can defy determinisms through reflexive analyses, that is, through the capacity to perform a critique of their conditions and dispositions (ibid.: 136–137). This reflexive analysis, he argues, should be a central concern for sociologists. Finally, he has argued that his writings and theorizations on social reproduction reflect the particular issues he has researched in an empirical way and should not be interpreted as a closed, ready-made model or as an attempt to produce a universally valid social theory (Bourdieu and Wacquant 1992: 159–161). Social change must therefore be investigated empirically as well, which is what he tried to do in part in *Homo Academicus* (Bourdieu 1984a).

Thus, the deterministic slant of his works originates basically in his research agenda, but there are open doors to investigate social change. However, if we wish to explore these alternative avenues, we encounter a model that depicts social agents actively though unthinkingly producing their own position as dominated individuals (symbolic violence) as a result of social processes that are described in an abstract, a-contextual and de-personalized way. This is, I would argue, because a model where meanings are totally arbitrary and pre-given by some external social structure precludes the possibility of exploring how interpretations and ideologies are imposed, fought upon or changed. In short, Bourdieu's implicit theory of meaning needs to be unpacked. If we wish to pay attention to the processes of meaning creation and negotiation, it is necessary to focus upon situated practice, that is, on the actual social loci where such processes take place, an analytical dimension that Bourdieu has so far avoided (if not strongly criticized). Probably, he has avoided it because attention to situated, interactional detail brings to the fore the problems of interpretation, that is, the fact that in social practice meanings appear often as unfinished and ambivalent. True enough, the recognition of these problems may lead many authors to embrace an uncritical relativism, which is what Bourdieu strongly criticizes. However, the solution is not to throw out the baby with the bathwater. We need an analytical framework that gives the situated side of social practice its due weight, and a framework that accepts the creative and ambivalent character of practice as an analytical starting point so that we can understand how creativity and ambivalence is managed, exploited, precluded or eliminated in situated interaction.

Bourdieu's analyses tend to dissolve or eliminate the ambivalence of the practices analyzed. This has not been identified as an issue, at least in these terms, either by Bourdieu or his commentators. In *The Logic of Practice*, Bourdieu does emphasize the ambiguous and indeterminate character of symbols (1990: 17), and argues that practical logic exploits "the polysemy of the symbols that it uses", particularly through metaphor and analogy (ibid.: 261). However, this idea is only applied to the analysis of rituals in order to argue that anthropologists have traditionally gone too far in trying to find a coherence in the use of symbols that is not natural to practice. He does not exploit the potential of this idea in a positive way, that is, in terms of the practical procedures that social actors deploy, successfully or not, to produce and sustain particular definitions of situations, these procedures being largely of a semiotic kind. I would argue that the problem originates in the core of Bourdieu's model, namely the idea that the objective truth of class relations is somehow dressed up under a particular veil of symbolic relations (Bourdieu 1991a: 136) that actually allows the objective relations to operate in a misrecognized form. Although this idea apparently opens up the possibility of acknowledging two competing views on a given state of affairs (that is, in terms of how it is symbolically apprehended by participants and how it is inserted within a particular configuration of power relations), the truth is that Bourdieu gives much more weight to the latter.

This is so despite the fact that he argues that the sociologist's job is precisely to scrutinize the relationship between the two, i.e. between the analyst's schematic abstractions (on how social structures work) and the agents' own experience –what he calls the epistemological break, whereby analysts must seek to bridge the distance between these two aspects. Additionally, his use of the notion of struggle sometimes seems to imply that the significance or value of particular elements can be seen as ambivalent or contingent because a particular social group may be able to change the rules of the game to further its own interests. For him, agents can achieve change if they "act on the social world by acting on their knowledge of this world", i.e. through political struggles that put forward alternative forms of representation of the world through language (Bourdieu 1991c: 127). This possibility entails necessarily the existence of competing constructions and interpretations of social phenomena, thus opening up the possibility of considering whether some practices may constitute the expression of a revolutionary struggle or not. Despite these implicit acknowledgements of the problematic character of meaning, his writings tend to resort to generalizing explanations that discard the situated perceptions of agents.

It is these problems and contradictions that cause difficulties when it comes to considering what kinds of political action may be relevant to address particular social problems, as we are unable to consider in what conditions and through which procedures changes (of whatever sort) can be encouraged. For instance, from the perspective of politicians, social workers and the like, it is not enough to conclude that their target populations or policy partners do things as they do simply because they have incorporated particular patterns of practice or discourse as a result of their social origins and conditions. Precisely what they need to know is where the unassailable social determinants begin to loosen their grip and hence how they actually come to have a grip in the first place so that more "gripful" alternatives can be pursued. *The processes* that lead social groups and individuals to adopt particular practices or discourses rather than others (sometimes, even when the choices run against the interests of all the parties involved) should be the central concern of an applied sociology

A deeper understanding of how particular practices acquire their value, how the habitus actually incorporates its dispositions and how fields contribute to the reproduction of power relations would help us to tackle many of the questions that we expect sociology to answer. This is what I have tried to develop in this study by combining the ideas of Fairclough (1992a, 1992b), Goffman (1959, 1974), Bakhtin (1981, 1986) and Bourdieu himself (1990, 1991a) to analyze practice both as produced and as productive of local orders of discourse where these processes of meaning creation and negotiation take shape.

I have argued that Bourdieu's model does not help us to describe and understand the subtle social processes that produce exclusion. Nor does it help us to distinguish between modalities and degrees of exclusion. Nor does it point towards possible ways of preventing it or solving it once it emerges. Moreover, his writings do not provide us with any clue as to how alternative social spaces could be put to work and what general principles could inspire such initiatives: would a political party do? an NGO? a new form of cooperative entrepreneurship? a new form of community government? new legislation on private property?

However, his works do point towards an interesting hypothesis which can serve, in turn, as an important tip for any political scheme aimed at tackling these issues: that the dynamics of all social spaces are more or less directly connected with the field of socioeconomic relations and with the political field. This means that whatever political initiatives we may wish to put forward, we must take into account how they fit within this complex network of power relations. It means that the potential subjects of the policies we may wish to devise will not be easily misled into participating in setups where they are simply lectured, entertained, taught useless skills or counseled to be aware of what they already know and feel everyday. The proposals must *make sense*, which means that they must be both structurally and symbolically inserted in a process of integration that provides space for strategic maneuvering by participants. This does not mean that people must just make money or expect to make money out of these initiatives, but that they constitute a means for people to engage in meaningful relations which include an acceptable material situation or a realistic perspective of one.

I believe that these very general principles could be applied to explore all the "problems" associated with the youth mentioned in this book, whether they are inadequate attitudes towards work, gender discrimination or anti-Catalan feelings. Each of these issues would probably need a sensitive study of its most relevant components. However, this analysis has also shown that none of them can be treated in isolation. We have seen that the different aspects of social identity are constructed through patterns of practice and speech genres that incorporate them all in an inextricable way. Possibly, this means that holistic and interdisciplinary approaches should not only be applied in the restricted spaces of academic speculation, but also in those areas where decisions are taken and positive actions are initiated.

Conclusions

The argument I have been developing up to this point leads to the following conclusion: different languages, linguistic varieties and speech styles serve to say and do different things. Certainly, this statement needs qualifying. Otherwise, it could be mistakenly associated with 18th and 19th century evolutionists, who saw languages as the expression of their speakers' state of "civilization". The idea that each language possesses the resources and the potential to express the unique culture or the worldview of its speech community has survived up to our days. It is often mentioned by minority language activists to claim that their language makes a specific contribution to human culture. However, when doubts are raised about the adequacy of a given language to accomplish certain expressive functions, the same activists may well voice the (apparently contradictory) claim that all languages are equally complex and hence capable of expressing any nuance of meaning one might like to put forward. What I am arguing does have connections with these old debates; but there are differences of substance, namely differences in what I understand by language, by saying and even by doing. This is not the moment to engage in a full-blown epistemological discussion. What I will do is to give a few indications of how I think we could develop a framework to understand the connections between what people speak, on the one hand, and what they do and say, on the other. I will also argue that this is important to address the kind of social problems I committed myself to addressing at the beginning, such as the anti-social behavior of some youth cliques and relations of inequality in terms of gender, ethnicity and class. Basically, I will argue that any policy initiative aimed at promoting a minority language, gender equality or less problematic forms of youth culture must take into account the fact that social practices are inserted in complex fields of relations, such as the ones analyzed in chapter 7 that constitute the workings of local contexts in subtle ways.

In part 1, I undertook a detailed study of what two groups of people did and said in a very concrete context, that is, in their leisure activities. In part 2 I analyzed how these people spoke, and particularly how they used the various speech styles and languages available in their context. In part 3, I speculated about the ways in which the patterns of social and linguistic practice analyzed were socially located. In the first part, my focus was not on the actual activities people engaged in, but on the various forms of self-display that participants organized and the ideologies they constructed. The distinction is important, as social actors often see their actions in terms of some practical purpose they may be pursuing, such as having a laugh, courting, getting drunk, parking the car, passing an exam, earning "a few bucks". My own conception of doing and seeing has followed the ideas of Goffman and symbolic interactionists, who see social actors as producing particular definitions of situations, issuing claims about what (or who) they are and about what counts as legitimate representations of reality. In short, they see social actors as producers of meanings, as "meaners" (Halliday 1978: 139), as people engaged in producing the world in which they live.

From this viewpoint, social interaction is very complex and can be analyzed from a myriad of perspectives. I chose to focus on how people "produced" themselves as gendered beings because I thought that this was the most important dimension in that context. It was the key to understand why it made sense to the Rambleros and the Trepas to talk like they talked, to choose some conversation partners and not others, to engage in given activities and reject others. This is how it emerged that many social interactions, such as games of verbal and physical aggression, appeared to make sense because some men were interested in displaying their strength and their abilities before others. Drug taking and the use of non-standard or taboo forms of speech were used to project a transgressive and independent character. The ethos of aggression and transgression was present in narratives, forms of dress and music tastes. On the other hand, many women sought to organize events where it was possible to show personal interest in participants so as to establish, develop and display friendships. As a result, the forms of talk organized by women and men were of a considerably different character. I also indicated that participation in masculine and feminine activities was not necessarily determined by people's sex. There was the possibility of crossing the symbolic boundaries established on the basis of the belief that given practices were "naturally" associated with a given sex. However, one had to be careful when crossing these boundaries, as most individuals had an interest in establishing and protecting the legitimacy of the identity they were constructing for themselves, such that they might (and sometimes did) respond aggressively to gender crossers, i.e. people adopting forms of behavior that (allegedly) contradicted their own claims about what constitutes a right man or woman. A group of Trepas men and women were developing forms of contestation against the traditional forms of gender identity. Drawing on feminist and leftist discourses, they were trying to develop new forms of participation and new types of social activity that involved alternative forms of gender display and the re-negotiation of old ones. In this small group, men would avoid the most aggressive forms of self-display, while women would adopt some traditionally masculine patterns of interaction and language use.

These struggles on what counted as legitimate gender identities were clearly of a symbolic kind. True enough, the interests behind these struggles were somehow connected with struggles over the control of material resources and access to powerful positions in society as a whole. At this point, however, what is of interest in the particular contexts studied is that the manifestations of these struggles took the form of negotiations and clashes over meanings and interpretations that affected almost any element involved in people's social performances: dress, posture, gesture, make up, taste, language, accent.

Considering that, as Halliday (ibid.) argues, language is the most powerful resource for making meaning, and bearing in mind that language played a key role in most of the social situations analyzed in this study, I assumed that the way language was used in the context studied must have played an important role in the construction of identities and ideologies, and in the *struggles* over those identities and ideologies. Of all the many perspectives in which we can approach language, I was particularly interested in the way people used their linguistic repertoire of languages, language varieties and speech styles in these processes of meaning making and of struggles over meaning. Does the fact of using argot, speaking in an Andalusian accent, using a variety of Catalan or Spanish have anything to do with what people want to say, and hence with the social reality they are trying to bring about in particular situations? If so, how? From a traditional linguistic perspective, the answer would be "no", as traditional linguistics has always seen form and meaning as totally separate realities and as connected by purely arbitrary conventions. From the perspective of linguistic anthropologists, the answer would be "yes", as there are tones of evidence showing that people may use particular linguistic forms to display adherence to particular identities and ideologies. My own position is that we should go a bit further, that is, towards acknowledging that linguistic varieties are *not only* used to "signal" particular identities and allegiances, but that they are essential components of the meaning resources that constitute these identities and ideologies. Why is it important to look at it in that way? To move on with this argument, it is useful to review what we saw in part 2.

In part 2, I explored in more detail how the Rambleros and the Trepas used the linguistic varieties that were available in their social milieu and how their linguistic behavior connected with the different cultural practices found in part 1. I found that the Rambleros men tended to use a form of Spanish that recalled the Andalusian accent, whereas the Rambleros women tended to speak in a rather standard style. On the other hand, most Trepas, both men and women, tended to incorporate many expressions of inner-city argot in their youth slang. I could not find any explanation for these linguistic differences in terms of the regional origin of people's families. On the other hand, I observed that the use of these styles correlated roughly with the diverging patterns of gender identity I had found. This means, for instance, that stylized Spanish (i.e. Spanish with Andalusian features) was being used along with the Rambleros men's endeavors to produce and sustain situations where their own ideas on masculinity were asserted and treated as valid. Stylized Spanish appeared as coupled with the ways of saying and doing that the Rambleros men produced. This was so much so that the Andalusian accent was much diminished in situations where the Rambleros did not feel the need to produce ritual aggressions or transgressions. Additionally, the Trepas appeared to use more argot when they wished to emphasize their image as transgressive people, as social rebels who rejected mainstream values and who identified with the lower classes, the ones who created this new language that expressed the meanings of their resistance to oppression.

In chapter 4 I have shown how the appropriation of these styles served to construct particular views of the world and to impose particular forms of relationship within the groups. That is, they were an essential constitutive element of the existing local orders of discourse. The Rambleros men had imposed a given order on women that protected their own forms of display and controlled the modes of expression that were given legitimacy within the group. Their *simple truth*, supported by the ironical meanings of stylized Spanish, imposed a male-centered view of what enjoyment was about, including what types of identity displays were acceptable (face-threats, swearing, naturalness, simple forms of dressing). On the contrary, the politicized Trepas, both men and women, had established a local order that rejected simplified versions of masculinity and sought to reinterpret peer-group practices in emancipatory terms. In this context, women had been able to create their own spaces independent from men's activities, thus creating a gender separation that was resented at times by people from both "sides". Here the hybridization of argot with political discourses -involving rather complex and creative intertextualities- allowed the Trepas to achieve the symbolic balance between the need to honor generally accepted peer-group values (transgression and rejection of dominant discourses) and the politically correct attitudes they were furthering.

My claim here is therefore that people constantly develop linguistic resources to produce and reproduce the meanings that they seek to construct. These linguistic (meaning making) resources are developed mainly in an *ad hoc* fashion, i.e. as communicative needs emerge in particular social situations. New linguistic expressions are thus continually created to serve the expressive needs of those who create them and therefore use them. They will become socially marked if they are only relevant to the interests of one particular social group. They will become situationally marked if they are used only in very specific situations. Maybe we can already call these linguistic creations *genres*, a concept that we can use to designate the sociolinguistic conglomerates that incorporate any dimension of linguistic form and any dimension of meaning, including the identities, situations, intentions and ideologies constructed by social actors. Thus, speech genres are the linguistic (including textual and paralinguistic) materials that are activated by speakers in their ordinary interactions (see also Pujolar 1999). And a speech style is formed by a multiplicity of speech genres, which may come to share some formal features (such as phonological and articulatory features, characteristic textual configurations, a set of vocabulary items), but whose specific existence is easier to perceive or to identify in so far as they appear in situations ascribed to some meaningful social category, such as a social group or a given sphere of activity.

These speech styles therefore contain not only one of the many ways in which speakers could "express" some meaning. The most characteristic meanings produced by the relevant community with its own speech style will hardly be realizable in any other form, at least in a way that makes sense to the concrete participants of the interactions where such meanings have to be made available. Does this amount to a radical position of linguistic relativism? It does not, if we take into account that my point of departure is not that meaning comes exclusively from language (as traditional linguistics implicitly presupposes), but from the process of language using that involves constant renovation (i.e. creation of new meanings out of the old ones) and restructuring (i.e. creation of new forms of expression out of the old ones). This is what Bakhtin's dialogical conception of language allows us to do, particularly through what he calls the process of reaccentuation, whereby speakers transform the semantic quality of the "voices" that they incorporate into their own utterances.

This is why we have seen that the speech styles described were incorporated and reinterpreted by speakers in different ways. Each group tended to construct a relatively coherent set of social meanings associated with each style, but these meanings were by no means uniform, unequivocal or fixed. They were constantly open either to contestation or refinement. The issue here is not so much the old discussion about whether particular speech styles and dialects are capable of or appropriate for producing particular meanings. For example, the use of Andalusian features in formal arenas has become quite common in the Spanish media since the eighties. However, I have also seen students in oral presentations being misunderstood by their fellow students as trying to be funny just because of their Andalusian accent. Rather than seeing these events as simple instances of social prejudice, it is more useful to appreciate that the students concerned had misunderstood the intention of the speaker precisely because that accent was often used to produce a particular type of performance outside the classroom. This integration between languages, ideologies, identities and contexts is not necessarily limiting for speakers, as this example suggests. It also allows for the establishment of social relationships which would otherwise be difficult or impossible to establish if accents or styles were not available or involved no special connotations.

It is also possible to speak about processes of *appropriation*, the processes whereby particular speech styles were taken up by speakers. From this perspective, some styles were presented as very clearly identified with the meanings one sought to construct and others were somehow "centrifuged" as symbolizing meanings against which one antagonized. Thus, the socially constitutive function of the speech styles described could be noticed when people emphasized the Andalusian accent or the use of argot in particular situations; but it was even more noticeable when speakers incorporated and combined them as alien voices in their discourse (i.e. in their narratives, jokes and dialogues). So the Rambleros could emphasize the use of argot in pretend-games where lower class marginal characters were evoked, characters which they considered as different from themselves. The Trepas, in contrast, presented themselves as real argot speakers and incorporated Andalusian accents to depict *other* types of people: ignorant, conservative, sexist, racist characters (which they presented in a negative fashion), or authentic characters (which they presented in a more positive fashion).

If we look at the multiplicity of speech styles present at any point in a given society, we will be seeing what Bakhtin called *heteroglossia*, a very diverse and constantly changing set of speech forms that roughly follow social boundaries of all types. This linguistic stratification is likely to pose difficult problems if we approach it with a purely taxonomic attitude and seek to represent it through lists, maps or graphics. After all, there is no reason to assume that many speech styles do not overlap or may not be seen as having relationships of inclusion with others. What I am talking about is something that is quite different from dialects, languages or (a more general term) linguistic varieties. As I see it, the distinction coincides with Halliday's distinction between diatypic and dialectal varieties, the former being defined according to use, the latter according to users. Of course, traditional classifications of languages, dialects and sociolects are based on many questionable (and often questioned) assumptions about how given users can be taken as users of whatever variety. Additionally, the framework I have adopted does not allow me to see users in any other way than as in interaction with other users (and therefore as the product of these interactions). From this perspective, it is difficult to arrive at any meaningful definition of, say, what the Catalan or Spanish languages *are*, that is, a definition based on the symbolic potentials of these languages. Languages and dialects constitute, therefore, categories that are meaningful for participants to designate what they perceive (usually on the basis of linguistic forms, but not exclusively so) as distinct ways of speaking, the distinction being relevant to make sense of many social and institutional practices. It is possible that a given speech style becomes so identified with a particular social group that it ends up receiving a name and being reified into something (a dialect, a language) about which one can mobilize resources or write poetry. However, the normal state of affairs will be that linguistic varieties will contain a number of speech styles according to the variety of social activities in which they are spoken. This is, as I understand it, what Gumperz' has recently argued in his bid to rethink linguistic relativity:

> ...there are a complex set of inter-relations and causal strands that link meaning, context, culture, and society together. ... Different social networks in the same society, city or street are likely to yield ... different meaning systems, provided they persist over time and become "institutionalized"... The simple association of one tribe, one culture, one language, which was implicit in the older Humboldtian and Sapir-Whorfian traditions, then breaks down. We can have speakers of the same language fractionated by interpretive subsystems associated with distinct social networks in complex societies,

and conversely, we can have social networks that transcend cultural and grammatical systems to create shared interpretive systems beneath linguistic diversity. (Gumperz 1996: 361)

It is from this perspective that I explored, in chapter 5, the social meanings attached to the use of Catalan and Spanish. It emerged that both languages were used to produce or evoke a wide range of situations or contexts. However, because the Rambleros and the Trepas had had a restricted access to social milieus and situations where Catalan was used, they were familiar with a restricted set of Catalan speech styles, and therefore to less varied meaning resources in this language. Most of these young people had had access to Catalan through the school, the media and other formal domains. Moreover, we must take into account that the peer-group constitutes one of the typical contexts where formal discourses are questioned or ridiculed. This was probably the reason why the various formal Catalan voices that constituted the common experience of these working-class youths were being mimicked and derided in various ways, as could be easily detected when analyzing their codeswitching practices. To put it in the technical terms I have defined, Catalan voices were being incorporated and reaccentuated as alien voices, as voices belonging to social groups other than themselves and as constructing meanings that did not match the ones they intended to construct.

As a result, many people perceived Catalan as a silly, unmasculine, unexpressive language, such that it was hard to speak it without evoking problematic characters and meanings (in a similar way as it is sometimes difficult to talk seriously with an Andalusian accent). This analysis explains, to some extent, why many young people are perceived as resisting the policies of linguistic promotion established in Catalonia. This form of resistance to official policies probably emerges more out of these subtle, implicit and often unconscious processes than out of some form of political position taking in the traditional sense of the term "political".

In chapter 6, we have seen that most Rambleros men tended to avoid using Catalan, while most Rambleros women sought to display positive attitudes towards using it, although they did not find many opportunities to do so. Some Rambleros men expressed an opinion against the use of the Catalan language. This might be taken as the reason why they almost never used it. However, it is important to remember that this opinion was not shared by all the Rambleros men and, moreover, that a general opinion in favor of the Catalan language (as occurred amongst the politicized Trepas or the Rambleros women) did not result in a very substantial increase in its use in the lives of those concerned. On the contrary, it seems that the predominant patterns of language choice (leading Catalan speakers to accommodate to Spanish speakers) combined with the restricted range of speech styles associated with Catalan constrained linguistic behavior in a more decisive way, thus contributing to the marginalization of this language in the peer-group context. This provides, incidentally, further evidence that the subtle processes of development and incorporation of speech styles in social interaction are quite different from what most people refer to when they talk about what language they speak to whom and why. These two types of phenomenon have to be treated very differently; which does not mean that they are not connected, as is shown by the usual comment that when a person changes language one gets the impression that the person has also changed character. Generally speaking, a change of language and a change of speech style must be accompanied by a change in the speech genres available, as well as a significant reorientation of the intertextual relations that the speaker and the audience can draw upon, such that a different situation is effectively projected. It is probably from this perspective that we can begin to explore the sociopolitical consequences of language policies, not only in terms of who possesses the legitimate competence, but also in terms of what range of cultural practices are legitimized and delegitimized as a consequence of linguistic regulations.

However, to address these issues from a wider political perspective, it is necessary to introduce additional elements into the analysis. The notion that social relations are constructed mainly by linguistic and other semiotic means has often been taken to imply that individuals have considerable freedom as to the meanings they can produce (a point often raised by Bourdieu against symbolic interactionism). Probably because meaning is often seen as something purely psychic that resides in people's minds, it is true that many sociolinguistic and anthropological studies describe people's practices as if they were the products of free choice. However, as Fairclough (1992a) points out, discourses are material entities. The fact that we see discourses, or semiotic productions, as constituted by symbolic elements does not preclude the fact that these are realized in material practices that are subject to the possibilities and limitations of social actors in terms of capacities, abilities and resources.

The exploration of the conditions that made particular meanings or discourses possible, impossible, likely or improbable was undertaken in part 3.

It was also in this part where the political implications and applications of the analysis could be discussed. I interpreted the practices of the Rambleros and the Trepas as particular forms of position taking within the field of youth culture. I explored the relationship between this field and other fields (education, the job market, and the linguistic market) on the basis of Bourdieu's conception of fields as both autonomous and interrelated spaces of struggles and competition for symbolic and material profits. Here I argued that a substantial part of the practices analyzed could be seen as the participants' forced response to social exclusion. This exclusion had been caused by educational failure and by the difficulties of finding a good position in the job market. While these difficulties were not comparable to those of the so-called drop-outs, petty delinquents and other marginal groups, it was clear that these young people generally saw little advantage in investing in middle-class values and patterns of behavior. In that situation, it made more sense to invest in forms of transgressive behavior which put dominant values in question (and which further endangered their chances to integrate in the job market). This need to invest in some socially meaningful undertaking points towards what appears to be a basic principle of human social existence, as suggested by Bourdieu:

> ... This I hold against a finalist, utilitarian vision of action which is sometimes attributed to me. It is not true to say that everything that people do or say is aimed at maximizing their social profit; but one may say that they do it to perpetuate or to augment their social being. (Bourdieu 1993: 274)

The Rambleros and the Trepas were thus striving to create, in a more or less collaborative way, social spaces that allowed some form of meaningful participation. In these social spaces, i.e. within the two cliques, the values and meanings dominant in the wider society could be either suspended, derided or denied. Hence the predominance of a transgressive ethos which allegedly subverted middle and upper-class cultural forms but which also showed, in many aspects, their dependence on them.

These considerations, however, should not prevent us from acknowledging that the response of some Trepas to their social conditions was considerably creative and complex. They had reinterpreted their situation as that of the victims of capitalist oppression, thus giving rise to a complex reframing of their position, whereby transgressive activities were reinterpreted as political subversion. At the same time, their investment in the values of some sections of the political field (those of the revolutionary groups where they had participated) had also led them to renegotiate significant elements of their personal relationships: old patterns of couple relations, gender relations and ethnolinguistic relations had been subjected to critique and had been reconstituted. Unfortunately, this creative and positive response did not contribute to improving their social position, at least during the time I studied them. On the contrary, sometimes it appeared that their emphasis on displaying subversion through speech and physical appearance made them less eligible for wage-earning employment.

Despite the fact that Bourdieu's model is not always helpful in providing a detailed understanding of how these processes work, these findings do point towards some useful implications and applications in terms of practical policy design. Whether the problems one wishes to address have to do with preventing risky and anti-social behavior amongst the young, sexist attitudes or the subordination of the Catalan language, some general observations can be made. Firstly, as the notion of *habitus* suggests, many aspects of our practice are the products of very subtle processes of which social actors are not fully aware and which they cannot fully control. The means to raise awareness of these aspects of practice in order to change them will certainly require not only compliance, but also active participation on the part of those concerned. Secondly, all patterns of social behavior take shape as individuals engage in some form of meaningful participation in particular social milieus, not as a result of mere indoctrination (as many official campaigns seem to imply). By meaningful participation I mean engagement in social activities that can be seen as constituting a local social field where the stakes are worth gambling for and where the individual can correspondingly contribute in an active and positive way. Whether policy designs orient themselves towards creating new fields, or towards facilitating access to desired fields that already exist, or towards changing some problematic practices of established fields (which is often quite difficult to do), these designs must take into account that social fields are never fully autonomous, but that they are articulated with other fields and especially with the field of socioeconomic relations.

This means that the policies aimed at addressing the social problems mentioned must be connected with the processes of struggle over possession (and definition) of symbolic and economic capital for those affected. With regard to people from low economic extraction, it means facilitating or ensuring access to economic resources and opportunities for social advancement, which also means integration in the social groups that intervene in some way or other in the production and distribution of these resources. In the case of the Catalan language, the promotion of Catalan does not only involve ensuring that people learn it at school, but also that they can be integrated in Catalan-speaking networks where it is meaningful to speak Catalan to develop one's relationships and the economic base to sustain them. To make this possible, it is probably necessary to change the perceptions of Catalan speakers as to what using Catalan means, particularly the perception that the language has to be kept for native speakers only, and probably the perception that only monolingual conversations are normal. The processes of language choice that arise from these perceptions tend to reduce the presence of the Catalan language in many milieus and, moreover, to foster the impression that not everybody has the right to speak it. The case of gender equality would be similar in the sense that the social milieus where gender relationships are experiencing important changes are located mainly in middle and upper class networks (though important inequalities remain in these areas as well). Additionally, it is obvious that gender equality is not only advancing because people are increasingly understanding and "aware", but also because many women are getting access to enough economic resources, such that they can negotiate their relationships with their partners and friends from a stronger position. It is also possible to regulate some areas of economic activity so that unskilled and poorly paid jobs are not so gender marked as they are now. However, such a policy would be difficult to implement in a social milieu where the satisfaction of the labor force is really what counts less and where people would not stand to gain from changing some of their cultural practices. Similar observations can be made in relation to the most problematic forms of youth culture, such as heavy drug-taking and risky behavior. The connections between social exclusion and the most extreme forms of anti-social behavior were detected by sociologists many years ago.

However, there are other dimensions to these problems that must be taken into account. Again, by developing Bourdieu's notion of *habitus*, we might well be able to build a relevant understanding of them. Policy makers are certainly aware that it is often too late to address some problems in a satisfactory way, particularly when they affect individuals who are already adults and whose attitudes and dispositions become less and less likely to change. It would be useful to develop a clearer idea of the ways in which cultural patterns are incorporated, of what experiences and what conditions are more important, and of what elements are easier or harder to deal with. In any case, it seems obvious that only long-term policies can be really effective, and also policies that are really sensitive to the particular contexts they target. I am talking here about a form of *dialogical politics* where target populations are given the possibility of actively participating in defining forms of intervention that are relevant to their local contexts and that provide them with resources to invest in alternative forms of identity. The question is, therefore, whether it is possible to create social spaces that encourage reflexivity about and commitment to emancipatory practices in ways that are relevant to local cultural traditions and are connected with access to economic resources.

It is not the right place here to go into the details of what such initiatives should look like. My intention was to develop a framework on the basis of which they could be conceptualized. I believe that a context sensitive analysis of social practices such as the one presented here can be useful to build an understanding of the cultural patterns of particular communities in ways that can be later used to engage in a meaningful dialogue with these communities to address particular social problems. One important implication of this study is, I believe, that an adequate understanding of the cultural practices of a given social group should include an assessment of their linguistic repertoire and of the way they use it to construct their identities, relationships and worldviews. It is very common for official bodies to be dismissive or merely tolerant of the linguistic styles and varieties spoken especially by communities of a low economic stratum. However, it is precisely the community's repertoire that provides them with the symbolic resources with which they make sense of their everyday life and which must constitute the starting point upon which meaningful political initiatives can be collaboratively devised. The way in which a community uses its linguistic repertoire reflects and contributes toward constructing the relationships between the community and the rest of society, whether these relationships are of conformity or of resistance.

In some contexts, particularly (though not exclusively) in multilingual ones, it may also be necessary to assess the desirability to regulate linguistic usages or to consider the impact of regulations that are already in place, even when they are implicit and rarely identified as an issue. The findings of this study suggest that any political initiative aimed at regulating linguistic usages can have profound effects on any community, as it may contribute to transforming the linguistic repertoire and hence the existing patterns of social relations (in both positive and negative ways). From this perspective, we should be aware that linguistic regulation can be a means of ideological control (see also Pujolar 1997c). By this I am not suggesting that politicians or pressure groups should abstain from regulating linguistic usages. This would amount to a kind of linguistic liberalism which, like any form of liberalism, would give the upper hand to the most powerful linguistic communities and their cultural forms. What seems clear is that we need to develop a deeper understanding of the connections between the use of particular language varieties and their associated cultural practices.

I believe that, from this perspective, it may also be possible to reconsider some traditional beliefs about language and culture that have always had (for good or for bad) a significant weight in the social and political arenas. The old ideas on the correspondence between languages and worldviews have had an enormous political influence in the modern period, as they have contributed to the creation of most nationalist movements and nation states. From another perspective, linguists such as Sapir contributed a lot to establishing the idea that all languages were equal in terms of their structural complexity and of their capability of expressing complex ideas. There is, I believe, some truth in all these positions, but I also feel that we need to go beyond the very general, abstract (and often vague) statements which have traditionally been made in relation to this issue. We need to put these principles, so to speak, in context; that is, to explore in more detail how the language-and-culture connection actually works in particular cases. This is what I have tried to do in this study by analyzing the social and linguistic processes that take place in a very concrete social setting.

It is probably not too soon to deploy important resources to study the ideological underpinnings of linguistic usages. In the last half of the 20th century, migration movements from developing to developed countries have made the latter much more culturally diverse than they used to be. At the same time, the advances in communication technologies are very much changing the way we perceive our position in the world. Multilingual communities and cross-cultural contacts are becoming the rule rather than the exception. This does not necessarily mean that the world is becoming a better place to live in as people of different cultures get to know each other and learn about each other. It is clear that new forms of cultural domination and marginalization are being created, as economic power and communication technologies are not equally distributed. But even in the best scenario we can imagine, linguistic and cultural diversity will need to be addressed politically at many levels ("politically", I mean, in the wider sense of the term, which includes not only the policies of governments, but also the initiatives of pressure groups, community movements and the spaces for so-called *life-politics*). I think that sociolinguistic researchers and social scientists in general will need to refine their methods and concepts to face up to the challenges of this new world.

Appendix

Original version of quotations translated from Catalan

...només per posar un exemple significatiu, pel que fa a les generacions més joves, que la introducció i l'adopció del llenguatge contracultural i, en definitiva, d'un idiolecte generacional, és duta a terme exclusivament en espanyol. (Argente et al. 1979: 256).

Ens trobem, per tant, davant d'una pràctica usual que aboca a molts a una òbvia traïció d'encuny lingüístic -a parer d'alguns autors- encara que per a molts sigui d'arrel inconscient, i l'hagin anat interioritzant d'acord amb les exigències marcades com *de bona educació* per una determinada societat; bona educació que no amaga altra cosa que una estratègia socialitzadora per tal de coaccionar la tria lingüística en el fet de la comunicació. (Erill et al. 1992: 101)

Original version of extracts given in English

Extract 2
Joan: *y otro el habla*
Pablo: *qué habla!*
Noia1: *qué habla* [diverses veus]
Noia2: *(...) de hablar*
Pablo: [més alt] *qué habla!*
Andrés: *(muérete) guarra, zorra y toas esas cosas.* [rialles i veus]
Ricardo: *he he he he he*
Mateo: *cómeme la polla ha ha ha >ha ha* [rialles generalitzades]
Ricardo: *>ho ho ho ho ho ho!*

Extract 4
Raquel: *para estar too el día de pie · toa noche por ejemplo si vamos a bailar o tal · >con tacones · minifalda*
Luis: *<tu quiereh ir con minifalda pa estar sentá[?]*
Raquel: *mmmm hombre · pero* [Luis laughs] *· >joer*
Paula: *<no >(xx) pero de vez en cuando*
Raquel: *<es que · tú no- tú nunca has ido >con- · con- · con tacones*
Pablo: *<si quieres ir con tacones · [...]*

Extract 5
Paula: *lo- lo que no voy a hacer · lo que no voy a hacer · yo no soy la que entra en el grupo ·* [noia riu] *· es ella · · si- si es ella pues · yo no voy a irla a lamerla el culo para que se quede*
Pablo: *haaala que vulgar!*
Raquel: *no además · además yo digo una*

Extract 6

Patricia: joo què sé · jo coses · · yo el fi- quan deia fill de puta era quan em pegava amb un cla- quan
estava clavant un clau i em pegava amb el martell · i deia fill de puta · o quan em queia algo a terra
allò · · però no deia fill de puta allò va · venga · fill de puta · o dir me la suda no ho deia mal tampoc

Extract 7

*Luis: somoh máh · cortaos de otro patrón somo más brutos no[?] máh · · nos gusta pergarnos meternos
entre nosotros · cuando no sabemos de que hablar insultarnos para pa picarnos y tal · · · pues sí ·
somo · máh · [Ell riu] · d- bueno ya has visto que · ir por ahi no[?] · no saber qué hacer · Riquini ·
me vah a comer la polla · · y ya el otro se mosquea · (me da) · que te pego bum · · · (claro) nunca ·
pero eh máh- máh que ná entre nosotros o sea nunca noh metemo con la gente o · · · pa divertirnos
pa · · · pa (que) siempre hay algo de qué reir no[?] pueh · · cuando no sabemo de qué reir pue · in-
sultarno [Ell riu] · · sin hacerla- o seaa · sin mala intención nunca no[?] · · tu ya lo hah visto no[?]
· incluso · incluso gente que no venga y (no) está al caso se la puede pasar bien se puede reir · ve-
nir en metro y metiendono unoh con otroh · · y la gente está por ahí escuchando pueh ri- riéndose y
tal.*

Extract 10

*Paula: metido · mira · nosotras hemos salido · solas · y nos hemos puesto a imitarnos las unas a las
otras · en la manera de bailar · · yy nos hemos · y nos hemos sacado los defectos*

Extract 11

*Irene: pero yo aquí no me bajo eh[?] porque sé que me bajo · hala tía que no sé qué no sé cuantos · si
(no) os metéis con el culo · os meteréis con las piernas*
*Luis: y tú te lo tomarías a mal por qué · [Irene: sí] porque piensas que nosotros no (noh) gustaría verte
con faldas?*
*Joan: no igual porque quieres vestir como quieres y no quieres que la gente te lo comente así te lo eche
así*
Irene: claro
Raquel: porque es que se están toa la tarde metiéndote con la falda de la Irene
Irene: al final · te amargas · y no te la pones [altres veus]

Extract 12

*Irene: que nosotras nos metemos con vosotros y os sienta · os sienta tope de mal · sin embargo a nosot-
no · vosotros os metéis con nosotras y no nos puede sentar mal porque joder!*

Extract 13

*Luis: eh que es otra fieht- són máa · · máh de tacataca no[?] máh · má en plan lolailo fumar mucho
petardos y tal · y armar laa · la bulla por la calle · · · meter con gent- bueno · · · metersee ir cantan-
do por la calle y la que alguien salta pué armarla no[?] yy · · armar la bronca no? er- · eeeh pasa ·
· pueh lo típico de la mili no[?] que · la hicimo en Segovia y · somos del segundo del 90 · eeh · y
venía uno de otro reemplazo · · íbamos aa o a armarla siempre · · o · somos de paracas · pueh nosotros de artillería · y había una historia montá de de · de peleas de hace años no[?] · · donde están
los de aviación · pues han ido tal pab · ahí por le rollo · · · uy teníamos una de bronca y ya nos íbamos p'allá y · y a armarla ya eh que íbamoh*
Joan: os meteis en broncas así en plan

Extract 14

Luis: pueh demuéhtrame la diferencia que hay entre tú ·
Raquel: es que tú >(xx la razón)
*Luis: <tú te puedes meter conmigo y cuando llegue un momento me mohquee y te digo mira o te callah
o te parto la cabeza*
Raquel: pero yo no soy capaz de decirte eso
Paula: porqué · porqué ·
Raquel: porque yo soy >de otra manera
Paula: <luis · >(xx) yo te digo otra cosa
Luis: <bueno · vale · digo otra cosa > · no la fuerza vale
Paula: <yo te · yo te di- >yo te digoo
Raquel: <(es que yo) te >digo te parto la cabeza

Paula: <que te parto la cabeza >y te pones a reir
Luis: <vale · no la fuerza · no la fuerza ella se mete conmigo y le digo >sí · sí[?]
  Raquel: <y encima me la parte · · sabeh [Ella riu]

Extract 15
See extract 6

Extract 16
Silvia: no · por ejemploo · anoche natalia me estaba contando que estaba muy deprimida no[?] porque
se veía · que no tenía estudioos y que · bueno que no tenía estudios pues s- · que se lo parecía a ella
no[?] y · o sea que estaba muy mal cuando se encontraba que no tenía trabajo · que los estudios
los tenía a medias · que · que debía ponerse a trabajar pero que no había encontrado curro · y que
· tampoco se ha puesto a buscarlo no[?] · y eso- es un poco todo · estábamos hablando así · más
porque la vi un poco deprimida le pregunté que qué le pasaba (xxx) · y le pregunté que · pues · ·
que qué le pasaba no y · · · y por eso no[?] e- ellos se estaban haciendo un porro pues nosotras qué
vamos a hacer pues · empezamos a hablar no[?] · también hacía que no la veía desdee antes dee
navidad y todo no[?] · cómo le había ido el pueblo y eso le pregunté no[?] si había ido al pueblo ·
y ella me dijo pues a mi lo mismo
Joan: igual las chicas estáis como mucho

Extract 17
Silvia: pero a lo mejor quedamos · y en- (va) hemos quedado la natalia y yo · ah[!] pues la clara · pues
ahora también me voy no sé qué · o la patricia no[?] ah[!] · pues yo también me voy entonces pues
quedamos cuatro o cinco y entonces ya sí que se arma · si emp- empezamos otra vez a hablar de
penas · con mucha gente · pues · · noo no puede ser tampoco no[?] entonces pues claro aprove-
chamos el momento no[?] · de decir · ahora · vamos a hablar no[?] · · en cinco minutos · a ver qué
· · però tampoco no es tan

Extract 21
Jaume: lo que passa que las tías · ho fan · en moments que a lo millor estem tots junts · a- por lo menos
ahir va ser això no[?] · estem tots junts i de repent pues · els veus · i nosaltros allí no[?] flipant no[?]
· i a lo millor jo vull parlar amb el chimo a lo millor estic dos dies · aguantant-me · sense parlar per-
què hi ha més gent · i no ho faig tenir (xxx) · ho faig per no tallar el rotllo de la gent no[?] · o sinó li
dic ei chimo vem- · al matí què fas · tal · vale pues baixa que vull parlar amb tu no[?] · I ja està
no[?] · · que no · no és dissimular com diguéssim no[?] · · però és per no agobiar la penya perquè jo
estic amb la gent

Extract 22
Luis: él y yo por ejemplo · y eh para- · cuando si algunah · bueno hemoh salido juntoh loh doh soloh ·
sin mah gente · · y ha sido para hablar cosas dee · o sea · · digamoh · para desahogar · para contar
cosah · (x) contar cosah a lo mejor porque necesitaba contárselah a alguien y mira pues ·

Extract 23
Paula: yo con su nariz no me he metido ·
Irene: exactamente
Andrés: con mi nariz · con mi forma de bailar · · con mis dientes · · con mis dientes con mi forma de
bailar con mi forma de vestir · con mi forma de ser pues lo que sea

Extract 24
Luis: igual que la tere cuando decía el curro no[?] eh · me voy al curro y eeeh la risa · el curro joé ni
que fueraa · de minero no[?] [Ell riu] · por lo que hace · · a (veo) · eso del · lo que tú decíah en el- ·
en las hojas aquellas el · peta

Extract 27
Irene: no sé · · és que bebe mucho eh[?] [Joan: m?] · que beben mucho · · la bebida es otra cosa ee · · ·
Joan: beben más los chicos >que las chicas
Irene: <que las chicas · · aunque la tere se lleva la palma también [Ella riu] · >no sé porqué ·
Joan: <tu · vas mucho de agua ·
Irene: hombre yo también bebo no[?] · de vez en cuando · · pero jolines · yo · una vez me puse mala · · y
nunca más · ya lo he dicho · nunca más · y encima con tequila · y ya dije que nunca más · o sea · ·

no me en-· me encontr-· fué en castelló · fue en semana santa y iban · todos uaaaa [Ella riu] *un pedo impresionante no[?]· · y me encontraba es que me encontraba · · es que no me encontraba vamos no me encontraba era una cosa de · · no porque era otro y otro y como estaba bueno pues otro y otro · y no te das cuenta no te das cuenta yy · · ·*

Joan: *(x) es lo que decía con una amigo mío · cuando te das cuenta ya no te das cuenta*

Irene: *que va · y yo se lo digo muchas veces eh[?] · · que no beban tanto · · joder pues (si) no bebes ·* [veu tonta] *si no sé qué · (si) no sé cuantos · (xx) [...] yo muchas veces he hablado con ellos eh[?] · · con el ricardo por ejemplo he hablado · pero por qué bebes y tal no sé qué no sé · · y qué vas a hacer · · y qué vas a hacer pues · te lo pasas bien · oye no te lo pasas bien bebiendo yo me lo paso mal · · porque yo bebo · · y después estoy por los suelos · · pa estar por los suelos · pues no bebo oye · · te lo pasas mal bebiendo · · ellos se lo pasan bien · · y parece que no estén oye pero cuando beben · parecen que no estén es-· están ajilipollaos · · · · no sé · es una cosa que ·*

Extract 28

Jaume: *sempre he estat al carrer des de que era petit no? · sempre he (tractat) més amb la gent del carrer no[?] · fins que va haver una temporada que · com vaig veure que · que gent del carrer · estaveen · · traient coses molt xungues de drogues i tal no[?] xungues · pues · ja vaig deixar la gent del carrer i vaig anar · a l'esplai no[?] i · o sigui · · va durar una temp- u- una època que anava amb gent de l'esplai i gent del carrer però a- a partir de catorse anys [...] no io io · ho vai fer io és que · · la gent veia que · ho feia per · · per fers- per fer-se més gran no[?] · I jo això ho veia una xorrada porque no · no entenia perquè la gent volia ser superior als demés no[?] · · no perquè (xxx) per exemple io fumant porros no me considero més gran que els demés no me considero superior a ella que no fuma no[?] o sigui · fumo perquè m'agrada y punto no[?] · i la gent va començar a fer aquestes coses · per sentir-se superior a la gent no[?] a vegades · · i va camb- i · la gent va canviar de ser també · i va ser quan jo vaig deixar-los no[?] o sigui · no em va agradar com eren i · em vaig anar d'aquesta gent · · que eren · més o menys com jo alguns no[?] · al final va acabar malament · lo que vam quedar del grup · (xx s'havien quedat) el chimo i jo no[?] o sigui · no va ser per això*

Extract 29

Pepe: *és que · · clar és er · es que · jo mat- jo no[?] per exemple · a partir de · d'escoltaar · · lo que és punki · de si escoltes · panki llavors · t'arriba potato no[?] potato fan regue · regue vitoriano i sii escoltes potato també · com que escoltes · kortatu fan una versió dels specials i comences a escoltar ska · i com que escoltes skaa doncs · acabes · escoltant sul i · i música mod també · i com que escoltes punki doncs acabes escoltant hard-core · i si escoltes hard-core guarro · acabes escoltant · · greencore i acabes escoltant trash metal · i si escoltes · hard-core també acabes escoltant hard-core melòdic · · clar · · · ·*

Joan: *és com una família del punk per >dir-ho així*

Pepe: *<no · no no no · · sii · el el- el eska és anterior · el- al panki · · i el heavy es anterior · · el hard-core sí que és posterior però · no és que siguin de la família sinoó que · que clar es-· es van juntant no[?]*

Joan: *es van · · entreteixint (xx) · · · [guitarra flamenca]*

Pepe: ah i la història de la música celta la música celta clar · ens tira mogollón a tothom · a tothom

Extract 30

Salva: [cançó, cridant molt alt] *(s) en la calle y en el bar · agobiando sin parar · esta guerra hay que acabar · (xx) hasta el final · · · · · cuando salimos del portal · a la vuelta hola qué tal · (no sé qué les va a xx) para aplicar (la) ley marcial · · · · todos somos sospechosos · todos somos peligrosos · · · entrarán al (local) · acusaos de traficar · y si no lo han encontrado no lo podrán denunciar · · · · · ya sabes como vivir · si no te quieres morir · has (pensao) en (xx) · no (xx) resistir · · · · · todos somos sospechosos todos somos peligrosos · · · · · lucha · lucha · lucha · lucha · lucha · lucha · lucha · lucha · lucha · lucha · lucha· lucha · lucha · lucha · lucha · lucha · · · · lucha · lucha · lucha · lucha · lucha · lucha · lucha · lucha · lucha · lucha · lucha · lucha · luchaaaaaaaaaaaaaaaaa- aa · lucha ·*

Extract 31

Clara: yo es que · los tíos de ahí los que conozco son · el salva · y eso el salva sí lo hace · y e-· o sea de diferente manera pero lo hace el salva se preocupa mucho eh[?] · · mucho mucho es muy maricón en eso · · y luego el pepe el · y el pepe se- se preocupa muchísimo · (de-) por lo menos él está bien · · no[?] · · · creo que · no

Extract 32

Clara: era un invitado · · y laa · natalia dijo · pues · · somos tal tal tal tal tal · · y el aleix · y yo · natalia · el aleix es un chico · dice ya pero · es diferente · · · eso la natalia montes · (x) es diferente · no a mi no me- no a mi me importaría que · · y tu sabes como es la natalia vamos que no le vean ni · ni ni ni · ni el tobillo eh[?] · · es una pasada · · ·

Joan: sí és bestial · · · molt interessant

Extract 45

Paula: no pero tú a mi no me digas que no porque es verdá he ido a tu casa y tú te has quedado sentado
Pablo: vale ·
Paula: cómo que vale · y por qué >en tu casa te quedas sentado?
Pablo: <sí · · (porque) sí
Peri: porque lo han acostrumbrado así=
Andrés: =porque es su casa ·
Paula: no- pues vale · también me quedaré yo la próxima vez · · y que lo haga too tu madre · te parece bien?
Pablo: yo no te he dicho nunca nada[!] ·
Irene: [Ella riu] >hostia
Pablo: <te he dicho yo alguna vez algo[?]=
Paula: =pe- pero es que te parece bien pablo que yo >fuera a tu casa y me quedara sentada?
Pablo: <yo nunca te he dicho nada [Irene riu]
Luis: tú- tú un momento · tu seguro-
Mateo: tu es que te has- ya estás >sacando el tema de >quicio
Luis: <cálla mateo esperate
Pablo: <too ha sio- too ha sido cuando hemos comido en mi >terreno que has
Mateo: <>está sacando el tema de quicio ya
Pablo: <ido y dices uy · hoy no he hecho nada · qué habrá dicho tu madre? y digo qué va a decir · nada[!]
Paula: pero eso me ha pasado muy pocas veces

Extract 51

Pepe: yo le- · le doy mucha razón a la magda · y es más · · nno me quedo contento · con la · con la con la solución que damos de que bueno es normal · es normal · · que si este   ul tema- al tema que me está preocupando · yo veo que el salva · me va a entender mejor · que el jaume [>Silvia: claro pues se lo dirás a él] <no no · pues no me quedo contento con eso   porque creo quee · · · >por lo menos por mi parte no espera espera
Silvia: <tu- · yo creo que tu subconsciente ya te lleva directamente o sea [Pepe: sí · pero es que aparte · pero es que-] · vale que te lleve · a la primera persona que tienes delante se lo vas a contar · si es un amigo tuyo no? [Pepe: sí · pero es que no · pero creo que no] · pero · a lo mejor no te entiende tan bien · como te podría entender él · si se lo explicas a >él
Magda: <>pues entonces no es colega
Pepe: <sí pero creo- · pero creo que es más que eso creo que es más que eso porque · igual · igual es por donde va la magda no? · y a lo que la magda · a lo que la magda aspira · pero yo lo que me encuentro · es que a veces · yo · no le comento · a la magda · tal cosa · no porque ella · no sea afín en este tema conmigo · sinó porque me siento cortado y digo · uy! · a ver si a la magda hablándole de esto · no estoy · no estoy · hablando de más no? · entonces · yo creo que hay un problema añadido [Silvia: también · puede que sí] · hay un

Extract 52

Clara: currarnos esta historia no y es y es una contradicción que tengo todavía no? · · que de coño porque la sociedad iría tan bien y no sé qué no sé cuantos · · no? · y como tía pienso que tal tal tal no? pues me voy a currar esto y lo otro · · peroo · ff- · pues como tía · pues me llamo Anita y entonces · · yo tengo mis limitaciones y paso dee · de · · · de castigarme no? · qué pasa[!] yo tengo que seguir viviendo y · yo quiero vivir lo mejor posible · no? · y que · mi calidad de vida sea buena · · y paso de batallar es que · no puedo · · y · y me como la cabeza eh? · pero

Josep: pero · pero en canvi per exemple

Extract 66

Salva: la coordinadora se habla catalán · · generalmente no[?] pero la gente de santa coloma · · habla
todos castellano · · la gente de sants hablan todos catalán · · no sé depende no[?] · yo creo que
también va por el barrio · · porque santa coloma pues · son todos unos garrulos · · y en sants pues
són todos · [To més alt, cantat] *muy así muy hipis muy catalanistas y*
Joan: tu experiencia del catalán en la

Extract 67

Jaume: a partir de catorse anys · vai fer la meva penya no[?] de la penya que era de · · de l'esplai · alla-
vors pues el meuu vocabulari a lo millor va canviar una mica · més · · a- al principii era més *callejero* no[?] · va canviar una mica més · · i va ser en plan de · no kumba però · en plan d- · o sigui *típico
esplai* no[?] o sigui [veu xava] una mica així (d'aquella-) · · però això va estar poc t- poc temps i ·
despues · amb la gent que sempre m'ha anat bé · ha sigut amb tios · més o menys ·que no d- que són
com jo no[?] i · per això que noo · la meva parla no és molt · · · és simple no és una cosa · rebuscada
ni res no[?]

Extract 75

Silvia: pues yo hablo castellano · casi siempre · · no tengo problemas para el c- para hablar catalán
pero a veces me cuesta no[?] · según qué palabras porque no estoy habituada a hablarlo no[?] ·
bueno habituada · · si yo- si tengo que hablarlo lo hablo o sea · no es que prefiera que me hablen
en castellano · qué va · es que me da igual no[?] · peroo · des de pequeña siempre he hablado en
castellano en mi casa no[?] · mi madre mi padre es de gerona · no[?] mi madre es de · · de málaga
no[?] entonces mi madre siempre hablaba en castellano y con nosotros igual · y sin embargo con
mis tíos pues hablamos el catalán no[?] mi (padre) pues (x) lo mismo · y · pues con la gente · según
· si hablo en catalán pues hablo en catalán · si hablo en castellano · pues · en castellano pero · me
siento mucho más cómoda hablando en castellano no[?] · porque · me sé expresar mejor · · · pero ·
no no es por otra cosa ahí
Joan: y en la escuela no te representó ningún problema >cuando lo introdujeron o
Silvia: <(cuand-) · que va nunca · desde- ya desde pequeñaa ya · cuando yo empecé a hacer clases de
catalán · pues · en el egebé no[?] · yy · yo hacía

Extract 76

Magda: porque no me sient- · no es que no lo sepa hablar · porque sí · lo sé hablar · pero es que yo
estoy pensado en castellano por qué estoy hablando en catalán si estoy pensando en castellano ·
porque lo traduzco y digo palabras que · como no las sé traducir las cambio[?] no · yo quiero decir
la palabra que estoy pensando · y no és porque yo no quiera que hablen catalán · a mi que me hablen me da igual · bueno a veces · no me da igual · peroo hablarlo yo en · · · cuando debo y ya
está cuando busco curro y estas cosas

Extract 77

Jaume: *con ella* · amb ella parlo en castellà no[?] · amb el chimo parlo català amb tu · català i a vegades
si comença en castellà en castellà · no tinc un idioma · propi no[?] per parlar · o sigui · · me puc ex-
pressar com vulgui en castellà i en català · (lo poc) que sé ho faig no[?]

Extract 78

Mateo: ui hosti menudo ridículo · cuando me lo hacían hablar · · yo no quería la mayoría de veces es
que (xx) que pasaba dee salir a · y había veces quee · cualquier ejercicio así · le decía · no no no lo
he hecho · solo por el mero hecho dee no salir allíi a hacer el · ridículo
Joan: y en · · en las · bueno en la

Extract 79

Clara: no noho sé · perquèee · · · perquè · yo me daba cuenta de qu- · de no[?] de que lo que estaba
haciendo era · era utilizar pues pues una historia solo por verguenza · · no[?] · pues hablar un
idioma que nunca he hablado · (pues lo que hice) fue quitarme la verguenza · y ya está · (es decir
no es) · no es que cambiara de · idea · yo era super consciente · de porque yo utilizaba de porque
yo soy anarquista · eh[?] yo · · me conozco mucho · o sea me paso (toas las) horas del día · dedica-
das a mi no[?] · y me conozco mucho · si es por verguenza pues · o bien di que es por verguenza · · ·
o bien rompe con la verguenza · · · quiero decir que no se me abrió la luz

Extract 80

Patricia: passo perquè · també · no em posa- no em ve de gust posar-me a barallar dee la importància del català perque m'enviaran a la merda · · vaig a l'escola i els hi començo a dir que · van- han de parlar en català perquè no sé què no sé quantos i em tiren un totxo al cap [rient] · · és lo mateix que deien de · *porque las feministas* no sé què no sé quantos i el que et poden tirar és una ampolla · és lo mateix · llavors més val fer-ho d'una altra manera · pues és parlar en cat- parl- els hi parles d'en tant en tant en català · · hi ha gent que · que sí quee · que potser

Extract 81

Clara: bueno amb el ayats ell sempre ha parlat en català · i un dia amb mi em va començar a parlar que · ui uixxx · *quieto[!]* [Els dos riem] *(te voy xxx) dos hostias · (vete a) militar (x) lo que tu quieras pero · a mi no me líes ·* clar perquè a més tu · tu parles · · més o menys eh[?] · pues com has començat a parlar amb una persona · *fíjate yo · yo tenía un novio que era · medio gitano · pero lo c- · pero lo conocí hablando · en catalán · ·*

Joan: vols dir gitano castellanoparlant perquè si vas a gràcia · o a sants · >· els manolos parlen en català

Clara: <*castellanoparlante · · · castellanoparlante total y absoluto · · y* sempre parlàvem en català · perquè no · (no[?] eh) · i · *y cuando hablábamos en castellano pues · no podíamos ·*

Joan: [ric] · és bestial això

Extract 82

Patricia: un cop hi ha molt de contacte amb una person- · per exemple jo amb la clara començo a parlar en català amb ella i em sona fals · · parlar-li en cata- tenir una conversa amb ella en català · i a ella m- i a ella igual llavors clar després amb una persona tornar-li obligar a parlar-li- parlar-li amb un altre idioma

Extract 83

Guille: és que jo que sé jo amb l'edu per exemple · que és una persona no[?] que · · més o menys · tenim un rotllo així · guapo no? · i em poso amb ell a parlar amb català i acabo parlant amb castellà [riu] i · al principi no al principi no em passava · al principi amb català no[?] · però després al · barrejant-se no[?] amb més gent · doncs · o estàs explicant algo ii · comences amb una persona a parlar-li en castellà perquè estàs acostumat a parlar-li en castellà · i de cop i volta li cànvies en català no[?] · però és que · nni me'n donc compte no[?] · · no sé jo penso que es parla · molt de tot

Extract 85

Luis: eh que nunca me ha *entrao y cuantoo · mâh me cuehta una cosa mâh la aborrehco no[?] · · y no huy- · no hay manera · · ah · bueno · loh que sean catalanihta · o sean independentihta me da lo mimmo por ello no[?] [...] nunca me hu gustao el catalán ni · · · lo- lo entiendo a veceh lo hablo pero no · · · se puede decir que odio las cosah catalana* [rialleta] · *en pocah palabrah algunah cosa · · todo lo que tiene nada que ver con fanatimmos y · como el barça como o sea así ·*

Cambrer: (esto no tiene nada que ver) te gustan más las catalanas que el catalán

Luis: también eh verdá [Jo ric] · · · *lah catalana sí be- eso sí que me guhta · · sí sí · lah catalanah me encantan*

Extract 86

Pablo: no me gusta el catalán yo qué sé · · · o sea lo tienes que aprender porque estás en cataluña pero simplemente · o sea es como si te obligaran · · y a mi como no me gusta que me obliguen · pues · a lo mejor no me gusta por eso · · pues igual que el latín el latín yo le tengo asco · · porque me obligaron o sea no me gustaba a mi · y claro en- en

Extract 87

Luis: profesore muy maniáticoh que · · decían lo típico [veu gutural] eh quee · con el franquihmo noh costó mucho ahora que podemos · pue venga catalán · venga catalán · · y (qué) culpa tenemos los demá hombre · déhano tranquilo · ·

Joan: bueno a ver · luego tengo así otras · preguntas sueltas que

Extract 88

Ricardo: es lo que digo yo yo- · (o sea) si estuvieses · o sea con- · con gente que está hablando todo el día catalán pues acabarías hablando el catalán · · (lo que pa- aquí) vale · aquí nos cachondeamos · y tal e · ah · sale mal esta palabra ee · que no sé qué que · (x) a mi me gusta e- · y · me parece que *soy uno de los pocos que me gusta el catalán · o sea no- · o sea yo no hablo por el hecho de que (te da) · · no sé · pero a mi me gusta o sea a mi me gusta oir una conversación en catalán · [...] bueno y · como al pablo que no sé quien más que no · se ve que no les gusta el catalán · a mi si me gusta · (x) es eso que noo · hombre yo con (x) algun un cliente · me pasa lo mismo que al andrés como eh-* tamoh de camarero pues · pues a veceh pues sí que hablas el catalán no[?] · aunque metas gamba-zoh no[?]*

Extract 89

Paula: sí · · si eel · · l- los de recepción hablan entre ellos en catalán · pero a lo mejor estoy hablando yo con ellos · · y por ejemplo eh- · ellos [dubte] · a lo mejor ellos están hablando en catalán no[?] y llego yo · y si me tienen que decir algo me lo dicen en castellano · y yo se lo digo a ellos · que no hace falta que- · que os pongáis a hablar conmigo en castellano · pero · es la costumbre ya · · y siempre me han · a lo mejor llego- y- bueno llego yoo bueno llega otro quee · y le hablan en caste-llano

Extract 90

Salva: pues · no sé porque · · · yo qué sé si el catalán es · la lengua de aquí · · habría que hablarla no[?] · y no porque diga · porque esto es cataluña hay que hablarla no? · sinó · · por decir · joder que sa-no que es · saber- poder hablar dos idiomas no? · · y aparte pues que a mi me interesa porque · no sé hablar catalán · · y · y aprovecho eso no[?] · y bueno y además sabiendo pues · · que el- el ayats si yo digo sanahoria · no se va a reir de mi no[?] · · o quee · claro que no se van a reir de mi por-que (claro) · están peces como yo

Extract 91

Aleix: una altra · · s'intenta parlar en català per raons polítiques fdiguessim · per reivindicar · peer- per lo que parlàvem · · (xxx tu estarás) amb una història · però tu intentes (treballar a xxxx més global) no [?] · o sigui si hi ha una gent que treballa per una història · · tu no vas a despreciar · tu vols que la gent entengui la teva tu entens el sentit de l'altra · llavors · uns perquè estem per laa història dee reivindicar el català · altres · perquè diuem bueno · jo sóc castellanoparlant però · · aquí hi ha una gent que sempre ho havia parlat · · i els (reivindica) com per treballar-ho no? · llavors al nivell del mili kk revolta al moc · (tothom) · (doncs) la idea és aquesta Jo: i es realitza la idea · amb una

Extract 92

Guille: clar · · a mi és el que em passava · o què sé · joo de petit tenia amics · per exemple uns amics de la escala que eren castellans no[?] · · iii · no sé · jo el sentia parlar amb castellà i · em donava pal contestar-li amb català no[?] no sé per quina raó · i acabava parlant en castellà · · i potser no feia ben fet no[?] perquè igual el xaval aquell volia aprendre el català · m'entens[?] · però · · jo què sé · · · no sé per què ho feia · però ho fas
Magda: un respeto · un (xxx)

Extract 93

Pepe: és curiós perquè · · jo veig una persona que- que el- · la seva llengua és el català · i li començo a parlar en català · ara això ja no em passa tan com abans no[?]· però com abans el parlava molt pitjor que ara · doncs · · semblava que diguessin pobret no[?] I em parlaven sempre en- amb castellà · i això és bueno de mala educació i és · · em sembla que és · una facta de respectee · m- molt gran no[?] · quan militava passava això · quan estava a la lliga em passava això · · · [Acord de guitarra flamenca] [...] sí · però és · això és sempre lo que passa és que · per lo que et deia abans de què t'a-naven tallant el rotllo · · fins quee · fins que lal- · fins que tu ets més fort que la vergonya · · i passes dee · · de tallar-te tu mateix el rotllo no? llavors si tu parles català amb algú · i aquest és catal- aquest- parla sempre català · i et contesta en castellà · tu passes igualment · continues parlant català · fins que el tiuu · se n'adona no[?] · · o no o dir-li por qué me contestas en castellano · no[?] · · [acords de guitarra flamenca]
Joan: sí · · · i quina necessitat hi ha · vull

Extract 94

Clara: vull dir el discurs del · aleix es · · que cadascú · parli com vulgui no sé què no sé quantos · pero la meva cult- · o sea no[?] · i jo per això · parlo sempre català · (val vui dir) tú si vols parla sempre · en castellà · · vale · jo llavors parlo sempre català

Extract 96

Irene: jolines a mi me ha costado · qué quieres que te diga · llegar a a a quinto · · vamos a- jolines años de estudio y estudio no[?] · y ahora · eh que ara no lo dejo · segurísimo · · yy trabajar pues sí me gusta no[?] · he aprendido muchas cosas · · pero creo quee · lo que tenía que aprender ahí · ya lo he aprendido · · ahora ya siempre es lo mismo lo mismo lo mismo lo mismo · lo que yo estaba comentando com mi madre es que me gustaría o sea a mi me gustaría seguir trabajando · pero · en otro sitio no[?]

Extract 97

Joan: de la escuela taller a donde tú vas a ahora pues · es bastante diferente
Salva: sí · un cambio de la hostia. · · No sé es que · · es acostumbrarse no[?] · · porque claro (entré) en el trabajo y · · estaba pues · joder · ahora irse a la plaza · unos porros · · una cervezas y (xxx) de la hostia porque claro no te pues marchar · · yy es ponerte e- en situación no[?] de decir · ahora estoy en un curro serio y que no · que no me puedo pasar · y en la escuela taller pues estaba como · como quería no[?] · pero es · no sé es acostumbrarse no[?] · igual es un poco de resignación pero · ·
Joan: la experiencia de la escuela taller

Notes

[1] See Bastardas (1985, 1986), Boix (1993), Erill et al. (1992) and Pujolar (1995a).

[2] Esteva (1973: 152) provides some official data on birth rates. In 1970, in Barcelona, where the majority of the population was still Catalan born, only 25,37% of children born alive came from Catalan couples, while 45,40 % came from immigrant couples, a proportion of 1 to 1,8. The remaining births corresponded mainly to mixed couples.

[3] Actually, it is arguable that they should be called "immigrants" at all, having moved within the boundaries of a single state, although Castilian speakers often define themselves as such as well. Kathryn Woolard (1989) and Rodríguez-Gómez (1993) have analyzed how the term "immigrant" is used in Barcelona to construct cultural differences in terms of language, ethnicityand social class. This is probably comparable to the use of the term "immigrant" in other contexts, which attests to the fact most Catalan researchers see themselves as a nation despite not having a state (see Pujolar 1995b).

[4] In Catalonia, it is difficult to get comparable data on language use at different periods of time because different surveys conducted by different institutions often phrase the questions differently. Strubell's data are based on the 1975 census. The data of the Institut d'Estudis Metropolitans de Barcelona (1991, 1997) are drawn from two official surveys. Finally, Argenter et al.'s data are based on a survey carried out by the Institut d'Estudis Catalans on 500 young people. 1975 data correspond to respondents' declared "family language"; 1986 to their declared "first" language; 1991 and 1997 to their "habitual" language, and 1996 to the language spoken "at home". Strubell only gives data on the proportion of Catalan speakers in 1975. Despite these problems, Argenter et al.'s data on young people does suggest that the Catalan-speaking population effectively decreased in the period studied. The survey from the Institut d'Estudis Metropolitans de Barcelona (1997a, 1997b: 62) on the whole of Barcelona Metropolitan Area confirms that, amongst people between 18 and 29 years of age, the percentages of Catalan speakers was 6 % lower than the that of whole adult population, while the percentages of Spanish speakers was 2 % higher and the percentage of bilinguals 4 % higher as well.

[5] These are the figures for young people in the Barcelona Metropolitan Area. "Working status" includes house workers, the unemployed and military conscripts. The chart shows how young people gradually drop or finish their studies and start

working or looking for jobs, although many try to combine both. "Both" status includes students who are studying and working or claim to be looking for work.

[6] In his well-known poetical style, Bakhtin affirms that the "utterance is a link in the chain of speech communion" (1986: 94). I believe that the use of a metaphor of ritual is significant here. Bakhtin and Goffman's works contain very striking coincidences of perspective which are sometimes hidden by their different vocabularies. The idea of action as oriented both to past and present is also present in Schutz' social phenomenological thinking, but has not been developed in the ethnomethodological traditions (Atkinson 1988).

[7] I use the generic masculine in quotations written in this form and also in my own text when it contains anaphoric relationships with such quotations.

[8] Since then, a few studies have appeared which focus on difference of language choice patterns in same-sex groups in Catalan schools (Woolard 1994; Vila 1996). Aracil (1983) reflected about the trend found amongst women from the *Rosselló* region, who had taken to raising their children in French. Some romanists had found a similar trend in Occitan-speaking areas. See Forsthuber (1991) for a very interesting discussion on the ideological, basically androcentric, underpinnings of some occitanist debates. Deprez (1994), Heller and Lévy (1994), Vilardell (1998) and Woolard (1989) provide interesting insights of gender-mediated experience of bilingualism in linguistically-mixed families.

[9] *Vitoria* (in Basque, *Gasteiz*) is one of the main cities of the Basque Country.

[10] Although I did not find any data about the amount of more or less stable rock bands existing in Barcelona, I have reason to believe that it is very high and that the Trepas' initiative is by no means extraordinary. In my home town, there was a weekly concert all year round of local groups of all styles. Most of the groups came from an area which has only some 40,000 inhabitants and not all the existing groups participated. Jones (1990) also suggests that organizing bands is a very widespread phenomenon among young English people. It is also significant that, in the two-year period in which I gathered information about groups for my research, the band performed in public only twice, which shows to what extent its function was more to organize involvement than to eventually build a musical career.

[11] This may help us to understand, for instance, Johnson's perception of male gossip:

... when I once introduced two male friends, I was intrigued by their ability to talk for over half an hour, revealing, in the process, relatively little about themselves beyond this shared interest in sport. (Johnson 1994: 146)

[12] Tusón (1985b) identifies this feature as originating in the southern Spanish Andalusian dialect, spoken by approximately half of Barcelona's immigrant population (which is 40 percent of the total population). Nevertheless, it has now become common in many colloquial forms of Spanish and is used by some politicians and television presenters.

[13] The problems of definition are voiced by many authors of dictionaries of unconventional language (see Chapman 1986; León 1992; Thorne 1990).

[14] There are some curious mismatches in the ways these terms are used in both Catalan and Spanish. The dictionary or academic meaning of *argot* commonly refers to what English dictionaries consider as "slang", while the word *caló*, which originally denominated the language of the Romany people, seems to be the equivalent to English "argot". Nevertheless, the Trepas would never call their speech *caló*, but *jerga* or *argot*, which corresponds to the English usage (see *Diccionari de la Llengua Catalana* 1983; León 1992; *The Collins English Dictionary* 1986).

[15] In Pujolar 1997a I provide a list of a number of argot items (and their deffinitions) that I found in the talk of the Trepas and the Rambleros.

[16] *La penya* (Spanish *la peña*) originally designated groups of people, usually men, who regularly met in particular cafés, as well as some voluntary societies devoted to recreational activities (e.g. football and bull-fighting fan clubs) (see *Diccionari de la Llengua Catalana* 1983; Moliner 1991). The most famous of them are the ones who participate in the *Sanfermines* festival of Iruña, which has of late become for many young people a kind of "Mecca". In any case, the meaning of the word seems to have shifted to designate 'the people', 'the gang', 'the folks', 'the crowd', 'the buddies' and so on.

[17] In my data, when people were animated *as* speaking Catalan or Spanish, the choice of language usually coincided with the reported language, and always so if the voice was animated through codeswitching. Irene and Alicia reproduced their mothers' Catalan with a switch, the latter with a Tarragonian accent. Patrícia animated in Catalan the "thoughts" of a Spanish speaker deciding to speak Catalan.

Pepe and Clara accurately reported dialogues with Catalan speakers with whom they tried unsuccessfully to speak Catalan.

[18] There is no reference to such an animal in the Catalan edition of Peterson *et al.* (1983). Although it might correspond to a dialectal denomination of a known species, it is more probably an elaboration of the insult *"mussol!"* 'owl'.

[19] However, the existing public images of these fashions are usually exaggerated, as is implied by terms such as *urban tribes*. I heard Pepe and Salva complain about the stereotyping and exaggerated treatment that youth groups receive in the press. Although it is true that some discos and bars attract the most enthusiastic followers of a particular movement, natural groups of young people are usually diverse, at least according to my own experience. So if I said that the Rambleros *were* heavies and the Trepas *were* punks, I would have to overlook many members who would clearly oppose such a statement (first of all, women), and I would probably overlook the fact that both heavies and punks did listen to a very varied range of music styles. Being heavy or being punk implies particular modes of participation and involvement in social activities where particular music styles and ideas become relevant. Nevertheless, it does not exclude the possibility of developing other tastes and relationships.

[20] It was also my impression that the particular type of Spanish spoken in working class neighborhoods was made to sound in the back of the mouth and the throat, a feature exaggerated in dramatizations of Andalusian speakers. Catalan was, at least, not *backed* so much and it is significant that the Catalan funny voices were usually produced by bringing the sounding space of the voice forward and to the nasal cavity. This recalls Bourdieu's (1991a: 86—87) remarks on *la gueule* 'the throat' and *la bouche* 'the mouth' as contrasting patterns of vocality between the working classes and the bourgeoisie, with their corresponding overtones of masculinity and femininity respectively.

[21] "Passive bilingualism" is often referred to as "the bilingual norm" as well (Woolard 1989; Pujolar 1991b).

[22] Amparo Tusón, in a personal conversation, reported to me cases where the opposite actually happens, that is, that people may feel freer to negotiate their linguistic behavior with close friends as there is no question of being misinterpreted and of endangering a well established relationship.

[23] The interviews were not centered on the language issue, but many other issues (some of them just as delicate, such as drug-taking) were discussed in it.

[24] Of course, the teaching of Catalan could benefit a lot from developments in the field of Language Teaching which have superseded the traditional error-centered approaches (see Nussbaum 1990). Joan Argenter (1991), the chairman of the Philological Section of the Institut d'Estudis Catalans (the equivalent of the Catalan language academy), has also suggested that traditional attitudes towards linguistic correctness may thwart the efforts towards linguistic normalization. He has argued that philologists and language teachers should consider the implications of the fact that Catalan is a second language for many of its users.

[25] The question of the self-assessment of competence points towards other lines of interpretation I cannot pursue here. For instance, I have observed that speakers of majority languages, such as Spanish, English and French, seem to regard foreign language learning (and using) as exaggeratedly problematic as compared with speakers of less widespread languages.

[26] The Spanish army is not only unpopular amongst pacifist groups, but amongst most native Catalans for other complex reasons. However, for the Rambleros men, the *mili* 'the service' was a favorite topic of discussion, in particular with respect to its adventurous side: how they endeavored to break the rules and get away with it, how they managed to get the most comfortable posts and leave regimes, how they got involved in get-togethers and brawls with other soldiers, stories of heavy drug taking and so on. The military service actually provided a space where multiple, new and exciting forms of transgression were possible, thus becoming a source for anecdotes, songs and expressions for later life that could be shared for mutual enjoyment and for a symbolic assertion of one's transgressive capabilities. Incidentally, the military service is one of Spain's traditional sites for the expression of anti-Catalan ideology. Insulting, nicknaming and bullying Catalans is a deeply rooted tradition both amongst officials and conscripts, which is an indication of how aggressive masculinity involves a complicity with authority.

[27] Here the question arises again of whether Catalan speakers adopted substantially different modes of participation in the activities of the group. Certainly, the difference was not as visible as the contrast between the genders. In the group, Catalan speakers generally seemed to play more passive roles, happily going along with the others' initiatives and topics of conversation. Nevertheless, the issue needs studying further, as this circumstance could be the product of mere chance. To date, I have no knowledge of any study on the ritual structure of Catalan-speaking groups.

[28] The term "*convivència*", which has no clear translation in English, conveys a sense of harmonious and friendly co-existence. It is a key word in Catalan politics, as it is used as a kind of euphemism to talk about the relationships between "Cata-

lans" and "Immigrants" without explicitly acknowledging that such a division exists. Part of its rhetorical force comes from the fact that it does not sound necessarily political, as it is used to refer to building relationships in many other senses (within a couple, between neighbors, between the peoples of the world and so on). In autumn 1989, it became a fighting word used against a nationalist party which demanded the recognition of Catalonia's right to self-determination. The underlying suggestion was that such a move could damage the existing constitutional political consensus in Spain and also the relationships between the two groups in Catalonia which do not officially exist.

[29] This wording seems to express both modesty and a certain insecurity with regard to Catalan, an attitude which is very widespread even amongst Catalan speakers. However, it would be difficult to say that Pepe's Catalan in this particular extract was less than very good. Apart from the fact that he got his meaning across well, fluently and without hesitations, there was not a single item of the Spanish interferences usually punished by teachers of Catalan (although there were some borrowings originating in slang).

[30] I do not see any reason to believe that that the Catalan education system of the 1980s was operating in a substantially different way from that of other industrial societies. A recent survey conducted in Barcelona showed that the percentage of children of manual workers who went to university was approximately half that of skilled workers and a third of that of managers and professionals (Argenter et al. 1999).

[31] Bourdieu does not make clear what can count as a field or in what ways aspects of practices or social relationships can be seen as located in particular fields rather than others. Thus he treats as conceptually comparable things that are obviously quite different, such as the educational field and the linguistic field. My analysis reflects this yet unresolved aspect of his framework.

[32] I devised this chart on the basis of data on a) active population according to age and b) estimated unemployment according to age. *Active population* refers to those effectively on the job market, either working or willing to work according to the census. Estimated unemployment is based on the *Enquesta de la Població activa* 'Survey of Active Population' and includes people who have been looking for a job for at least four weeks and whose availability is verified 15 days after the questionnaire is answered (Direcció General de Joventut 1991: 35).

[33] In another survey conducted in 1996 in Barcelona on a random sample of 500 young people aged between 17 and 25, we found that 201 had dropped or finished

their studies and were either working or looking for work. Of these, only 41 (20.4 %) had a permanent contract or were working in their family's business, 60 were unemployed (29.8 %) and 100 (49.8) had various forms of temporary contract (Argenter et al. 1999).

[34] I understand that a classroom, a relationship or a social situation characterized by the fact that it contains members of both sexes has to be seen as *sex-mixed*. In the way I have defined "gender" in this book, a male-only classroom could contain individuals of different "genders" and hence could be seen as *gender-mixed*.

[35] Dreyfus and Rabinow (1993) also argue that, because of the assumption that practices are reproductive, Bourdieu applies interpretive procedures that are circular and tautological. Any action becomes forcibly a bid to acquire cultural or economic capital, and any denial of the workings of structures becomes proof of the hidden, masked workings of these structures.

[36] Hasan (1998) provides an elaborate argument of how Bourdieu's writings on language and the linguistic market contain serious contradictions with regard to what he sees as the origin of meaning. She argues, successfully in my view, that he treats language as if it was merely an onomastic system (i.e. with signs simply naming elements of reality external to language), where the connection between linguistic form and content is fully arbitrary and, consequently, where the social values attached to particular varieties originate in purely external (i.e. social) factors. As a result, what Bourdieu does is to import into his own conception of meaning the most problematic assumptions of the narrow formal linguistics that he is so strongly criticizing, which treats language (i.e. the linguistic system) as if it was independent from its use in social life. The only difference is, according to Hasan, that Bourdieu only considers the external factors and dismisses the internal ones as irrelevant, thus keeping the traditional separation between internal and external linguistics though from the "opposite side", as it were.

References

Antich, José
    1994   *El Virrei*. Barcelona: Editorial Planeta S.A.

Aracil, Lluís V.
    1965 [1982]Conflicte lingüístic i normalització lingüística a l'Europa nova. In Aracil (ed.), 23–38.
    1979 [1982]Educació i sociolingüística. In Aracil (ed.), 129–217.
    1983   *Dir la realitat*. Barcelona: Edicions dels Països Catalans.

Aracil, Lluís V. (ed.)
    1982   *Papers de sociolingüística*. Barcelona: La Magrana.

Argente, Joan A.
    1991   Debat sobre la normalització lingüística: ple de l'Institut d'Estudis Catalans 18-IV-1990. Barcelona: Ed. Institut d'Estudis Catalans.

Argente, Joan Albert; Castellanos, Jordi; Jorba, Manuel; Molas, Joaquim; Murgades, Josep; Nadal, Josep Mª, and Sullà, Enric
    1979   Una nació sense estat, un poble sense llengua? in *Els Marges* no. 15. Barcelona: Editorial Curial, 3–13.

Argenter, Joan; Bargalló, Helena, and Pujolar, Joan
    1999   Tria de llengua, discurs i identitat entre joves barcelonins (2ª Fase). Unpublished Research Report. Barcelona: Institut d'Estudis Catalans.

Auer, Peter
    1984   *Bilingual Conversation*. Amsterdam: John Benjamins.
    1988   A conversation analytic approach to code-switching and transfer. In Heller (ed.), 187–213.
    1990   A discussion paper on code alternation. Paper presented at the 1st seminar of the European Science Foundation Network on Code-switching, Basel, January 1990. Strasbourg: European Science Foundation.

Bakhtin, Mikhail
    1981   *The Dialogic Imagination*. Ed. M. Holquist, trans. C. Emerson and M. Holquist. Austin: University of Texas Press.
    1984a   *Rabelais and his World*. Trans. Hélène Iswolsky. Bloomington: Indiana University Press.
    1984b   *Problems of Dostoevsky's Poetics*. Emerson, C. (ed. and trans.) Manchester: Mancester University Press.
    1986   *Speech genres and other late essays*. Ed. M. Holquist, trans. C. Emerson and M. Holquist. Austin: University of Texas Press.

334   *References*

Ballart, Jordi
1996   An urban accent in a bilingual setting: the case of Xava Catalan. Unpublished MA Dissertation. Salford, England: University of Salford.
Barth, Fredrik
1969   Introduction. In Barth (ed.) *Ethnic Groups and Boundaries*, 9–38. Oslo and London: Universitetsforlaget and George Allen & Unwin.
Bastardas, Albert
1985   *La bilingüització de la segona generació immigrant: realitat i factors a Vilafranca del Penedès.* Barcelona: La Magrana.
1986   *Llengua i inmigració: la segona generació immigrant a la Catalunya no-metropolitana.* Barcelona: La Magrana.
1991   Planning change in codeswitching: theoretical and practical inferences from the Catalan case. In ESF Scientific Networks: *Papers for the symposium on code-switching in bilingual studies: theory, significance and perspectives.* Vol 1. Strasbourg: European Science Foundation, 93–124.
1996   *Ecologia de les llengües. Medi, contactes i dinàmica sociolingüística.* Barcelona: Edicions Proa.
Benet, Josep
1995   *L'Intent franquista de genocidi cultural contra Catalunya.* Barcelona: Publicacions de l'Abadia de Montserrat.
Blom, Jan-Peter and Gumperz, John J.
1972   Social meaning in linguistic structures: code-switching in Norway. In Gumperz and Hymes (eds.), 407–434.
Boix, Emili
1989   Tria i alternança de llengües entre joves de Barcelona: normes d'ús i actituds.Ph.D. Thesis. Universitat de Barcelona.
1990   Language choice and language switching among young people in Barcelona: concepts, methods and data. In the *Papers for the workshop on concepts, methodology and data.* Brussels: European Science Foundation, Network on Code-switching and Language Contact, 209–226.
1993   *Triar no és trair. Identitat i llengua en els joves de Barcelona.* Barcelona: Edicions 62.
Bourdieu, Pierre
1972   *Esquisse d'une théorie de la pratique. Précédée de trois études d'etnologie kabyle.* Geneva: Droz.
1979   *La Distinction: critique sociale du jugement.* Paris: Éditions de minuit.
1984a   *Homo academicus.* Paris: Éditions de Minuit.
1984b [1993]*Sociology in question.* London: Sage publications.

1987   What makes a social class? On the theoretical and practical existence of groups. In Berkeley Journal of Sociology n. 32,. 1–18.

1988a   Program for a sociology of sport. In *Sociology of sport journal* 5, no. 2: 153–161.

1988b   *Homo academicus*. English edition. Cambridge and Oxford: Polity Press and Basil Blackwell.

1980 [1990]*The logic of practice*. Cambridge and Stanford: Polity Press and Stanford University Press.

1991a   *Language and Symbolic Power*. London: Polity Press.

1991b   Censorship and the imposition of form. In Bourdieu (1991a), 137–159.

1991c   Did you say 'Popular'? In Bourdieu (1991a), 90–102.

1993   Concluding remarks: for a sociogenetic understanding of intellectual works. In Calhoun, Lipuma and Postone (eds.), 263–275.

Bourdieu, Pierre; Darbel, Alain and Schnapper, Dominique

1966   *L'amour de l'art. Les musées d'art européens et leur public*. Paris: Éditions de Minuit.

Bourdieu, Pierre and Passeron, Jean-Claude

1964   *Les héritiers. Les étudiants et la culture*. Paris: Éditions de Minuit.

1970   *La Reproduction. Éléments pour une théorie du système d'enseignement*. Paris: Les Éditions de Minuit.

Bourdieu, Pierre and Wacquant, Loïc

1992   *An Invitation to Reflexive Sociology*. Cambridge: Polity Press.

Bourhis, Richard

1984   Cross-cultural communication in Montreal: two field studies since bill 101. In *International Journal of the Sociology of Language* vol. 46, 33–47.

Breen, Marcus

1991   A stairway to heaven or a highway to hell? Heavy metal rock music in the 1990s. Cultural Studies vol. 5, no. 2, 191–204.

Brittan, Arthur

1989   *Masculinity and Power*. Oxford: Basil Blackwell.

Brown, Penelope and Levinson, Stephen

1987   *Politeness. Some Universals in Language Usage*. Cambridge: Cambridge University Press.

Bruner, Edward and Kelso, Jan

1980   Gender differences in graffiti: a semiotic perspective. In Kramarae (ed.),. 239–252.

Calhoun, Craig; Lipuma, Edward and Postone Moishe (eds.)

1993   *Bourdieu: Critical Perspectives*. Cambridge: Polity Press.

Calsamiglia, Helena and Tusón, Amparo
  1980   Ús i alternança de llengües en grups de joves d'un barri de
            Barcelona: Sant Andreu del Palomar. In *Treballs de
            Sociolingüística Catalana* no.3, 11–82. València: Editorial 3 i 4.
  1984   Use of languages and code-switching in groups of youths in a Barri
            of Barcelona: communicative norms in spontaneous speech. In
            International Journal of the Sociology of Language vol. 47, 105–
            121.
Cameron, Deborah
  1992   *Feminism and Linguistic Theory*. Second Edition. London: The
            Macmillan Press Ltd.
  1994   Verbal hygiene for women: linguistics misapplied?. In *Applied
            Linguistics* Vol. 15 No. 4, 382–98.
  1997   Performing gender identity: young men's talk and the construction
            of heterosexual masculinity. In Johnson and Meinhof (eds.), 47–64.
Cameron, Deborah; Frazer, Elizabeth; Harvey, Penelope; Rampton, MBH and
        Richardson, Kay
  1992   *Researching Language*. Issues of Power and Method. London and
            New York: Routledge.
Carulla, Mireia
  1990   *The Catalan language today*. Departament de Cultura. Barcelona:
            Generalitat de Catalunya.
The Collins English Dictionary.
  1986   London and Glasgow: William Collins & Sons LTD.
Chapman, Robert (ed.)
  1986   *New Dictionary of American Slang*. London and Basingstoke:
            Macmillan Press.
Cheshire, Jenny
  1982   *Variation in an English dialect: a sociolinguistic study*. Cambridge:
            Cambridge University Press.
Chouliaraki, Lilie and Fairclough, Norman (in press) *Discourse in late modernity:
            rethinking Critical Discourse Analysis*. Edinburgh: Edinburgh
            University Press.
    (forthcoming) "On Hasan's 'The disempowerment game: a critique of
            Bourdieu's view of language" in *Linguistics and Education* vol. 10,
            no. 2.
Cicourel, Aaron V.
  1993   Aspects of structural and processual theories of knowledge. In
            Calhoun et al. (eds.), 89–115.
Coates, Jennifer and Cameron, Deborah (eds.)
  1988   *Women in their Speech Communities: New perspectives on
            Language and Sex*. London: Longman.

Coates, Jennifer
1988 Gossip revisited: language in all-female groups. In Coates and Cameron (eds.), 94–122.

Codó, Eva
1998 Analysis of language choice in intercultural service encounters. Unpublished dissertation. Universitat Autònoma de Barcelona.

Collins, James
1993 Determination and contradiction: an appreciation and critique of the work of Pierre Bourdieu on language and education. In Calhoun, Lipuma and Postone (eds.), 116–138.

Connell, R. W.
1987 *Gender and Power*. Cambridge: Polity Press and Basil Blackwell.

Departament de Cultura
1991 *Estudis i propostes per a la difusió de l'ús social de la llengua catalana*. Vol. 2. Barcelona: Generalitat de Catalunya.

Departament de Treball
1995 *Anuari*
1994 *. Informació estadística del departament de Treball*. Barcelona: Generalitat de Catalunya.
1996 *Anuari 1995. Informació estadística del departament de Treball*. Barcelona: Generalitat de Catalunya.

Deprez, Christine
1994 *Les enfants bilingues: langues et familles*. Paris: Crédif.

De Klerk, Vivien
1992 How taboo are taboo words for girls? In *Language and Society* vol. 21, 277–289.
1997 The role of expletives in the construction of masculinity. In Johnson and Meinhof (eds.), 144–158.

Diccionari de la Llengua Catalana
1983 Barcelona: Enciclopèdia Catalana S.A.

Direcció General de Joventut
1991 *La Joventut de Catalunya en Xifres (1994)*. Departament de la Presidència. Barcelona: Generalitat de Catalunya.

Drew, Paul and Wootton, Anthony (eds.)
1988 *Erving Goffman. Exploring the Interaction Order*. Cambridge: Polity Press.

Dreyfus, Hubert and Rabinow, Paul
1982 *Michel Foucault: Beyond Structuralism and Hermeneutics*. Brighton. Harvester Press.
1993 Can there be a science of existential structure and social meaning? In Calhoun, Lipuma and Postone (eds.), 35–44.

Easthope, Antony
1986   *What a Man's Gotta do. The Masculine Myth in Popular Culture.*
          Boston. Unwyn Hyman Ltd.
Eckert, Penelope
1980   Diglossia: separate and unequal. In *Linguistics* Vol. 18, 1053–1064.
1989   *Jocks and Burnouts. Social categories and identity in the high
          school.* New York: Teachers College Press.
Erill i Pinyot, Gustau; Farràs i Farràs, Jaume and Marcos i Moral, Ferran
1992   *Ús del català entre els joves a Sabadell.* Departament de Cultura.
          Barcelona: Generalitat de Catalunya.
Esteva, Claudi
1973   Aculturación y urbanización de inmigrados en Barcelona. Cuestión
          de etnia o cuestión de clase? In *Ethnica* no. 5, 135–189.
Fairclough, Norman L.
1989   *Language and Power.* London: Longman.
1992a   *Discourse and Social Change.* Cambridge: Polity Press.
1992b   Introduction. In Fairclough (ed.), 1–29.
Fairclough, Norman L. (ed.)
1992   *Critical Language Awareness.* London: Longman.
Ferguson, Charles A.
1959   Diglossia. In *Word* vol. 15, 325–340.
Ferrer i Gironès, Francesc
1985   *La persecució política de la llengua catalana. Història de les
          mesures preses contra el seu ús des de la Nova Planta fins avui.*
          Barcelona: Edicions 62.
Fishman, Joshua A.
1964   Language maintenance and language shift as a field of inquiry. In
          Linguistics vol. 9,: 32–70.
1967   Bilingualism with and without diglossia: diglossia with and without
          bilingualism. In *Journal of Social Issues* vol. 23, 29–38.
Forsthuber, Bernadette
1991   Spracheinstellungen von Frauen im französisch-okzitanischen
          Sprachkonflikt. Unplublished Dissertation Geisteswissenschaftliche
          Fakultät. Universität Wien.
Foucault, Michel
1972   *The archaeology of knowledge.* London: Tavistock Publishers.
1979   *Discipline and Punish: the Birth of the Prison.* Harmondsworth:
          Penguin Books.
Frith, Simon
1987   Towards an aesthetic of popular music. In Leppert, Richard and
          McClary, Susan (eds.), 133–150.

Frith, Simon and Goodwin, Andrew (eds.)
1990   *On Record. Rock, Pop and the Written Word*. London: Routledge.
Frith, Simon and McRobbie, Angela
1978/9   Rock and sexuality. In *Screen Education* no. 29, 3–19.
Funes i Artiaga, Jaime
1982   *La Nova Delinqüència Infantil i Juvenil*. Barcelona: Rosa Sensat/ Edicions 62.
Gal, Susan
1979   *Language Shift*. New York: Academic Press.
Gardiner, Michael
1992   *The Dialogics of Critique. M.M. Bakhtin and the Theory of Ideology*. London and New York: Routledge.
Gardy, Philippe and Lafont, Robert
1981   La diglossie comme conflit: l'exemple occitan. In *Langages* no. 61, 75–91.
Gabinet d'Estudis Socials
1991   *Enquesta a la Joventut de Catalunya (1990)*. Direcció General de Joventut. Barcelona: Generalitat de Catalunya.
Gilligan, Carol
1982   *In a Different Voice: Psychological Theory and Women's Development*. Cambridge, Mass.: Harvard University Press.
Gluckman, Max
1963   Gossip of scandal. In *Current Anthropology* vol. 4 no. 3, 307–315.
Goffman, Erving
1957   Alienation from interaction. In *Human Relations* vol. 10 pt. 1, 47–60.
1959 [1969]*The presentation of self in everyday life*. London: Allen Lane The Penguin Press.
1967   *Interaction Ritual*. New York: Anchor Books.
1974 [1975]*Frame Analysis. An essay on the organisation of experience*. Harmondsworth: Penguin Books.
1981   *Forms of talk*. Oxford: Blackwell.
Goodwin, Marjorie H.
1990   *She-Said-He-Said. Talk as Social Organisation among Black Children*. Bloomington and Indianapolis: Indiana University Press.
Grillo, Ralph (ed.)
1989   *Social Anthropology and the Politics of Language*. London: Routledge.
Gumperz, John J.
1982   *Discourse strategies*. Cambridge: Cambridge University Press.

1996   Introduction to part IV. In Gumperz, John J. and Levinson, Stephen
            C. (eds.) *Rethinking linguistic relativity*. Cambridge: Cambridge
            University Press, 359–373.

Gumperz, John J. (ed.)
1982   *Language and Social Identity*. Cambridge: Cambridge University
            Press.

Gumperz, John J. and Hymes, Dell (eds.)
1972   *Directions in Sociolinguistics: the Ethnography of Communication*.
            New York: Holt, Rinehart and Winston Inc.

Halliday, Michael A. K.
1978   *Language as Social Semiotic*. London: Edward Arnold.

Hasan, Ruqaiya
1998   The disempowerment game: Bourdieu and language and literacy. In
            Linguistics and Education. Vol 10, no. 1.

Heller, Monica
1982   Negotiations of language choice in Montreal. In Gumperz (ed.),
            108–118.
1985   Ethnic relations and language use in Montréal. In Wolfson and
            Manes (eds.), 75–90.
1988   Strategic ambiguity: code-switching in the management of conflict.
            In Heller (ed.),77–96.
1994   *Crosswords. Language, Education and Ethnicity in French
            Ontario*. Berlin: Mouton de Gruyter.
1999   *Linguistic minorities and modernity: a sociolinguistic ethnography*.
            London: Longman.

Heller, Monica (ed.)
1988   *Codeswitching. Anthropological and Sociolinguistic Perspectives*.
            Berlin: Mouton de Gruyter.

Heller, Monica and Lévy, Laurette
1994   Les contradictions des mariages linguistiquement mixtes: les
            stratégies des femmes franco-ontariennes. In *Langage et Societé* 67,
            53–88.

Hewitt, Roger
1986   *White Talk Black Talk. Inter-racial Friendship and Communication
            amongst Adolescents*. Cambridge: Cambridge University Press.

Hill, Jane H. and Hill, Kenneth C.
1986   *Speaking Mexicano: Dynamics of Syncretic Language in Central
            Mexico*. Tucson: University of Arizona Press.

Hughes, Linda
1988   'But that's not REALLY mean': competing in a cooperative mode.
            In *Sex Roles* vol. 19, 669–687.

Hymes, Dell
    1964a   Directions in (ethno-) linguistic theory. In Romney and D'Andrade (eds.), 6–56.

Institut d'Estadística de Catalunya
    1992   *Anuari estadístic de Catalunya (1991)*. Barcelona: Generalitat de Catalunya.
    1993   *Anuari estadístic de Catalunya (1992)*. Barcelona: Generalitat de Catalunya.

Institut d'Estudis Metropolitans de Barcelona
    1991   *Enquesta Metropolitana (1986). Condicions de Vida i hàbits de la població de l'àrea metropolitana de Barcelona. Volum 20: Transmissió i coneixement de la llengua catalana a l'àrea metropolitana de Barcelona.* Coord. María Jesús Izquierdo, Fausto Miguélez and Marina Subirats. Bellaterra: Àrea Metropolitana de Barcelona and Institut d'Estudis Metropolitans de Barcelona.
    1997a   *Enquesta de la regió metropolitana de Barcelona (1995).* Coord. Lucía Baranda. Institut d'Estudis Metropolitans de Barcelona. Diputació de Barcelona. Vol. 3.
    1997b   *Les condicions de vida dels joves metropolitans.* Coord. Lucía Baranda. Barcelona: Institut d'Estudis Metropolitans de Barcelona, Diputació de Barcelona i Pla Jove.

Instituto Nacional de Estadística
    1998   *Banco de datos tempus. PAE. Encuesta de población activa (principales resultados). Parados Catalunya Tasas (1976–1998).* http://www. Ine.es/tempus/welcome.html.

Jackson, David
    1990   *Unmasking Masculinity. A Critical Autobiography*. London: Unwin Hyman.

Johnson, Sally
    1994   A Game of Two Halves? On men, football and gossip. In *Journal of Gender Studies* vol. 3, No. 2, 145–54.
    1997   Theorizing language and masculinity: a feminist perspective. In Johnson and Meinhof (eds.),. 8–26.

Johnson, Sally and Meinof, Ulrike H. (eds.)
    1997   *Language and Masculinity*. Oxford: Blackwell.

Jones, Deborah
    1980   Gossip: notes on women's oral culture. In Kramarae (ed.), 193–198.

Jones, Simon
    1990   Music and symbolic creativity. In Willis, Paul (ed.) *Common Culture: Symbolic Work at Play in the Everyday Cultures of the Young.* Buckingham: Open University Press, 59–83.

Kramarae, Cheris (ed.)
1980   *The Voices and Words of Women and Men.* Oxford: Pergamon Press.

Labov. William
1972   *Language in the Inner City.* Philadelphia: University of Pennsylvania Press.

Lafont, Robert
1977   Sobre el procés de patoisització. In *Treballs de Sociolingüística Catalana* no.1. Ed. 3 i 4. València,: 131–136.

León, Víctor
1992   *Diccionario de Argot Español.* Madrid: Alianza Editorial.

Leppert, Richard and McClary, Susan (eds.)
1987   *Music and Society. The Politics of Composition, Performance and Reception.* Cambridge: Cambridge University Press.

Lever, Janet R.
1974   Games children play: sex differences and the development of role skills. Ph.D. Thesis. Department of Sociology. Yale University.

Lipuma, Edward
1993   Culture and the concept of culture in a Theory of Practice. In Calhoun et al. (eds.), 14–34.

Lyman, B
1973   Civilisation: contents, discontents and malcontents. In *Contemporary Sociology* vol. 2, 360–6.

Maltz, Daniel N. and Borker, Ruth A.
1982   A cultural approach to male-female miscommunication. In Gumperz (ed.), 196–216.

Marí, Isidor
1989   Per arribar a conversar en català. In Avui 05/03/1989. Barcelona:

Martín Rojo, Luisa
1996   Jargon. in Verschueren, Jeff, Östman, Jan-Ola, Blommaert, Jan and Bulcaen, Chris (eds.) *Handbook of Pragmatics* vol. 2. Amsterdam: John Benjamins.

Martin-Jones, Marilyn
1989   Language, power and linguistic minorities: the need for an alternative approach to bilingualism, language maintenance and shift. In Grillo (ed.), 106–125.

Milroy, Lesley
1980   *Language and Social Networks.* Basil Blackwell Ltd. Oxford.

Miró, Josep; Sena, Ernest and Miralles, Frederic
1974   *La Catalunya Pobra.* Barcelona: Editorial Nova Terra.

Moliner, María
1991   *Diccionario de Uso del Español.* Madrid: Editorial Gredos S.A.

Moll, Aina
    1989   El bilingüisme passiu en un xip. In *Avui* 23/02/1989. Barcelona:
Mollà, Toni and Palanca, Carles
    1987   *Curs de sociolingüística 1*. Alzira: Edicions Bromera.
Morson, Gary Saul and Emerson, Caryl
    1990   *Mikhail Bakhtin. Creation of a Prosaics*. Stanford: Stanford
                University Press.
Nussbaum, Luci
    1990   Contacte de llengües a la classe de francès. Una aproximació
                pragmàtica.Ph.D. Thesis. Universitat Autònoma de Barcelona.
                Bellaterra.
Overing, J.
    1986   Men control women? The "catch 22" in the analysis of gender. In
                International Journal of Moral and Social Studies vol. 1, 135–156.
Payrató, Lluís
    1996   Català col·loquial. Aspectes de l'ús corrent de la llengua catalana.
                València: Universitat de València. 3ª edició.
Peterson, Roger; Mountfort, Guy and Hollom, P.A.D.
    1983   *A Field Guide to the Birds of Britain and Europe*. William Collins
                Sons & Co. Ltd. London. Catalan version,
    1989   *Guia dels Ocells dels Països Catalans i d'Europa*, revised and
                adapted by Francesc Giró, Rosa Llinàs and Jordi Sargatal.
                Barcelona: Edicions Omega SA.
Phillips, Angela
    1993   *The trouble with boys. Parenting the men of the future*. London:
                Pandora, Harper Collins.
Pla Fulquet, Joan
    1995   L'obertura de la [a] a Barcelona: el xava i altres varietats. In Turell,
                Teresa (ed.) *La sociolingüística de la variació*. Barcelona: PPU,
                139–159.
Potter, Jonathan and Wetherell, Margaret
    1987   *Discourse and Social Psychology. Beyond Attitudes and Behaviour*.
                London: Sage Publications.
Pujolar, Joan
    1991a   Ús de la llengua catalana dins l'àmbit empresarial a la ciutat
                d'Olot.Unpublished dissertation. Universitat Autònoma de
                Barcelona. Bellaterra.
    1991b   Language choice patterns in equal encounters among bilingual
                university students in Catalonia.M.A. Dissertation. Lancaster
                University. Lancaster.

| 1993 | L'estudi de les normes d'ús des de l'Anàlisi Crítica del Discurs. In *Treballs de Sociolingüística Catalana* no. 11. València: Editorial Tres i Quatre, 61–78. |

1995a   The identities of 'la penya': the voices and struggles of young working-class people in Barcelona. Unpublished Ph.D. Thesis. Lancaster University.

1995b   Immigration in Catalonia: the politics of sociolinguistic research. In *Catalan Review, International Journal of Catalan Culture*. IX, 2: 39–59.

1997a   *De què vas, tio?* Barcelona: Empúries.

1997b   Masculinities in a multilingual setting. In Johnson and Meinhof (eds.).:86–106.

1997c   Dialogismo y bilingüismo: explorando las relaciones entre lengua e identidad en el contexto catalán. In Carbó, Teresa y Martín Rojo, Luisa (eds.) *El análisis del discurso en España hoy*. Special editions of *Discurso: teoría y análisis*. Autum 1996–Spring 1997. Mexico D.F.: Universidad Nacional Autónoma de Mexico,. 183–212.

1999   Els gèneres verbals: reflexions sobre la seva significació per a una teoria de l'ús social del llenguatge. In Llengua i Literatura 10. Barcelona: Institut d'Estudis Catalans.

Rabinow, Paul
1984   "Introduction" in Rabinow, Paul (ed.) *The Foucault Reader*. London: Penguin Books, 3–29.

Rafanell, A. and Rossich, Albert
1990   Quin futur hi ha per a la llengua catalana? In Revista de Catalunya no. 37, 21–6.

Rahola, Pilar
1989   Bilingüisme passiu. In *Avui* 06/03/1989. Barcelona:

Rampton, M. B. H.
1991   Interracial Panjabi in a British adolescent peer-group. In *Language in Society* vol 20 no.3, 391–422.

1995   *Crossing. Language and ethnicity among adolescents*. London: Longman.

1998   Language crossing and the redefinition of reality. In Auer, Peter (ed.) *Code-switching in conversation. Language, interaction and identity*. London and New York: Routledge, 290–317.

Recolons, Lluís, et al.
1979   *Catalunya: home i territori*. Barcelona: Editorial Blume.

Rodríguez-Gómez, Mª Guadalupe
    1993   Immigrant workers constructing a nation: class formation, the construction of social persons, and the politics of the past in Santa Coloma de Gramenet. Unpublished PhD Thesis. Department of Anthropology. University of Chicago.

Romaine, Susan
    1989   *Bilingualism*. London: Basil Blackwell.

Roman, Leslie G.
    1988   Intimacy, labor and class: ideologies of feminine sexuality in the Punk slam dance. In Roman, Christian-Smith and Ellsworth (eds.), 143–184.

Roman, Leslie G. and Christian-Smith, Linda (eds.) with Ellsworth, Elizabeth,
    1988   *Becoming Feminine. The Politics of Popular Culture*. London: The Fallmer Press.

Romney, A. Kimball and D'Andrade, Roy G. (eds.)
    1964   Transcultural Studies in Cognition. In *Special Edition of the American Anthropologist* vol. 66, no.3 pt. 2.

Saladrigas, Xavier
    1997   L'ús del català en la música pop-rock (1987–1994). In *Treballs de Sociolingüística Catalana* 13, 57–75.

Scotton, Carol Myers
    1988   Codeswitching as indexical of social negotiations. In Heller (ed.), 151–186.

Sebba, Mark
    1993   *London Jamaican*. London: Longman.

Sheldon, Amy
    1992   Conflict talk: sociolinguistic challenges to self-assertion and how young girls meet them. In *Merrill-Palmer Quarterly* no. 38, 95–117.

Shepherd, John
    1987   Music and male hegemony. In Leppert and McClary (eds.), 151–172.

Straw, Will
    1990   Characterizing Rock music culture. The case of Heavy Metal. In Frith and Goodwin (eds.), 97–110.

Strubell, Miquel
    1981   *Llengua i població a Catalunya*. Barcelona: Edicions la Magrana.

Talbot, Mary
    1998   *Language and Gender: An Introduction*. Cambridge: Polity Press.

Tertilt, Hermann
    1996   *Turkish Power Boys. Ethnographie einer Jugendbande*. Frankfurt am Main: Suhrkamp Taschenbuch.

Thorne, Barrie
  1993   *Gender Play. Girls and Boys in School*. Buckingham: Open
            University Press.
Thorne, Tony
  1990   *Dictionary of Contemporary Slang*. Soho: Bloomsbury Publishing.
Torras, Maria Carme
  1999   Selection of medium in conversation: a study of trilingual service
            encounters. Unpublished dissertation. Universitat Autònoma de
            Barcelona.
Trudgill, Peter
  1974   *The social differentiation of English in Norwich*. Cambridge:
            Cambridge University Press.
Turell, Maria Teresa
  1984   *Elements per a la recerca sociolingüística a Catalunya*. Barcelona:
            Edicions 62.
Tusón, Amparo
  1985a   Language, community and school in Barcelona. Ph.D. Thesis.
            University of California. Berkeley.
  1985b   El repertori lingüístic de la ciutat de Barcelona. In Pubblicazioni
            del Dipartimento di Scienze del Linguaggio (ed.) *Formazione
            dell'insegnante di lingue in ambiente di lingue in contatto*. Serie
            Ricerche 5. Università di Roma "La Sapienza", Bargatto. Roma,
            63–87.
  1990   Catalan-Spanish code-switching in interpersonal communication. In
            *Papers for the Workshop on Impact and consequences: broader
            considerations*. Brussels: European Science Foundation, Network
            on Code-switching and Language Contact, 167–187.
Uchida, Aki
  1992   When 'difference' is dominance: a critique of the 'anti-power-based'
            cultural approach to sex differences. In *Language in Society* vol.
            21, 547–68.
Vallverdú, Francesc
  1980   *Aproximació Crítica a la Sociolingüística Catalana*. Barcelona:
            Edicions 62.
  1989   El bilingüisme passiu en qüestió? In *Avui* 16/02/1989 Barcelona:
  1990   *L'ús del català: un futur controvertit*. Barcelona: Edicions 62.
Vila, Ignasi
  1993   *La normalització lingüística a l'ensenyament no universitari de
            Catalunya*. Servei de Difusió i Publicacions. Barcelona: Generalitat
            de Catalunya.

Vila, Francesc Xavier
1996   When Classes are over. Language choice and language contact in bilingual education in Catalonia. Ph.D. Thesis Vrije Universiteit. Brussels.

Vilardell, Elisenda
1998   Canvi i manteniment de la llengua en parelles lingüísticament mixtes a Sabadell. Unpublished dissertation. Universitat Autònoma de Barcelona. Barcelona.

Voloshinov, Valentin N.
1971   Reported Speech. In Mateika, Ladislav and Pomorska, Krystyna (eds.) *Readings in Russian Poetics: Formalist and Structuralist Views*. Cambridge: M. I.T. Press.

Wacquant, Loïc
1992   Toward a social praxeology: the structure and logic of Bourdieu's sociology. In Bourdieu and Wacquant, 1–59.

Whorf, Benjamin Lee
1971   *Language, thought, and reality*. Selected writings of Benjamin Lee Whorf. Massachussets: The M. I.T. Press.

Williams, Glyn
1992   *Sociolinguistics: a Sociological Critique*. London: Routledge.

Williams, Raymond
1973   Base and superstructure in Marxist cultural theory. In *New Left Review* vol. 87, 3–16.

Williams, Robin
1988   Understanding Goffman's methods. In Drew and Wootton (eds.), 64–88.

Willis, Paul
1977   *Learning to Labour*. Westmead: Saxon House.

Wodak, Ruth (ed.)
1989   *Language, power, and ideology: studies in political discourse*. Amsterdam and Philadelphia: J. Benjamins Pub. Co.

Wolfson, Nessa and Manes, Joan (eds.)
1985   *Language of Inequality*. Berlin: Mouton Publishers.

Woolard, Kathryn
1985a   Language variation and cultural hegemony: towards an integration of sociolinguistics and social theory. In *American Ethnologist* vol. 12, No. 4, 738–48.
1985b   Catalonia: the dilemma of language rights. In Wolfson and Manes (eds.), 91–110.
1989   Doubletalk: Bilingualism and the Politics of Ethnicity in Catalonia. Stanford: Stanford University Press.

1994   Gendered peer-groups and the bilingual repertoire in Catalonia. In
            Silberman, Pamela and Loftin, Jonathan (eds.) *Proceedings of the*
            Second annual Symposium About Language and Society (SALSA
            II). University of Texas. Austin, 200–220.
1995   Changing forms of codeswitching in Catalan comedy. In *Catalan*
            Review, International Journal of Catalan Culture IX, 2: 223–252.
1999   Simultaneity and bivalency as strategies in bilingualism. In *Journal*
            of Linguistic Anthropology 8(1), 3–29.

Woolard, Kathryn and Gahng, T. -J.
1990   Changing language policies and attitudes in autonomous Catalonia.
            In *Language in Society* 19, 311–330.

Woolf, Virginia
1927 [1974]*To the Lighthouse*. London: The Hogarth Press Ltd.

Index